PEACE IS POSSIBLE

PEACE
IS POSSIBLE

A Reader on World Order
edited by Elizabeth Jay Hollins
Grossman Publishers
New York 1966

"On Death and Death Symbolism: The Hiroshima Disaster" by Robert Jay Lifton,
is reprinted by special permission of the William Alanson White Psychiatric Foundation Inc. and the author from *Psychiatry* (1964) 27:191-210. Reprinted in *The
American Scholar*, Winter 1965.

"National Security and the Nuclear-Test Ban" by Jerome B. Wiesner and Herbert F.
York, copyright © 1964 by Scientific American, Inc., is reprinted with the permission of the authors.

"Population and Poverty" by Kenneth Boulding, from the magazine *The Correspond-
ent*, Fall 1965, is reprinted with the permission of the author.

"Salvation on the Campus" by J. Glenn Gray from *Harper's Magazine*, May 1965,
is reprinted with the permission of the author.

"A Radical Frame of Mind" by Rochelle Gatlin is reprinted with the permission of
Saturday Review, October 16, 1965, and of the author.

"The Prevention of World War III" by Kenneth Boulding is reprinted with the permission of the *Virginia Quarterly Review*, Winter 1962, and the author.

"Group Psychology and the Elimination of War" by Jerome D. Frank is reprinted
with the permission of the *International Journal of Group Psychotherapy*, January
1964.

The interview with Robert Pickus is reprinted with the permission of *Mademoiselle*.

The introduction by Grenville Clark to *World Peace through World Law* by Grenville Clark and Louis B. Sohn is reprinted with the permission of the Harvard University Press.

The encyclical *Pacem in Terris* by Pope John XXIII is reprinted with the permission
of the Paulist Press, New York.

The address by Paul Tillich at the Pacem in Terris Convocation, and the speeches of
Abdul Monem Rifa'i, George F. Kennan, Adam Schaff, Abba Eban and the excerpt
from the speech of Muhammed Zufrula Khan all made at this same convocation are
reprinted with the permission of the Center for the study of Democratic Institutions,
Santa Barbara, California.

"The Wedding of the World's Civilizations" by F. S. C. Northrop is reprinted with
the permission of *Main Currents in Modern Thought*, May-June 1965.

"Four Problems in Lawmaking for Peace" by Louis Lusky is reprinted with the permission of the *Political Science Quarterly*, from Vol. LXXX, No. 3, pages 341-356.

"The U.N. of Dag Hammarskjöld is Dead" by Hans J. Morgenthau, © 1965 by The
New York Times Company, is reprinted with the permission of the author.

Acknowledgments

The quality and degree of thanks that go to my husband, Harry B. Hollins, are so great that they cannot be adequately represented under acknowledgments. In addition to the constant pressures of his own demanding work as manager of the World Law Fund, he has given me help and support in every stage of this project from first to last. He has been my editor and my consultant, at the same time allowing the choice of materials and the direction of my comments to remain entirely my own.

I am deeply indebted also to Saul H. Mendlovitz. In the course of countless conversations over the past several years he has taught me a great deal about the subject here dealt with, to which he has given his full commitment.

My thanks go to Betty Reardon and to Chloe Zerwick, both of the World Law Fund, who each read the manuscript of my comments making valuable critical remarks. And in a very personal way I would like to thank Nancy Wilson Ross, who knows how rare and how valuable is the gift of *attention* and who gave it to me more than once when I asked.

This whole book is made out of the concentrated study, the knowledge and the intensive thought of others, and I am indebted to all of them. I have tried, as much as possible, to acknowledge this indebtedness throughout the book as I went along. But it has not always been possible. As I am not a professional, and as I brought to my connecting comments the background of a rather wide and varied reading over a good many years, I have absorbed, and now reflect as my own, certain thoughts, now and then an illuminating phrase, once or twice the ghost of a sentence, which I recognize as having come from somewhere, but I do not know where. I would like to make a special acknowledgment of indebtedness to those unnamed contributors.

To Grenville Clark

who has repeatedly had the sensitivity to
foresee the requirements of the future, the
courage to identify himself with those
requirements, the sagacity to cast them in
form of practical action; who has the fairness
to treat with respect every person, the belief
in reason to appeal to the reason of his
fellow men; who has held a permanent conviction
that the individual can act; who has made
of the law, throughout his life, a means
to realize the essential values,

with lifelong admiration and affection,
this Reader is dedicated.

Contents

PEACE IS POSSIBLE

INTRODUCTION

One might say that this book has been compiled for myself or for someone like myself. It is an effort to find some way of looking at the present world scene that is realistic and reasonably coherent, yet to which I can give moral assent and toward which I would seek to influence action if I could. I have no special competence for this task; it is with the voice of the ordinary concerned person that I speak, and with his mind that I have read and continue to read, for this is an unfinished subject.

We all recognize that societies today—whether we think of an urban megalopolis such as New York City, or one of the new nations of Africa—are changing in almost all their basic dimensions at a rate unprecedented in history. We all know in a general way, although few have absorbed its full significance, that science and technology have brought about rapid and drastic changes in the given conditions of life which affect every part of it and are of such a magnitude that they are comparable to a mutation. This mutation which we are undergoing, whether we recognize it or not and whether we like it or not, contains hitherto undreamed of possibilities for wide betterment of man's life on earth, and it contains hitherto undreamed of and very actual possibilities for profound disaster. The basic psychological challenge before us is that these new conditions force us to make drastic changes in certain deeply ingrained habits of behavior and thinking. The economist Kenneth Boulding puts it succinctly: "If the human race is to survive, it will have to change its way of thinking more in the next 25 years than it has in the last 25,000."

Growth is possibly the chief cause of our predicament, and the fact of growth in itself is not to be deplored. It declares that mankind is an experiment that has (so far) succeeded. Man has covered the earth, and the congestion, the pressure of man in contact with man everywhere, forces evolution. It is the very roundness of the earth that forces convergence. Imagine for a moment that the earth were a flat disk of infinite size; life could spread out endlessly in a loose unorganized way, without pressure or development. But the earth is *round*, a globe. Man, this unfinished still-evolving creature, today suddenly meets himself everywhere. Idea encounters idea. Life "inrolls upon itself," to use Teilhard de Chardin's phrase, and the consequent congestion and tension has always, thus far, been met by evolutionary change. But the institutions that man has to date evolved for himself are inadequate and everywhere have broken down. To meet this crisis—and it is *our* crisis, *now*—we must bring to bear the two special attributes that man, more than any other form of life, has been developing over his long evolutionary history: "consciousness" (or "awareness") and "reason."

I think of this book as a Reader, which means "a collection of instructional materials," this one having a controlling subject. A theme that runs through this Reader is the idea of *system change*, and system change as rapidly as possible, to meet our urgent need. Let me illustrate. Here in the United States we are just beginning to see that the problems of the cities transcend the boundaries of the cities and, indeed, often those of the states which theoretically contain those cities. In a postelection column (Fall, 1965) entitled "Can Lindsay Succeed?" (as mayor of New York) Walter Lippmann pointed out that "the real city in fact lies in three states and comprises many little cities, many suburbs and myriads of villages. The needs and interests of the urban conglomerations of our era have outgrown the political structures which have come down to them from a very different past." At this level we are waking up; and, let us hope, *beginning* to do something about it. We also see (and many have seen for a long time) that there are certain problems formerly handled by the nation state that now transcend the power of the nation state to handle adequately. But we seem less prepared to do something about this, although the problems escalate with appalling speed. The reasons for this are roughly two: we are trapped in confused habits of thought about what we really mean by sovereignty, and we are not yet aware of mankind as an entity, a community. This awareness is still emerging.

What are the most pressing problems facing the world community where there seems a breakdown in our ability to handle them?

Danger of nuclear war—the New Fact, as the philosopher Karl Jaspers calls it.

The impossibility for any nation to protect the lives and property of its citizens from outside aggression. One of the basic factors that brought the nation state into being was that it could provide this security. Today this is no longer so.

The threat to identity, *i.e.* the threat to smaller nations of unwanted domination and interference by others.

Hunger. And with this goes the need for conservation and best use of the earth's resources, all of which requires *planning* (until recently a dirty word in government) on a *world scale.*

Population control. We have reached a point where, if man merely multiplies, we will go under. Even in procreation, "awareness" is now called for.

Poverty and illiteracy, which demand a massive attack and which are intimately linked with hunger and with population control. An Indian official said that the coming of electricity to a certain village had reduced the birth rate; before that, there had been nothing else one could do after dark.

Human rights and civil rights and race relations—unfortunately very linked. Belated progress is lately being made in the United States, but does the present situation in Rhodesia concern only Rhodesia and does not the present world system exacerbate these problems?

The threat to human values that is posed by the sheer *size* of the arms race and the cold war (quite apart from the danger of escalation in the recurring hot wars). The manipulation of our lives, the enormousness of the bureaucracies that are engendered, the imperviousness of the situation to personal desire or choice, the general impersonality that rubs out individuality—evidenced, for instance, in the statistics about overkill—this threat to our human quality is acutely felt, especially by young people.

Of all these issues it is my intention to focus on war prevention. Not only does the existence of nuclear weapons and their modern delivery systems make war the most devastating and omnipresent problem warping our lives in subtle as well as obvious ways, but there is good reason to believe that most of the other grave world problems have a better chance of yielding were this one dealt with. Their relevance to war prevention is bluntly this: the present world system of competing national armaments *costs* so much in resources, brain power and sheer human energy—diverted from urgently needed constructive purposes—that human society cannot turn these in adequate supply on anything else. There is a connection between an annual world expenditure of 150 billion dollars for unproductive (destructive) purposes and the possibility of raising the standards of living for two thirds of the world now living on bare subsistence level; there is a connection between this expenditure and averting the probability of death by starvation for literally millions of persons in the next two decades unless an unprecedented effort is made to control the population explosion and expand the production of food. Even in the United States, "the richest country in the world," for the first time since World War II many find that the economy is straining its capacity to produce. In *The New York Times* this morning (Wednesday, December 29, 1965) are two modest headlines on page one: "War Costs May Cut City's School Aid" and, conversely, "Shift of Defense Funds to Domestic Programs Hinted if War Were to Slacken." Even in the United States, it would seem, we are having difficulty affording war and the Great Society, and it must be remembered of course that active war accounts for only a small part of the cost of the competitive armaments system.

It is less simple to demonstrate the connection of war prevention with civil rights and human rights and race relations in the world community. Yet the problems are interwoven. The potential explosive violence of these issues if they remain neglected are cause for most horrible war. At the same time, modern war destroys these values themselves. Human rights are annihilated in modern war. Civil rights rest basically on law and justice, not force. Genocide remains genocide whichever race perpetrates it. And, in any circumstances whatsoever, the war system itself *creates* a problem between personal liberty and national security, so that even without World War III but with a continuance of military-political struggles there arises the possibility of living in a garrison state. Moreover, in these great as in lesser problems, it is a matter of *attention:* when war and the threat of war dominate our attention it is sapped from elsewhere. Walter Lippmann ended his column about the changes that must take place in New York with the conclusion that, *given an environment of peace,* there is a chance of achieving them.

Most of us agree war is bad, but what do we do about it? The great problems and their solutions today are immensely complicated. Much of the most pertinent thought and data is highly specialized and outside the area of reading of the average person unless it happens to fall within his particular field. And much relevant matter that does come his way has only a small part of its full significance because it comes to him fragmentary, isolated, like one piece of a picture puzzle, forming no cohesive over-all point of view. Both these difficulties are particularly true when it comes to thinking seriously about this, the most urgent problem of our time—the eradication of war. Moreover, this problem appears so large, so appalling, so complex, so beyond the power of the mere citizen to affect in any way that we do not confront it. Yet on this, more than on any other great problem facing us today, do we need fresh thinking rather than stock attitudes—attitudes which, on examination, may not prove relevant to the realities after all.

Until very recently War/Peace problems have been dealt with almost entirely by experts and even by them on a piecemeal basis. Where the subject entered the educational structure at all it would be as one unrelated bit at a time: arms control and disarmament, or peace-keeping forces, or current international law (without reference to enforcement or peace-keeping or disarmament), or economic development, etc. Valuable peace research, such as that at the Center for Conflict Resolution at the University of Michigan, has been conducted on limited theoretical problems, but, not only has our total peace research been minuscule in comparison with our war research, it has not been utilized in a broad frame of reference. During the last two or three years, however, largely through the initiative of the World Law Fund in New York, universities, colleges and schools in this country and to a lesser extent in other countries have begun to assume the responsibility for a serious educational program on war prevention with emphasis on looking at the whole problem as an interrelated piece. Those who have most deeply studied this larger picture have come increasingly to say that what is required is not merely an adjustment of this part or of that, nor—far worse—an upping in size of the old system, but a true system change, *from* a system of competing national armaments and unlimited national sovereignty *to* some system of world order based on the principles of justice and world law.

What does this involve, what are the risks, what are the advantages? . . . weighed against the risks and advantages of our present course. And to make the comparison fairly we must consider the *trend*, where in each case we would most likely be 20 to 30 years from now. What the new system might look like, how we might come to it, what have we to build on, is this a proper course for man, is it *necessary?* All these are questions of vital importance to everyone. They cannot be left solely to government, nor to research, nor to the academic community. A share of responsibility must be assumed by citizens in all areas of life, for the solution to our dilemma is basically a political decision which requires a broad understanding by many people of the position we are in and of the alternatives.

We need tools to do our own thinking. During the past five or six years, out of my own concern and because the circumstances of my life have brought me into working contact with others who were deeply concerned, I have had occasion to do considerable reading. These articles are culled from many dealing with the same subjects with approximately the same conclusions. They are offered because they served me as tools, and therefore I hope they may serve you. They are deliberately very varied, both in scope and in depth, and they cut across many disciplines since this is a book designed, not for the specialist, but for the man or woman as human being, in our time, facing revolutionary changes that present an enormous but not insuperable challenge for evolutionary response on our part.

Each of these articles has interest in itself, many of them great interest, but they are of far greater interest, and greater significance, when taken together. It is intended they be read in the order presented, but they do not form an inflexible doctrinaire argument; instead you will observe that they steadily interweave, reinforcing each other, throwing sidelights on each other, fleshing each other out, thus creating a *way of thinking* with responsible authority behind it.

World order is a big subject for anyone, particularly a nonprofessional like myself, to organize. I have followed what seemed to me the most natural course, one which most nearly recapitulates my own—and I believe most persons'—development. Section One, therefore, attempts to look as succinctly as possible at the most glaring of our ills which cry out for world cures. It is a depressing picture. It cannot help but be. Civil rights here at home is not dealt with because it does not require world solutions. Nor the mess of our cities. But these, like everything else, suffer from our consuming involvement in the war system. Next, having faced our predicament, we go on, in Section Two, first to admit that we must make a drastic change and then to look at as clear definitions as possible of a better alternative. The idea of a world order based on the principles of law and of justice instead of on force and the threat of force seems so right and so reasonable that one's instinct is to accept it at once. But another part of one's instinct is to raise doubts. Some of the doubts are caused by true dilemmas to which there are no perfect solutions; some by insufficient understanding of how something so untried might actually work, fears of how it might go wrong, what would be the losses as well as gains; some of the doubts are due to long entrenched habits of thought; some are real difficulties which require working out where the way is not yet clear. Section Three, therefore, which deals with these matters, is muddled and groping. But it is encounter with the difficulties that brings to light both to what degree mankind as an entity can be thought to already exist and what shape we wish to give to world order. The prospect of a world system that would prevent war becomes curiously actual. Section Four deals with how we can move toward it. Throughout I have interspersed my own comments, sometimes citing authorities not included in the Reader, sometimes merely giving my own feelings, for this is a discussion in which we must all engage—with these writers and with each other.

World order is also a new subject. We need images and terms in which to think about it, handles to get hold of it by. The very term "system change" is such a handle—it helps us to grasp the subject as well as to describe what we have to do. I have made use of a few such handles which seem genuinely descriptive and I have used a few additional terms that are currently in use among those who discuss these matters, since you will meet them in other reading. Although this is a layman's book compiled by a layman, nothing has been avoided *only* because it was technical; when we see that something has vital meaning for us we can master it, so I have no hesitation about the "difficulty" of the article by Wiesner and York. But, on the whole, technical points which are the domain of experts are not the concern here. I believe, however, that a careful reading of these materials which, being current in swift-moving events may be perishable in small details but not in their core, will present quite clearly the most basic relevant facts, will reveal the areas of greatest difficulty and will indicate certain guidelines for a solution. Furthermore, I hope that from this background some of you will continue to increase your understanding of the subject both through more specialized works now in existence and through new books and articles as they are published.

One thing is clear—what we must seek is a recognition in the mind, not only of the responsible statesmen but of the ordinary citizen who must influence those statesmen, that the coming of the atomic age has completely changed the nature of the world as we knew it, and we must use our best human attributes to make adequate response to that change.

Here are the beginnings of a road map that is not yet complete.

I

WHERE WE ARE

These first articles describe aspects of the unprecedented situation we are in which challenges the full use of our "awareness" and "reason." All indicate that the problems that underlie them require world solutions and this in itself imposes a difficulty as we are not yet used to thinking in world terms. But it is essential that we become truly conscious of these realities— i.e. admit them into our immediate personal mind, not just into our storehouse of facts—if we would live as responsible persons today.

F or myself, statistics, no matter how closely I read them—*e.g.* 149 million fatalities in the first few minutes (Secretary of Defense Robert McNamara, Feb. 18, 1965. And it is noteworthy that by "fatalities" the government here means *immediate* deaths)—never convey a real picture of what a nuclear exchange, even a "limited" one, would be like. The bombs dropped on Hiroshima and Nagasaki were extremely small in relation to those in our possession today, a mere one thousandth of the destructive power. Nonetheless, to date, they provide what is fortunately the only data on the meaning of the new weapons in human terms that we have to study.

Dr. Lifton, a psychiatrist and associate professor at Yale, is primarily interested in individual psychological experience in historic change and in "extreme situations." This article is part of a larger study of the psychological effect of the Hiroshima atom bomb on the survivors or—more literally to the specially coined Japanese word—on the "explosion-affected person (or people)." This then is a record by a trained specialist of what it is like to be a *survivor* of a nuclear attack, to actually experience the overwhelming and prolonged encounter with death that inevitably accompanies it.

There is an additional significance. No one concerned with religion or with existential values or with the thought "What is the meaning of life" can avoid facing the implications of this article. Dr. Lifton points out that there is an interrelationship between the way in which we look at death and the way in which we conduct life that has been recognized by philosophers for centuries but has received little study from psychiatrists, although it is a problem peculiarly relevant to our age. Here, he says, "I will do no more than state a few principles that I have found a useful beginning for comprehending the Hiroshima experience, relating it to universal human concerns, and examining some of the impact on our lives of the existence of nuclear weapons."

On Death and Death Symbolism: The Hiroshima Disaster

ROBERT JAY LIFTON

The larger a human event, the more its significance eludes us. In the case of Hiroshima's encounter with the atomic bomb—surely a tragic turning point in man's psychological and historical experience—the meaning is perhaps only now, after nineteen years, beginning to reveal itself. Yet the event has much to teach us in our struggle to cope with a world altered more than we realize, and made infinitely more threatening, by the existence of nuclear weapons. I shall describe here a portion of a larger study of the psychological effects of the atomic bomb in Hiroshima, and shall focus upon what I believe to be the central psychological issue in both the actual disaster and its wider symbolism—the problem of death and dying.

The study of death and death symbolism has been relatively neglected in psychiatry and psychoanalysis: in addition to familiar emotional resistances, death confronts us with an issue far beyond our empathic and intellectual capacities. But whatever the difficulties, the nuclear age provides urgent cause for new efforts to enhance our understanding of what has always been man's most ineradicable problem.

I conducted the investigation from April to September of 1962, mostly in Hiroshima itself. This was the last six months of a two and one-half year stay in Japan, the greater part of which was spent investigating psychological and historical patterns of Japanese youth. The Hiroshima study consisted primarily of individual interviews with two groups of atomic bomb survivors: one group of thirty-three chosen at random from the list of more than 90,000 survivors (or *hibakusha*) kept at the Hiroshima University Research Institute for Nuclear Medicine and Biology; and a group of forty-two survivors selected because of their prominence in dealing with A-bomb problems or their capacity to articulate their experiences—physicians, university professors, city officials, politicians, writers and poets, leaders of survivor organizations and peace movements.

Hibakusha, a coined word, by no means an exact equivalent of "survivor" (or survivors), but, literally, "explosion-affected person" (or people), conveys in feeling a little bit more than merely having encountered the bomb, and a little bit less than having experienced definite physical injury from it. By official definition, the category of *hibakusha* includes four groups considered to have had possible exposure to significant amounts of radiation: those who were within the city limits then defined for Hiroshima, an area extending from the bomb's hypocenter for 4,000, and in some places 5,000, meters; those who were not then in the city, but within fourteen days entered a designated area extending for about 2,000 meters from the hypocenter; those who were engaged in some form of aid to, or disposal of, bomb victims at various stations then set up; and those who were *in utero,* and whose mothers fit into any of the first three groups. I tried to learn all I could, too, from a variety of sources and in various informal ways, about the extraordinary constellation of influences relating to the bomb felt by the city's inhabitants during these intervening years.

Work in a foreign culture must, of course, depend heavily upon assistance from local individuals and groups. In Hiroshima the sensitivities inherent in the situation of an American psychiatrist's undertaking a study of reactions to the atomic bomb made such assistance particularly imperative. Meetings and interviews were arranged, wherever possible, through personal introduction. And with the randomly selected group, my first contact with the survivor was made through a visit to the home with a Japanese social worker from Hiroshima University, when I briefly explained (either to the survivor himself or to a family member) my purpose in undertaking the work, and arranged for a later meeting at the office I maintained in the city. The consistently cooperative responses I encountered were, I believe, importantly related to my having conveyed to both colleagues and research subjects my sense of personal motivation in the study, my hope that it might shed light on these difficult problems and in a small way contribute to the mastery of nuclear weapons and the avoidance of their use.

Interviews generally lasted two hours, and I tried to see each research subject twice. They were conducted in Japanese, with a research assistant to interpret; the great majority (particularly with subjects in the randomly selected group) were tape-recorded, always with the subject's consent. While I attempted to ask certain questions of all subjects, I encouraged each person to associate freely to whatever ideas and emotions were brought up.

I shall discuss in this paper, in sequence, the psychological aspects of four different stages of experience with death—that is, of what I have called the permanent encounter with death. Then, in the latter portion, I shall attempt to suggest a few general principles in the difficult area of the psychology of death and dying, essentially derived from this investigation but by no means limited to the Hiroshima experience.

IMMERSION IN DEATH: The overwhelming immersion in death directly following the bomb's fall began with the terrible array of dead and near-dead in the midst of which each survivor found himself. Important here was the extreme sense of surprise and unpreparedness: because, following an air raid alarm, an all-clear signal had been sounded just a few minutes before; because of the psychological sense of invulnerability all people tend to possess, even in the face of danger; and because of the total inability of anyone to anticipate the unprecedented dimensions of the weapon about to strike. The number of deaths, both immediate and over a period of time, will probably never be fully known. Variously estimated from 63,000 to 240,000 or more, the official figure is usually given as 78,000, but the city of Hiroshima estimates 200,000; the enormous disparity is related to the extreme confusion at the time, to differing methods of calculation, and to underlying emotional influences at times affecting the estimators. But anyone exposed relatively near the center of the city could not escape from the sense of ubiquitous death around him—from the blast itself, from radiant heat, and from ionizing radiation. For instance, if one were with 1,000 meters (0.6 miles) from the hypocenter, and out-of-doors (that is, without benefit of shielding from heat or radiation), more than nine tenths of the people around one were fatalities; and if unshielded at 2,000 meters (1.2 miles), more than eight of ten people around one were killed. For those indoors, mortality was lower, but even then to have a 50 per cent chance of escaping both death and injury, one had to be about 2,200 meters (1.3 miles) from the hypocenter. Therefore the most significant psychological feature at that point was the sense of a sudden and absolute shift from normal existence to an overwhelming encounter with death.

Recall of the experience was extremely vivid, despite the seventeen-year interval. But for those closest to the hypocenter, first memories of the event were frequently no more than that of a sudden flash, an intense sensation of heat, the recollection of being knocked down or thrown across the room and finding oneself pinned under debris, or simply of awakening from an indeterminate period of unconciousness. Nonetheless, many stressed (partly, undoubtedly, with retrospective reconstruction) feelings related to death and dying—such as: "My first feeling was, 'I think I will die'"; "I was dying without seeing my parents"; and "I felt I was going to suffocate and then die, without knowing exactly what had happened to me."

Beyond this sense of imminent individual death was the feeling of many that the whole world was dying.

A science professor, covered by falling debris, found himself temporarily blinded:

*My body seemed all black, everything seemed dark, dark all over. . . .
Then I thought, "The world is ending."*

A Protestant minister, himself uninjured, responded to the mutilation and destruction he saw everywhere around him:

The feeling I had was that everyone was dead. The whole city was destroyed. . . . I thought all of my family must be dead—it doesn't matter if I die. . . . I thought this was the end of Hiroshima—of Japan—of mankind.

And a woman writer:

I just could not understand why our surroundings had changed so greatly in one instant. . . . I thought it might have been something which had nothing to do with the war, the collapse of the earth which it was said would take place at the end of the world, and which I had read about as a child. It was quiet around us. In fact there was a fearful silence, which made one feel that all people and all trees and vegetation were dead.

This "death silence" was consistently reported by survivors. Rather than wild panic, most described a ghastly stillness and a sense of slow motion: low moans from those incapacitated, the rest fleeing, but usually not rapidly, from the destruction, toward the rivers (whose many branches run through the city), toward where there were thought to be family members, authorities of some sort, medical personnel, or simply accumulations of people; or in many cases merely moving along with a gathering crowd and with no clear destination. This feeling of *death in life* was described by a store clerk as follows:

The appearance of people was . . . well, they all had skin blackened by burns. . . . They had no hair because their hair was burned, and at a glance you couldn't tell whether you were looking at them from in front or in back. . . . They held their arms bent [forward] like this [and he proceeded to demonstrate their position] . . . and their skin— not only on their hands, but on their faces and bodies too—hung down. . . . If there had been only one or two such people . . . perhaps I would not have had such a strong impression. But wherever I walked I met these people. . . . Many of them died along the road—I can still picture them in my mind—like walking ghosts. . . . They didn't look like people of this world. . . . They had a special way of walking—very slowly. . . . I myself was one of them.

Characteristic here is the other-worldly grotesqueness of the scene, the image of neither-dead-nor-alive human figures with whom the survivor closely identifies himself. Similar emotions were conveyed by the frequently expressed imagery of a Buddhist hell—or as one man put it, "I was not really alive."

We are struck here by the intensity of feelings of helplessness and abandonment—not simply in themselves, but rather helplessness and abandonment in the face of threatened annihilation. The *hibakusha* fears annihilation of his own self, and also his sense of relationship to the world of people and objects in which he exists. He anticipates the annihilation of both the field or context of his existence and his attachment to it—reminding us of what the existentialists mean when they speak of "being-in-the-world," and also reminding us of recent psychoanalytic stress on the significance of the "nonhuman environment." And he fears the annihilation of that special set of feelings and beliefs that both relate him to others and allow for his sense of being a unique and particular person—in other words his sense of inner identity. This *anticipation of annihilation*—of self, of being, of identity—was related to overwhelming stimuli, an ultimate sense of threat that has been referred to by such names as "basic fear," and "the fear of the universe."

Indeed, so overwhelming was this experience that many would undoubtedly have become psychotic were it not for the extremely widespread and effective defense mechanism I have called "psychic closing-off." In the face of grotesque evidences of death and near-death, people simply ceased to feel. They had a clear sense of what was happening around them, but their emotional reactions were unconsciously turned off.

A physicist compared the process to an overexposed photographic plate. A clerk who witnessed others dying around him at a temporary first-aid area said, "I just couldn't have any reaction . . . you might say I became insensitive to human death." And the woman writer quoted before described "a feeling of paralysis that came over my mind."

The unconscious process here is that of closing oneself off from death itself; the controlling inner idea, or fantasy, is, "If I feel nothing, then death is not taking place." Psychic closing-off is related to the defense mechanisms of denial and isolation, as well as to the behavioral state of apathy. But it deserves to be distinguished from these by its sudden, global quality, by the protective symbolic screen it throws out enabling the organism to resist the impact of death—that is, to survive psychologically in the midst of death and dying. It may well represent man's most characteristic response to catastrophe: at times life-enhancing, or even, psychologically speaking, life-saving; but at other times, particularly when prolonged and no longer appropriate to the threat, not without its own dangers. Certainly the investigator of nuclear disaster finds himself experiencing a measure of such closing-off, as indeed does the reader of an account such as this one.

Psychic closing-off has, however, its limitations even as a protective reaction. It cannot entirely succeed in neutralizing either the threatening stimuli from without nor those from within—the latter taking the form of self-condemnation—of guilt and shame. For at the very beginning of the atomic bomb experience there is initiated a need for justifying one's own survival in the face of others' deaths, a form of guilt that plagues the atomic bomb survivor from then on. *Such quick self-condemnation intensifies the lasting imprint of death created by this early phase of atomic bomb exposure.* Contained within this imprint is something very close to witnessing in actuality that which ordinarily takes place only in psychotic fantasy—an end-of-the-world experience. Normally a projection of inner psychological "death" onto the outside world, the process is here reversed so that an overwhelming external experience of near-absolute destruction becomes internalized and merged with related tendencies of the inner life.

A type of memory that symbolizes this relationship of death to guilt is contained in what I have called the *ultimate horror*—a specific image of the dead or dying with which the survivor strongly identifies himself, and which evokes in him particularly intense feelings of pity and self-condemnation. The scene may include his own family members, or anonymous people in grotesque physical array; or, as was frequent, pitiful images of women and children, universal symbols of purity and vulnerability, and especially so in Japanese culture.

One particular form of "ultimate horror" seemed to epitomize the association of death and guilt. It was the recollection of requests of the dying which could not be carried out, most specifically their pleas for a few sips of water. Water was withheld not only because of survivors' preoccupation with saving themselves and their own families, but because authorities spread the word that water would have harmful effects upon the severely injured. The request for water by the dying, however, has special significance in Japanese tradition, as it is related to an ancient belief that water can restore life by bringing back the spirit that has just departed from the body. These pleas were therefore as much psychological expressions of this belief as they were of physical need; indeed, one might say that they were pleas for life itself. The survivor's failure to acquiesce to them, whatever his reasons, could thus have the psychological significance to him of refusing a request for the privilege of life—while he clung so tenaciously to that same privilege.

INVISIBLE CONTAMINATION: The second encounter with death took the form of *invisible contamination*. Almost immediately after the bomb fell—sometimes within hours or even minutes, often during the first twenty-four hours, and during the following days—*hibakusha* became aware of a strange form of illness. It consisted of nausea, vomiting, and loss of appetite; diarrhea with large amounts of blood in the stools; fever and weakness; purple spots on various parts of the body from bleeding into the skin (purpura); inflammation and ulceration of the mouth, throat, and gums (orapharyngeal lesions and gingivitis); bleeding from the mouth, gums, nose, throat, rectum and urinary tract (hemorrhagic manifestations); loss of hair from the scalp and other parts of the body (epilation); extremely low white blood cell counts when these were taken (leukopenia) and in many cases a progressive course until death. These symptoms of irradiation, and particularly the associated fatalities, aroused in the minds of the people of Hiroshima a special terror, an image of a weapon that not only kills and destroys on a colossal scale but leaves in the bodies of the exposed deadly influences which may emerge at any time and strike down their victims. This image was made particularly vivid by the delayed appearance of these radiation effects—often two to four weeks after the bomb fell—in people who had seemed in perfect health, externally untouched by atomic bomb effects.

No one at first understood the cause of the symptoms, and in the few functioning medical facilities, isolation procedures were instituted in the belief that they were part of some infectious gastrointestinal condition. Ordinary people also suspected some form of epidemic, possibly in the nature of cholera. But very quickly, partly in response to word-of-mouth information and misinformation about the atomic bomb, people began to relate the condition to a mysterious "poison" emanating from the weapon. Whatever their idea of cause, survivors were profoundly impressed by the fact of others dying around them and the way in which they died: a gruesome form of rapid bodily deterioration that seemed unrelated to more usual and "decent" forms of death. They were struck particularly by the loss of scalp hair, the purple spots on the skin, and the way in which victims appeared to remain conscious and alert almost to the moment of their death. As a middle-aged electrician relates:

> There was one man who asked me for help and everything he said was clear and normal. . . . But in another three hours or so when I looked at him he was already dead. . . . And even those who looked as though they would be spared were not spared. . . . People seemed to inhale something from the air which we could not see. . . . The way they died was different . . . and strange.

Some were intrigued by the weirdness of the symptoms—as in the case of a doctor quoted in a later written account:

> I know it is terrible to say this, but those spots were beautiful. They were just like stars—red, green, yellow, and black . . . all over the body, and I was fascinated by them.

But the predominant feeling among survivors was that they were imminently threatened by this same "poison"—as conveyed in such statements as: "Soon we were all worried about our health, about our bodies—whether we would live or die"; "I thought, 'sooner or later I too will die'. . . . I never knew when some sign of the disease would show itself"; and, "We waited for our own deaths."

The nature of the death symbolism here was revealed in three rumors which swept Hiroshima during the period immediately following the bomb. The first rumor simply held that all those who had been exposed to the bomb in the city would be dead within three years. The psychological message here was: none can escape the "poison"; the "epidemic" is total; all shall die.

But a second rumor, even more frequently related to me, and, I believe, with greater emotion, was that trees, grass, and flowers would never again grow in Hiroshima; from that day on the city would be unable to sustain vegetation of any kind. The message here was: nature was drying up altogether; life was being extinguished at its source—suggesting an ultimate form of desolation which not only encompassed human death but went beyond it.

The third rumor, closely related to the other two, held that for a period of seventy or seventy-five years Hiroshima would be uninhabitable. Here was the sense that Hiroshima was to become totally deurbanized—literally, devitalized—that the bomb's invisible contamination had deprived the involved area of its life-sustaining capacity.

Other rumors, particularly during the first few days after the bomb fell, expressed further ramifications of these emotions: there would be new attacks with "poison gases" or "burning oil"; America would next drop a "cold bomb" (or "ice bomb") which would freeze everything so that everyone would die. There was even a rumor that America would drop rotten pigs so that, as one man put it, "everything on the earth would decay and go bad." These additional rumors conveyed the sense that the environment had been so fundamentally disturbed, and the individual sense of security (and invulnerability) so threatened, that further life-annihilating assaults must be anticipated.

We may thus summarize the psychological aspects of the second encounter with death: fear of epidemic contamination to the point of bodily deterioration; a sense of individual powerlessness before an invisible, all-enveloping, and highly mysterious poison; the sense, often largely unconscious and only indirectly communicated, that this *total contamination* must have a supernatural, or at least more-than-natural, origin, must be something in the nature of a curse with which one's group is afflicted as a punishment for some wrongdoing that has offended the supernatural forces which control life and death. This was occasionally made explicit in, for instance, survivors' Buddhist references to misbehavior in previous incarnations; it was implicit in their repeated expressions of awe, in the elaborate mythology they created around the event, and in their various forms of self-condemnation.

"A-BOMB DISEASE:" The third encounter with death occurred with later radiation effects, not months but years after the atomic bomb, and may be summed up in the scientifically inaccurate but emotionally charged term, "A-bomb disease." The medical condition that has become the model for "A-bomb disease" is leukemia, based upon the actual increased incidence of this always fatal malignancy of the blood-forming organs, first noted in 1948 and reaching a peak between 1950 and 1952. The symptoms of leukemia, moreover, resemble those of acute radiation effects, sharing various manifestations of blood abnormalities, as well as the more visible and dreaded "purple spots" and other forms of hemorrhage, progressive weakness, and fever, although leukemia differs from acute irradiation in that it inevitably results in death.

Psychologically speaking, leukemia—or the threat of leukemia—became an indefinite extension of the earlier "invisible contamination" of which we have spoken. And individual cases of leukemia in children have become the counterpart of the "ultimate horror" described in relation to the first moments of the experience, symbolizing once more the bomb's desecration of the most pure and vulnerable—of childhood itself. Indeed, Hiroshima's equivalent of an Anne Frank legend has developed from a case of leukemia in a twelve-year-old girl, Sadako Sasaki, which occurred in 1954; her death led to a national campaign for the construction of a monument (which now stands prominently in the center of Hiroshima's Peace Park) to this child and to all other children who have died as a result of the atomic bomb.

And just at the time that the incidence of leukemia was recognized as diminishing and approaching the normal, evidence has accumulated that the incidence of other forms of cancer has been increasing among survivors—including carcinoma of the stomach, lung, thyroid, ovary, and uterine cervix. Leukemia is a rare disease (even with its increased incidence, only 122 cases were reported in Hiroshima between 1945 and 1959), but cancer is not; and should the trend continue, as appears likely, the increase in cancer will undoubtedly give further stimulus to various elaborations of death symbolism, just as some of these were beginning to decline. Thus, we again see evoked the feeling that the bomb can do anything, and that anything it does is likely to be fatal.

Other medical conditions have been thought to be produced by delayed radiation effects: impairment in the growth and development of children; a variety of anemias and of liver and blood diseases; endocrine and skin disorders; impairment of central nervous system (particularly mid-brain) functions; premature aging; and a vague but persistently reported borderline condition of general weakness and debilitation. The exact consequences of radiation effects remain in many areas controversial, and are still under active investigation by both American and Japanese groups. What concerns us here, however, is the association in the minds of survivors of any kind of ailment with atomic bomb effects—whether it be fatigue, mild anemia, fulminating leukemia, or ordinary cardiovascular disease; whether there is no apparent scientific relationship to radiation effects, whether such a relationship may be presumed as probable, or whether such a relationship is possible but inconclusive. Bodily concerns of survivors are also intensified by the continuous publicizing of "A-bomb disease" by the mass media and by survivor and peace organizations, often in the form of lurid reports of patients dying in the "A-bomb hospital" (a special facility set up for the exposed population) of "A-bomb disease." Even though the relationship between the actual condition and the atomic bomb effects may be questionable, the ordinary survivor tends to identify himself directly with the victim and with the process of dying. As one man stated, "When I hear about people who die from A-bomb disease . . . then I feel that I am the same kind of person as they."

The survivor thus becomes involved in a vicious circle on the psychosomatic plane of existence: he is likely to associate even the mildest everyday injury or sickness with possible radiation effects; and anything he relates to radiation effects becomes in turn associated with death. The process is accentuated, although not created, by the strong Japanese cultural focus upon bodily symptoms as expressions of anxiety and conflict. The psychosomatic dilemma can also take on complicated ramifications. For instance, some survivors develop vague borderline symptoms, inwardly fear that these might be evidence of fatal "A-bomb disease," but resist seeking medical care because they do not wish to be confronted by this diagnosis. When such a pattern occurs in relationship to physical disease, we usually refer to it as "denial of illness"; but here the "illness" being denied is itself likely to be a symbolic product of psychological currents; and the "denial" is a specific response to the associated death symbolism. Others become involved in a lifelong preoccupation with "A-bomb disease," sometimes referred to by Hiroshima physicians as "A-bomb neurosis"; they become weak and sometimes bedridden, focus constantly upon their blood counts and bodily symptoms, and struggle with an intricate inner balance between the need for their symptoms as an expression of various psychological conflicts on the one hand, and the anxious association of these symptoms with death and dying on the other. At best, survivors find themselves constantly plagued with what we may call the "nagging doubt" about the possibility of radiation effects, and look upon themselves as people who are particularly vulnerable, who cannot afford to take chances.

Beyond their own sense of impaired body-image, survivors fear that this impairment will manifest itself in subsequent generations. Genetic effects from the A-bomb are a controversial and unresolved issue. Fortunately, studies on comparative populations have revealed no increase in abnormalities among children of survivors. But it is widely known that such abnormalities can be caused by radiation, and there are again the problems of variation in medical opinion (a few Japanese pathologists think that some evidence of increase in genetic abnormalities exist), and of lurid, sometimes irresponsible, journalistic reports. There is, however, one uncomfortably positive genetic finding among significantly exposed survivors, that of a disturbance of sex ratio of offspring, the significance of which is difficult to evaluate. Still another factor in survivors' psychological associations has been the definite damage from radiation experienced by children exposed *in utero,* including the occurrence of microcephaly with and without mental retardation; this phenomenon is, scientifically speaking, quite unrelated to genetic effects, but ordinary people often fail to make the distinction.

We may say that, at this third level of encounter with death, the sudden "curse" we spoke of becomes an *enduring taint*—a taint of death that attaches itself not only to one's entire psychobiological organism, but to one's posterity. Although in most cases able to live, work, marry, and beget children in more or less normal fashion, survivors have the sense of being involved in an *endless chain of potentially lethal impairment* which, if it does not manifest itself in one year—or in one generation—may well make itself felt in the next. Once more elements of guilt and shame become closely involved with this taint; but rather than a product of an acute epidemic-like experience, the whole constellation is perceived as a permanent and infinitely transmissible form of impaired body substance.

IDENTITY OF THE DEAD: This brings us to the fourth level of encounter, that of a lifelong identification with death, dying, and with an anonymous group of "the dead." Indeed the continuous encounter with death, in the sequence described, has much to do with creating a sense of group identity as *hibakusha,* or survivors. But it is an unwanted, or at best ambivalent, identity, symbolized externally by disfigurement—that is, by keloid scars which, although possessed only by a small minority of survivors, have come to represent the stigmata of atomic bomb exposure.

A central conflict of this *hibakusha* identity is the problem of what I have come to speak of as *survival priority*—the inner question of why one has survived while so many have died, the inevitable self-condemnation in the face of others' deaths. *For the survivor can never, inwardly, simply conclude that it was logical and right for him, and not others, to survive. Rather, I would hold, he is bound by an unconscious perception of organic social balance which makes him feel that his survival was made possible by others' deaths: if they had not died, he would have had to; and if he had not survived, someone else would have.* This kind of guilt may well be the most fundamental to human existence. Additional factors also contribute greatly to guilt feelings: the survivor's relief, even joy, that it was the other and not he who died; previous death wishes he may have had toward parents who denied him nurturence he craved, or toward siblings who competed for this nurturence, whether guilt is directly experienced in relationship to the actual death of these family members, or indirectly through unconsciously relating such wishes to the death of any "other," however anonymous.

In ordinary mourning experiences, and in most ordinary disasters, this guilt may be resolved through the classical psychological steps of the mourning process. But my impression was that here such resolution has been either minimal or at best incomplete. As in other mourning experiences, survivors have identified themselves with the dead (both as specific people and as an anonymous concept), and have incorporated the dead into their own beings; indeed we might say that survivors have imbibed and incorporated the entire destruction of their city, and in fact the full atomic bomb experience. But they have found no adequate ideological interpretation—no spiritual explanation, no "reason" for the disaster—that might release them from this identification. They have felt compelled virtually to merge with the dead and to behave, in a great variety of ways, *as if* they too were dead. Not only do they judge all behavior by the degree of respect it demonstrates toward the dead, but they tend to condemn almost any effort that suggests strong self-assertion or vitality, that is, which suggests life.

The *hibakusha* identity, then, in a significant symbolic sense, becomes an identity of the dead—taking the following inner sequence: I almost died; I should have died; I did die, or at least am not really alive; or if I am alive it is impure for me to be so; and anything I do that affirms life is also impure and an insult to the dead, who alone are pure. Of great importance here, of course, is the Japanese cultural stress upon continuity between the living and the dead; but the identity sequence also has specific relationship to the nature of the disaster itself.

Yet one must not conclude that all survivors are therefore suicidal. This is by no means the case, and I was in fact struck by the tenacity with which *hibakusha,* at all of the stages mentioned, have held on to life. This identification with death—this whole constellation of inwardly experienced death symbolism—is, paradoxically enough, the survivor's means of maintaining life. In the face of the burden of guilt he carries with him, and particularly the guilt of survival priority, his obeisance before the dead is his best means of justifying and maintaining his own existence. But it remains an existence with a large shadow cast across it, a life that, in a powerful symbolic sense, the survivor does not feel to be his own.

GENERAL PRINCIPLES: The interrelationship between the anticipation of death and the conduct of life has been recognized and commented upon by generations of philosophers, although mentioned with surprising infrequency in psychiatric work. There are many signs that this psychiatric neglect is in the process of being remedied, and the significance of problems in this area so impresses itself upon us in our present age that matters of death and dying could well serve as a nucleus for an entire psychology of life. But I will do no more than state a few principles that I have found a useful beginning for comprehending the Hiroshima experience, relating it to universal human concerns, and examining some of the impact upon our lives of the existence of nuclear weapons. Attempting even this much is audacious enough to warrant pause and examination of some rather restraining words of Freud:

> *It is indeed impossible to imagine our own death; and whenever we attempt to do so we can perceive that we are in fact still present as spectators. Hence the psychoanalytic school could venture on the assertion that at bottom no one believes in his own death, or, to put the same thing in another way, that in the unconscious every one of us is convinced of his own immortality.*

These words from his essay, "Thought for the Times on War and Death," were written in 1915, about six months after the outbreak of World War I, and have found many recent echoes. (Merleau-Ponty, the distinguished French philosopher, has said, "Neither my birth nor my death can appear to me as *my* experience . . . I can only grasp myself as 'already born' and 'still living'—grasping my birth and death only as prepersonal horizons.")

Profound as Freud's words are, psychological investigations of death may have been unduly retarded by them. For they represent the kind of insight that, precisely because of its importance and validity, must be questioned further and even transcended. I believe it is more nearly correct to say that our own death—or at least our own dying—is not entirely unimaginable but can be imagined only with a considerable degree of distance, blurring, and denial; that we are not absolutely convinced of our own immortality, but have a need to maintain a *sense of immortality* in the face of inevitable biological death; and that this need represents not only the inability of the individual unconscious to recognize the possibility of its own demise but also a compelling universal urge to maintain an inner sense of continuous symbolic relationship, over time and space, to the various elements of life. Nor is this need to transcend biological life *mere* denial (although denial becomes importantly associated with it): rather it is part of the organism's psychobiological quest for mastery, part of an innate imagery apparently present in man's mind since the earliest periods of his history and prehistory. This point of view is consistent with that of Joseph Campbell, the distinguished student of comparative mythology, who has likened such innate imagery or "elementary ideas" to the "innate releasing mechanisms" described by contemporary ethologists. It also bears some resemblance to Otto Rank's stress upon man's long-standing need of "an assurance of eternal survival for his self," and to Rank's assertion that

"Man creates culture by changing natural conditions in order to maintain his spiritual self."

This sense of immortality may be expressed through any of several modes:

First, biologically—or, more correctly, biosocially—by means of family continuity, living on through (but in an emotional sense, *with*) our sons and daughters and their sons and daughters, by imagining (however vaguely and at whatever level of consciousness) an endless chain of biological attachment. This has been the classical expression of the sense of individual immortality in East Asian culture, as emphasized by the traditional Chinese family system, and to a somewhat lesser extent by the Japanese family system as well. But it is of enormous universal importance, perhaps the most universally significant of all modes. This biological mode of immortality never remains purely biological; rather it is experienced psychically and symbolically, and in varying degree extends itself into social dimensions, into the sense of surviving through one's tribe, organization, people, nation, or even species. On the whole this movement from the biological to the social has been erratic and in various ways precarious; but some, like Julian Huxley and Pierre Teilhard de Chardin, see it as taking on increasing significance during the course of human evolution. If this is so, individual man's sense of immortality may increasingly derive from his inner conviction, "I live on through mankind."

Second, a sense of immortality may be achieved through a theologically based idea of a life after death, not only as a form of "survival" but even as a "release" from profane life burdens into a "higher" form of existence. Some such concept has been present in all of the world's great religions and throughout human mythology. The details of life after death have been vague and logically contradictory in most theologies, since the symbolic psychological theme of transcending death takes precedence over consistency of concrete elaboration. Christianity has perhaps been most explicit in its doctrine of life after death, and most demanding of commitment to this doctrine; but intra-Christian debate over interpretation of doctrine has never ceased, with present thought tending toward a stress upon transcendent symbolism rather than literal belief.

Third, and this is partly an extension of the first two modes, a sense of immortality through one's creative works or human influences—one's writings, art, thought, inventions, or lasting products of any kind that have an effect upon other human beings. (In this sense lasting therapeutic influences upon patients, who in turn transmit them to their posterity, can be a mode of immortality for physicians and psychotherapists.) Certainly this form of immortality has particular importance for intellectuals conscious of participating in the general flow of human creativity, but applies in some measure to all human beings in their unconscious perceptions of the legacy they leave for others.

Fourth, a sense of immortality through being survived by nature it, self: the perception that natural elements—limitless in space and time—remain. I found this mode of immortality to be particularly vivid among Japanese, steeped as their culture is in nature symbolism; but various expressions of Western tradition (the Romantic Movement, for instance) have also placed great emphasis upon it. We can probably safely say—and here comparative mythology again gives us support—that there is a universal psychic imagery in which nature represents an "ultimate" aspect of existence.

These psychological modes of immortality are not merely problems one ponders when dying; they are constantly (if often indirectly or unconsciously) perceived standards by which we evaluate our lives. They thus enable us to examine the part played by death and death symbolism during ordinary existence, which is what we mean by the beginnings of a death-oriented psychology of life. Let us then put forth three propositions, all of them dealing with death as a standard for, or test of, some aspect of life.

1. Death is anticipated as a *severance of the sense of connection*—of the inner sense of organic relationship to the various elements, and particularly to the people and groups of people most necessary to our feelings of continuity and relatedness. Death is therefore a test of this sense of connection in that it threatens us with that which is most intolerable: *total severance*. Indeed all of the modes of immortality mentioned are symbolic reflections of that part of the human psychic equipment which protects us from such severance and isolation.

Another expression of the threat to the sense of connection represented by death is the profound ambivalence of individuals in every culture toward the dead. One embraces the dead, supplicates oneself before them, and creates rituals to perpetuate one's relationship to them, and (as we saw so vividly in the case of the Hiroshima survivors) to attenuate one's guilt over survival priority. But one also pushes away the dead, considers them tainted and unclean, dangerous and threatening, precisely because they symbolize a break in the sense of connection and threaten to undermine it within the living. These patterns too were strongly present in Hiroshima survivors (and can be found in general Japanese cultural practice), although less consciously acceptable and therefore more indirectly expressed. Indeed, in virtually every culture the failure of the living to enact the rituals necessary to appease the dead is thought to so anger the latter (or their sacred representatives) as to bring about dangerous retribution—punishment for this failure to atone for the guilt of survival priority.

2. Our second proposition is that death is a test of the meaning of life, of the symbolic integrity of the life one has been living. This is a more familiar concept, closely related to ideas that have long been put forth in literature and philosophy, as well as in certain psychoanalytic writings of

Freud, Rank and Jung; and it has a variety of manifestations. One is the utilization of a *way or style of dying* as an epitome of life's significance. In the Japanese *samurai* code, a heroic form of death in battle on behalf of one's lord was the ultimate expression of the meaning of life. Various cultures and subcultures have similarly set up an ideal style of dying, rarely perfectly realized, but nonetheless a powerful standard for the living. The anticipation of dying nobly, or at least appropriately—of dying for a meaningful purpose—is an expression of those modes of immortality related both to man's works (his lasting influences) and his biosocial continuity. Much of the passionate attraction man has felt toward death can, I believe, be understood as reflecting the sense that only in meaningful death can one simultaneously achieve a sense of immortality and articulate the meaning of life.

Timing and readiness play an important part. Can one visualize, in association with death, sufficient accomplishment to justify one's life? Or has life become so burdensome and devoid of meaning that death itself (whatever the style of dying) seems more appropriate? This was the case with a remarkable group of people undergoing surgery recently described by Avery Weisman and Thomas P. Hackett. These "predilection patients" were neither excessively anxious nor depressed, and yet correctly predicted their own deaths. For them, "death held more appeal . . . than did life because it promised either reunion with lost love, resolution of long conflict, or respite from anguish," and we are led to conclude that this psychological state interacted with their organic pathology and their reactions to surgical procedures to influence significantly the timing of their deaths. Their surrender to death, we may say, was related to their sense that they could no longer justify their continuing survival.

A classical literary expression of anticipated death as a test of the integrity of one's entire life (and one which has inspired many commentaries) occurs in Tolstoi's *The Death of Ivan Ilych*. Here the protagonist, in becoming aware of the incurable nature of his illness, reviews his past and is tormented by the thought that "the whole arrangement of his life and of his family, and all his social and official interests, might all have been false," and that the only authentic expressions of his life have been "those scarcely noticeable impulses which he had immediately suppressed." His lament in the face of approaching death is that of wasted opportunity ("I have lost all that was given me and it is impossible to rectify it") and existential guilt: the awareness of the enormous gap between what he has been and what he feels he might have been. But his torment disappears through a sudden spiritual revelation, his own capacity to feel love and pity for his wife and son. At that point, for Ivan Ilych, "death" disappears: "Death is finished . . . it is no more!" "Death" had meant emptiness, the termination of a life without significance; death has been transcended through a revelation that revivified Ivan Ilych's sense of immortality by transporting him, even momentarily, into a realm of what he could perceive as authentic experience, and one in which he could feel in contact with eternal human values of pity and love, whether these were derived from a theologically-defined supernatural source, or from man's own creative works and influences.

Highly significant in Ivan Ilych's search for integrity was his disgust for the lying and evasiveness of those around him concerning the true nature of his illness (and concerning everything else), his yearning for an end to "this falsity around and within him [which] did more than anything else to poison his last days." But we may say that his family members were incapable of acting otherwise, because their deception was also self-deception, their own need to deny death; and because they were immersed in their own guilt over survival priority in relationship to Ivan Ilych—guilt made particularly intense by their hypocrisy, lack of love for him, and relief that death was claiming him and not them. Similar emotions were present in his colleagues and friends immediately after his death: "Each one thought or felt, 'Well, he's dead but I'm alive!'" The one voice of integrity around Ivan Ilych was that of a simple peasant servant who made no effort to hide from him the fact that he was dying but instead helped him understand that death is, after all, the fate of everyone, that "We shall all of us die." Here we may say that the "survivor" lessens the emotional gap between himself and the dying man by stressing their shared destiny; this in turn enables the dying man to see his experience in relationship to the larger rhythms of life and death, and thereby awakens his biologically linked mode of immortality.

Very similar in theme to the death of Ivan Ilych, and probably influenced by it, is a recent Japanese film made by the accomplished director, Akira Kurosawa, *Ikiru* (To Live). The film is also about a dying man who critically reviews his life: a petty official whose past actions had been characterized by bureaucratic evasion, and who overcomes his self-condemnation by an almost superhuman dedication to a final task, the building of a park for children. He thus achieves his sense of immortality mainly by his "works," by the final monument he leaves behind for others (even though surviving fellow bureaucrats, who had actually tried to block the enterprise, claim complete credit for it). This form of immortality is more consistent with East Asian stress upon the contribution to the social order—and with the Japanese *deification of the human matrix*— than is the Western mode of spiritual revelation or faith expressed in the Tolstoi story. Moreover, in the sequence of the bureaucrat's behavior on discovering he was dying—first his withdrawal into petulant inactivity and then his extraordinary rush of productive energy—we find evidence of the East Asian tendency to deal with problems of despair over life and death by means of a polarity of purposeless withdrawal or active involvement, rather than by the more characteristically Western pattern of self-lacerating inner struggle against the forces creating despair. But concerning the problems of death and the sense of immortality, the essential message of *Ikiru* is not different from that of *The Death of Ivan Ilych*.

From the foregoing we can begin to recognize the wider meaning of the concept of the survivor. All of us who continue to live while people anywhere die are survivors, and both the word and the condition suggest a relationship that we all have to the dead. Therefore, the Hiroshima survivors' focus upon the dead as arbiters of good and evil, and invisible assigners of guilt and shame, is by no means as unique as it at first glance appears to be. For we all enter into similar commitments to the dead, whether consciously or unconsciously, whether to specific people who lived in the past or to the anonymous dead; or whether these commitments relate to theological or quasi-theological ideas about ties to the dead in another form of existence, or to more or less scientific ideas about a heritage we wish to affirm or a model we wish to follow. In any quest for perfection there is probably a significant identification with the imagined perfection of the dead hero or heroes who lived in the golden age of the past. Most of our history has been made by those now dead, and we cannot avoid calling upon them, at least in various symbolic ways, for standards that give meaning to our lives.

3. And a last proposition: death, in the very abruptness of its capacity to terminate life, becomes a test of life's sense of movement, of development and change—of sequence—in the continuous dialectic between fixed identity on the one hand and individuation on the other. To the extent that death is anticipated as absolute termination of life's movement, it calls into question the degree to which one's life contains, or has contained, any such development. Further, I would hold that a sense of movement in the various involvements of life is as fundamental a human need, as basic to the innate psychic imagery, as is the countervailing urge toward stillness, constancy, and reduction of tension which Freud (after Barbara Low) called the "Nirvana principle." Freud referred to the Nirvana principle as "the dominating tendency of mental life" and related it to the "death instinct"; but I would prefer to speak instead of polarizing psychic tendencies toward continuous movement and ultimate stillness, both equally central to psychic function. Given the preoccupation with and ambivalence toward death since mankind's beginnings, Freud's concept of the death instinct may be a much more powerful one than his critics will allow. At the same time it may yield greater understanding through being related to contemporary thought on symbolic process and innate imagery, rather than to older, more mechanistic views on the nature of instinct.

To express this human necessity for a sense of movement, I find it often useful to speak of "self-process" rather than simply of "self." I believe that the perpetual quest for a sense of movement has much to do with the appeal of comprehensive ideologies, particularly political and social ones, since these ideologies contain organized imagery of wider historical movement, and of individual participation in constant social flux. Yet ideologies, especially when totalist in character, also hold out an ultimate vision of utopian perfection in which all movement ceases, because one is, so to speak, *there*. This strong embodiment of both ends of the psychic polarity —of continuous movement as well as perfect stillness—may well be a fundamental source of ideological appeal. For in this polarity, ideologies represent a means of transcending linear time, and, at least symbolically, of transcending death itself. In the promise of an interminable relationship to the "Movement," one can enter into both a biosocial mode of immortality and a very special version of immortality through man's works, in this case relating to man's symbolic conquest of time. Nor is it accidental that ideologies appear and gather momentum during periods of cultural breakdown and historical dislocation, at which time there tends to be a sense of cessation of movement and of prominent death symbolism. Central to the revitalizing mission of ideologies is their acting out, in historical (and psychological) context, the classical mythological theme of death and rebirth.

In response to a threat of death, actual or symbolic, the psychic response is likely to be either that of stillness and cessation of movement, or else of frenetic, compensatory activity. The former was by far the most prominent in the Hiroshima situation, although the latter was not entirely absent. The psychic closing-off that took place right after the bomb fell was a cessation of psychic motion, or what might be thought of as a temporary form of sympolically "dying" to defend against the threat of more lasting psychological "death" (psychosis) posed by overwhelming evidence of actual physical death. The same may be said of the later self-imposed restraint in association with the identity of the dead, an identity whose very stillness becomes a means of carrying on with life in the face of one's commitment to death and the dead. But there were occasional cases of heightened activity, usually unfocused and confused, even at the time of the bomb. And later energies in rebuilding the city—the "frontier atmosphere" that predominated during much of the postwar period—may be seen as a somewhat delayed intensification of movement, although it must be added that much of this energy and movement came from the outside.

Can we say something more about these propositions concerning death, and about the various modes of immortality, as they apply to the nuclear age? I believe that from these perspectives we can see new psychological threats posed by nuclear weapons—right now, to all of us among the living.

Concerning the first proposition, that death is a test of our sense of connection, if we anticipate the possibility of nuclear weapons being used (as I believe we all do in some measure), we are faced with a prospect of being severed from virtually all of our symbolic paths to immortality. In the postnuclear world, we can imagine no biological or biosocial posterity; there is little or nothing surviving of our works or influences; and theological symbolism of an afterlife may well be insufficiently strong in its hold on the imagination to still fears of total severance. In my Hiroshima work I was struck by the inability of people to find adequate transcendent religious explanation—Buddhist, Shinto, or Christian—for what they and others had experienced. This was partly because of the relatively weak state of such theological symbolism in contemporary Japan, but perhaps most fundamentally because of the magnitude of the disaster itself. Whatever the mixed state of religious symbolism in the rest of the world, there is grave doubt whether the promise of some form of life after death can maintain symbolic power in an imagined world in which there are none (or virtually none) among the biologically living. This leaves only the mode of immortality symbolized by nature, which I found to be perhaps the most viable of all among Hiroshima survivors—as expressed in the Japanese (originally Chinese) proverb quoted to me by several of them: "The state may collapse but the mountains and rivers remain." And with all the other modes of immortality so threatened, we may raise the speculative possibility that, independent of any use of nuclear weapons, one outcome of the nuclear age might be the development of some form of natural theology (or at least of a theology in which nature is prominent) as a means of perpetuating man's innate need for a sense of immortality.

Concerning the second proposition, relating to the meaning and integrity of life, we find ourselves even more directly threatened by nuclear weapons. As many have already pointed out, nuclear weapons confront us with a kind of death that can have no meaning. There is no such thing as dying heroically, for a great cause, in the service of a belief or a nation, in other words for a palpable purpose—but rather only the prospect of dying anonymously, emptily, without gain to others. Such feelings were prominent among Hiroshima survivors both at the time of their initial immersion in death and during the months and years following it. They could not view their experience as purposeful, in the sense of teaching the world the necessity for abandoning nuclear weapons, but rather saw themselves as scapegoats for the world's evil, "guinea pigs" in a historical "experiment," or else as victims of war made infinitely more inhuman by the new weapon used. Part of their problem was the difficulty they had in knowing whom or what to hate, since, as one of my colleagues put it, "You can't hate magic." They did find in postwar Japanese pacifism an opportunity for organized rechanneling of resentment into a hatred of war itself; this was of considerable importance, but has by no means resolved the issue. The only consistent "meaning" survivors could find in all of the death and destruction around them was in the application of an everyday expression of East Asian fatalism—*"shikataganai"* ("it can't be helped")—which is a surface reflection of a profoundly important psychological tendency toward accepting whatever destiny one is given. But however great the psychological usefulness of this attitude, we can hardly say that it enabled survivors to achieve full mastery of their experience. Hiroshima survivors were the very antithesis of the "predilection patients" we spoke of before: rather than being ready for death, they found its intrusion upon life to be unacceptable, even absurd; and when seeming to embrace death, they were really clinging to life.

Considering the destructive power of present nuclear weapons and granting the impossibility of a meaningful nuclear death, is not life itself deprived of much of its meaning? Does not nuclear death threaten the deep significance of all our lives? Indeed, the attraction some feel toward the use of nuclear weapons might be partly a function of this meaninglessness, so that in a paradoxical way they want to "end it all" (perhaps realize their own end-of-the-world fantasies), to deny the very emptiness of the nuclear death toward which they press. Here the principle of individual suicide as an attempt to deny the reality of death is carried further to encompass nuclear suicide-murder as an attempt to deny the threat to meaningful human existence posed by these weapons.

And finally, in relationship to the proposition of death as a test of life's sense of movement, I think the matter is more ambiguous, although hardly encouraging. There is a sense in all of us, in greater or lesser degree, that nuclear weapons might terminate all of life's movement. Yet there is also, at least in some, a strange intensity and excitement in relationship to the confrontation with danger which nuclear weapons provide; and this, it might be claimed, contributes to a sense of movement in present-day life. But this exhilaration—or perhaps pseudo-exhilaration—is less a direct function of the nuclear weapons themselves than of the universal historical dislocation accompanying a wider technological revolution. In other words, there is in our world an extraordinary combination of potential for continuously enriching movement and development of self-process, side by side with the potential for sudden and absolute termination. This latter possibility, which I have called the *potentially terminal revolution,* has not yet been seriously evaluated in its full psychological consequences; and whatever its apparent stimulus to a sense of movement, we may well suspect that it also contributes to a profound listlessness and inertia that lurks beneath.

I am aware that I have painted something less than an optimistic picture, both concerning the Hiroshima disaster and our present relationship to the nuclear world. Indeed, it would seem that we are caught in a vicious psychological and historical circle, in which the existence of nuclear weapons impairs our relationship to death and immortality, and this impairment to our symbolic processes in turn interferes with our ability to deal with these same nuclear weapons. But one way of breaking out of such a pattern is by gaining at least a dim understanding of our own involvement in it. And in studying the Hiroshima experience and other extreme situations, I have found that man's capacity for elaborating and enclosing himself in this kind of ring of destructiveness is matched only by his equal capacity for renewal. Surely the mythological theme of death and rebirth takes on particular pertinence for us now, and every constructive effort we can make to grasp something more of our relationship to death becomes, in its own way, a small stimulus to rebirth.

꙳ ꙳ ꙳ ꙳

It has been the classic responsibility of a nation's government to guard the security of its citizens. To this end citizens have paid taxes, delegated power, and the government has maintained a military establishment. One of the extraordinary aspects of the unprecedented situation that confronts us is that the technological breakthroughs have made obsolete any notion of national security through national military means.

In the following article which appeared in October 1964, Jerome B. Wiesner and Herbert F. York, two eminent scientists who served as advisors to the Eisenhower and Kennedy administrations, set forth explicitly why this is so. They emphasize that although they "discuss the matter from the point of view of our country's national interest, [they] believe, however, that a Soviet military technologist, writing from the point of view of the U.S.S.R., could write an almost identical paper." In other words, it is a world problem due to the revolution in the technology of war itself. And they conclude:

"Both sides of the arms race are thus confronted by the dilemma of steadily increasing military power and steadily decreasing national security. It is our considered professional judgment that this dilemma has no technical solution." Recognition of this fact is essential before we can move on to the positive note on which the article ends.

National Security and the Nuclear-Test Ban

JEROME B. WIESNER AND

HERBERT F. YORK

The partial nuclear-test ban—the international treaty that prohibits nuclear explosions in the atmosphere, in the oceans and in outer space—has been in effect for a little more than a year. From July, 1945, when the first atomic bomb was set off in New Mexico, until August, 1963, when the U.S. completed its last series of atmospheric bomb tests in the Pacific, the accumulated tonnage of nuclear explosions had been doubling every three years. Contamination of the atmosphere by fission products and by the secondary products of irradiation (notably the long-lived carbon 14) was approaching a level (nearly 10 per cent of the natural background radiation) that alarmed many biologists. A chart plotting the accumulation of radioactive products can also be read as a chart of the acceleration in the arms race.

Now, for a year, the curve has flattened out. From the objective record it can be said that the improvement of both the physical and the political atmosphere of the world has fulfilled at least the short-range expectations of those who advocated and worked for the test ban. In and of itself the treaty does no more than moderate the continuing arms race. It is nonetheless, as President Kennedy said, "an important first step—a step toward peace, a step toward reason, a step away from war."

The passage of a year also makes it possible to place in perspective and evaluate certain misgivings that have been expressed about the effect on U.S. national security of the suspension of the testing of nuclear weapons in the atmosphere. These misgivings principally involve the technology of nuclear armament. National security, of course, involves moral questions and human values—political, social, economic and psychological questions as well as technological ones. Since no one is an expert in all the disciplines of knowledge concerned, it is necessary to consider one class of such questions at a time, always with the caution that such consideration is incomplete. As scientists who have been engaged for most of our professional lifetimes in consultation on this country's military policy and in the active development of the weapons themselves, we shall devote the present discussion primarily to the technological questions.

The discussion will necessarily rest on unclassified information. It is unfortunate that so many of the facts concerning this most important problem are classified, but that is the situation at this time. Since we have access to classified information, however, we can assure the reader that we would not have to modify any of the arguments we present here if we were able to cite such information. Nor do we know of any military considerations excluded from open discussion by military secrecy that would weaken any of our conclusions. We shall discuss the matter from the point of view of our country's national interest. We believe, however, that a Soviet military technologist, writing from the point of view of the U.S.S.R., could write an almost identical paper.

Today as never before national security involves technical questions. The past two decades have seen a historic revolution in the technology of war. From the blockbuster of World War II to the thermonuclear bomb the violence of military explosives has been scaled upward a million times. The time required for the interhemispheric transport of weapons of mass destruction has shrunk from 20 hours for the 300-mile-per-hour B-29 to the 30-minute flight time of the ballistic missile. Moreover, the installation of the computer in command and control systems has increased their information-processing capacity by as much as six orders of magnitude compared with organizations manned at corresponding points by human nervous systems.

It has been suggested by some that technological surprise presents the primary danger to national security. Yet recognition of the facts of the present state of military technology must lead to the opposite conclusion. Intercontinental delivery time cannot be reduced to secure any significant improvement in the effectiveness of the attack. Improvement by another order of magnitude in the information-processing capacity of the defending system will not make nearly as large a difference in its operational effectiveness.

The point is well illustrated by the 100-megaton nuclear bomb. Whether or not it is necessary, in the interests of national security, to test and deploy a bomb with a yield in the range of 100 megatons was much discussed during the test-ban debates. The bomb was frequently referred to as the "big" bomb, as if the bombs now in the U.S. arsenal were somehow not big. The absurdity of this notion is almost enough by itself to settle the argument. A one-megaton bomb is already about 50 times bigger than the bomb that produced 100,000 casualties at Hiroshima, and 10 megatons is of the same order of magnitude as the grand total of all high explosives used in all wars to date. Other technical considerations that surround this question are nonetheless illuminating and worth exploring.

There is, first of all, the "tactics" of the missile race. The purpose of a missile system is to be able to destroy or, perhaps more accurately, able to threaten to destroy enemy targets. No matter what the statesmen, military men and moralists on each side may think of the national characteristics, capabilities and morality of the other side, no matter what arguments may be made about who is aggressive and who is not or who is rational and who is not, the military planners on each side must reckon with the possibility that the other side will attack first. This means that above all else the planner must assure the survival of a sufficient proportion of his own force, following the heaviest surprise attack the other side might mount, to launch a retaliatory attack. Moreover, if the force is to be effective as a deterrent to a first strike, its capacity to survive and wreak revenge and even win, whatever that may mean, must be apparent to the other side.

Several approaches, in fact, can be taken to assure the survival of a sufficient missile force after a first attack on it. The most practical of these are: (1) "hardening," that is, direct protection against physical damage; (2) concealment, including subterfuge and, as in the case of the Polaris submarine missiles, mobility, and (3) numbers, that is, presenting more targets than the attacker can possibly cope with. The most straightforward and certain of these is the last: numbers. For the wealthier adversary it is also the easiest, because he can attain absolute superiority in numbers. A large number of weapons is also a good tactic for the poorer adversary, because numbers even in the absence of absolute superiority can hopelessly frustrate efforts to locate all targets.

There is an unavoidable trade-off, however, between the number and the size of weapons. The cost of a missile depends on many factors, one of the most important being gross size or weight. Unless one stretches "the state of the art" too far in the direction of sophistication and miniaturization, the cost of a missile turns out to be roughly proportional to its weight, if otherwise identical design criteria are used. The protective structures needed for hardening or the capacity of submarines needed to carry the missile also have a cost roughly proportional to the volume of the missile. Some of the ancillary equipment has a cost proportional to the size of the missile and some does not; some operational expenditures vary directly with size or weight and some do not. The cost of the warhead generally does not, although the more powerful warhead requires the larger missile. It is not possible to put all these factors together in precise bookkeeping form, but it is correct to say that the cost of missile, complete and ready for firing, increases somewhat more slowly than linearly with its size.

On the other hand—considering "hard" targets only—the effectiveness of a missile increases more slowly than cost as the size of the missile goes up. The reason is that the radius of blast damage, which is the primary effect employed against a hard target, increases only as the cube root of the yield and because yield has a more or less direct relation to weight. Against "soft" targets, meaning population centers and conventional military bases, even "small" bombs are completely effective, and nothing is gained by increasing yield. Given finite resources, even in the wealthiest economy, it would seem prudent to accept smaller size in order to get larger numbers. On any scale of investment, in fact, the combination of larger numbers and smaller size results in greater effectiveness for the missile system as a whole, as contrasted to the effectiveness of a single missile.

This line of reasoning has, for some years, formed the basis of U.S. missile policy. The administration of President Eisenhower, when faced with the choice of bigger missiles (the liquid-fueled Atlas and Titan rockets) as against smaller missiles (the solid-fueled Minuteman and Polaris rockets), decided to produce many more of the smaller missiles. The administration of President Kennedy independently confirmed this decision and increased the ratio of smaller to larger missiles in the nation's armament. During the test-ban hearings it was revealed that the U.S. nuclear armament included bombs of 23-megaton yield and higher, carried by bombers. Recently Cyrus R. Vance, Under Secretary of Defense, indicated that the Air Force has been retiring these large bombs in favor of smaller ones. There are presumably no targets that call for the use of such enormous explosions. . . .

Suppose, however, a new analysis, based on information not previously considered, should show that it is in fact necessary to incorporate the 100-megaton bomb in the U.S. arsenal. Can this be done without further weapons tests? The answer is yes. Because the U.S.S.R. has pushed development in this yield range and the U.S. has not, the U.S. 100-megaton bomb might not be as elegant as the Soviet model. It would perhaps weigh somewhat more or at the same weight would produce a somewhat lower yield. It could be made, however, and the basic techniques for making it have been known since the late 1950s. The warhead for such a bomb would require a big missile, but not so big as some being developed by the National Aeronautics and Space Administration for the U.S. space-exploration program. Such a weapon would be expensive, particularly on a per-unit basis; under any imaginable circumstances it would be of limited use and not many of its kind would be built.

The extensive series of weapons tests carried out by the U.S.—involving the detonation of several hundred nuclear bombs and devices—have yielded two important bodies of information. They have shown how to bring the country's nuclear striking force to its present state of high effectiveness. And they have demonstrated the effects of nuclear weapons over a wide range of yields. Among the many questions that call for soundly based knowledge of weapons effects perhaps none is more important in a discussion of the technical aspects of national security than: What would be the result of a surprise attack by missiles on the country's own missile forces? Obviously if the huge U.S. investment in its nuclear armament is to succeed in deterring an attacker, that armament must be capable of surviving a first strike.

A reliable knowledge of weapons effects is crucial to the making of rational decisions about the number of missiles needed, the hardening of missile emplacements, the degree of dispersal, the proportion that should be made mobile and so on. The military planner must bear in mind, however, that such decisions take time—years—to carry out and require large investments of finite physical and human resources. The inertia of the systems is such that the design engineer at work today must be concerned not with the surprise attack that might be launched today but rather with the kind and size of forces that might be launched against them years in the future. In addition to blast, shock and other physical effects, therefore, the planner must contend with a vast range of other considerations. These include the yields of the various bombs the attacker would use against each target; the reliability and accuracy of his missiles; the number and kind of weapons systems he would have available for attack; the tactics of the attacker, meaning the number of missiles he would commit to a first strike, the fractions he would allocate to military as against civilian targets and the relative importance he would assign to various kinds of military targets, the effects of chaos on the defender's capacity to respond, and so on. In all cases the planner must project his thinking forward to some hypothetical future time, making what he can of the available intelligence about the prospective attacker's present capabilities and intentions. Plainly all these "other considerations" involve inherently greater uncertainties than the knowledge of weapons effects.

The extensive classified and unclassified literature accumulated in two decades of weapons tests and available to U.S. military planners contains at least some observations on all important effects for weapons with a large range of yields. These observations are more or less well understood in terms of physical theories; they can be expressed in numerical or algebraic form, and they can be extrapolated into areas not fully explored in the weapons tests conducted by the U.S., for example into the 100-megaton range. As one departs from the precise circumstances of past experiments, of course, extrapolation becomes less and less reliable. Nonetheless, some sort of estimate can be made about what the prompt and direct effects will be under any conceivable set of circumstances.

Consider, in contrast, the degree of uncertainty implicit in predicting the number and kind of weapons systems that might be available to the prospective attacker. Such an uncertainty manifested itself in the famous "missile gap" controversy. The remarkable difference between the dire predictions made in the late 1950s—based as they were on the best available intelligence—and the actual situation that developed in the early 1960s can be taken as indicating the magnitude of the uncertainties that surround the variables other than weapons effects with which the military planner must contend. Moreover, these factors, as they concern a future attack, are uncertain not only to the defender; they are almost as uncertain to the attacker.

Uncertainties of this order and kind defy reduction to mathematical expression. A human activity as complex as modern war cannot be computed with the precision possible in manipulation of the data that concern weapons effects. What is more, the uncertainties about this single aspect of the total problem are not, as is sometimes assumed, multiplicative in estimation of the over-all uncertainty. Most, but not all, of the uncertainties are independent of one another. The total uncertainty is therefore, crudely speaking, the square root of the sum of the squares of the individual uncertainties.

In our view, further refinement of the remaining uncertainties in the data concerning prompt direct physical effects can contribute virtually nothing more to management of the real military and political problems, even though it would produce neater graphs. Furthermore, if new effects should be discovered either experimentally or theoretically in the future, or if, in certain peculiar environments, some of the now known effects should be excessively uncertain, it will be almost certainly possible to "over-design" the protection against them. Thus, although renewed atmospheric testing would contribute some refinement to the data on weapons effects, the information would be, at best, of marginal value.

Such refinements continue to be sought in the underground tests that are countenanced under the partial test ban. From this work may also come some reductions in the cost of weapons, modest improvements in yield-to-weight ratios, devices to fill in the spectrum of tactical nuclear weapons and so on. There is little else to justify the effort and expenditure. The program is said by some to be necessary, for example, to the development of a pure fusion bomb, sometimes referred to as the "neutron bomb." It is fortunate that this theoretically possible (stars are pure fusion systems) device has turned out to be so highly difficult to create; if it were relatively simple, its development might open the way to thermonuclear armament for the smallest and poorest powers in the world. The U.S., with its heavy investment in fission-to-fusion technology, would be the last nation to welcome this development and ought to be the last to encourage it. Underground testing is also justified for its contribution to the potential peaceful uses of nuclear explosives. Promising as these may be, the world could forgo them for a time in exchange for cessation of the arms race. Perhaps the best rationale for the underground-test program is that it helps to keep the scientific laboratories of the military establishment intact and in readiness—in readiness, however, for a full-scale resumption of the arms race.

Paradoxically one of the potential destabilizing elements in the present nuclear standoff is the possibility that one of the rival powers might develop a successful antimissile defense. Such a system, truly airtight and in the exclusive possession of one of the powers, would effectively nullify the deterrent force of the other, exposing the latter to a first attack against which it could not retaliate. The possibilities in this quarter have often been cited in rationalization of the need for resuming nuclear tests in the atmosphere. Here two questions must be examined. One must first ask if it is possible to develop a successful antimissile defense system. It then becomes appropriate to consider whether or not nuclear weapons tests can make a significant contribution to such a development.

Any nation that commits itself to large-scale defense of its civilian population in the thermonuclear age must necessarily reckon with passive modes of defense (shelters) as well as active ones (antimissile missiles). It is in the active mode, however, that the hazard of technological surprise most often lurks. The hazard invites consideration if only for the deeper insight it provides into the contemporary revolution in the technology of war.

The primary strategic result of that revolution has been to overbalance the scales in favor of the attacker rather than the defender. During World War II interception of no more than 10 per cent of the attacking force gave victory to the defending force in the Battle of Britain. Attrition of this magnitude was enough to halt the German attack because it meant that a given weapons-delivery system (bomber and crew) could deliver on the average only 10 payloads of high explosive; such a delivery rate was not sufficient to produce backbreaking damage. In warfare by thermonuclear missiles the situation is quantitatively and qualitatively different. It is easily possible for the offense to have in its possession and ready to launch a number of missiles that exceeds the number of important industrial targets to be attacked by, let us say, a factor of 10. Yet the successful delivery of only one warhead against each such target would result in what most people would consider an effective attack. Thus where an attrition rate of only 10 per cent formerly crowned the defense with success, a penetration rate of only 10 per cent (corresponding to an attrition rate of 90 per cent) would give complete success to the offense. The ratio of these two ratios is 100 to one; in this sense the task of defense can be said to have become two orders of magnitude more difficult.

Beyond this summary statement of the situation there are many general reasons for believing that defense against thermonuclear attack is impossible. On the eve of attack the offense can take time to get ready and to "point up" its forces; the defense, meanwhile, must stay on the alert over periods of years, perpetually ready and able to fire within the very few minutes available after the first early warning. The attacker can pick its targets and can choose to concentrate its forces on some and ignore others; the defense must be prepared to defend all possible important targets. The offense may attack the defense itself; then, as soon as one weapon gets through, the rest have a free ride.

The hopelessness of the task of defense is apparent even now in the stalemate of the arms race. A considerable inertia drags against the movement of modern, large-scale, unitary weapons systems from the stage of research and development to operational deployment. The duration and magnitude of these enterprises, whether defensive or offensive, practically assure that no system can reach full deployment under the mantle of secrecy. The designer of the defensive system, however, cannot begin until he has learned something about the properties and capabilities of the offensive system. Inevitably the defense must start the race a lap behind. In recent years, it seems, the offense has even gained somewhat in the speed with which it can put into operation stratagems and devices that nullify the most extraordinary achievements in the technology of defense. These general observations are expensively illustrated in the development and obsolescence of two major U.S. defense systems.

Early in the 1950s the U.S. set out to erect an impenetrable defense against a thermonuclear attack by bombers. The North American continent was to be ringed with a system of detectors that would flash information back through the communications network to a number of computers. The computers were to figure out from this data what was going on and what ought to be done about it and then flash a series of commands to the various interceptor systems. In addition to piloted aircraft, these included the Bomarc (a guided airborne missile) and the Nike-Hercules (a ballistic rocket). By the early 1960s this "Sage" system was to be ready to detect, intercept and destroy the heaviest attack that could be launched against it.

The early 1960s have come and yet nothing like the capability planned in the 1950s has been attained. Why not? Time scales stretched out, subsystems failed to attain their planned capabilities and costs increased. Most important, the offense against which the system was designed is not the offense that actually exists in the early 1960s. Today the offensive system on both sides is a mixture of missiles and bombers. The Sage system has a relatively small number of soft but vital organs completely vulnerable to missiles—a successful missile attack on them would give a free ride to the bombers. As early as 1958 the Department of Defense came to realize that this would be the situation, and the original grand plan was steadily cut back. In other words, the Sage system that could have been available, say, in 1963 and that should have remained useful at least through the 1960s would in principle have worked quite well against the offense that existed in the 1950s.

To answer the intercontinental ballistic missile, the Department of Defense launched the development of the Nike-Zeus system. Nike-Zeus was intended to provide not a defense of the continent at its perimeter but a point defense of specific targets. To be sure, the "points" were fairly large—the regions of population concentration around 50 to 70 of the country's biggest cities. The system was to detect incoming warheads, feeding the radar returns directly into its computers, and launch and guide an interceptor missile carrying a nuclear warhead into intersection with the trajectory of each of the incoming warheads.

Nike-Zeus was not designed to defend the 1,000 or so smaller centers outside the metropolitan areas simply because there are too many of these to be covered by the resources available for a system so huge and complicated. Nor was the system designed to defend the retaliatory missiles, the security of these forces being entrusted to the more reliable protection of dispersal, concealment, mobility and number. In principle, the defense of a hardened missile silo would have presented by far the simplest case for proof of the effectiveness of Nike-Zeus as advanced by those who contend that such a system can be made to "work." There would be no ambiguity about the location of the target of the incoming warhead. By the same token Nike-Zeus might have been considered for the defense of a few special defense posts, such as the headquarters of the Air Defense Command of the Strategic Air Command. These special cases are so few in number, however, that it had to be concluded that the attacker would either blast his way through to them by a concentration of firepower or ignore them altogether.

At the time of the conception of the Nike-Zeus system its designers were confronted with a comparatively simple problem, namely that of shooting down the warheads one by one as they presented themselves to the detectors. Even this simple problem had to be regarded as essentially unsolvable, in view of the fact that a 90 per cent success in interception constitutes failure in the inverted terms of thermonuclear warfare. At first, therefore, the designers of the offensive system did not take the prospect of an antimissile system seriously. Then the possibility that the problem of missile interception might be solved in principle gave them pause. Thereupon the designers of the offense began to invent a family of "penetration aids," that is, decoys and confusion techniques. The details of these and the plans for their use are classified, but the underlying principles are obvious. They include light decoys that can be provided in large numbers but that soon betray their character as "atmospheric sorting" separates them from the heavier decoys (and actual warheads) that can be provided in smaller numbers to confuse the defending detectors down to the last minute. Single rockets can also eject multiple warheads. Both the decoys and the warheads can be made to present ambiguous cross sections to the radar systems. These devices and stratagems overwhelmed the designed capability of the Nike-Zeus system and compelled its recent abandonment.

If the installation of the system had proceeded according to plan, the first Nike-Zeus units would have been operational within the next year or two. This could have been celebrated as a technical milestone. As a means of defense of a substantial percentage of the population, however, the system would not have reached full operational deployment until the end of the decade. In view of its huge cost the system should then have looked forward to a decade of useful life until, say, the late 1970s. Thus, in inexorable accordance with the phase-lag of the defense, the U.S. population was to be defended a decade too late by a system that might have been effective in principle (although most probably not in practice) against the missiles of the early 1960s.

The race of the tortoise and the hare has now entered the next lap with the development of the Nike-X system as successor to Nike-Zeus. The Advanced Research Projects Agency of the Department of Defense has been spending something on the order of $200 million a year on its so-called Defender Program, exploring on the broadest front the principles and techniques that might prove useful in the attempt to solve the antimissile problem. Although nothing on the horizon suggests that there is a solution, this kind of work must go forward. It not only serves the forlorn hope of develping an active anti-missile defense but also promotes the continued development of offensive weapons. The practical fact is that work on defensive systems turns out to be the best way to promote invention of the penetration aids that nullify them.

As the foregoing discussion makes clear, the problems of antimissile development are problems in radar, computer technology, missile propulsion, guidance and control. The nuclear warheads for the antimissile missile have been ready for a long time for delivery to the right place at the right time. Although it is argued that certain refinements in the existing data about weapons effects are needed, the other uncertainties all loom much larger than the marginal uncertainties in these physical effects. The antimissile defense problem, then, is one in which nuclear testing can play no really significant part.

The pursuit of an active defense system demands parallel effort on the passive defense, or shelter, front because the nature of the defense system strongly conditions the tactics of the offense that is likely to be mounted against it. To take a perhaps farfetched example, a Nike-Zeus system that provided protection for the major population centers might invite the attacker to concentrate the weight of his assault in ground bursts on remote military installations and unprotected areas adjacent to cities, relying on massive fallout to imperil the population centers. This example serves also to suggest how heavily the effectiveness of any program for sheltering the civilian population depends on the tactics of the attacker. Fallout shelters by themselves are of no avail if the attacker chooses to assault the population centers directly.

In any speculation about the kind of attack to which this country might be exposed it is useful to note where the military targets are located. Most of the missile bases are, in fact, far from the largest cities. Other key military installations, however, are not so located. Boston, New York, Philadelphia, Seattle, San Francisco, Los Angeles (Long Beach) and San Diego all have important naval bases. Essential command and control centers are located in and near Denver, Omaha and Washington, D.C. The roll call could be extended to include other major cities containing military installations that would almost certainly have to be attacked in any major assault on this country. The list does not stop with these; it is only prudent to suppose still other cities would come under attack, because there is no way to know in advance what the strategy may be.

The only kind of shelter that is being seriously considered these days, for other than certain key military installations, is the fallout shelter. By definition fallout shelters offer protection against nothing but fallout and provide virtually no protection against blast, fire storms and other direct effects. Some people have tried to calculate the percentage of the population that would be saved by fallout shelters in the event of massive attack. Such calculations always involve predictions about the form of the attack, but since the form is unknowable the calculations are nonsensical. Even for the people protected by fallout shelters the big problem is not a problem in the physical theory of gamma-ray attenuation, which can be neatly computed, but rather the sociological problem of the sudden initiation of general chaos, which is not subject to numerical analysis.

Suppose, in spite of all this, the country were to take fallout shelters seriously and build them in every city and town. The people living in metropolitan areas that qualify as targets because they contain essential military installations, and the people living in metropolitan areas that might be targeted as a matter of deliberate policy, would soon recognize that fallout shelters are inadequate. That conclusion would be reinforced by the inevitable reaction from the other side, whose military planners would be compelled to consider a massive civilian-shelter program as portending a first strike against them. Certainly the military planners of the U.S. would be remiss if they did not take similar note of a civilian-shelter program in the U.S.S.R. As a step in the escalation of the arms race toward the ultimate outbreak of war, the fallout shelter would lead inevitably to the blast shelter. Even with large numbers of blast shelters built and evenly distributed throughout the metropolitan community, people would soon realize that shelters alone are not enough. Accidental alarms, even in tautly disciplined military installations, have shown that people do not always take early warnings seriously. Even if they did, a 15-minute "early" warning provides less than enough time to seal the population into shelters. Accordingly, the logical next step is the live-in and work-in blast shelter leading to still further disruption and distortion of civilization. There is no logical termination of the line of reasoning that starts with belief in the usefulness of fallout shelters; the logic of this attempt to solve the problem of national security leads to a diverging series of ever more grotesque measures. This is to say, in so many words, that if the arms race continues and resumes its former accelerating tempo, 1984 is more than just a date on the calendar 20 years hence.

Ever since shortly after World War II the military power of the U.S. has been steadily increasing. Throughout this same period the national security of the U.S. has been rapidly and inexorably diminishing. In the early 1950s the U.S.S.R., on the basis of its own unilateral decision and determination to accept the inevitable retaliation, could have launched an attack against the U.S. with bombers carrying fission bombs. Some of these bombers would have penetrated our defenses and the American casualties would have numbered in the millions. In the later 1950s, again on its own sole decision and determination to accept the inevitable massive retaliation, the U.S.S.R. could have launched an attack against the U.S. using more and better bombers, this time carrying thermonuclear bombs. Some of these bombers would have penetrated our defenses and the American casualties could have numbered in the tens of millions.

Today the U.S.S.R., again on the basis of its own decision and determination to accept the inevitable retaliation, could launch an attack on the U.S. using intercontinental missiles and bombers carrying thermonuclear weapons. This time the number of American casualties could very well be on the order of 100 million.

The steady decrease in national security did not result from any inaction on the part of the responsible U.S. military and civilian authorities. It resulted from the systematic exploitation of the products of modern science and technology by the U.S.S.R. The air defenses deployed by the U.S. during the 1950s would have reduced the number of casualties the country might have otherwise sustained, but their existence did not substantively modify this picture. Nor could it have been altered by any other defense measures that might have been taken but that for one reason or another were not taken.

From the Soviet point of view the picture is similar but much worse. The military power of the U.S.S.R. has been steadily increasing since it became an atomic power in 1949. Soviet national security, however, has been steadily decreasing. Hypothetically the U.S. could unilaterally decide to destroy the U.S.S.R. and the U.S.S.R. would be absolutely powerless to prevent it. That country could only, at best, seek to wreak revenge through whatever retaliatory capability it might then have left.

Both sides in the arms race are thus confronted by the dilemma of steadily increasing military power and steadily decreasing national security. *It is our considered professional judgment that this dilemma has no technical solution.* If the great powers continue to look for solutions in the area of science and technology only, the result will be to worsen the situation. The clearly predictable course of the arms race is a steady open spiral downward into oblivion.

We are optimistic, on the other hand, that there is a solution to this dilemma. The partial nuclear-test ban, we hope and believe, is truly an important first step toward finding a solution in an area where a solution may exist. A next logical step would be the conclusion of a comprehensive test ban such as that on which the great powers came close to agreement more than once during 10 long years of negotiation at Geneva. The policing and inspection procedures so nearly agreed on in those parleys would set significant precedents and lay the foundations of mutual confidence for proceeding thereafter to actual disarmament.

❊ ❊ ❊ ❊

Kenneth Boulding, who is Professor of Economics at the University of Michigan and codirector of the Center for Research on Conflict Resolution, has written widely in the fields of economic policy and development. He has pointed out elsewhere that we think of the earth easily as a succession of spheres—a lithosphere, a biosphere, an atmosphere, and so on—and that it is a simple extension of this notion to think of the "econosphere" as the whole web of relations extending over the globe. The elements of the econosphere are the persons of the human population of the earth in their economic aspects, connected by an intricate web of exchange, payments, transfers and organizational roles and communications. The notion of the econosphere is essential to the concept of mankind, although it does not encompass all the relationships of what might be called the "homosphere," which is the sphere of mankind in all its relationships.

At this present stage of world development the whole question of the relationship between developed and underdeveloped areas needs the utmost attention for, as Nathan Keyfitz pointed out in the March 1966 issue of the *Bulletin of the Atomic Scientists*, there is real danger that mankind may become split into "Two Worlds on One Planet." How to cross the "four coinciding lines of income, race, culture and geography which separate the nationally poor from the middle classes of the world is today's problem."

In this short, simple piece below, Boulding expresses his view that, on our present course, the Population-Poverty crisis will reach a point-of-no-return within 10 to 20 years and "a major mobilization of intellectual resources is clearly indicated—something, for instance, at least on the scale of the Manhattan Project which produced the nuclear weapon— and the logical coordinator of such an effort is the United Nations." Although Boulding's first step does not require prohibitive sums, one must ask whether we will deal adequately with this crisis while so much of the world's resources both of brains and of energy are funneled into the war system.

I would call your attention to the last paragraph and to his view that it is not necessarily utopian to believe that we can develop common images of the future of man and common views of how we can move toward that future. Why this should be so will become clear, I trust, before the end of these materials. I would also call your attention to an earlier sentence and what follows it. "The major asset of the United Nations is that it is an enormous depository of legitimacy." The question of what constitutes a legitimate authority is one of great importance and elusiveness and it will haunt this Reader throughout, never entirely pinned down; yet in it lies the secret of our consent to any government whether it be a parent or a world body. Certainly, it would seem clear that brushing aside the United Nations and taking unilateral military action to settle a dispute by any member nation, particularly by a Great Power, eats away dangerously at that painstakingly acquired store of legitimacy and shows a curious callousness to world public opinion.

Population and Poverty

KENNETH BOULDING

It is hard to avoid pessimism about the immediate prospects for economic development in the tropical belt, even should circumstances be the most favorable. The principal obstacle to economic growth in these areas is the demographic upheaval produced by the introduction of chemical insecticides and malaria control. In many countries around the tropical belt, especially those that are most easily accessible, malaria was largely and rather quickly eliminated about 1950. The result was a spectacular decline in mortality rates, especially in infant mortality—without, however, any corresponding decline in birth rates. In many places, indeed, the birth rate has actually risen. This has led to an enormously distorted age distribution, and in many of these countries today half the population is under the age of fifteen, with the number of fourteen-year-old teenagers almost double the number of twenty-year-old young adults. This sudden burst at the lower end of the age pyramid has brought with it almost unbearable social burdens. In many of the tropical societies, for instance, literacy is declining, for the educational system simply cannot cope with the enormous numbers of children. The proportion going on to higher education is likewise almost bound to decline, in spite of strenuous efforts, because in a few years the number of young people of college age, or even of high school age, will be doubled—a rate of increase which the facilities for high school and college education cannot possibly match. A related but quite different sort of handicap is a shortage in the active labor force, which is likely to last for some time. Already a relatively small percentage of the population in these countries is available for internal development, and since the proportion of adults needed to rear and educate children is unlikely to decline in the near future, the prospects are very discouraging.

Perhaps the best hope would be a sharp reduction in the birth rate beginning almost immediately; and this is by no means off the agenda, now that relatively simple and cheap intrauterine devices for birth control are available. If we suppose a sharp reduction in birth rate, from the forty to forty-five per thousand which is all too common in these countries to, say, twenty per thousand in the next five years, then by 1980 or 1985 there will be relatively small cohorts of children and very large numbers in the labor force. This will be the moment to initiate development. A very rapid expansion in the educational system will be possible; a considerable labor force will be able to be spared for physical investment; and in a single generation, a large step could be taken toward entering the modern world. In many countries, however, should birth rates continue at their present rate over the next twenty years or so, the situation will be almost hopeless. Not only will there continue to be unmanageable numbers of children to feed, clothe, and educate, but even a large investment effort will hardly prevent a decline in the per capita capital stock. If the population doubles in twenty years, as can easily happen in some of these countries, the capital stock must also double if it is to keep pace. This means making a substantial investment effort just to stand still in per capita terms.

When we look at the structural situation, the outlook becomes even more gloomy. Most of these countries consist of what might be called a traditional rural sector, in which perhaps 80 per cent of the people live, and a more modern urban sector with about 20 per cent of the populace.

The sudden enormous influx of teenagers into the rural labor market, hitherto capable of incorporating only relatively fixed numbers of new entrants each year, is likely to disrupt it almost completely. The outcome will be either widespread unemployment among the rural youth or a general teenage exodus to the cities. The cities, however, are already expanding at an unprecedented rate, because of the phenomenon which I have called the "rural push"—that is, an increase in the rural population beyond what the traditional society can possibly take care of, with the result that surplus villagers are almost literally pushed into the cities. Some of the cities in these countries have been growing at the rate of 12 or 15 per cent per annum, which means they are doubling every five or six years. A city can hardly grow at this rate without collapsing into severe social disorganization. For one thing, the growth of employment opportunities lags far behind the rapid growth of population, and urban unemployment of a strictly structural nature, intractable to any ordinary monetary or fiscal management, is thus an almost inevitable feature of these burgeoning cities. A 20 per cent or even 25 per cent rate of urban unemployment is by no means uncommon in the major cities of the tropical belt. The wastage and disintegration of human resources which this represents is frightful to contemplate.

We have to recognize that economic development is fundamentally a learning process. If people are to enter the modern world, they have to absorb a wide range of new skills and new concepts. Innovation somehow has to break into the traditional network by which skills and concepts are transmitted—through the family, the face-to-face interaction of peers, and such informal agencies as the old men and the village meeting place. There are two major sources of new knowledge: the school system and the mass media—particularly, in poor countries, the radio, which can reach the illiterate as well as the literate and moreoever is relatively cheap. In fact I would not be surprised to find that radio is the most important agent of change in the world today. Unfortunately, it is a "teacher" which is subject to strong abuses. It can easily be exploited by paranoid nationalist leaders to divert people from seemingly insoluble real problems to never-never lands of national glory and aggressiveness. But, properly used, it can be an enormously important tool for realistic education and social transformation, and one suspects that its potentialities in this direction are far from fully explored.

What possible role might the United Nations play in these processes? The major asset of the United Nations is that it is an enormous depository of legitimacy. That is, in most parts of the world it carries an aura of authority and of intrinsic rightness; and it is able to bestow this, with varying degrees of success, on the undertakings it sponsors. The United Nations represents the aspirations of mankind for unity; it embodies and legitimizes the enormous yearning of mankind to avoid the scourge of war; and it is the forerunner of the world government towards which all the long-run forces of history seem to be leading. For all its organizational weakness, therefore, it is a major part of what might be called the world integrative system, and it has, as it were, a legacy coming to it from the future.

The economic analysis I presented earlier indicates that the major priority, and one in which the United Nations can be of great utility, is a world campaign for the reduction of birth rates. This, I suggest, is more important than any program of aid and investments. Indeed, if it is neglected, all programs of aid and investment will, I believe, be ultimately self-defeating and will simply increase the total amount of human misery.

We are, furthermore, enormously hampered in our efforts towards economic development not only by sheer ignorance of the details of existing social systems in the developing nations, but also by the absence of any really satisfactory theory of the organization of development. A major mobilization of intellectual resources is clearly indicated—something, for instance, at least on the scale of the Manhattan Project which produced the nuclear weapon—and the logical coordinator of such an effort is, again, the United Nations. I suggest, therefore, that the second priority be a massive ten-year research program in a number of countries, directed towards what might be called the social engineering of developmental institutions. Relatively speaking, neither of these two priorities should cost much: a billion dollars a year for ten years would probably be ample.

If these projects are reasonably successful, the great aid and investment push should come in the 1980s, with preparation for it beginning early in the 1970s. It is hard now to predict the exact form this intense effort would take, but I suspect that the major push would be in the biological sciences; for it is here that we seem to have the broadest horizon in development at the moment. Next to this probably comes the chemical industry and the development of new forms of construction involving plastics and other new materials. What are often thought of as the traditional industries of development, for instance steel and other heavy industries, may in fact be quite unimportant by 1980. This is something we cannot now predict with any assurance. But the one thing we must not do is to assume that the patterns of the past are necessarily going to be repeated in the future.

Whether the United Nations is the agency that can accomplish these things is still an open question. If it is to function effectively as an agent of socio-economic revolution, we must develop common images of the future of man and common views of how we can move towards that future. At the moment we have neither. The socialist countries have a very clear and almost certainly mistaken view of the future, while the capitalist world has a rather unclear and perhaps almost equally mistaken conception. Nevertheless, it appears that the social sciences have rapidly been developing images of the social system, and especially of the dynamics of the system, which are more realistic than any we have had before. Given this, it is not utopian to expect the eventual emergence of what might be called a rough world consensus about the future and what has to be done to achieve it. If the United Nations can early catch a vision of this consensus and of the tasks ahead, it will clearly be the agency most appropriate to undertake them.

※ ※ ※ ※

In a speech on November 22, 1965, to the Food and Agricultural Organ-ization (FAO) of the United Nations, Gunnar Myrdal, the noted Swed-ish economist, continues this discussion of the immediate crisis ahead with emphasis on hunger. He shows why the world is on a collision course in this respect and why, within a decade, "we will be skirting a disaster of such proportion as to threaten the peace and stability of the Western world." He states that "In spite of all tensions and clashes, we are now much more one world than we were a generation ago. Commu-nications have revolutionized our relations. We would have the sight of mass hunger brought into our homes on the television just as we did the murder of President Kennedy and later of Oswald." He alludes to cer-tain system changes—such as the international monetary system—which should and could be undertaken, and to what the underdeveloped coun-try should and could do more energetically for itself.

But paramount, he warns of our blindness and apathy to the out-come of the atomic race and the less publicized preparation for biologi-cal and chemical warfare, and to the gathering food crisis. We appear no more concerned than we do about our inevitable personal catastrophe of individual death. In individuals in regard to personal death this is healthy—it promotes life. But in members of a nation and of mankind this lack of concern is dangerously irrational and toward death.

The first part of the speech, which deals specifically with the work of FAO, is omitted. It is the second half which is given here.

1965 McDougal Memorial Lecture

GUNNAR MYRDAL

On these problems of international finance and trade I would have much more to say, both critically and constructively, and I will return to them in a few minutes for some more remarks. Let me first turn, however, to developments on another level of the rich countries' relations to the underdeveloped countries which I sense when I am traveling, meeting people and following the press in many different countries. I refer to the undercurrent of growing popular apathy to a more generous policy toward the poor countries. We who feel the seriousness of present trends and the paramount importance of much more international solidarity have special reasons to see and analyze this undercurrent with utmost candor.

In a sense we have been too successful in spreading our knowledge and simplifying it to the extent that it has become coined into a commonplace—stated and listened to as a sort of Sabbath-day religion, divorced from weekday practical life. Public men, teachers, preachers, leaders in all sorts of organizations, journalists, authors and, of course, politicians on solemn occasions all reiterate: that there is mass poverty in the underdeveloped countries almost beyond our grasp; that there is disease and illiteracy; that the income gap between developed and underdeveloped countries is not only very wide but continually widening; that, indeed, in recent years development in underdeveloped countries has tended to slow down instead of speed up; that, more particularly, food production in the underdeveloped regions is lower per head than before the war; that up to two thirds of the people in underdeveloped countries suffer from malnutrition and/or undernutrition; that food production in recent years has not kept pace with the population increase in Latin America, Asia and Africa; that regardless of whatever progress there is in the spread of birth control there will nevertheless be an increase in world population between now and the end of this century that will equal or exceed the current population, and that this population increase will mainly occur in the underdeveloped nations; that, consequently, their food supply will have to be more than doubled in order merely to preserve present grossly inadequate standards of nutrition; that double the present food supply will be needed as early as

1980, now only fifteen years off, to feed the increasing population and achieve a very modest improvement of nutritional levels; and so on. The recording of these facts is commonly supplemented by declarations that the ideal of social justice makes the international action to overcome the plight of underdeveloped countries a binding duty.

In the rich countries there must by now be few persons with even an average interest in public affairs who have not had these facts and that last moral judgment impressed upon them time and time again. They incorporate them in their world outlook but ordinarily they do not let them influence their preparedness for action, least of all action that would imply real sacrifice. Nowhere in the rich countries is aid to underdeveloped countries today dealt with as a major social and economic issue and in other terms than, on the one hand, relatively small-scale charity and, on the other hand, national interests, whether political interests to influence the underdeveloped countries' foreign and internal policy in one direction or another or commercial interests to get their share of such trade as accrues from assistance. Politicians, in particular, who have to watch the attitudes of the electorate, are conspicuously abandoning the Sunday religion when it comes down to practical political actions, leaving it to isolated, powerless individuals and groups to voice the unpopular demands for world solidarity.

The psychological paradox at which I hint would be worthy of intensive research, which has not been given it in any one of the rich countries so far as I know. I would like to venture a few observations expressing some tentative conclusions from my own thoughts on the matter. In spite of weekly religious and quasi-religious excursions, most people live in a narrow world and are crudely egoistic for themselves and those near them with whom they identify themselves; among those fairly well off even the needs of the poor in their own lands have been straining their loyalty. They feel even more indifferent to the notion that they should be responsible for the poor countries. They are aware, moreover, of the harsh and, as a rule, increasing economic inequality in most of the underdeveloped countries and have a feeling that the spokesmen for the poor countries, who mostly belong to the privileged strata, should do some equalization at home before they appeal for more international solidarity. There is particularly in the United States, which has had most experience in the field of large-scale aid ever since the Marshall Plan, a growing feeling that they receive little gratitude and sympathy in exchange for foreign aid. Often, a sort of historical analogy is applied by recalling how their own nations and other rich nations had to struggle for development through sacrifice and hard work without any outside aid: why should not the presently underdeveloped nations have to follow this same path, which would also do them good morally? This analogy is false, of course, since initial conditions are so vastly different, mostly to the great disadvantage of underdeveloped countries today. When people are informed of this they may then turn to the other extreme reason for nonconcernedness, namely, that aid to underdeveloped countries is a hopeless task, however much they would be prepared to give. To this is sometimes added that people in underdeveloped countries are inferior and not able to use the opportunity for development they have and that they are not too anxious to work hard.

These attitudes are rationalizations that are not founded on careful study of the facts and not even logically consistent and reconcilable: this is true of most people's attitudes on most social questions. But they are real or, rather, they cover the important reality that for the time being none of the rich nations is prepared to put aid to underdeveloped countries on a par with other, really important main items on the national budget. There are individuals and groups who would be prepared to do it, but they do not influence any political party or government. Likewise in the field of international trade, even if it were clear to the economist and the circumspect politician that concessions to the underdeveloped countries would be even in a rich nation's long-term interest, there are always vested interests built up to oppose such concessions and they are powerful, particularly when they can appeal to nationalist feelings. The delegations at this conference represent governments who have to respect how people in general think and feel. We who sense the necessity to proceed much more rapidly to action on a much broader scale are foolish if we don't take into account the psychological and political reality to which I refer.

We then have to face the further question of what we can do in order to change these attitudes. You cannot expect me, as a seasoned professor, to underrate the gradual and ultimate effectiveness of enlightenment. The Freedom from Hunger Campaign has already accomplished a certain impact on world opinion by getting such a great number of those who write and speak to repeat its basic message. We have to continue this effort in the service of truth, make it ever more specific, and draw ever more people into practical work.

Aside from this, there are a number of problems concerning the rich countries themselves, which they should be able to tackle more successfully. They should do it in their own interest but it would also make a greater generosity in their policies toward underdeveloped countries more possible. As I have already said, there is, in my opinion, no reason why rich countries should not have faster growth, full employment and a stable price level and why they should not be able to organize among themselves the international monetary system in such a way that they would not now be in the situation of finding reasons to keep down the financial flow of funds to underdeveloped countries for foreign exchange considerations. These are problems which the rich countries themselves can, and should, solve. The foreign exchange problems of underdeveloped countries are of a totally different nature: these countries are bound to be short of foreign exchange. Wanting to develop while being so short of resources, they can in general not abstain from controlling the use of the foreign exchange they can dispose of. It is not productive of intellectual clarity or of practical results to mix the two types of quite different problems together, as unfortunately has been done in many of the schemes worked out for monetary reform. This is often done for the good purpose of securing more financial funds for the poor countries and is often applauded by their own spokesmen. It is an illusion to believe, however, that more financial aid could be smuggled through by confused schemes of that type; the rich countries will not buy them. On the other hand, the poor countries have all interest in wishing the rich countries success in their endeavors to establish internal and external balance in their economies, as this would take away an inhibition for a financial outflow to the poor countries.

In the same way, the international trade problem is totally different in the poor and the rich countries, and there are reasons for what I have called a "double standard morality" in regard to commercial policy—for once a double standard to the advantage of the weak and not the strong as usually has been the case in our world. The rich countries should now take the consequence of their comparative strength—as Britain did more than a hundred years ago when it was ahead of all the world in development— and open their boundaries for the flow of commodities as well as capital, among themselves and in relation to the poor countries. They could do it, if they kept their economies in balance. During this approach toward free trade, they should even discriminate in favor of the underdeveloped countries by abolishing tariffs and other restrictions on imports from these countries as a first step. To ask for reciprocity is unreasonable; as one Indian statesman long ago stated at a GATT meeting: "equality between unequals is inequality." The poor countries cannot possibly abstain from protecting their sprouting industries. They also need protective trading blocks while the rich countries should afford to go a more direct way to freeing their own trade. Again, the underdeveloped countries have the greatest interest in the liberalization of trade among the rich countries, even if they have no possibility to participate in such a move.

At the same time, there is much the underdeveloped countries could do themselves in order to break down the reluctance on the part of people in the rich countries to come forward with more assistance. A few months ago the President of the World Bank, Mr. George D. Woods, in an address to the Bank's Governors where he noted that "the level of development assistance has been stationary for several years," said bluntly that "it is useless to attempt to sugarcoat the fact that in many of the underdeveloped countries, economic performance can be greatly improved." After having illustrated what he meant, he went on to stress that "it is the effectiveness of internal effort which to a large extent is going to determine the future of international development assistance." For my own part, and thinking particularly about the difficulty of overcoming the undercurrent of popular resistance in the rich countries against making substantial sacrifices to aid underdeveloped countries, I would give special emphasis to the urgency of increasing social discipline and rooting out corruption, on the one hand and, on the other hand, of complying better to the ideals of greater social and economic equality to which all underdeveloped countries are solemnly committed. Internal reforms in these directions would also greatly improve the chances to speed up development, particularly in agriculture. To this I will return.

Turning next to what will actually happen I want first to focus our attention on agriculture, not only because I am speaking to an audience with particular interest in this field but also because I believe it is there the greatest dangers are pending. The statistics on trends presented in FAO's *Third World Food Survey* two years ago and the recently published *The State of Food and Agriculture 1965,* together with all we know about the tremendous economic and social inhibitions and obstacles in the way of agricultural reform in the underdeveloped countries must lead to the conclusion that whatever the prospects are for substantially raising agricultural production in the somewhat longer run, the immediate prospects are gloomy. I believe we must have the candor to face the fact that, as a prominent American agricultural economist, Professor Earl L. Butz, who has often taken part in the meetings of FAO, has expressed it: "The world is on a collision course." And he continued:

> *When the massive force of an exploding world population meets the much more stable trend line of world food production, something must give. Unless we give increased attention now to the softening of the impending collision, many parts of the world within a decade will be skirting a disaster of such a proportion as to threaten the peace and stability of the Western world.*

In contemplating the threatening world food crisis we have to recall that, in several very big countries like India and Pakistan and many smaller ones, it would have already broken out had it not been for the availability of large-scale food imports granted without foreign exchange compensation, mainly under P.L. 480 from the surpluses in the United States.

An intensification of the food crisis would create an internationally intolerable situation. In spite of all tensions and clashes, we are now much more one world than we were a generation ago. Communications have revolutionized our relations. We would have the sight of mass hunger brought into our homes on the television just as we did the murder of

President Kennedy and later of Oswald. I have no doubt that when the crisis comes, people in the rich countries will suddenly respond in the way for which their Sabbath-day religion has prepared them.

If the lid of production restrictions is lifted, food production could rise very much in the United States. Canada, Australia and a few other countries are in a similar situation. But we should not expect these countries to send this food and carry the financial burden alone. It has been easy to vote billions for P.L. 480 in Congress, when it was riding the market of awkward food surpluses; it is different when the surpluses have disappeared and agricultural policy becomes directed toward an increase of production instead of a limit on production. Other rich countries will have to share the financial burden, but they will do it only if this food aid is internationalized—not by paying contributions into the United States' Treasury for a United States activity. Under these conditions it is well that we have an international agency, working under FAO auspices, The World Food Program, already in operation on an experimental scale, and that according to unanimous opinion it has been run economically and effectively.

Internationally organized food aid can, however, under no circumstances be a permanent solution of the problem: it can merely bridge over an emergency. As a Staff Economist in the U. S. Department of Agriculture, Lester R. Brown, has recently pointed out, the increase in grain consumption by 1980, necessary in order to meet the expected population increase and a modest rise of 10 per cent in per capita consumption, would boost grain production requirements by almost as much as the current output of North America and Western Europe combined. A similarly forbidding calculation could be made of the shipping facilities necessary for an extensive food aid program. The sharp impact of that type of flight into fantasy is that, even if for a short time the first shocks of the food crisis can be absorbed by aid from the rich countries, the very great increase in agricultural production, which is urgently needed if disaster is to be averted, must begin to take place in the vast underdeveloped regions.

How this is going to be accomplished is the main business of the agricultural ministries in underdeveloped countries, of this organization, and of the present Conference.

Even if reforms can have their full effects in the somewhat longer run, it is urgent that they be undertaken without delay and that they are planned in such a way that they will have as much result as possible, as quickly as possible. As a matter of fact, I feel much less concerned about how things will look at the turn of the next century. In the long run much will happen: we will perhaps have entirely new techniques to produce the food; the entire world situation will be different in all sorts of ways; forecasts are bound to be proven wrong; perhaps we may feel optimistic that things will in some way take a radically new turn as we have often seen happening before. It is the years to come in this decade and the next about which I am worried. In the short run our forecasts are more reliable and they point to danger of world calamity.

About the policy measures to be undertaken I will restrict myself to a few brief observations. I want first to emphasize that, contrary to the experience in the developed countries, what increase of food production there has been in the underdeveloped countries has mainly been due to an extension of the cultivated area, while the yields per acre have hardly risen at all; this is true even in a country like India with a very high man/land ratio and very low yields. New cultivable land is becoming scarce or else the costs of cultivating it are forbiddingly high. Yields are generally very low, which by itself should be reason for hope, if there could be such a change in agricultural technology that the yields would rise.

My second point is that while, of course, there is much technology available, the application of which is continuously proving itself to be of importance, nevertheless there is to a large extent need for a new technology that has to be invented and applied. This is due to two circumstances. For one thing, most of the underdeveloped countries are in the tropical and subtropical zones and there has been very little of that specialized and localized practical research which in the developed countries has made possible the rapid rise in yields. We are all aware of the disappointments that are often experienced when applying fertilizers, for instance, or trying to use seeds which should give bigger crops. Very much more programmed, practically directed, specialized and localized research into food production in these areas would be warranted.

Moreover—and this is too often overlooked even by agricultural experts—while from the beginning agricultural technology in the now developed countries could reckon with a decrease of labor in agriculture, most underdeveloped countries will have to adjust their technology to an agricultural labor force that for a generation will rise in numbers about as fast as the present very rapid population increase. This point deserves a few words of explanation.

Fortunately, the road seems now to be opening for a much more determined policy of spreading birth control among the masses. But we would deceive ourselves if we counted on a rapid change of fertility. Also, the relatively greater numbers of children, which is a reflection of the higher fertility up till now implies that the population increase has a tremendous momentum. The breaking distance is so long. This does not mean that a decrease in fertility would not always and immediately improve income per head and living levels, by lessening the dependency burden in the families, but it does imply that the birth curve in a nation will not be lowered as fast as if the age distribution were a more normal one, adjusted to a stable population. Finally, the effects on the labor force are delayed for fifteen years and will be very inconsequential for a whole generation. The future workers are already born or will soon be born.

To this comes the fact that industrialization in most of the underdeveloped countries, even if it proceeded much faster than it does, will not for decades absorb much additional labor. Under certain circumstances industrialization will even throw out more labor in traditional industry and craft than it gives new employment. This is no reason for not trying to industrialize as fast as possible: when once a higher level of industrialization is reached, industry will increasingly employ more labor. Meanwhile, however, a swelling flow of refugees from the countryside to the cities is not productive. . . .

My third observation is that a substantial and rapid increase in agriculture yields has rarely, if ever, occurred in traditional self-sufficiency farming, where illiteracy is prevalent and the relation between the farmer and his land is such that he has little possibility and little incentive to exert himself. Among the several institutional problems raised by this observation I would give high priority to the need for land reform in the broadest sense of the word. It would have a different direction in countries with different systems of ownership and tenancy and it has to be accompanied by other induced changes in regard to education, marketing, availability of credits, etc. It must often be costly in order to be effective in raising yields, and I think we should begin to consider whether international credits, which would have to be on a rather large scale, could not be given to make it more possible for underdeveloped countries to speed up land reforms and undertake all the other measures necessary to render these reforms really productive. But that assumes that these countries, or rather those in these countries who have the political power, begin to take seriously the urgent need for reorganization of the relations between the toiler and the land he tills. I think it is tragic—and a contributory cause of no small importance to the grave situation we face today—that local vested interests have made a sham of land reform in so many countries. FAO has for many years courageously and competently labored with land reform, and I have a feeling that in recent years it has been reaping results in a greater interest in many countries to do something effectively to solve the problem, even if in other countries I sense a tendency to try to forget about it and focus public attention only on the more technical problems.

Let me end my lecture by telling you of a thought that constantly and increasingly is pressing itself upon my mind and making me deeply disturbed. I fear that we are becoming accustomed to living on happily and attending to the business of the day while not giving much thought to the possibility or probability of the unthinkable ahead of us. To this category I reckon the outcome of the atomic armament race and the less publicized preparation for biological and chemical warfare; as time goes on without effective intergovernmental agreement to stop this development, improvements in technology must make it easier and cheaper for all sorts of countries to equip themselves for genocide. To this category of unthinkably menacing calamities belongs also the gathering food crisis. We seem to be taking the pattern from the entirely rational way in which we as individuals live on happily from day to day and work and enjoy ourselves, though we know we are soon approaching the personal catastrophe of death. Otherwise life would be unbearable; nothing can be done about it anyhow; and our nations and mankind do not perish with us but will survive. But this attitude is dangerously irrational, when we take it as members of a nation and of mankind. Social catastrophes are different from the certainty of death for the individual, as they can and should be averted. And if we do not use foresight and take measures against them, we all perish and there will be no posterity.

※ ※ ※ ※

I believe there is a relationship between the content of the foregoing articles and the plight of meaninglessness that so besets young people, particularly American young people, today. No wonder they are "alienated." The fact is that the society which the supposedly controlling adults represent has become not only death-oriented but morally insufferable. There is a split between what is preached and what is practiced. Lately young people have seen their own country commit, deny and later acknowledge the very actions it has most condemned and sought to punish in others—in Cuba, Vietnam and Santo Domingo. And they are told this hypocrisy is necessary for national security which also is already being invoked to stifle protest. In the values that they see in the adult world around them young people see the failure of the American myth (myth in the sense of guiding vision) of freedom, equality, justice, progress—and nothing to replace it.

I wonder what the effect would be if they did not feel the doom of nuclear war impending and if they saw before them the adventure of a new lap in man's development as what Boulding (and probably Teilhard de Chardin too) would call the "homosphere" struggled and very slowly emerged—if they saw themselves at the beginning of something new, not unwilling, unconsulted, ineffective participants at an end.

Although not directly related to war prevention perhaps the following short pieces—one by a university professor who is chairman of the Department of Philosophy at Colorado College and one by a student—should be read at this point. Nor can we doubt, were a decent vision offered them, what an enormous source of energy lies here.

Salvation on the Campus: Why Existentialism Is Capturing the Students

J. GLENN GRAY

"Our Tom looked like a bum when he came home for Christmas. His clothes were filthy, he was wearing a mandarin beard, and his hair hadn't been cut since September. Last fall we gave him permission to live alone off-campus and cook for himself. Now he has trench mouth, a bad case of athlete's foot, and some kind of mysterious virus."

Our neighbor was both exasperated and amused as she thus described her son, a senior at a famous Ivy League college. He is a superior student who had hitherto seemed anything but a beatnik. For years his parents have let him steer his own course and supported him financially at some sacrifice. What, then, is he rebelling against? Is this merely a ludicrous episode in his development or a sign of a severe disorder? His mother doesn't know.

Many other enlightened parents are equally perplexed by the bizarre actions of their college sons and daughters. Nor can professors and university administrators shed much light on the moods and motivations of students in the 'sixties. They have been baffled by the rioting at Berkeley last fall and other less publicized incidents elsewhere.

For today's student is a very different creature from his predecessors. In my own college days in the 'thirties, if I had come home at Christmas in Tom's condition, my parents would probably have had me committed to a different sort of institution. What lies behind the change?

For one thing, today's student is more affluent than we were, more comfortably housed, and better equipped with the materials of scholarship. But his college life is also more impersonal and competitive, less humane. It is harder for him to know his professors, the administration, or even his all too numerous fellow students. Learning is increasingly packaged and is sometimes referred to, shamelessly, as the "knowledge business." Knowledge itself expands at a rate that makes him feel like an impostor if he seeks to be broadly educated, and walls him off from others if he specializes. His professors are less attached to the institution where they teach and more to their disciplines. And they have less time to give him or the college. In this situation, the traditional college spirit—of either the rah-rah variety or the community of learners—may seem to the student as outmoded as the raccoon coat and the hip flask.

If he has reached the age of reflection, today's student is seeking above all to differentiate himself from the crowd. Thirty years ago it was distinctive merely to be a college man. Now he must struggle to be more than a grade-point average, an anonymous statistic with a college and home address. Often he expresses this yearning for uniqueness in ways that parents administrators, professors, and other outsiders consider illegitimate. Well publicized are the bearded, sloppily dressed students, defiant of even minimal administrative regulations, studious enough, but incontinent in their demands for alcoholic and sexual freedoms, fiercely insistent on leading their own lives.

Typical of this state of mind is a student's letter in a recent issue of our college newspaper. "The trouble is that they [administration and faculty] take it all as seriously as the rest of the piety we get about law and morality and the intellectual purpose of our existence. The most ironic thing on this campus is that they believe in their own hypocrisy. . . . One of the reasons that administration and much of the faculty alike draw grotesque pictures of students is that they probably have never talked with one, not that they'd listen if they did. For years the same situations occur, the same opinions are given, the same pleas are voiced, and the same nothing happens."

The desire for self-definition often goes hand in hand with an inner need—more or less conscious—for a compelling authority to make freedom meaningful. In the 'thirties, economic pressures for existence and our opposition to the fascist menace rescued us from this dilemma. In the 'forties there was the war and, afterward, the threat of the Bomb to distract attention from inner conflicts. For some students in the 'sixties the civil-rights struggle has become a Cause—a clear-cut issue on which to act and to argue. But as yet this movement has not reached anything like the numbers nor hit with anything like the impact that we experienced with fascism, communism, the war, and the Bomb.

Lacking an embracing cause and a fervent ideology, the student's search for a durable purpose is likely to become aggressive, extremist, at times despairing. It can easily turn into preoccupation with subjective feelings and plain egotism. As André Gide has put it, "Each human being who has only himself for aim suffers from a horrible void." Paradoxical as it sounds, the real problem of our college youth is to discover some authority, both private and public, that will make possible authentic individuality.

Their favorite rebel

I have learned something about this search over the past fifteen years as one of the professors conducting a senior seminar called Freedom and Authority. Before generalizing, perhaps I should say a word about Colorado College, where I teach philosophy. It is a fairly typical small, private liberal-arts institution, founded in 1874 by New England Congregationalists before Colorado was a state. It has long since cut loose from church ties, drifting—like Grinnell, Carleton, Pomona, and others—into secularism. Our students are drawn from many states; after Colorado, California and Illinois contribute the most.

We are not as selective as the Ivy League colleges nor as equalitarian as the state institutions. Since—like those of most private colleges—our costs are high, our students come largely from upper-middle-class families. (Some are shockingly rich. A few years back when we banned automobiles for freshmen, a Texas girl wired our admissions committee, requesting in good faith that she be permitted to bring her private airplane.)

I was originally lured out here by a dean who painted an enticing picture of Back Bay Boston accents mixed with Western ranch drawls. But the percentage of students from ranches, farms, and the working class has steadily declined, and drawls are now rare. In sum, our students and their families are, economically and socially, very much like you who are reading this magazine. They represent an important—if not typical—sample of American college students.

Our Freedom and Authority seminar is a very freewheeling, wide-ranging course. Though we constantly change the readings, a few books have remained by nearly unanimous consent from the beginning. The first of these is Plato's account of the trial, imprisonment, and death of Socrates in the *Apology, Crito,* and end of *Phaedo.* These short dialogues, conveniently grouped in one paperback, are probably exerting a profounder influence on the campus today than such bestsellers as Golding, Salinger, and Baldwin, which bloom and fade in campus popularity.

Why does Socrates appeal to contemporary students? They respond to his fearless assertion of his right to determine his own conduct despite powerful opposition from the majority of his fellow citizens. The conflict

between individual freedom and sociopolitical authority which he drama-
tizes expresses their own central dilemma. These students have outgrown
the discipline of parents. In college, various authorities—the college administration, campus mores, and student cliques—vie for their allegiance.
They are also uneasily conscious of the different standards of the professional and business worlds they are about to enter. The sensitive student,
confused by these uncertain values, is thrilled when Socrates, the original
rebel who became the "father" of philosophy, tells his fellow Athenians
that he loves and cherishes them, but chooses to obey only his vision of the
right and good. Socrates' example can still engender a revolutionary fervor
in youthful hearts. It was hardly an accident that the campus rebellions at
Berkeley and earlier at the University of Colorado were led by philosophy
majors.*

Less acceptable to my students than Socrates' idea of freedom is his
concept of authority, which leads him to refuse a proffered escape from
prison after he has been sentenced to death. He likens the laws of Athens
to parents, who must always be obeyed even if they chastise their children
unjustly. At this point, my students begin to protest, and their identification with Socrates is broken. As one of them put it last fall, "I can't imagine anything less comparable to my parents than the U. S. government."

There are exceptions. One girl, for example, last November reconciled
the seeming contradictions in Socrates' philosophy in this fashion: "In the
Apology individual determination of conduct challenges and defeats all
other values, including Athenian law. However, the reverse is not what
happens in the *Crito*. Here, Athenian law is weighted *with* his personal
laws of conduct *against* a solitary value, his life. His natural desire to flee
for his life, not his individualism, is challenged here. . . . As part of his
personal conduct code, Socrates could not destroy Athenian law simply
because it was being used to destroy a lesser value, his life on earth. 'To
injure in turn when ill-treated' was against his moral structure also, so that
his personal conduct code forced him to abide by Athenian law. Of the
three values considered in the *Apology* and the *Crito,* Socrates held individual determination of conduct most important, Athenian law second,
and his own life least important."

All of us blessed her, a rank beginner in philosophy, for the kind of
insight that an unburdened mind often brings to a complex issue. In the
ensuing discussion, her classmates were intellectually persuaded that Socrates' freedom was sustained by his lifelong membership in the community of Athens. But how could his example be helpful today? Since patriotism is hardly an operable emotion among contemporary students,

* *Similarly, the unprecedented student demonstration at Yale in March was
a protest against the administration's failure to give tenure to an admired
philosophy teacher.*

Socratic freedom, though intellectually appealing, does not in the end provide a satisfying answer. After all, Socrates was an old man with secure roots in a small community, a situation quite opposite to that of young people in our huge, fast-changing, incredibly complex society.

"Just like my old man"

As a contrast to Socrates, we study *The Death of Ivan Ilych,* Tolstoi's powerful short story in which a modern man must face an agonizing death with no resources save the polite conventions of an artificial society. Slowly dying, daily more isolated and desperate, Ivan asks:

> *"Then what does it mean? Why? It can't be that life is so senseless and horrible. But if it really has been so horrible and senseless, why must I die and die in agony? There is something wrong!*
> *"Maybe I did not live as I ought to have done," it suddenly occurred to him. "But how could that be, when I did everything properly," he replied, and immediately dismissed from his mind this, the sole solution of all the riddles of life and death, as something quite impossible.*

But he cannot dismiss these fears for long.

> *He lay on his back and began to pass his life in review in quite a new way. In the morning when he saw first his footman, then his wife, then his daughter, and then the doctor, their every word and movement confirmed to him the awful truth that had been revealed to him during the night. In them he saw himself—all that for which he had lived—and saw clearly that it was not real at all, but a terrible and huge deception which had hidden both life and death. This consciousness intensified his suffering tenfold.*

In the end, Tolstoi rescues Ivan from utter meaninglessness and absurdity via his own (Tolstoi's) passionate faith in primitive Christianty. But this does little to alleviate the atmosphere of controlled terror and doom.

The story has a stunning impact on our students. If they find Socrates wholly admirable but a size larger than life, Ivan is all too human, the anonymous Everyman of our day, painfully contemporary. I have overheard more than one of my students breathe, "My God, he is just like my old man!" They do not identify with him for he is too much like adults they know and dislike—a portrait of what modern life may force them eventually to become. Though they hardly aspire to be heroes like Socrates, they desperately want to escape being victims like Ivan.

The sin of phoniness

Ivan's "inauthentic" life has become a rich source for the Existentialists in their indictment of modern society. On the campus Existentialism— which is both a mood and a metaphysics—is compounded of anxiety about being lost in the crowd and the lack of closeness or intimacy with fellow students. Sometimes, the despairing response to these feelings is sexual promiscuity; more often it is expressed in eccentric dress and flamboyant behavior. Such climates of opinion are contagious and often attract spurious reactions. These can be downright funny, as in the reported case of the student who used to telephone his girl friend and say, "Honey, I'm in the abyss again. How about going out for a beer?"

But in fact the underlying mood is quite different from the perennial depressions of late adolescence. These students are anxiously concerned with the problem of being themselves. Authenticity is the element of Existentialism that strikes the deepest note for them. The highest virtue is honesty with themselves and others while phoniness in whatever form is the greatest vice. "The thing that's wrong with this class," a senior burst out recently, "is that none of us is spontaneous. We're all trying to be so clever and to impress each other. I think we are simply afraid to be ourselves. I'm sick of my own pretending."

To be a genuine or authentic person is not primarily a moral matter, in the sense that older Americans think of morality. For Existentialists authenticity means freely choosing what is one's own in behavior, attitude, and mode of living, however singular these may appear to others. The kind of society we are building—or that is being built around us—is, for them, a major obstacle to the attainment of authentic individuality.

Triggers of self-discovery

The difficult art of becoming oneself can hardly be more than begun by the age of twenty-two or twenty-three. Hence the important question is: How long does the search continue? Graduates of our Freedom and Authority seminar often write to their old professors and many of them return to campus annually, from as far away as Pennsylvania and California. We hold an informal seminar with them at Homecoming, usually based on a book which we have assigned in advance.

Surprises about the future development of one's students are the rule for a college professor. But I am still disconcerted when the students I counted on fail me and the least promising prove to be "late bloomers."

In the last category is a pretty Connecticut girl who seemed quite unremarkable when she left my seminar section a couple of years ago and proceeded to a government job in Washington. Soon afterward an FBI agent came to my office for a routine loyalty check and I gave him the expected replies. But meanwhile someone denounced her as an associate of Communists at college, and she was subjected to a thorough investigation. She secured help from the American Civil Liberties Union, an organization she had first heard of in our course. The investigation ended harmlessly at a hearing where one government agent testified that she was "an innocuous person."

When she returned to campus last spring for a visit this characterization was much on her mind. "That agent was right," she told me. "Up till now I have been just that, an innocuous person, but I intend to be innocuous no longer." She asked me to support her application for law school, which she entered last fall. She had decided to become a defender of civil liberties in a private capacity, not to practice law. This winter she wrote me long letters displaying an unsuspected spirit and passion and marking her as a person who has attained security of mind. She has already resolved not to take the loyalty oath required of members of the bar in the state where she is studying, to make a court case of the matter. She has also become a militant pacifist. It was apparently the description of her as "innocuous" that triggered all these responses—all dormant in her college days.

The death of President Kennedy had a similar transforming effect on another unlikely student whose undistinguished college career included a troubled progress through my Freedom and Authority course. He married and went to work for a national soap company where he was rising rapidly. But the Kennedy assassination disrupted his world. Soon afterward he wrote me asking for "a philosopher's point of view." "I felt a strong sense of identity with him," he wrote, expressing a feeling widespread at that time. "Perhaps this is because he was young, or because we shared similar political views (weak and irresolute as mine are) or because he was an 'intellectual' President, or because . . . I felt guilt because of his murder, and I feel dead because of his death."

He had tried, he said, to cope with the disaster, to reason it through, but in vain. "I usually end up saying 'God damn,' with an incredulous shake of the head. Surely there must be more grief written in people's hearts than what is written on their faces. Aside from a few hours at the funeral, all seems to be normal with the people I see and know. But for me this one act had made all other acts irrelevant and trivial; it has displaced time with paranoia, good with evil, relative simplicity with incomprehensibility, an ideal with dirt."

He could no longer remain in the business world. Despite his wife and children, he decided to return to graduate school to prepare himself for work in international education. He is now immersed in the study of foreign languages and Existentialism. Wearing a heavy beard, he has lost all resemblance to the young executive of a year ago. For the first time in his life, he told me recently, he is truly "engaged" in discovering the meaning of existence through commitment to thought and action rather than middle-class drift.

These two cases are, of course, exceptions. Relatively few of our young alumni have made much progress toward attaining a distinctive individuality after leaving college. The demands of business and professional life on the men, of homemaking and child-rearing on the women, tend either to halt the search or even to induce surrender to reigning values. It would seem that the very prosperity which permits college students to spend time pondering important issues of existence acts as a sedative in their early adulthood. Affluence, not religion, might be called the opiate of the 'sixties. The immediate requirements of making a living and getting ahead in the status race seem to dull the passions and despair which obsessed many of them in college. There is, of course, nothing surprising in this. Many of us escape the need to give meaning to our existence through the age-old expedient of producing the next generation and letting them struggle with the problem.

The appeal of nothingness

The existentialist preoccupation with the Absurd, Nothingness, *Angst*, etc.—at least as metaphysical concepts—did not until recently have much of a grip on the English-speaking countries. When I first began teaching the leading Existentialists about 1950, interest in a Kierkegaard, Heidegger, or Sartre was likely to be a matter of either curiosity or fashion. Their very names were strange and most Americans had difficulty pronouncing the word Existentialism. In those years my colleagues frequently asked me to give a coffee-break explanation of the movement.

Now discussions are far more earnest and passionate. I conduct a Wednesday evening seminar on Existentialism at my home. Frequently I have to push the students out after several hours, if I am to simmer down and get any sleep that night. Often they continue heated arguments elsewhere till the small hours. In colleges all over America, courses dealing with Existentialists are currently very popular, to the disgust of the disciples of Language Analysis—an Oxford import—who once felt confident of dominating academic philosophy. The rapid availability of translations from German and French Existentialist writings and sales of large editions attest to the surprising new demand.

What accounts for it? Undeniably, there is a large element of the modish, for Americans have always been susceptible to philosophic imports from the Continent and England. (In philosophy, it has been said, we are still largely a colony of Europe.) I must also admit, rather shame-facedly, that even philosophy is not immune to the attraction of "the hottest thing in town." After the war it was Oxford Analysis, now it is Existentialism.

There is, however, much more to the matter. Existentialists draw their insights and inspiration from literature rather than science. They are concerned with the individual and with personal experience in an age that threatens to overwhelm individuality. This is why they attract so many American playwrights and novelists who have begun the process of Americanizing the European mood. Because the specific possibilities and frustrations of our everyday life are sharply different from those in France or Germany we were slow to accept the Existentialist mood and metaphysics. Now that our writers have succeeded in "translating" them into our American idiom, we are feeling their delayed impact.

The students I know best seem to have an intuitive grasp of what Heidegger and Sartre mean when they write of man's exposure to Nothingness. In a few extreme cases Nothingness means a profound feeling of disengagement with American culture, if not Western civilization itself. Other students who say in the privacy of my office, "I am at the end of my rope," are feeling only a temporary despair, perhaps little more than the romantic storm and stress of late adolescence. Sometimes I respond with a gentle joshing, and refuse to take them too seriously. With others I am far from sure.

The latter group includes students who often do superb work in my classes but who are quite as likely to be on academic probation as on the Dean's list. (One of them recently spent three semesters in the near-failing and three in the excellent category.)

These are brilliant, alienated young people. Generally, they do not care for Karl Jaspers, the Existentialist who identifies himself most closely with conventional philosophy. They respond to the philosophers radically at odds with the whole tradition of modern culture. They want Kierkegaard's either-or—the leap of faith or gross sensuality; Satre's good faith or self-deception; Heidegger's nearness to Being or nihilism.

The ablest student I ever taught at Colorado College was of this kind. He wrote better commentaries on these philosophers than are found in the published literature. His poems, which I alone was allowed to see, were also first-rate. But it was a trial to keep him in college from one semester to another. Again and again he would disappear into the mountains, by himself for days. My wife and I constantly feared his suicide. When he finally graduated I easily secured fellowships for him to three graduate schools. He turned down all of them and proceeded to wander over the country, supporting himself at odd jobs. In his college years I was, in effect, struggling with him for his very soul; it is now sadly clear that I lost.

Turning inward

In an earlier day, before the disillusionment with communism, some such students found release in action, in attachment to a utopian authority which gave them a feeling of belonging. For others, the crude menace of Hitler served to unite them with Western values. Today a few find a sense of belonging in Southern racism. Others in the civil-rights movement or in the Peace Corps with its opportunities for genuine service.

What these students need above all is action, not further study, yet how can I counsel them to give up their studies before the degree? To serve with any significance in our specialized society they will need more formal schooling than they have or want before they have "found" themselves. The plight of dropouts on the lower academic rungs is well known. Equally poignant is the problem of those at the top—often even in graduate school—who do not know where they are headed nor whether they should stay in college at all.

Ironically, our technological society appears to widen the spheres of freedom while making it even harder to escape from the toils of "the system" as students call it. Students today travel far more than we did in the 'thirties and 'forties; learn and see more and participate in a much larger range of activities. At an early stage the choice of many different careers is open to them. But once they have chosen anything specific, whether it be a "major" or marriage, they are soon past the point of no return.

In this situation Existentialism appeals. Its deepest conviction is that through his choices each individual makes himself. Its emphasis is not only on the absurd character of social reality, in some cases, of the world as a whole, but also on Possibility. In an inner sense everyone determines his own course. He can choose to lead an authentic existence or choose to be lost in the crowd. If the overwhelming majority opt for the latter condition, this does not prevent the exceptional person from standing alone as an authentic "single one." To a man, Existentialists are against group activities. They never tire of reminding us that "existence" literally means to "stand out from."

"I have decided that I am simply different from all the others," a brilliant youth told me the other day, explaining how even his close friends saw no point whatever to his poetry. "I must think and write for myself from now on." Both resolution and pathos were in his voice.

What, if not absurd?

I doubt that Existentialist philosophy can ultimately satisfy the search for authority. So far, few of these thinkers have provided guidelines for social or political action, though all of them stress the necessity for individual commitment. However, for students who are not yet able or ready to act, Existentialism offers a great deal. At the least it presents an escape from the morass of conformity, *la dolce vita,* boredom, and the meaningless competitiveness in which they see so many of their elders caught.

Furthermore, those who go behind Sartre to the Danish and German originators of this movement discover a choice between an absurd or tragic view of human destiny. The absurd view is that existence is finally meaningless and futile, a defiant if admirable gesture in a void. The tragic conviction acknowledges the fragile and exposed character of individuality but discovers meaning and purpose in the individual's struggle to locate himself in nature and society. Though his personal life is of short duration, and subject to chance and misfortune while it lasts, his actions are of great importance in the moral sum of things. Tragedy links us to what has been in the history of our species and binds us in faith to the future. It teaches that there are things worth living and dying for, ideas, ancestors, and descendants.

On the other hand, the metaphysical idea that "life is a tale told by an idiot, full of sound and fury, signifying nothing" can do none of these things. The conviction of absurdity cuts all ties to history and nature and with them the nerve of meaningful action. Which version of Existentialism will be accepted by students in the rest of the 'sixties?

The answer will be important. It has been a favorite taunt of European critics that in America there are no tragedies, only mistakes. The quality of current experience is rapidly dissipating any remaining truth in this ancient charge. Yet young people inevitably find it hard to learn the price in pain and suffering necessary to pay for the tragic vision. Falling into a persuasion of absurdity and meaninglessness is, on the surface at least, much easier. The polar choices again are between the life of Socrates and that of Ivan Ilych.

That the tragic and absurd should be competing for students' minds in the 'sixties is not surprising, when one remembers that many of their parents were fighting World War II while they were infants and that they have grown up in a world changing at an incredible pace. Indeed, were young people not constitutionally adaptable and preoccupied with the immediate present, they would be in a much worse plight than they are. The wonder is that so many are sane and resilient.

Rift between generations

Nevertheless, there has hardly been a time, in my experience, when students needed more attention and patient listening to by experienced professors than today. The pity is that so many of us retreat into research, government contracts, and sabbatical travel, leaving counsel and instruction to junior colleagues and graduate assistants. In so doing we deepen the rift between the generations and at the same time increase the sense of impersonality, discontinuity, and absence of community that makes college life less satisfactory in this decade than it used to be. What is needed are fewer books and articles by college professors and more cooperative search by teacher and taught for an authority upon which to base freedom and individuality.

After surviving so many turbulent decades of this century, some of us may feel a certain confidence that the present will prove no harder than the past has been. But we should remind ourselves that peace and affluence have their own perils as surely as do wars and depressions. Though our students increasingly come to us better prepared in the traditions of Western civilization, how many of them care more deeply about these traditions than did students in the bad old days? My pessimistic sense of catastrophe has lessened somewhat since 1960, but I find that deep uneasiness about the course of American higher education has grown. Nowadays nearly everyone looks to education for salvation as once we looked to religion or to a political ideology. But before we succeed in building the great society, we shall need to resolve the doubt and bafflement about its validity and worth in the minds of those now in college who should serve as leaders. Many of the harassed young men and women I teach, at any rate, have not yet decided what sense, if any, their existence has.

A Radical Frame of Mind

ROCHELLE GATLIN

Mrs. Gatlin was graduated summa cum laude from San Francisco State College in June, 1965. This is her commencement address. She is now a graduate student in American Civilization at the University of Pennsylvania.

College students of the 1960s are different from those of ten years ago. Specific issues in which questions of ethics are sharply defined have impelled them to reject the beat-style withdrawal of the 1950s. To paraphrase Crane Brinton, "Many of the new generation have thrown themselves into movements like the Peace Corps, civil rights, disarmament, and international government. They do this often to the accompaniment of words of despair and anger, but their deeds belie their words." Many of the same students who heroically went to Mississippi last summer were carried out of Sproul Hall last winter. Although the Berkeley Free Speech Movement contained a few hipsters and revolutionary zealots, there was a surprisingly large proportion of what U.C. graduate Michael Miller calls the most intellectually serious and morally alert students on campus, who demand the most from the university, who are concerned with putting knowledge of the past to work in the present and who believe that the educational process should provide a continuum between ideas and social action.

Fortunately demonstrations, sit-ins, and arrests are not the only ways to affect university and social reform. The Free Speech Movement was a dramatic event that occasioned sensational headlines, but at other institutions less publicized programs have been initiated. For example, the Committee for an Ideal Campus at Brandeis University in Massachusetts is an officially recognized organization, which receives a budget from the associated student body. Some of the programs of this committee include: compiling a critique of professors and courses, tabulating a student-faculty poll intended to ascertain what issues concern the campus community, making plans for a national convention of similar student groups, and initiating the Spinoza Institute—which will offer nongraded courses and seminars next fall in the Modern Cinema, Eastern Thought, Psychedelic Stimulants, and the History of Peace Movements.

In its first Statement of Purpose, the Committee for an Ideal Campus summed up principles which are advanced by student reformers and university critics all over the country. This statement says in part:

> *We believe that the ideal university is an intellectual community of teachers and students . . . knowledge is advanced as a force which is personally relevant and meaningful, not as a commodity which is produced and marketed. . . .*
>
> *By virtue of its intellectual freedom, the university can serve society as a center of independent thought and criticism. The members of the university may challenge undesirable customs and values, offer suggestions for their improvement, and exercise their rights as citizens to participate in social and political action.*

Obviously the constant scrutiny of university and social practices found in the above declaration may lead to unrest, but I do not believe that unrest is something that can or should be "remedied" by suppression. To state this positively, the effect of current student unrest may be a critical analysis—even exposé—of hypocritical practices in relation to traditional American values of peace, equality, and individual freedom. For example, it took the Freedom Riders and the registering of disenfranchised Southern Negroes—and unfortunately the murder of a few white Northerners—to focus the country's attention on the wide discrepancy between the ideal and the practice of equality.

One characteristic of socially alert students is their dissatisfaction with and even discarding of the liberalism of Woodrow Wilson, Franklin Roosevelt, and Clark Kerr. Stanley Kauffmann has expressed the growing irrelevance of liberalism with its optimistic belief in progress by saying that although liberal sentiments are unimpeachable, they are almost irresponsible in the light of existing conditions—the contemporary equivalent of a hundred Hail Marys to avert the Black Plague. To many students, there is something ineffectual about the liberal bureaucrat with his tools of mediation and compromise. Furthermore (as Michael Miller has said in a recent article in *Dissent*), "the more militant students regard liberalism with something less than satisfaction. They believe it to be somehow implicated, if only by default, in the heritage of nightmares that compose modern history—Auschwitz, Hiroshima, the Cold War, McCarthyism."

But student radicals do not look to bureaucratic, puritanical Russia or to unindustrialized, overpopulated, and poverty-ridden China as models. Not Marx, but Gandhi and Thoreau are their mentors. Their goal is to eliminate the divorce between the political and the personal; no definite programs, no slogans, only a direct emotional response to hyopcrisy and injustice.

This graduating class joins with others throughout the country in facing tasks that require a radical and experimental frame of mind, guided by generous social impulses. We must find workable ideas to replace the myths that have been outrun by technology and social upheaval; we must develop a social vision less shallow than the duty to spend money to keep the economy going; and we must emphasize that although education might *sometimes* produce practical innovations beneficial to our health and material comfort, it should *always* produce greater understanding of the human condition and promise.

II

CHANGE – TO WHAT?

We have seen that human beings are confronted with a totally new situation which makes the prevention of war not only desirable but necessary. In a summary way we have looked at that situation. Now we must consider our response. The articles in this section fall into two groups: a) on accepting the need for change and the general direction of that change, and b) some views of world order.

F irst, Kenneth Boulding stands back and considers the relations between nations as a system, *i.e.* a set of correlated factors and principles forming a complex unity. The system under which nations operate is still the system of unilateral national defense which, due to the technological breakthroughs of the last twenty years, he finds to have a high built-in probability of disaster. A chief obstacle to any effort toward system change that would normally be made is the mechanism termed by psychiatrists "denial"—the doom is so large that we do not really believe it or pay much attention to it. This is what Myrdal speaks of. It is, of course, akin to the "psychic closing-off" referred to by Lifton as felt by many shortly after the bomb fell—with this significant difference: whereas the "closing-off" saved many from becoming psychotic in the face of existing horror and was therefore *toward* life, "denial" of the present danger when there is still possibility for remedial action is obviously *against* life.

When we are in a jam which is so terrifying we choose to ignore it, it does not help to keep pointing out how terrible it is. But if we can be shown that there is a way out, that we are not inevitably doomed, our paralysis is broken and all sorts of energies are released. Boulding outlines in very general terms what he sees as five stages of the way out—all leading *from* a system of unilateral national defense *to* a new system. You will notice that his first three stages are *extremely* unstable and even stage four fraught with difficulty. I personally take some exception to his use of the term "Utopia" as illusory and therefore slightly to be derogated. The point is that the famous Utopias were conceived when there was no possibility of achieving them, which gave the term a shady name. Now, for the first time, there is a pressing need combined with a real possibility of achieving something which in the *past* would have been considered "Utopian"—although of course it would not be so in any "ideal" sense, having problems of its own.

To me, the real point of this article is his pinpointing of system change, together with a major block to it, and his recognition of our need to be *able to visualize*, in as much detail as possible, the alternative to paralysis.

This article was first published in 1962.

The Prevention of World War III

KENNETH BOULDING

When we talk about preventing something we imply two things. We imply, first, that there is a dynamic system which is now proceeding that, if allowed to proceed unchanged, will result in an event which is regarded as undesirable and which, therefore, we want to prevent. We imply also that it is possible to change the dynamic system in question and replace it by another dynamic system in which the unwanted event does not occur. Thus, suppose we find ourselves driving toward a railroad crossing and suddenly we see the red lights flashing and a train approaching. Our dynamic system at the moment consists simply of velocity and direction. We are proceeding, say at 50 miles per hour, toward the crossing. The distant early warning system of our eyes informs us the crossing is dangerous. The knowledge which we have of our existing dynamic system informs us that if it continues we will arrive at the crossing at the precise moment when the train is there. The combination of a distant information system coupled with the simple dynamics of automobiles enables us, however, to prevent the disaster. We do this by putting on the brakes long before we get to the crossing. This in effect changes the dynamic system under which we have been operating. It introduces a new variable into it, indeed a new dimension, deceleration. Because of this, we are able to prevent the disaster, as we are able to avoid simultaneous occupancy of the crossing by ourselves and the train.

We must be careful, of course, in applying the analogy of a simple psycho-mechanical system like a man driving a car to the enormous complexities and uncertainties of the international system. However, the international system is still a system, even though it has important random elements in it. Because it is not entirely random, it has elements of predictability. One of the greatest difficulties lies precisely in the stochastic nature of the system. We are driving a car, as it were, that may or may not respond to brakes according to whether dice held by the driver indicate "respond" or "fail." The situation is made all the more difficult by the fact that we face here a stochastic system with a very small universe, that is, a very small number of cases. Stochastic systems with a large number of cases can be treated by the theory of probability. We have a pretty fair idea, for instance, how many people are going to die in automobile accidents next year, although we do not know exactly who they are.

The problem of reducing the total number of automobile accidents is a very different kind of problem from the one that faces the driver of the preceding paragraph. Nevertheless, even with our present knowledge it would not be difficult to design an automobile and a road system which would kill, let us say, 20,000 people a year instead of 40,000. What we would be doing here would be to reduce the probability of disaster on the part of a single individual. It is by no means impossible to think of the international system in a rather similar way, and to talk about the things we can do to reduce the probability of disaster. What we mean by this is that if we had a very large number of planets roughly identical with our own we could postulate changes in the system which would reduce the number of cases in which disaster occurred. This would be the analogue of treating road deaths as a public health problem and seeking to reduce their probability. As far as we know, however, we do not have a large number of planets like ours and for our purposes at least there is only one. Hence, reducing the probability of disaster does us very little good if the disaster actually occurs. The problem of stochastic systems with a small number of cases has received insufficient attention in the theoretical literature. It is precisely this kind of system, however, with which we have to deal in international affairs.

I believe the present international system to be one which has a significant probability built into it of irretrievable disaster for the human race. The longer the number of years we contemplate such a system operating, the larger this probability becomes. I do not know whether in any one year it is 1 per cent, 10 per cent, or even 50 per cent. I feel pretty sure, however, that it is of this order of magnitude, not, shall we say, of the order of magnitude of .01 per cent. The problem of system change, therefore, is urgent and desperate, and we are all in terrible danger. This is largely because of a quantitative change in the parameters of the international system under which we now live. This is still essentially the system of unilateral national defense in spite of the development of the United Nations and certain international organizations. Unilateral national defense is workable only if each nation can be stronger than its potential enemies in its home territory. This is possible under two circumstances. The first is that the nations must be far enough away from each other, and the extent to which their power declines as they operate further away from their own home bases must be sufficiently great. Then each nation can be stronger than the other *at home* with on-the-spot forces because of the fact that in a nation's home territory the enemy operates at a certain disadvantage. There is a second condition, however, which is that each nation must be able to dominate an area around its home base equal in depth to the range of the deadly missile. Because of quantitative changes in these conditions even in the last few years the system of unilateral national defense has become infeasible on a world scale. No nation is now far enough away from potential enemies to be sure that it can dominate even its own territory. Furthermore, the range of the deadly missile is rapidly reaching 12,500 miles, which means that the second condition cannot possibly be fulfilled. The condition which unilateral national defense attempts to establish, therefore, which I call *unconditional viability,* is now no longer possible.

The urgent and desperate nature of the present situation is created by the universality of the disaster with which we are threatened. The system of unilateral national defense has never given permanent security. The rise and fall of nations and empires is a testament to this fact. Indeed, looking with a large historical eye, one may say that unconditional viability has never existed except perhaps for brief periods and the best that unilateral national defense could do for any society was to postpone disaster. The situation of the individual society, that is, is rather analogous to that of the individual, whose life, on this earth at any rate, must also end in irretrievable disaster, that is, in death. Where we have a large number of individuals, however, death for the individual is not death for the race. In fact death for the individual is necessary if the race is to survive. Where the number of individuals becomes smaller and smaller, however, there comes to be a critical point where death for the individual is also death for the race and the irretrievable disaster which the individual suffers is likewise irretrievable disaster for the species. The unilaterally defended national state now seems to me to have got to this stage in its development. It is no longer appropriate as a form of organization for the kind of technical society in which we live. Its death throes, however, may destroy the whole human race. The age of civilization out of which we are passing was characterized by a large number of nation-states or independent political organizations practicing unilateral national defense. Because of the large number of these organizations there were always some being born and always some ready to rise into the places of those which suffered disaster. With the number of effectively independent nation-states now reduced to two or perhaps at most three, the possibilities of irretrievable disaster become much greater.

The problem which we face, therefore, is how to effect a system change in the international order, or perhaps we should say the world political order, sufficient to lower the probability of disaster to a tolerable level. The critical problem here might be described as that of "system perception." To revert again to the analogy of the car and the railroad cross-ing, if the driver of the car does not see that he is approaching the crossing, if the warning lights are not working, and if he cannot see the train ap-proaching, he will naturally not take any steps to avert the disaster. The world problem here is perhaps psychological rather than mechanical. There is a fairly widespread sense abroad of impending doom. The doom, however, is so large that we do not really believe it and we go about our daily actions as if it did not exist. This is the mechanism, as Jerome Frank has pointed out, known to the psychologists as "denial." Up to a point this is actually healthy. We all know that we are going to die sometime and we may die tomorrow; but we act pretty much as if we are going to live forever. We do not spend much time in taking tearful farewells and in writing our last wills and testaments. We plan ahead for months and even for years, in spite of the fact that these plans may never come to fruition. This perfectly legitimate response to uncertainty becomes pathological when it prevents us from taking steps which would postpone disaster or make it less likely. The man who is afraid that he has a cancer but who will not go to a doctor because he might find out that he has one is a good example. Where the prospect of disaster, therefore, is so vague or so uncer-tain that it merely results in pathological denial, it is necessary to bring the actor to a more realistic appraisal of the system within which he is acting.

If the problem of "denial" is to be overcome, it is necessary to do more than merely scare people with horrendous pictures of the possible future. Indeed, the more horrendous the picture which is drawn, the more it is likely to result in denial and pathological inactivity. The future which faced our driver at the railroad crossing was also horrendous, but instead of denying this and continuing on his way he presumably applied the brakes, that is, initiated a system change. The problem in the international system is that we seem to have no brakes. That is, it is hard for people to visualize the nature of the system change which is necessary for survival. This, then, is one of the major tasks today of the political scientist, the philosopher, the journalist, and the prophet: to give the people an image of changes in the international system which seem small enough to be fea-sible yet large enough to be successful. It is not useful to picture Utopias which seem utterly unattainable—this perhaps is the main difficulty with the World Federationists—even though the function of Utopias in provid-ing a constant driving force in social dynamics should not be underesti-mated. The present situation, however, calls not for Utopia, but for politi-cal solutions. Indeed, one of our great difficulties today is that we have too many Utopias. We need to think, therefore, in terms of a world social contract: that is, a minimum bargain between the contending parties which will give the world a sufficient system change to relieve it from the intolerable burden which it now bears. This social contract does not even have to be explicit or contractual. It can begin by being tacit; indeed, one can argue that a world social contract already exists in a tacit embryo form. We can visualize perhaps the following five stages of development.

I. The stage of tacit contract. In systems which have an inherent instability, such as duopoly in the relations of firms, or a bipolar system of mutual deterrence in the relations of states, it is often possible to maintain a quasi-stable position for a long time through tacit contract: that is, through mutually consistent unilateral behavior on the part of each party. A quasi-stable position is like that of an egg on a golf tee—it is stable for small disturbances but not for large. For considerable periods of time, however, the disturbances may be small enough so that Humpty-Dumpty does not fall. Comes a slightly larger disturbance, however, and all the King's horses and men cannot put him together again. The international system under the Eisenhower administration exhibited this kind of quasi-stability. An important element in that stability was a tacit agreement between the United States and the Soviet Union to do nothing effective about civil defense. We agreed, in effect, that our civilian populations should be mutually exchanged as hostages, for we each had the power to destroy large numbers—at least half—of each other's civilians. This meant that the chance of deliberate nuclear war was very small, though the chance of accidental war was appreciable; indeed, the missiles almost went off on at least two occasions. A natural accident, such as a large meteor, or an electronic breakdown, or a social accident, such as a mad pilot, or a political accident, such as an unwise commitment to an irresponsible third party, could under these circumstances easily set off a mutual exchange of nuclear weapons, so that the system could not be regarded as more than a temporary expedient.

Another example of tacit contract was the mutual suspension of nuclear tests, recently broken by the Soviet Union. Here the fear, perhaps, of world opinion, and the fear also of the technical consequences of an uncontrolled race for technical development of weapons, created a temporary tacit agreement. We have had similar tacit agreements in regard to spheres of influence and intervention in third-party quarrels. The United States did not interfere in Hungary, nor the Soviet Union in Egypt during the Suez crisis. The Russians allowed themselves to be thrown out of the Congo, and are not threatening to be more than a nuisance in Cuba. The conflicts in Korea and Vietnam were temporarily settled by latitudinal partitions. The Arab-Israeli conflict does not become an arena of the cold war. All these represent systems of mutuality of conduct which might be classified as tacit agreement.

II. The fate of the tacit agreement on nuclear testing, and what looks like the impending fate of the tacit agreement on civil defense, is a testimony to the inherent instability of the tacit agreement in the long run. It is something like the gentleman's agreement in economic competition, which suffers from the defect that not all people are gentlemen. The danger is that in the absence of organization between contending parties their only means of communication is by a "threat system." A threat system, which is characteristic of unilateral national defense, is based on the proposition, "If you do something bad to me I will do something bad to you," by contrast with an exchange system, which is based on "If you do something good to me I will do something good to you." Both systems tend to lead to consummation, but whereas the consummation of exchange is an increase of "goods" the consummation of threats is an increase of "bads." War is mainly the result of the depreciation in the credibility of threats in the absence of their consummation; and hence a threat system has a basic instability built into it, which tacit contract may postpone but cannot ultimately avoid. The great problem, therefore, is how to get rid of threat systems. This, I suspect, happens historically mainly by their being overlaid with other systems of relationship—trade, communication, organization—until they fall so much to the bottom of the pile that they are no longer significant.

The essential instability of threat systems and the weakness of tacit agreements, therefore, make it highly desirable to pass into the second stage of formalized agreement, and the building of what might be called "peace-defending" organizational structures. The first of these obviously is an arms control organization designed at first perhaps only to limit the present arms race but capable of the ultimate hope of policing genuine disarmament. We could begin, perhaps, with an organization for the prevention of accidental war. This will be a joint organization of the major armed forces of the world. Once this has been accomplished, a major system change is under way. It is the organizational disunity of the armed forces of the world which constitutes the real threat to humanity. If they were united they might threaten us with a great many disagreeable consequences but they would not threaten us with extinction. An arms control organization, therefore, would be the beginning of a very powerful social change. It would constitute the formal recognition of the fact that unilateral national defense is no longer possible. Once this initial break is made, system change may be expected to take place quite rapidly. It may be that we shall have to look forward to a substantial separation of the armed forces organization from the states which they are supposed to defend, and which they can no longer defend. Just as we solved the problem of religious wars by the separation of church and state, so we may be able to solve the problem of nuclear war by the separation of the armed forces from the state. The plain fact is that today the threat which the armed forces of the world present to their own civilian populations is much greater than any conflict among the nations. Arms control will be the beginning of the recognition of this social fact.

III. Arms control must move fairly rapidly into disarmament; otherwise it will be unstable. The organization of the world armed forces will be a loose and unstable one at first, and it will always threaten to break up. It may be, of course, that the major pressure towards disarmament will come from the economic side. Once the threat of war is removed by arms control and by organizational unity of the world armed forces, the economic burden of maintaining these monstrous establishments will seem intolerable, especially in view of the fact that it is the arms burden (equal to the total income of the poorest half of the human race!) which perhaps prevents the world from really tackling the problem of economic development and which condemns hundreds of millions of people and their descendants to live in misery. One looks forward, therefore, to the third stage of rapid and total disarmament, under the arms control organization. There are many difficult problems involved in this which have not been worked out and on which research desperately needs to be done. One research program is on the way at the moment on the broad problems of the economics of disarmament, conducted by Professor Emile Benoit of Columbia University. The United Nations is about to inaugurate a similar study. However, the organizational and social-psychological problems involved are very great and quite unprecedented. Growth is always much easier than decline and the problems of adjustment involved in a rapid decline in the world's armed forces still have to be faced. These problems, however, are difficult rather than insoluble.

IV. Even universal total disarmament, however, is not enough, for this too is likely to be unstable even though disarmament itself will reduce many of the sources of conflict, especially those which arise out of strategic considerations. It will not eliminate all conflicts by any means. In a world as divided as this, ideologically and economically, we may expect serious conflicts continually to arise. These conflicts will constantly present the temptation to the losing side to resort to violence and to redevelop organized armed forces. If disarmament is to be stable, therefore, there must be a system of conflict control. Conflict control is one of the essential functions of government. It is not, however, the only function. In thinking of world government, this is probably where we ought to begin. In the early stages it is more important to establish conflict control than to establish justice or to solve all social problems. Conflict control as a function of government has been inadequately studied and identified. This is perhaps because the study of conflict systems themselves is still in its infancy. However, this is a rapidly developing body of social science and one hopes that it may be possible in the not-too-distant future to develop a substantial body of knowledge on the identification and control of conflict systems. The problem, of course, is the identification of conflict processes in early stages before they become pathological. There are very difficult problems here in the definition of the pathology of conflict, as this, of course, goes very deep into our value systems. Conflict which is regarded as pathological by one person may not be so regarded by another. If, however, we regard violence as generally a sign of pathological conflict, we may be able to identify the processes of social dynamics which lead toward it, and we may therefore be able to interpose counterweights which will correct these processes. We may revert once more to the analogy of the car at the crossing. We need to develop both perception of dangers ahead and also organizations which can act as brakes. These processes have been fairly well worked out in industrial relations, where a whole profession of mediators and conciliators and personnel experts has come to being. There is no reason why these principles should not be applied in other fields of social life and especially to the conflict of states.

V. The last stage, of course, is true world government, capable not only of controlling conflict but of expressing and developing the common concerns and aims of mankind. At the moment this seems to be a long way off. Fortunately, the prevention of war does not depend, I think, on the establishment of full world government. If the stages of development which I have outlined can be pursued rapidly enough, war may be postponed for longer and longer periods until the postponement becomes indefinite by the establishment of a true world government. We must therefore find halfway houses and quarterway houses which are moderately habitable. We must not allow Utopian longings to deprive us of political bargains. The actual negotiation of the world social contract is going to be a long and arduous business. We need to put many more resources into this than we are now doing. Nevertheless, there is something here which can be done. There is a road which leads somewhere. If we are to break out of the apathy, irrationality, and despair which beset us, we must gain a vision of that road of escape and make at least one step along it. This is the great significance of the growing movement for peace research. Just as we no longer accept depressions as "acts of God," wholly unpredictable and uncontrollable, so we need no longer accept mass violence as unpredictable and uncontrollable. The fact that we cannot yet predict or control it should stir us to a great intellectual effort in this direction, for this way lies hope. The only unforgivable sin in the present crisis of mankind is despair.

༝ ༝ ༝ ༝

Next, in a deeply thought-provoking article, Jerome Frank, Professor of Psychiatry at Johns Hopkins University School of Medicine, examines, from the standpoint of his own area of special competency, two factors of extraordinary importance for the elimination of war: group standards and group cohesiveness. He points out that whereas the standards of most nations place a high value on peace, they attach a still higher one to the defense of the moral convictions, ideals and mores of the group and that therefore wars will never be abolished by appeals to the human desire for peace.

The job facing us is two-pronged: to alter or to reinterpret group standards which support war, bringing them into closer relation with the new facts, and to develop *alternative ways* of defending one's society and one's values that are compatible with the nuclear age. Here, surely, is the nub.

Konrad Lorenz, in his extraordinarily interesting and valuable book, *On Aggression*, has made clear that the original function of the instinct of aggression—its positive use in evolution—was to insure the spacing out of members of the same species. But very few living creatures engage in killing members of their own kind as man does. Evolution, in the interests of species preservation, has introduced inhibitive mechanisms. It is significant that in the cultural evolution of peoples the earliest and most important imperatives, of the Mosaic or any other law, are not commandments but *prohibitions*. In almost all living things the species-preserving instinct of aggression is retained but made harmless by a complex of other instincts giving rise to various forms of ritualization of conflict between members of the same species. Only the rat engages in ferocious wars with its own kind as does man. And in rats these clan fights serve no constructive purposes whatever but are the aggressive instinct gone wild, without life-preserving checks.

It may well be that the need, of which Jerome Frank speaks in the article below, of each side to create the stereotype of the enemy as a monster who is sub-human, i.e. *non*-human, has to do with a buried recognition of the force of this fundamental law of species preservation. We have to create the fiction that the enemy is not of our species.

In relation to the development of alternate ways of defending one's society, I believe there is much to be learned from expert research into ritualization of aggression. Provided it is kept totally divorced from war, it is possible that the "space race" may be a most propitious ritualization of aggressive conflict between the United States and the Soviet Union, for instance.

And for ourselves: from the brief analysis Frank gives of four wide-spread group standards supporting war we are able to view our own attitudes more clearly and possibly to reassess them. He goes on to consider what can be done towards changing group standards in a way that would make war less likely.

Every sentence of this article has underlying it the importance of what each single individual can do. Dr. Frank says, in effect, now is a time to stand up and be counted.

Group Psychology and the Elimination of War

JEROME D. FRANK, M.D.

In considering the most urgent problem of our time—the prevention of war—the clinician is inclined to view war as a form of aberrant human behavior and to explore the ways in which psychopathological processes in individuals may foster it. He may speculate, for example, on how the mechanism of denial impedes full realization of the destructiveness of nuclear weapons, how the "repetition compulsion," aggravated by anxiety, may hamper the search for new solutions, and how the psychopathology of national leaders, such as Hitler, may heighten their warmaking propensities.

On further thought, however, it becomes increasingly clear that individual psychopathology cannot cast much light on the question of war. For one thing, mentally healthy national leaders are fully as capable of leading a nation to war as unbalanced ones. For another, war is a group activity. Individuals fight, but they do not wage war. This is reserved for organized groups.

Nor can one assume that war is pathological. Many sociologists and political scientists have taken psychologists to task for their unspoken assumption that peace is the natural state of human societies and that war is a kind of affliction that strikes them from time to time. They suggest that it would be more accurate to view war and peace as states of society that have alternated with monotonous regularity, as if each contains within it processes that inevitably lead to the other. Furthermore, war has not been an unmitigated evil. It may have been essential to the continuance of organized societies, for it strengthened social solidarity, which erodes in peace time, and has performed many other vital social functions. Today the elimination of war has become a requirement for human survival, but this may be only because it has become so destructive that it has lost whatever positive social values it may have once possessed.

Psychologists and psychiatrists are frequently admonished not to meddle with questions of war and peace because knowledge gained from individuals and small groups is not applicable to large social systems. And indeed there is much force in this admonition. As one goes from the individual to the group to the nation, new phenomena emerge and principles applicable at one level may be irrelevant at another. We must also recognize, however, that no adequate theory of international behavior exists at this time. Therefore, until the irrelevance of psychological knowledge has been demonstrated, it seems to me that we have both the right and the duty to try to contribute what we can from our own area of competency. Only by testing the limits of our thinking will we discover what is pertinent and what is not.

I should like to touch on two areas of group psychology that may be pertinent to the elimination of war: group standards and group cohesiveness.

The power of group standards to affect the perceptions and behavior of group members is apparent even in artificially composed, ephemeral therapy groups. We know how standards of candid expression of feelings, responsibility for one's behavior, and mutual respect play a crucial part in helping patients to correct faulty attitudes and behavior. So, it is not surprising that the standards and values of organized societies powerfully affect the perceptions and behavior of their members. For example, what to the Communists are wars of liberation against capitalist-imperialist oppressors, to Americans are cynical exploitations of popular discontent by a sinister worldwide conspiracy against peace and freedom, masterminded by a small group of power-hungry leaders. To Americans, nuclear missiles in Turkey are purely defensive, while those in Cuba are obviously aggressive. To Russians, of course, these weapons appear exactly the reverse.

Group standards do more than determine the perceptions and behavior of the group members. In a real sense, they give meaning to life. Each member of a group internalizes its values. They become part of himself, and their loss represents a kind of psychological death that many find much harder to contemplate than losing their lives in defense of their values, an attitude summed up in the slogan, "Better dead than Red." One of the unfortunate consequences of this propensity is that groups will go to extreme lengths to defend ideals to which they have committed themselves, and the more abstract the issue, the more intense the commitment seems to be. Wars fought for food, loot, or territory have probably been less bitter and inexorable on the whole than those fought over ideological differences.

The standards of most nations place a high value on peace, but they attach a still higher one to the defense of the moral convictions, ideals, and mores of the group. It follows that wars will never be abolished by appeals to the human desire for peace. Mankind has yearned for peace as strongly throughout history as we do today, but this has not led to the slightest reduction in the frequency and deadliness of wars. The elimination of war, then, requires the modification of group standards supporting war and the development of alternative ways of defending one's society and one's values that are compatible with the nuclear age.

Let me now briefly consider four widespread group standards supporting war that have been socially useful in the past but have become very dangerous in the nuclear age. The first is absolute national sovereignty, the right of each nation to pursue its "vital interests" regardless of the effects of this pursuit on the "vital interests" of other nations. Advances in weapons technology, communication, and transportation have made this concept obsolete. No nation can protect itself from fallout carried by nuclear explosions anywhere in the world; armed space satellites can be constructed at any time; and it will soon be possible to influence climate all over the world. Today no nation can be secure at the expense of the security of other nations. Yet such is the power of group standards that nations must be persuaded to relinquish aspects of their sovereignty that, in fact, they no longer possess.

A second very powerful group standard is that under certain circumstances war is both a feasible and a proper way of pursuing the interests of one's group. The conviction of its practicality rests on age-long human experience. Until the twentieth century, societies could successfully defend their values by war. The intellectual insight that, "No one can win a modern war," as General Curtis LeMay has put it, makes little headway against the group standard of war's feasibility, engrained by millennia of human experience.

Furthermore, the group standards of all modern societies sanction war as morally justified. People everywhere have been taught from earliest childhood that the right and proper response to a threat to the integrity of one's own nation is to destroy the threatening nation. Conscience, in short, is on the side of war, and unless this is recognized, we are not going to make much headway in abolishing it.

The third group standard which supports war is a corollary to the second. It equates armed strength with determination and courage. The way to convince an enemy that you cannot be intimidated is to build more weapons. Leading scientific authorities, as well as President Kennedy, have said that beyond a certain point increase in military strength does not increase national security and may actually decrease it. However, since national group standards equate armed strength with courage, disarmament becomes a sign of weakness or surrender and those who advocate it are cowards; thus the elimination of war requires breaking the link between courage and arms.

The strength of the influence of a group's standards on its members depends on its cohesiveness. Humans seem to have a strong drive to group formation, perhaps based on the simple fact that they cannot survive in isolation. This is quite apparent in therapy groups. I am repeatedly amazed at the rapidity with which strangers, all of whom have difficulties with others, congeal into a group and how reluctant they are to disband after they have been meeting for a while.

One aspect of the human tendency to form cohesive groups may increase the likelihood of wars, and this is the rejection of the outsider. All group creatures from ants to men view the stranger with suspicion and are impelled to close ranks against him. Group therapists have learned that one does not lightly introduce new members into an established group. Careful preparation of both group and newcomer may be necessary to forestall painful consequences.

If groups tend to react adversely to strange individuals, it is scarcely surprising that they are suspicious of strange groups with different standards and customs. It is easy to view another group as hostile. The existence of a hostile group, in turn, causes the threatened group to close ranks, a fact instinctively exploited by political leaders, who may manufacture an enemy in order to consolidate their power.

It seems as if before one group can to go war against another it must label the adversary as in some respects non-human; otherwise, killing members of the enemy group would be in some sense an attack on oneself. So, wars are regularly preceded by mounting recriminations until at the onset of hostilities each group has cast the other into the stereotype of the enemy. The image of the enemy is remarkably similar no matter what nation is in the role. He is always a kind of subhuman monster: cunning, crafty, and cruel. The degree of correspondence of the image of the enemy to his actual characteristic varies from case to case. Nazi Germany was closer to it than we were initially, but we destroyed Germans no less indiscriminately and ruthlessly than they did us. This highlights the unfortunate fact that enemies act toward each other in ways that confirm their reciprocal image.

Another implication of group cohesiveness for the problem of war is that it inhibits personally destructive or group disruptive behavior by the group's members.

Every society has rules or laws for settling potentially disruptive conflicts. It is worth emphasizing in this connection that obedience to law does not rest simply on the police power of the state. Obedience to law seems to spring primarily from what has been called the habit of obedience, which probably in turn is rooted in a sense of a community of interests and values. For example, between the evacuation of the Nazis from Copenhagen and the restoration of the police there was an interregnum in which there were no police for several days, and yet there was no increase in crime. I stress this point because I think some tend to place too much emphasis on a world police power as a means for assuring peace. A world police force will indeed be necessary, but it may not have to be very powerful, just as the unarmed police in England are able to control armed criminals.

This very sketchy and incomplete analysis suggests certain directions of effort toward the elimination of war, of which I should like to mention three. First, we should work to build a sense of world community, on which obedience to world law must ultimately rest. While the major obstacle to this today is the existence of a deep-seated and perhaps irreconcilable conflict between the Communist and Western worlds, the problem is aggravated by mutual fear and mistrust, some of which might be reduced even in the face of the basic conflict. Any success in this direction will not only increase the chances for progress toward a world community but may reveal that some aspects of the conflict are not as irreconcilable as they appear to be at present.

One has to start very modestly, and the best place to begin seems to be the promotion of increased international communication and cooperation. Interchanges of performing artists, cultural, scientific and technical missions, students and the like may do something to foster the sense of international community by diminishing mutual feelings of strangeness, but they also may backfire. Increased contact can help to disclose and correct mutual distortions and diminish mutual ill will by yielding favorable experiences to the participants. It can also, however, confirm the reality of certain areas of conflict and unearth hitherto unsuspected ones, and it can intensify misconceptions and heighten mutual antagonisms because of the universal tendency to perceive only that information which tends to confirm one's preconceived ideas. Contact between members of different societies also creates opportunities for unintended slights and insults resulting from lack of awareness of social forms, proper word usage, and the like. It is especially important in face-to-face contacts with members of other groups to avoid behavior which humiliates them, and this includes doing things for them without giving them a chance to reciprocate. This may be one reason why the American foreign aid program has earned us so little gratitude. The Peace Corps seems to have learned this lesson and is proving effective in winning friends.

Especially effective in promoting a sense of community are genuinely cooperative activities to attain goals that all nations want but none can achieve alone. In this connection, the famous Robbers Cave experiment is relevant. This was an experiment in a boys' camp in which children who were strangers were rapidly formed into two organized warring groups through having them defeat each other in games under dubious circumstances. Various efforts were then made to break down the mutual hostility. It was found that merely increasing contact between the groups had no effect, or even reinforced their mutual antagonism. However, by creating situations in which the whole camp had to cooperate to survive, the antagonism was rapidly broken down. For example, the camp water supply was surreptitiously interrupted and all the boys had to find and remedy the trouble, or the camp truck, on which the camp depended for supplies, managed to stall in a ditch, and the whole camp had to get on the tow rope and pull it out.

Fortunately, modern technology has opened up opportunities for analogous cooperation among nations toward superordinate goals. The International Geophysical Year was one, and space offers innumerable others. Although only a tiny beginning, it is encouraging that Russia and the United States have agreed to cooperate in charting and predicting the weather. Accurate long-range weather forecasting represents a genuine superordinate goal since it would bring tremendous benefits to all countries; yet none can accomplish this by itself. The greater the number of these cooperative activities, the more rapidly the sense of world community will develop, and this will become a powerful inhibitory influence on efforts to settle international disputes by violence.

Secondly, we must strengthen group standards and values within societies that break the link between violence and courage. There is some evidence that this is possible. In the psychiatric sphere there is the convincing experiment of Wilmer (1958), who was able to create group standards in an admission ward in a naval hospital that interdicted violence by either patients or staff. Since many patients came to this ward in a highly excited state, this was far from easy, but in his ten months of direction of this ward he never once had to put a patient in seclusion or in restraints, and renunciation of violence enhanced the self-respect of both patients and staff. On a larger scale, the nonviolent campaigns led by Gandhi in India and King in the United States are pertinent. From the psychological standpoint, perhaps their most impressive aspect was that both succeeded in creating group standards which divorced courage from violence. Refusal to resort to violence became the sign of firmness of will; resort to violence was a sign of cowardice. Furthermore, as studies of the sit-in movement in this country have shown, nonviolent behavior can powerfully strengthen self-esteem and be a way of expressing contempt for one's opponent. Although the implications of these findings for the prevention of war are admittedly remote, they suggest that a breakthrough in conflict management has been achieved that holds great promise.

Finally, we must strenuously attack group standards supporting the morality of war. It is easy to show intellectually that modern war is not a workable way of resolving international conflicts. The facts demonstrate beyond doubt that, as almost all political and many military leaders have affirmed, war is no longer a possible means of pursuing national goals. It is much more difficult to convince mankind that war has lost its moral justification, because the group standards justifying war are maintained by powerful emotions and only appeals with an emotional component can change them. Those of us who, as therapists or scientists, place a high value on objectivity, find it difficult to make such appeals. But group standards, like personal attitudes, are largely impervious to purely intellectual arguments.

The group standard supporting the morality of war is the doctrine that a war is justified if its possible good effects outweigh its harmful ones. This doctrine of the "just war" has enabled religions to sanction any war, because any war that "our side" engages in is "just" by definition; otherwise we would not be fighting. It is therefore important to hammer home the point that, as most religious leaders agree, a "just" nuclear war is impossible, because no conceivable good it might accomplish could outweigh the harm it would inflict on mankind. We must never let people forget that nuclear weapons are weapons of genocide.

Merton has made this point most effectively in a poem entitled "Chant to be Used in Processions around a Site with Furnaces." It is a monologue by a commander of a Nazi extermination camp who was hanged for genocide. He concludes:

> *You smile at my career but you would do as I did if you knew your-self and dared*
> *In my day we worked hard we saw what we did our self sacrifice was conscientious and complete our work was faultless and detailed.*
> *Do not think yourself better because you burn up friends and enemies with long-range missles without ever seeing what you have done*

If there is any such thing as immorality, it is certainly immoral to plan to kill millions of people immediately, to condemn millions of others to a lingering, horrible death infinitely worse than death in a gas chamber, and to blight future generations for centuries to come. Tamerlane, Genghis Khan, and Hitler could exterminate whole peoples without violating their own moral standards, but a society that values the worth of the individual cannot defend itself by these tactics without destroying its own moral basis, even if some remnant should survive. If we really have a superior way of life, it will prevail in a disarmed world; if we do not, nuclear war will not save it.

The elimination of nuclear war requires changes in deeply ingrained group standards, and these can only be brought about by groups within societies. We know from studies of group influence, such as the Asch experiment, that a single individual has great trouble defying a unanimous group consensus. The pressure of this consensus may be so strong as to make him doubt the evidence of his own eyes. Just one ally who supports him, however, enables him to stand his ground. Working for the elimination of war requires the espousal of group values which contradict many currently dominant ones, so the support of kindred spirits is vital. Fortunately, there are now groups working for peace that represent every shade of opinion. If you believe, as I do, that the days of Western civilization, and perhaps of humanity itself, are numbered unless the world achieves universal disarmament soon, I urge you to waste no time in joining the peace group of your choice.

※ ※ ※ ※

The following short statement by Robert Pickus who is national coordinator of Turn Toward Peace, appeared as an interview in Mademoiselle back in 1961. It goes right to the heart of several often confused points, but I would particularly call attention to this: "It's tragic that so few intelligent people have been willing to start at that point—ruling out organized violence as a solution and then saying, 'all right, what do we do instead?'"

I would like to ask, with deep respect, of all those who have been carrying the burden of protest for the whole of us, "After protest, what?" Protest and civil disobedience are of great importance to the country as well as to the conscience of the individual. In foreign policy especially where we often do not have a direct chance in the ballot box, it is a way of voting, a way of expressing our choice. It is my personal feeling that all Americans, in the future, will be deeply indebted to the protesters. For the fact that Norman R. Morrison burnt himself to death before the Pentagon, and the North Vietnamese made a stamp with his picture on it (a moving, young, white, American face) so that his protest, and the fact of other protests, is *known* throughout Asia, may well be what saves *all* Americans from being spat on at some future date in a large portion of the globe. It destroys the stereotype of "American as enemy" that would otherwise exist. This in itself must make any peace that comes easier to implement.

Interview with Robert Pickus

But are men good enough to get rid of violence, to get rid of war?

Those are two different questions. We've got rid of slavery, but we still have exploitation, and in one form or another we're likely to have it always. But the move from a world that accepts slavery to a world that rejects it and is working on problems of exploitation is an important move. Isn't it possible that we could get rid of war, while people went on being nasty to their wives, occasionally kicking stray dogs? Wouldn't that still be an important advance? I'm not talking about saintliness or the best of all possible worlds when I talk of getting rid of war. I'm talking about the minimal understandings necessary if the human story is to go on. We've got to recognize that organization for war is no longer right and no longer rational, that we must turn our energies to developing alternate methods for the defense of our values. The startling thing is that in almost every other area of life we've already rejected violence. In penology we don't think punishment is the real answer any more. We don't throw the mentally ill into chains. The kind of pacifism I mean is already working in most other areas of life. It's only here in the question of war that there's been a failure of thought. Beat a child? No. But jump into a plane and destroy a city of a million human beings . . . yes sir!

Aren't there any causes worth the sacrifice of
human life through warfare?

It isn't the sacrifice of human life that's at stake—most pacifists are willing to put their own lives quite literally on the line in order to further their beliefs—it's your phrase "through warfare." The point is, can causes we care for be furthered by war? To me it's clear that they can't. You only collaborate in spreading the very attitudes and actions you wanted to stop. It isn't even a moral question of whether war is right or wrong, but does it work? And I say no.

Assuming war can't serve our values, still they are under attack. . .

That's the problem we must think about. It's tragic that so few intelligent people have been willing to start at that point—ruling out organized violence as a solution and then saying, "All right, what do we do instead?" All our intellectual efforts have been set in the context of one basic assumption: that organization for war is still right and rational for people holding democratic values—by which I don't mean voting, but a view of what a human being is and why there's dignity and value simply in the fact of being human. If this is the ground you stand on, then you have to rule out mass-organized violence and start searching for an alternative. The trouble with many pacifists is that they haven't faced the consequences of renouncing the violent solution.

Do you think war has ever achieved what people wanted it to?

I can't make an absolute statement about violence in the preatomic past, but I will about now. Herman Kahn's book, *On Thermonuclear War,* has done the peace movement a great service by carrying the premises involved in the use of violence to their logical conclusion. He's demonstrated that a commitment to violence today is not limited, not discriminate, not proportionate; that if you go along that road you must be willing to accept the final results. I think many people assume that somehow it'll never happen—even though so much of the whole life of our society is organized around war; still say, *"But* it's unthinkable. The whole point in preparing for war is to prevent war." But Kahn says, in effect, "Nonsense, you can't prepare for war intelligently unless you face the fact that it may come. And if it comes, this is what it will cost, and we must do something about the cost."

⚹ ⚹ ⚹ ⚹

Nonetheless, at least some of those who have acted by protest, whether pacifist or not, must "face the consequences of renouncing the violent solution" and dig beyond protest for an alternative. The rest of this book is occupied with that digging beyond.

※ ※

Everyone who has thought about the subject seriously knows that ultimately we will have to evolve some system of world order based on laws or rules. Every society, from the beginning of time, has required some system of order, greater or less, so that the individuals who compose it may be free to carry on their lives. There is no doubt that the world has already in some respects become one society, mankind having met himself everywhere in his triumphant spread over the globe. From the point of view of a world society, however, nation states are interrelated parts, not self-sufficient and sovereign wholes. This requires an adjusted way of thinking about a great many things.

Amid wide diversity of opinion there is growing agreement among the best informed and most responsible persons of many nations, including the Soviet Union, on a few simple points: that the system of competing national armaments has become not only obsolete but too costly and too dangerous to keep; that disarmament is essential and must be permanent; and that this requires some authority to administer it. Furthermore, there is growing recognition that there are other world problems closely tied to the prevention of war—such as the guarantee of outer space for peaceful purposes and the responsibility of rich nations to aid in closing the widening gap between "haves" and "have-nots"—all of which also require some authority to administer them. The question is: how much authority and how might it affect the absolute autonomy of the nation state? The Russians, as I see it, talk about one simple world law that would establish disarmament and forbid overt aggression by any state against another. In the *Disarmament Proposals of the Soviet Union as of March 1, 1964,** for instance, disarmament is unequivocally sought. But the international authority to administer it appears extremely weak. This is consistent with the Soviet view of coexistence as the solution to the problem of war. It is important to realize that this word, for all the ambiguity and propaganda overtones that have become attached to it, expresses the overwhelming desire for peace of the Rus-

* Comparison and Evaluation of Current Disarmament Proposals *by Marion H. McVitty, published by the World Law Fund, is a short, instructive book on this subject.*

sian people and their government's recognition of it. Harrison Salisbury makes this point plain*:

"*The harsh truth is that between 20,000,000 and 25,000,000 Russians died in World War II. But this was not the only cost in lives. So staggering was this blow to the Russian birthrate and normal rate of population increase that Russia lost an additional 20,000,000 lives —the deficit in births directly attributable to the consequences of the savage war.*

"*Thus, World War II is calculated to have cost Russia a population loss—actual and expected—of nearly 45,000,000. No country in modern times has suffered so severe a loss. Not even the devastating famines of China have taken such a toll. All the countries of Europe together did not suffer a fraction of such casualties in World War I.*

"*The only catastrophe which can be compared with that suffered by Russia is the catastrophe which the world has not suffered—the catastrophe of nuclear devastation, with its estimates of death tolls running to 50 to 60 per cent of national populations.*

"*With the memories of World War II so vivid, with the country still suffering so horribly from war wounds, nothing stirred Russian emotions so profoundly as threat of war.*" Peace, therefore, became "*the dominant theme of Soviet propaganda throughout the cold war years. Supposedly, the target was the United States and the other 'imperialist' governments of the West, the 'warmongers' who were said to be threatening the outbreak of global conflict. Actually, however, the propaganda was chiefly designed to convince the Russian people that their own government was doing everything possible to prevent a new World War. Diplomats in Moscow during these years felt that the only factor which might really shake the Soviet Government was a mass conviction on the part of the war-weary people that Stalin was leading them back into war.*"

My own understanding is based on moderate reading and a mere sixteen days in the Soviet Union in May 1966, but it is my strong impression that this is the feeling that exists today. To the Soviet citizen—whether the concerned, intelligent lawyer or educator, or the young woman interpreter whose childhood during the war was spent as a refugee in the

* Russia—by Harrison E. Salisbury, a Nations Today book, published by Macmillan Company, New York 1965—p. 85 and p. 95.

Urals or in Siberia, or the ordinary "man in the street"—the word coex-istence expresses a dominant concern for peace and is shorthand for the hope that both the Communist and Western worlds will develop along their characteristic lines without fearing the other or being interfered with by the other; that they will enter a peaceful competition and eventually a cooperation in improving the lot of mankind; that the fundamental differences between them will be eroded with the passing of time.

You will find a statement about coexistence by the Polish Communist Adam Schaff in the last section of this Reader. As a formula to replace war, however, it does not appear to the serious thinkers of the West (as opposed to the Communist world) as sufficiently organized for safety. It leaves too much vague. In the West, particularly in the United States, there are considerable official pronouncements about law, world law, but it has not been spelled out. *The U. S. Disarmament Proposals as of March 1, 1964* raise so many problems about inspection that they could reasonably appear to the Russians as not genuinely to seek disarmament. Indeed it can be fairly said that, to date, no government has made a proposal that was adequate or to which the government itself appeared genuinely committed. Until that happens who can judge how other governments might respond? With the emergence of China as a nuclear power, the Soviet Union herself might choose more safeguards than coexistence provides. What China's position might become in even the near future no one knows. But the fundamental needs of the Chinese people are not so extraordinarily different from those of other people, and China cannot voluntarily remain apart nor be deliberately excluded from world society indefinitely.

However one looks at it, the vital question remains: just how much supranational or world authority do we need for the purpose of war prevention? Part and parcel of this question is the consideration of what kind of world order, and by what steps arrived at, do we want—for it is bound to come, in one form or another, if we survive at all.

It is my strongly held conviction that what we must aim at is a world order based on justice and voluntarily arrived at, not imposed by force, and one that allows diversity—what Norman Cousins calls "a world safe for its differences." It is a further condition that all major sectors of mankind must find benefit in the new system if a stable peace is to be achieved. Not only will the peace not be stable otherwise, but there would be insufficient incentive to take the risks and make the effort of will and imagination to bring the new system into being.

Many thoughtful people believe that mankind is so embedded in old habits of thought that it will not make—through the nation-states which are now its highest authorities—the necessary effort until after an appalling Third World War or some catastrophe so great as to be almost comparable. It may be possible, however, to learn before, not after, the fact.

※ ※

The next item merits the most careful study. It is a summary of what is generally recognized as the most complete and scholarly plan to date for a disarmed world under enforceable law.

In 1945 Grenville Clark, a prominent New York lawyer who had already had a distinguished career,* saw that the Charter of the newly created United Nations did not give that organization the powers necessary to fulfill the purpose for which it was intended—*i.e.* to preserve peace at the world level. Believing the weaknesses of the Charter to be of the utmost importance, he called a conference of private citizens to discuss the matter at his home in Dublin, New Hampshire. After evolving, during the next few years, certain basic ideas that were expounded in his small book A *Plan for Peace,* and in response to requests for a large and comprehensive work, he enlisted the close cooperation of Louis B.

* In 1916 Grenville Clark was the prime mover of the "Plattsburg movement" to train volunteer officers at their own expense prior to U.S. entry into World War I which he saw to be inevitable. This project proved so valuable that it was soon formally incorporated into the army. After wartime service he returned to private practice in New York as partner in his own law firm of Root, Clark, Buckner and Ballantine. In 1940, almost singlehanded, he conceived, wrote and engineered the passage of the Selective Service Act, our first peacetime draft, as he again saw that the United States was unprepared for her inevitable part in World War II. He served as special assistant to Secretary of War Henry L. Stimson during World War II. Subsequently, during the McCarthy period, he was prominent in the defense of many civil liberties cases. Well ahead of general recognition of the need, he became a leader in the creation of the Legal Defense Fund of the N.A.A.C.P. for civil rights cases.

Sohn*, then a young professor at the Harvard Law School with whom he had kept in touch since the Dublin Conference in October 1945. Aided by an initial research grant from The Ford Foundation, they set to work to examine the basic minimum requirements for peace in the world community. In 1953 and in 1956 they issued documents which were widely circulated for comment and criticism in many countries. The whole was then revised and combined in the book, *World Peace through World Law* which was published in 1958 by the Harvard University Press. This book, in whole or in part, has been translated into thirteen languages and has received scholarly reviews in many countries including the U.S.S.R.

The authors cast their proposals in the form of a revision of the United Nations Charter—article by article, with the reasoning behind each choice, and with seven annexes dealing with new authorities which they deem essential. However, the authors emphasize that their requirements for peace need not be accomplished through Charter revision but could be embodied in a special treaty on disarmament and its enforcement leaving a United Nations freed of peace-keeping responsibility to perform the many humanitarian and important functions it now has.

The Introduction, by Grenville Clark, which follows below, is designed to summarize the basic principles and essential features of the authors' plan for peace. You will notice that Clark states even more forcibly a point made by Boulding: that in order to move from our present predicament people must be shown a way out, and in full detail.

A prime motive for this book is that the world is far more likely to make progress towards genuine peace, as distinguished from a precarious armed truce, when a detailed plan adequate to the purpose

* Louis B. Sohn came as a young lawyer from Poland in 1939 to be an instructor at Harvard Law School. He took part in the founding United Nations Conference at San Francisco in 1945, was consultant to the U.N. Secretariat in 1948, and Legal Officer of the Codification Division of the U.N. in 1951. He is now Bemis Professor of International Law at Harvard Law School and is a consultant to the U. S. Arms Control and Disarmament Agency and to the Office of International Security Affairs in the Department of Defense.

is available, so that the structure and functions of the requisite world institutions may be fully discussed on a world-wide basis.

He stresses that such a plan must be so framed that it is *acceptable* to the nations and *adequate* to do the job. The area of enforceable world law, as viewed by this plan, is strictly limited to war prevention although assisting agencies are set up to deal with the world's other grave problems.

Clark and Sohn take what is sometimes called the radical approach —that is, they believe that a plan has greater chance of *acceptance* by the nations if it can be shown in advance to be *adequate* both to keep the peace and safeguard the rights of all concerned. It is easier, and safer, in their opinion to take a big step clearly defined so that the nations know to what they are committing themselves rather than to advance in small and uncertain degrees. Moreover the tremendous benefits of the change cannot be enjoyed until it is achieved.

No system is perfect in all particulars. Any reader of *World Peace through World Law* becomes aware that the authors have, in every particular, weighed one possible choice against another and selected what they judged the *relative* best for the whole plan. Some thoughtful persons may have reservations on the size of their world peace force, despite the careful safeguards surrounding it. And others may query whether necessary internal revolutions will be able to take place within this proposed framework, although the authors have restricted the world authority from interference with internal affairs. But by being able to examine a whole structure we are aided in pinpointing problems for further study.

There are at least four reasons why the Clark-Sohn plan merits careful consideration:

1) The total estimated annual cost of Clark and Sohn's world peace forces and supporting institutions is well under 20 billion dollars. This figure is opposed to the estimated annual military expenditures by the nations of more than 140 billions. The indicated annual savings of well over 100 billions is surely a factor to be reckoned with at a time when two thirds of the world's population lacks the basic necessities. You will note in the Introduction that provision is made for a World Development Authority which would employ 25 billions, or less than one quarter of the annual savings.

2) Careful study of the Clark-Sohn plan reveals that it has "some-

thing for everybody." Although no nation would like every particular of it, and each nation does have to give up something, at the same time each nation on balance does stand to gain. There is an inducement for the large nations and for the small, for the "haves" and the "have nots," for the capitalist and the communist. For this reason it may prove in the end more acceptable (realistic) than a more gradual approach. Saul Mendlovitz discusses this particular point in Section IV.

3) The plan's attempt at *completeness* brings into focus the interlocking nature of the international system. Because it depicts in detail the character of the proposed system it serves as a "model" by which to examine the requirements for genuine peace.

4) Regardless of any chance for acceptance of this plan or a similar plan in the near future, having a clear vision of what could be exerts a pull toward it and enables us to move.

The Introduction below is from the second edition (1960) of *World Peace through World Law*. It has been slightly edited, with the authors' consent, for inclusion here. I have also tried to incorporate the authors' latest thinking (as of April 1966) on certain technical points: 1) in view of the fact that there are in 1966 one hundred and twenty-nine independent nation states as compared to the ninety-nine which existed in 1960, the up-dated formula which they propose for representation in the Revised General Assembly is given in a footnote; 2) several changes in their proposal for the disarmament process are incorporated into the Introduction as here given; and 3) at the suitable place I have indicated (a) the reduction in strength of their proposed United Nations Peace Force, and (b) the increase (largely for developmental purposes) in the proposed annual budget of the United Nations which changes, as of April 1966, they would make as compared to April 1960.

The authors emphasize, however, that these changes do not affect the fundamental philosophy or basic plan as set forth in the first and second editions of *World Peace through World Law*.

Introduction to World Peace Through World Law

GRENVILLE CLARK

This book sets forth a comprehensive and detailed plan for the maintenance of world peace in the form of a proposed revision of the United Nations Charter. The purpose is to contribute material for the world-wide discussions which must precede the adoption of universal and complete disarmament and the establishment of truly effective institutions for the prevention of war. . . .

The fundamental premise of the book is identical with the pronouncement of the President of the United States on October 31, 1956: "There can be no peace without law." In this context the word "law" necessarily implies the law of a world authority, *i.e.* law which would be uniformly applicable to all nations and all individuals in the world and which would definitely forbid violence or the threat of it as a means for dealing with any international dispute. This world law must also be law in the sense of law which is capable of enforcement, as distinguished from a mere set of exhortations or injunctions which it is desirable to observe but for the enforcement of which there is no effective machinery.

The proposition "no peace without law" also embodies the conception that peace cannot be ensured by a continued arms race, nor by an indefinite "balance of terror," nor by diplomatic maneuver, but only by universal and complete national disarmament together with the establishment of institutions corresponding in the world field to those which maintain law and order within local communities and nations.

A prime motive for this book is that the world is far more likely to make progress toward genuine peace, as distinguished from a precarious armed truce, when a *detailed* plan adequate to the purpose is available, so that the structure and functions of the requisite world institutions may be fully discussed on a world-wide basis. Consequently, this book comprises a set of definite and interrelated proposals to carry out complete and universal disarmament and to strengthen the United Nations through the establishment of such legislative, executive and judicial institutions as are necessary to maintain world order.

Underlying principles

The following are the basic principles by which Professor Sohn and I have been governed.

First: It is futile to expect genuine peace until there is put into effect an effective system of *enforceable* world law in the limited field of war prevention. This implies: (a) the complete disarmament, under effective controls, of each and every nation, and (b) the simultaneous adoption on a world-wide basis of the measures and institutions which the experience of centuries has shown to be essential for the maintenance of law and order, namely, clearly stated law against violence, courts to interpret and apply that law and police to enforce it. All else, we conceive, depends upon the acceptance of this approach.

Second: The world law against international violence must be explicitly stated in constitutional and statutory form. It must, under appropriate penalties, forbid the use of force by any nation against any other for any cause whatever, save only in self-defense; and must be applicable to all individuals as well as to all nations.

Third: World judicial tribunals to interpret and apply the world law against international violence must be established and maintained, and also organs of mediation and conciliation—so as to substitute peaceful means of adjudication and adjustment in place of violence, or the threat of it, as the means for dealing with all international disputes.

Fourth: A permanent world police force must be created and maintained which, while safeguarded with utmost care against misuse, would be fully adequate to forestall or suppress any violation of the world law against international violence.

Fifth: The complete disarmament of all the nations (rather than the mere "reduction" or "limitation" of armaments) is essential for any solid and lasting peace, this disarmament to be accomplished in a simultaneous and proportionate manner by carefully verified stages and subject to a well-organized system of inspection. It is now generally accepted that disarmament must be universal and enforceable. That it must also be complete is no less necessary, since: (a) in the nuclear age no mere reduction in the new means of mass destruction could be effective to remove fear and tension; and (b) if any substantial national armaments were to remain, even if only 10 per cent of the armaments of 1960, it would be impracticable to maintain a sufficiently strong world police force to deal with any possible aggression or revolt against the authority of the world organization. We should face the fact that until there is *complete* disarmament of every nation without exception there can be no assurance of genuine peace.

Sixth: Effective world machinery must be created to mitigate the vast disparities in the economic condition of various regions of the world, the continuance of which tends to instability and conflict.

The following supplementary principles have also guided us:

Active participation in the world peace authority must be universal, or virtually so; and although a few nations may be permitted to decline active membership, any such nonmember nations must be equally bound by the obligation to abolish their armed forces and to abide by all the laws and regulations of the world organization with relation to the prevention of war. It follows that ratification of the constitutional document creating the world peace organization (whether in the form of a revised United Nations Charter or otherwise) must be by a preponderant majority of all the nations and people of the world.

The world law, in the limited field of war prevention to which it would be restricted, should apply to all individual persons in the world as well as to all the nations—to the end that in case of violations by individuals without the support of their governments, the world law could be invoked directly against them without the necessity of indicting a whole nation or group of nations.

The basic rights and duties of all nations in respect of the maintenance of peace should be clearly defined not in laws enacted by a world legislature but in the constitutional document itself. That document should also carefully set forth not only the structure but also the most important powers of the various world institutions established or authorized by it; and the constitutional document should also define the limits of those powers and provide specific safeguards to guarantee the observance of those limits and the protection of individual rights against abuse of power. By this method of "constitutional legislation" the nations and peoples would know in advance within close limits what obligations they would assume by acceptance of the new world system, and only a restricted field of discretion would be left to the legislative branch of the world authority.

The powers of the world organization should be restricted to matters directly related to the maintenance of peace. All other powers should be reserved to the nations and their peoples. This definition and reservation of powers is advisable not only to avoid opposition based upon fear of possible interference in the domestic affairs of the nations, but also because it is wise for this generation to limit itself to the single task of preventing international violence or the threat of it. If we can accomplish that, we should feel satisfied and could well leave to later generations any enlargement of the powers of the world organization that they might find desirable.

While any plan to prevent war through total disarmament and the substitution of world law for international violence must be fully adequate to the end in view, it must also be *acceptable* to this generation. To propose a plan lacking in the basic essentials for the prevention of war would be futile. On the other hand, a plan which, however ideal in conception, is so far ahead of the times as to raise insuperable opposition would be equally futile. Therefore, we have tried hard to strike a sound balance by setting forth a plan which, while really adequate to prevent war, would, at the same time, be so carefully safeguarded that it *ought* to be acceptable to all nations.

It is not out of the question to carry out universal and complete disarmament and to establish the necessary new world institutions through an entirely new world authority, but it seems more normal and sensible to make the necessary revisions of the present United Nations Charter.

Main features of the whole plan

In harmony with these underlying principles, the most important specific features of the proposed Charter revision may be summarized as follows:

(1) *Membership.* The plan contemplates that virtually the whole world shall accept permanent membership before the revised Charter comes into effect—the conception being that so drastic a change in the world's political structure should, in order to endure, be founded upon unanimous or nearly unanimous approval.

The assurance of assent by a great preponderance of the nations and peoples of the world would be accomplished by the revised Articles 3 and 110 providing: (a) that every independent state in the world shall be eligible for membership and may join at will; (b) that the revised Charter shall come into force only when ratified by five sixths of all the nations of the world, the ratifying nations to have a combined population of at least five sixths of the total world population and to include all the twelve nations which then have the largest populations. The assurance of permanent membership would be provided by the revised Article 6 whereby no nation, once having ratified the revised Charter, could either withdraw or be expelled.

The practical result would be that the plan would not even become operative until active and permanent support had been pledged by a great majority of all the nations, including as the twelve largest nations Brazil, France, the Federal Republic of Germany, India, Indonesia, Italy, Japan, Pakistan, the People's Republic of China, the United Kingdom, the U.S.A., and the U.S.S.R. . . .

With so large a preponderence in the number and population of the ratifying nations, it is reasonable to suppose that within a few years after the ratification of the revised Charter, there would be no nonmember nations whatever. For it seems clear that few, if any, nations would wish to stand out when at least five sixths of all the nations of the world, having over 90 per cent of its population, had agreed to the new plan for world peace.

The likelihood that there might not be a single nonmember nation is made the greater by the proposed requirement (under revised Articles 2 and 11) that every one of the necessarily small minority of nonmember nations shall, nevertheless, be required to comply with all the prohibitions and obligations of the disarmament plan. This provision that *every* nation in the world shall completely disarm and shall comply with the plan for the substitution of world law for international violence is deemed fundamental, since if even one small nation were permitted to possess the new weapons of mass destruction, such fears and suspicions might remain as to prevent the adherence of others, and the entire plan might be frustrated. . . .

(2) *The General Assembly.* A radical revision is proposed as to the powers, composition and method of voting of the General Assembly . . .

The plan calls for imposing the final responsibility for the enforcement of the disarmament process and the maintenance of peace upon the General Assembly itself, and gives the Assembly adequate powers to this end. These powers would, however, be strictly limited to matters directly related to the maintenance of peace. They would *not* include such matters as regulation of international trade, immigration and the like, or any right to interfere in the domestic affairs of the nations, save as expressly authorized by the revised Charter in order to enforce disarmament or to prevent international violence where a situation which ordinarily might be deemed "domestic" has actually developed into a serious threat to world peace.

To ensure the observance of these limitations, the delegated powers would be enumerated and defined in the revised Charter; while, as still further protection, there would be an explicit reservation to the member Nations and their peoples of all powers not thus delegated "by express language or clear implication.". . .

As above mentioned, the principle is followed that all the *main features* of the whole plan shall be included in the revised Charter itself as "constitutional legislation," having in mind that the nations will be more likely to accept the plan if all its principal provisions are clearly set forth in the constitutional document itself. The effect would be to bind the nations in advance not only to all the fundamentals but also to many important details, and thus to leave for the General Assembly a more limited legislative scope than might be supposed.

Since, however, the General Assembly, even with elaborate "constitutional legislation," would need to have some definite legislative powers, the plan calls for a revision of the system of representation in the Assembly.

For it cannot be expected that the larger nations would consent to give the Assembly even very limited *legislative* powers under the present system whereby Albania, Costa Rica, Iceland, Liberia, etc., have an equal vote with the United States, the Soviet Union, India, the United Kingdom, etc.

The purpose is, by abolishing the present system of one vote for each member Nation, to substitute a more equitable system, and thus to make the nations more willing to confer upon the General Assembly the limited yet considerably increased powers that it would need.

The proposed plan of representation takes account of relative populations but is qualified by the important provisions that no nation, however large, shall have more than thirty Representatives and that even the smallest nation shall have one Representative. The upper limit of thirty would be imposed partly because weighted representation is not likely to be accepted by the smaller nations unless the differences in representation between the majority of the nations and the largest nations are kept within moderate limits, and also because without some such limitation, the General Assembly would be of so unwieldy a size as to be unable to transact business. At the other extreme the purpose is to ensure that even the very small nations shall have some voice.

The proposed formula* divides the 99 nations, generally recognized in early 1960, as independent states or likely soon to be so recognized, into six categories according to relative populations, with representation as follows:

The 4 largest nations........30 Representatives each........120
The 8 next largest nations....15 Representatives each........120
The 20 next largest nations.... 6 Representatives each........120
The 30 next largest nations.... 4 Representatives each........120
The 34 next largest nations.... 2 Representatives each........ 68
The 3 smallest nations....... 1 Representative each........ 3

99 nations   551 Representatives

* *Because in 1966 the number of independent nation states had risen to 129, the authors' revised formula for representation is as follows:*

The 4 largest nations........30 Representatives each........120
The 10 next largest nations....12 Representatives each........120
The 15 next largest nations.... 8 Representatives each........120
The 20 next largest nations.... 6 Representatives each........120
The 30 next largest nations.... 4 Representatives each........120
The 40 next largest nations.... 3 Representatives each........120
The 10 smallest nations....... 1 Representative each........ 10

129 nations   730 Representatives

Over a period of years, the authors have studied many plans for determining representation by various formulas that would take account of such factors as relative literacy, relative wealth as measured by per capita income, etc. We have concluded, however, that the introduction of any such other factors would raise so many complications and involve such uncertain and invidious distinctions that it is wiser to hold to the less elaborate formula herein proposed.

We have also studied numerous suggestions for a bicameral world legislation in which the nations would have voting power in one house in proportion to their populations, but equal voting power in the other house irrespective of their size. Modifications of this plan in the shape of a system of double voting in a single house have also been studied. After weighing these alternatives, we conclude that the one-chamber solution herein proposed (together with representation which takes account of relative populations, but is modified by the proposed system of categories and the proposed maximum and minimum number of Representatives) is not only simpler, but also is probably as fair an arrangement as any other. However, we hold no dogmatic views on this difficult subject, the essential point being that there must be some radical, yet equitable, change in the present system of representation in the General Assembly as a basis for conferring upon the Assembly certain essential, although carefully limited, powers of legislation which it does not now possess.

As to the method of selection of the Representatives, it is proposed that a system of full popular election shall be gradually introduced. This would be done under a three-stage plan providing: (a) that in the first stage all the Representatives would be chosen by the respective national legislatures of the member Nations; (b) that in the second stage at least half the Representatives would be chosen by popular vote of those persons qualified to vote for the most numerous branch of the national legislature; and (c) that in the third stage all the Representatives would be chosen by the same sort of popular vote. The first two stages would normally be of twelve years each (three four-year terms of the General Assembly) but could each be extended by eight years by a special vote of the Assembly. The popular election of all the Representatives would, therefore, normally become mandatory twenty-four years after the ratification of the revised Charter and in any case not later than forty years after the revised Charter comes into force.

With regard to the terms of service of the Representatives, it is proposed that they shall serve for four years. . . .

Two full-time Standing Committees of the General Assembly would be constitutionally provided for, namely, a Standing Committee on the Peace Enforcement Agencies and a Standing Committee on Budget and Finance. The former would be a "watchdog" committee to exercise legislative supervision over the process and maintenance of disarmament and over the United Nations Peace Force. The latter would have vital functions in submitting to the Assembly recommendations as to the amount and apportionment of each annual budget for all the activities of the strengthened United Nations.

With relation to the powers of the revised General Assembly, a clear distinction would be made between legislative powers and powers of recommendation. The *legislative* powers would be strictly limited to matters directly related to the maintenance of peace, whereas the extensive powers of mere recommendation now possessed by the Assembly would be retained and even broadened. To this end, the Assembly's legislative authority would, as above mentioned, exclude any regulation of international trade, immigration and the like and any right to interfere in the domestic affairs of the nations, save only as strictly necessary for the enforcement of disarmament or, in exceptional circumstances, for the prevention of international violence.

On the other hand, as distinguished from the power to legislate, the General Assembly would have the right to make nonbinding recommendations on any subject which it deemed relevant to the maintenance of peace and the welfare of the world's people.

(3) *The Executive Council.* It is proposed to abolish the present Security Council and to substitute for it an Executive Council, composed of seventeen Representatives elected by the General Assembly itself. This new and highly important organ would not only be chosen by the Assembly, but would also be responsible to and removable by the Assembly; and the Council would serve for the same four-year terms as the Representatives in the Assembly.

Special provision would be made for representation of the larger nations, whereby the four largest nations (China, India, the U.S.A. and the U.S.S.R.) would each be entitled at all times to have one of its Representatives on the Council; and four of the eight next largest nations (Brazil, France, West Germany, Indonesia, Italy, Japan, Pakistan and the United Kingdom) would in rotation also be entitled to representation, with the proviso that two of these four shall always be from nations in Europe and the other two from nations outside Europe. The remaining nine members would be chosen by the Assembly from the Representatives of all the other member Nations and the non-self-governing and trust territories under a formula designed to provide fair representation for all the main regions of the world and to ensure that every member Nation, without exception, shall in due course have a Representative on this all-important Council.

In contrast to the voting procedure of the present Security Council, whereby any one of the five nations entitled to "permanent" membership has a veto power in all nonprocedural matters, the decisions of the new Executive Council on "important" matters (as defined in paragraph 2 of revised Article 27) would be by a vote of twelve of the seventeen Representatives composing it, with the proviso that this majority shall include a majority of the eight members of the Council from the twelve member Nations entitled to fifteen or more Representatives in the Assembly and a majority of the nine other members of the Council. All other decisions would be by a vote of any twelve members of the Council.

The Executive Council would constitute the *executive arm* of the strengthened United Nations, holding much the same relation to the General Assembly as that of the British Cabinet to the House of Commons. Subject to its responsibility to the Assembly, the new Council would have broad powers to supervise and direct the disarmament process and other aspects of the whole system for the maintenance of peace provided for in the revised Charter. . . .

(4) *Economic and Social Council, Trusteeship Council.* These two Councils would be continued, but with a somewhat different composition than under the present Charter designed to provide a better-balanced representation on these Councils. . . .

Like the Executive Council these two other Councils would be directly responsible to the Assembly. Their responsibilities would be enlarged; and their usefulness would be enhanced by reason of the greatly increased funds which would be available to them under the proposed new revenue system.

(5) *The Disarmament Process.* The proposal includes a highly developed and detailed plan for general and complete disarmament, to be carried out under adequate inspection by every nation in the world without exception step by step over a six-year period.

During the first year after the coming into force of the plan, an Inspection Service would be organized and would conduct an arms census whereby every nation would supply a complete list of its armed forces, armaments and armament production facilities, but without being required to disclose the location of certain secret installations. In each six-month period thereafter 10 per cent of any and all military organizations would be disbanded, and 10 per cent of all armaments and armament-making facilities would be destroyed or converted to other uses. The result would be that at the end of the five-year actual disarmament period (six years after the coming into force of the plan) no nation would possess any *military* forces whatever and the only military force in the world would be the United Nations Peace Force.

This complete elimination of all national *military* forces would, however, be without prejudice to the retention by every nation of such lightly armed internal police forces as are needed for internal order only—subject to careful restrictions as to the maximum size of such police forces relative to population and as to the character of the weapons permitted to them.

After completion of the arms census an arms truce would take effect, under which all nations would be legally bound not to increase their existing armed strength. Then would follow the above-mentioned ten disarmament stages of six months each, during each of which there would be a 10 per cent across-the-board arms reduction, applying equally to all categories of military units, armaments and armament production facilities.

During each of the ten periods of six months, every nation would give the Inspection Service advance notice of the specific military units, armaments, armament facilities and excess internal police forces which it proposes to eliminate in that period, in order to comply with the 10 per cent reduction requirement. When these proposals have been checked and found adequate, the proposed reductions would take place under the direct supervision of the Inspection Service. During each six-month period the Inspection Service would also conduct a thorough inspection of a region, chosen by a decision of the Inspection Service, comprising one tenth of the territory of each nation, in order to verify the accuracy of the initial arm census (which, for each nation, would contain a separate inventory for each of ten substantially equal regions into which the nation would be divided). The purpose and effect would be, therefore, that after five years all national military strength (and all internal police forces in excess of the prescribed limits) would have been eliminated, and the original arms census would have been completely verified.

This step-by-step reduction would provide every nation with an effective safeguard against cheating by others, since each stage would have to be completed by *all* nations before *any* nation could be called upon to begin the next stage. Provision would be made for delaying the whole process (by one or more postponements in no case exceeding six months) until any noncomplying nation was brought into line.

A portion of the eliminated national armaments would be turned over to the United Nations Peace Force, which would be built up to its full strength during the same period as that of the disarmament process. Another portion, consisting of all the nuclear weapons which have not been destroyed, all nuclear materials contained in destroyed nuclear weapons, and all nuclear materials from which nuclear weapons could be made, would be turned over to a civilian agency, to be known as the United Nations Nuclear Energy Authority. In both cases, fair compensation would be paid. All the rest of the eliminated national armaments would simply be destroyed. . . .

The disarmament plan also includes provision for a United Nations Nuclear Energy Authority with dual functions: (a) to assist the Inspection Service in guarding against possible diversion of nuclear materials to any war-making purpose, and (b) to promote the world-wide use of nuclear materials and processes for peaceful purposes. To these ends, the Nuclear Energy Authority would have wide powers to acquire by purchase at a fair price all nuclear materials in the world, with the obligation to have them put to use at fair rentals for peaceful purposes in all parts of the world under arrangements that would apportion the materials fairly and safeguard them against seizure. It is contemplated that this new Authority, having wider scope and membership than the International Atomic Energy Agency established in 1956, would take over the personnel and functions of that Agency. . . .

A new feature of the disarmament plan, made necessary by the recent penetration of outer space and its potentialities for the future, is a proposed United Nations Outer Space Agency. The broad objectives sought are: (a) to ensure that outer space is used only for peaceful purposes, and (b) to promote its exploration and use for the common benefit of all the people of this earth, rather than for the benefit of any nation or any part of mankind.

The Outer Space Agency would, subject to the over-all authority of the General Assembly and the Executive Council, be under the "direction and control" of a United Nations Outer Space Commission. This Commission, like the Inspection Commission and the Nuclear Energy Commission, would be composed of five members appointed for five-year terms by the Executive Council subject to confirmation by the General Assembly and would be removable at will by the Council. . . .

(6) *A World Police Force.* The plan is framed upon the assumption that not even the most solemn agreement and not even the most thorough inspection system, or both together, can be *fully* relied upon to ensure that every nation will always carry out and maintain complete disarmament and refrain from violence under all circumstances. Moreover, it must be recognized that even with the complete elimination of all *military* forces there would necessarily remain substantial, although strictly limited and lightly armed, internal police forces and that these police forces, supplemented by civilians armed with sporting rifles and fowling pieces, might conceivably constitute a serious threat to a neighboring country in the absence of a well-disciplined and heavily armed world police.

In short, our conception is that if police forces are necessary to maintain law and order even within a mature community or nation, similar forces will be required to guarantee the carrying out and maintenance of complete disarmament by each and every nation and to deter or suppress any attempted international violence. In consequence, detailed constitutional provision is made for a world police, to be organized and maintained by the strengthened United Nations and to be called the "United Nations Peace Force." This world police force would be the only *military* force permitted anywhere in the world after the process of national disarmament has been completed. It would be built up during the above-described "actual disarmament stage," so that as the last national military unit is disbanded the organization of the Peace Force would simultaneously be completed.

Annex II provides in detail for the organization and maintenance of the proposed United Nations Peace Force—for its recruitment and pay, its terms of service, its maximum and minimum strength, and for its training, equipment, disposition and functions. This Peace Force would consist of two components—a standing component and a Peace Force Reserve—both of which would, save in the most extreme emergency, be composed solely of volunteers.

The standing component would be a full-time force of professionals with a strength of between 200,000 and 600,000, [1966 figures: 200,000 to 400,000] as determined from year to year by the General Assembly. The proposed term of service for its enlisted personnel would be not less than four or more than eight years, as determined by the General Assembly, with provision for the re-enlistment of a limited number of especially well-qualified personnel.

In respect of the composition of the standing component, assurance would be provided through various specific limitations in Annex II that it would be recruited mainly, although not exclusively, from the smaller nations. These limitations would include: (a) a provision whereby the number of nationals of any nation (including any non-self-governing or trust territory under its administration) serving at any one time in the standing component shall not exceed 3 per cent of its then existing total strength; (b) a provision that the number of nationals of any nation in any one of the three main branches (land, sea and air) of the standing component shall not exceed 3 per cent of the then existing strength of such main branch; (c) a provision that the number of nationals of any nation serving at any one time in the officer corps of either of the three main branches of the standing component shall not exceed 3 per cent of the then existing strength of the officer corps of such main branch; and (d) a provision that not less than 2 per cent or more than 10 per cent of the total strength of the standing component shall be nationals of the nations or nation constituting any one of eleven to twenty regions into which the whole world would be divided by the General Assembly pursuant to paragraph 9 of Article 26 of Annex I.

The units of the standing component would be stationed throughout the world in such a way that there would be no undue concentration in any particular nation or region, and, on the other hand, so as to facilitate prompt action for the maintenance of peace if and when required. Proposed specific provisions in this respect include: a direction that the standing component shall be stationed at military bases of the United Nations so distributed around the world as to facilitate its availability in case prompt action to prevent or suppress international violence is directed by the General Assembly (or in certain circumstances by the Executive Council); a provision that no such base shall be situated within the territory of any nation entitled to fifteen or more Representatives in the General Assembly, thus ensuring that no United Nations military base would be located in any of the twelve largest nations; a provision that all the territory of the world outside that of the twelve largest nations shall be divided by the General Assembly into eleven to twenty regions for the special purpose of distributing elements of the standing component between such regions, with the proviso that not less than 5 per cent or more than 10 per cent of the total strength of the standing component shall be stationed in bases in any one of those regions, save only when the Peace Force has been duly called upon to take action.

In order to ensure the greatest possible security for the standing component, provision would be made that its units be located to the greatest extent possible on islands or peninsulas, or in other easily defensible positions.

The mobility of the standing component would be of great importance, in order that its widely distributed units could be promptly brought together into a formidable force in the event of any serious threat of international violence or serious defiance of the authority of the world organization. The equipment of the standing component should, therefore, include an ample number of large and swift aircraft for the long-distance transport of men and supplies, and in voting the annual budgets for the Peace Force the General Assembly would have authority to provide for this need.

As distinguished from the active or standing component, the Peace Force Reserve would have no organized units whatever, but would consist only of individuals partially trained and subject to call for service with the standing component in case of need. It would have a strength of between 600,000 and 1,200,000, [1966 figures: 300,000 to 600,000] as determined by the General Assembly. Its members would be recruited subject to careful provisions as to geographical distribution identical with those applicable to the standing component. The proposed term of service of its enlisted personnel would be for not less than six or more than ten years, as determined by the General Assembly. They would receive a minimum amount of basic training during the first three years of their term of service and some further training during the remainder of their terms, but except for these training periods would remain in their home countries on a stand-by basis subject to call.

The officers of both components would be selected, trained and promoted with a view to "ensuring an officer corps of the highest possible quality" with adequate opportunity for the selection as officer candidates of highly qualified men from the rank and file.

Specific provision would be made for adequate pay and allowances for the personnel of both components, all pay and other compensation (including retirement pensions) to be free from all taxation.

It is contemplated that the United Nations Peace Force shall be regularly provided with the most modern weapons and equipment, except that its possession or use of biological, chemical or any other weapons adaptable to mass destruction, other than nuclear weapons, would be forbidden, special provision being made, as hereafter mentioned, for the use of nuclear weapons in extreme circumstances. The initial weapons and equipment of the Peace Force would come from the transfer of weapons and equipment discarded by national military forces during the process of complete disarmament. Subsequent supplies would be produced by the United Nations in its own production facilities through a separate agency to be established by the General Assembly and called the United Nations Military Supply and Research Agency. This Agency would engage in research relative to the development of new weapons and relative to methods of defense against the possible use by any nation of prohibited weapons clandestinely hidden or produced.

With regard to the use of nuclear weapons by the Peace Force, the solution proposed is that neither component shall normally be equipped with any kind of nuclear weapons, but that some such weapons shall be held in reserve in the custody of a civilian agency for use only under the most careful precautions. This agency would be the Nuclear Energy Authority which would be authorized to release any nuclear weapons for possible use by the Peace Force only by order of the General Assembly itself, and then only if the Assembly has declared that nuclear weapons (which might have been clandestinely hidden or clandestinely produced) have actually been used against some nation or against the United Nations, or that such use is imminently threatened. While it may be argued that nuclear weapons should be part of the regular equipment of a world police force so that it could immediately crush by ruthless action any defiance of the world law, this solution has been rejected as being no more consistent with the purpose of the Peace Force than the regular equipment of a city police force with weapons whereby thousands of citizens could be killed in suppressing a riot.

It is also realized that it can be persuasively argued that nuclear weapons should not be even potentially available to the Peace Force. On balance, however, it is believed wise to make it *possible* for the Peace Force to use nuclear weapons in extreme circumstances provided that, as called for by the above-described proposals, such possible use is safeguarded with the utmost care.

The immediate direction of the Peace Force would be entrusted to a committee of five persons—to be called the Military Staff Committee—all of whom would have to be nationals of the smaller nations, *i.e.* of those nations entitled to less than fifteen Representatives in the General Assembly. Beyond this safeguard, however, the Military Staff Committee would always be under the close control of civilian authority, *i.e.* of the Executive Council. Still further, the General Assembly, through its Standing Committee on the Peace Enforcement Agencies, would exercise a general supervision over the work of the Military Staff Committee and over the

Executive Council itself in respect of the organization and all the activities of the Peace Force. In short, the plan includes the utmost precautions for the subordination of the military direction of the Peace Force under all circumstances to civilian authority as represented by the Executive Council and the General Assembly.

While a world police force, well-equipped and strong enough to prevent or promptly to suppress *any* international violence is, we believe, indispensable, the danger that it might be perverted into a tool of world domination is fully recognized. It is with this danger clearly in mind that meticulous care has been taken to surround the proposed Peace Force with the above-mentioned careful limitations and safeguards, so as to make its subversion virtually impossible.

Even with these elaborate safeguards, it is realized that the danger of possible misuse of the Peace Force cannot be *wholly* eliminated any more than every *conceivable* danger of violation of the disarmament process can be eliminated. However, in order to achieve complete national disarmament and genuine peace, *some* risks must be taken. What we have attempted is to reduce these to the very minimum. On the one hand we have sought to provide for a world police so strong as to be capable of preserving peace in any foreseeable contingency. On the other hand, we propose such careful checks and limitations that there would be every possible assurance that the power of this world police would not be misused.

It will be seen that, despite all the proposed safeguards, this plan calls for a world police that would be a strong and effective fighting force in case of need. The idea of some people that a world peace force somewhat similar as to arms and functions to the United Nations Emergency Force of 1957-1960 might suffice is, we believe, unsound and untenable. Even in a world in which all national military forces were abolished, there would, as above mentioned, necessarily remain internal police forces of substantial strength which would probably need to possess a considerable number of rifles and even a few machine guns. In addition there would remain literally millions of sporting rifles and revolvers in the hands of private persons and thousands of nonmilitary airplanes, large and small. Accordingly, it is conceivable that, even with total disarmament, an aroused nation with a strong grievance could marshal quite a formidable armed force even if no one in it possessed any weapon stronger than a rifle. And while it is true that any such force, even of a million men, could not withstand a well-armed contingent of the world police of even one twentieth its strength, that contingent in order to suppress the aggression promptly and with minimum injury would need to be a genuine fighting force, well equipped and highly disciplined.

Moreover, there would remain a lurking suspicion for some time at least that despite the most efficient world inspection system some nation or nations had contrived to hide or might produce secretly some forbidden weapons. In these circumstances it seems perfectly clear that in order to provide the necessary assurance to obtain general assent to universal and complete disarmament, it will be essential to provide a world police of such strength and armament as to be able *quickly* and *certainly* to prevent or suppress *any* international violence. We firmly believe that on no cheaper terms can universal and complete disarmament be achieved, while it is equally clear that without total disarmament, genuine peace is unattainable. We submit, in short, that a strong and well-armed police force is part of the indispensable price of peace and that the sooner the world faces up to this conclusion the better it will be for all peoples.

(7) *The Judicial and Conciliation System.* In accordance with the conception that the *abolition* of national armaments is indispensable to genuine peace, and that if such armaments are abolished other means must be simultaneously provided for the adjudication or settlement of international disputes and for "peaceful change," provision is made for a world system of conciliation and adjudication.

In proposing such a system, recognition is given to the existence of two main categories of international disputes, namely: (1) those disputes which are capable of adjudication through the application of legal principles, and (2) the equally or more important category of disputes which cannot be satisfactorily settled on the basis of applicable legal principles.

With respect to those international disputes which are susceptible of settlement upon legal principles, it is proposed to empower the General Assembly to *direct* the submission of any such dispute to the International Court of Justice whenever the Assembly finds that its continuance is likely to endanger international peace. In case of such submission, the Court would have compulsory jurisdiction to decide the case, even if one of the parties should refuse to come before the Court.

The International Court of Justice would also be given authority to decide questions relating to the interpretation of the revised Charter; and to decide disputes involving the constitutionality of laws enacted thereunder. Compulsory jurisdiction would also be conferred upon the Court in certain other respects as, for example, any dispute relating to the interpretation of treaties or other international agreements, or as to the validity of any such treaty or agreement alleged to conflict with the revised Charter. . . .

In respect of the enforcement of the judgments of the International Court of Justice, it is proposed that the General Assembly (or in certain special circumstances the Executive Council) could direct economic sanctions or, in the last resort, action by the United Nations Peace Force to ensure compliance. Any such action would, however, be limited, if at all possible, to air or naval demonstrations and would involve actual military operations against a noncomplying nation only if absolutely necessary.

With regard to the other main category of international disputes, *i.e.*

those inevitable disputes which are not of an exclusively legal nature, it is proposed to establish a new tribunal of the highest possible prestige, to be known as the World Equity Tribunal. To this end it is proposed that the Tribunal shall be composed of fifteen persons elected by the General Assembly pursuant to safeguards and an elaborate procedure designed to ensure the choice of individuals whose reputation, experience and character would furnish the best assurance of impartiality and breadth of view. Thus no two of them could be nationals of the same nation, and it would be required that at least ten of the fifteen must have had more than twenty years of legal experience as judges, teachers of law or practicing lawyers. In addition, the General Assembly would be restricted in its choice to a list of persons nominated by the member Nations upon the recommendation of a committee in each member Nation which would have to include representatives of its principal judicial tribunals and legal associations, and of its leading academic, scientific, economic and religious organizations. Beyond this, the General Assembly would be required to pay due regard to the geographical distribution of the members of the Tribunal, so as to ensure fair representation of all the principal regions of the world.

To ensure the independence of the members of the World Equity Tribunal, they would be elected for life, subject only to the possibility of dismissal if, in the unanimous opinion of his colleagues, a member is no longer able properly to perform his functions or has ceased to fulfill the required conditions of his tenure.

In ordinary circumstances this World Equity Tribunal could not make binding decisions, as distinguished from recommendations, except with the consent of the parties. But provision is made that if the General Assembly votes by a large special majority, *i.e.* by a three-fourths majority of all the Representatives then in office (including two thirds of all the Representatives from the twelve largest nations), that the carrying out of the Tribunal's recommendations is essential for the preservation of peace, the recommendations of the Tribunal shall become enforceable by the same means as a judgment of the International Court of Justice.

The purpose of this important departure is to supplement other methods for settling *nonlegal* international disputes (such as negotiation, conciliation and agreed arbitration) by providing an impartial world agency of so high a stature that, under exceptional conditions involving world peace, its recommendations may be given the force of law.

Through the adoption of these proposals in respect of both legal and nonlegal international disputes, world institutions would at last exist whereby *any* nation could be compelled to submit *any* dispute dangerous to peace for a final and peaceful settlement; and the world would no longer be helpless, for lack of adequate machinery, to deal by peaceful means with any and all dangerous disputes between nations.

In order to provide means for the trial of individuals accused of violating the disarmament provisions of the revised Charter or of other offenses against the Charter or laws enacted by the General Assembly, and to provide safeguards against possible abuse of power by any organ or official of the United Nations, provision is also made for regional United Nations courts, inferior to the International Court of Justice, and for the review by the International Court of decisions of these regional courts.

The proposal is for not less than twenty or more than forty such regional courts to have jurisdiction in regions to be delineated by the General Assembly, each regional court to be composed of not less than three or more than nine judges. The judges of these courts would be appointed by the Executive Council from a list of qualified persons prepared by the International Court of Justice, with the provisos that not more than one third of the judges of any such court could be nationals of the nations included in the region of the court's jurisdiction, and that no two judges of any such court could be nationals of the same nation. Their appointments (which would be subject to confirmation by the General Assembly) would be for life, subject only to dismissal for cause by a vote of two thirds of all the judges of the International Court.

The regional United Nations courts, together with the International Court of Justice, would introduce a regime of genuine and enforceable world law in respect of all *legal* questions likely to endanger world peace, while the World Equity Tribunal would, as above mentioned, provide means for the authoritative and compulsory settlement of nonlegal situations seriously dangerous to peace.

In addition to these judicial agencies, it is proposed to establish a World Conciliation Board which could be voluntarily availed of by the nations, or to which the General Assembly could refer any international dispute or situation likely to threaten peace. The functions of this new Board would be strictly confined to mediation and conciliation; and, if it failed to bring the disputing nations to a voluntary settlement, resort could be had to the International Court of Justice or the World Equity Tribunal, as might be most suitable in view of the nature of the issues involved.

In order to achieve genuine peace we must have more than total and universal disarmament and more than an effective world police. We must also have world tribunals to which the nations can resort with confidence for the adjustment or decision of their disputes and which, subject to careful safeguards, will have clearly defined authority to deal with any dispute which is dangerous to peace even if a nation does not wish to submit to the jurisdiction of the appropriate tribunal.

(8) *Enforcement and Penalties.* The plan envisages a variety of enforcement measures, including the prosecution in United Nations regional courts of individuals responsible for a violation of the disarmament provisions.

In order to aid the Inspection Service in the detection and prosecution of any such violators, it is proposed to have a civil police force of the United Nations with a strength not exceeding 10,000. This force would be under the general direction of an Attorney-General of the United Nations, to be appointed by the Executive Council subject to confirmation by the General Assembly. The Attorney-General, besides having supervision over the civil police force, would be responsible for making arrangements with national authorities for assistance in the apprehension of persons accused of offenses against the revised Charter and the laws and regulations enacted thereunder and for the detention of such persons pending trial. Provision would also be made for Assistant Attorneys-General of the United Nations who would be assigned to each regional court.

In case of a serious violation of the revised Charter or any law or regulation enacted thereunder for which a national government is found to be directly or indirectly responsible, the General Assembly could order economic sanctions against the nation concerned. In extreme cases the Assembly (or the Executive Council in an emergency and subject to immediate review by the Assembly) would also have authority to order the United Nations Peace Force into action. Any such enforcement action would correspond to the above-mentioned action available for the enforcement of judgments of the International Court of Justice or of the recommendations of the World Equity Tribunal for the settlement of a dispute when the General Assembly has decided that a continuance of the dispute would be a "serious danger" to peace.

(9) *World Development.* The plan further provides (revised Articles 7 and 59 and Annex IV) for the establishment of a World Development Authority, whose function would be to assist in the economic and social development of the underdeveloped areas of the world, primarily through grants-in-aid and interest-free loans. This Authority would be under the direction of a World Development Commission of five members to be chosen with due regard to geographical distribution by the Economic and Social Council, subject to confirmation by the General Assembly.

The World Development Commission would be under the general supervision of the Economic and Social Council which would have power to define broad objectives and priorities. Since that Council would be composed of twenty-four Representatives, of whom twelve would come from the member Nations having the highest gross national products and twelve from among the Representatives of the other member Nations selected with due regard to geographical distribution, there would thus be reasonable assurance that account would be taken both of the views of those nations contributing large shares of United Nations revenue, and also of the nations most in need of the Authority's assistance.

This proposed World Development Authority could, if the General Assembly so decided, have very large sums at its disposal, since the Authority's funds would be allocated to it by the Assembly out of the general revenues of the United Nations. With the large resources which the Assembly could and should provide, the World Development Authority would have the means to aid the underdeveloped areas of the world to the extent necessary to remove the danger to world stability and peace caused by the immense economic disparity between those areas and the industrialized regions of the world.

While universal, enforceable and complete disarmament, together with adequate institutions and methods for the peaceful settlement of disputes, are certainly indispensable, no solid and stable peace can be assured by these means alone. There is also required a more positive approach through the amelioration of the worst economic ills of mankind. To this end, the new World Development Authority, together with the Nuclear Energy Authority, would serve as important arms of the strengthened United Nations.

(10) *A United Nations Revenue System.* It would obviously be futile to establish the proposed new world institutions called for by the plan (including the United Nations Peace Force, the Inspection Service, the World Development Authority, the Nuclear Energy Authority, the Outer Space Agency, the World Equity Tribunal and the World Conciliation Board) unless a well-planned system is provided for their sufficient and reliable financial support. Such a system should also, of course, provide for the adequate support of the already existing organs and agencies of the United Nations which would be continued and, in some cases, would have enlarged functions and responsibilities. These include the revised General Assembly itself, the strengthened International Court of Justice, the Economic and Social Council, the Trusteeship Council, the Secretariat and the various specialized agencies already affiliated with the United Nations.

The United Nations Peace Force, with an assumed strength for its standing component of, say, 400,000 (midway between the proposed constitutional maximum of 600,000 and minimum of 200,000) and with an assumed strength for the Peace Force Reserve of, say, 900,000 (midway between the proposed constitutional maximum of 1,200,000 and minimum of 600,000) would alone require some $9 billion annually. The minimum annual amount required for the General Assembly and Executive Council, the judicial system, the Secretariat, the Inspection Service, the Nuclear Energy Authority, the Outer Space Agency and the other organs and agencies other than the World Development Authority may be estimated at $2 billion. To this should be added a large amount on the order of $25 billion which should be annually appropriated by the General Assembly for the proposed World Development Authority in order to make a real impression on the vast problem of mitigating the worst economic disparities between nations and regions.

Upon first impression, this assumed $25 billion figure for world development may appear high, but is in fact moderate if the purpose is to accomplish a substantial change in the living conditions of the more economically underdeveloped areas of the world. This is so because, before the machinery for supplying any such amount can become operative, there will probably be an increase in world population to nearly 4 billion, by which time the number of people living in poverty relative to the standards of the industrialized nations will certainly be not less than 2 billion. Accordingly, the annual expenditure of $25 billion to improve the condition of these people would represent only about $12 per captia which is little enough to accomplish any substantial improvement in their living standards.

It is apparent, therefore, that the reasonable expenses of a world authority adequately equipped to deter or suppress any international violence, to administer a comprehensive system for the peaceful settlement of all disputes between nations and *also* to do something substantial for the economic betterment of the underdeveloped parts of the world, could easily run to $36 billion per annum. And while this amount would be less than one half the 1960-61 budget of a single nation—the United States—it would, nevertheless, be so large a sum that reliance for supplying it should not be placed on a system of yearly contributions by the separate governments of nearly one hundred nations. Apart from a World Development Authority, the maintenance of a high level of efficiency and morale by the proposed Inspection Service, the Peace Force, the Nuclear Energy Authority and the Outer Space Agency would be of crucial importance; and it would indeed be folly to set up these and other vital organs without reliable machinery for supplying the necessary funds. To this end, a carefully devised *collaborative* revenue system is proposed.

A chief feature of this system would be that each member Nation would assign in advance to the United Nations all or part of certain taxes designated by it and assessed under its national laws. Each nation would undertake the entire administrative function of collecting the taxes thus assigned to the United Nations, these taxes to be paid directly to a fiscal office of the United Nations in each member Nation. In this way it would be unnecessary to create any considerable United Nations bureaucracy for this purpose.

Another important feature would be an *over-all limit* on the maximum amount of revenue to be raised in any year, namely, 2 per cent [1966 figure: 3 per cent] of the gross world product (total value of all goods produced and services rendered) as estimated from year to year by the above-mentioned Standing Committee on Budget and Finance of the General Assembly.

The General Assembly would adopt the annual United Nations budget covering all its activities, and would determine the amounts to be supplied by the taxpayers of each member Nation for that budget. These amounts would be allotted on the basis of each member Nation's estimated proportion of the estimated gross world product in that year subject to a uniform "per capita deduction" of not less than 50 or more than 90 per cent of the estimated average per capita product of the ten member Nations having the lowest per capita national products, as determined by the Assembly. A further provision would limit the amount to be supplied by the people of any member Nation in any one year to a sum not exceeding 2½ per cent of that nation's estimated national product. . . .

A more detailed explanation of this revenue plan is set forth in Annex V. It is believed that the plan would be effective to provide reliable and adequate revenues for the strengthened United Nations without involving the creation of a United Nations revenue-raising bureaucracy.

(11) *Privileges and Immunities.* Annex VI relates to the privileges and immunities of the United Nations itself and of the greatly expanded personnel (including the United Nations Peace Force) which, under the revised Charter, would be in the service of the United Nations.

For the successful operation of an effective world organization to maintain peace, a body of genuinely international servants of high morale is clearly essential. To this end, it seems advisable to provide constitutionally and in some detail not only as to the privileges and immunities of the United Nations as an organization, but also as to the rights and privileges of all United Nations personnel and the limitations thereon.

(12) *Bill of Rights.* Annex VII contains a proposed Bill of Rights having a two-fold purpose: (a) to emphasize the limited scope of the strengthened United Nations by an explicit reservation to the member Nations and their peoples of all powers not delegated by express language or clear implication; and (b) to guarantee that the strengthened United Nations shall not in any manner violate certain basic rights of the individual, that is to say of any person in the world.

The reason for the former is to make doubly sure that the authority of the United Nations shall not be enlarged by indirection, but shall be confined within the limits set forth in the revised Charter.

The latter set of provisions would not extend to any attempted protection of the individual against the action of his own government. It may be argued that the time has come for a world organization to guarantee to every person in the world and against any authority whatever a few fundamental rights—such as exemption from slavery, freedom from torture and the right to be heard before criminal condemnation. We have not, however, thought it wise to attempt so vast a departure; and the proposed guarantees relate solely to possible infringements by the United Nations itself. Against such violations it does seem advisable and proper to have the explicit assurances which would be provided by Annex VII.

The assurances thus provided would include: guarantees, in considerable detail, of the right of fair trial for any person accused of a violation of the revised Charter or of any law or regulation enacted thereunder; a guarantee against double jeopardy, *i.e.* against being tried twice for the same alleged offense against the United Nations; and also a prohibition against any *ex post facto* law of the United Nations, *i.e.* against any law making criminal an act which was not criminal at the time the act occurred.

Provisions would also be included against excessive bail and any cruel or unusual punishment, including excessive fines; and the death penalty would be specifically prohibited. In addition, a remedy would be provided against unreasonable detention through a provision securing the right of any person detained for any alleged violation of the revised Charter or of any law or regulation enacted thereunder to be brought without undue delay before the appropriate United Nations tribunal to determine whether there is just cause for his detention.

Unreasonable searches and seizures would also be forbidden, subject to the proviso that this prohibition shall not prejudice searches and seizures clearly necessary or advisable for the enforcement of total disarmament.

Finally, it would be provided that the United Nations shall not restrict or interfere with freedom of conscience or religion; freedom of speech, press or expression in any other form; freedom of association and assembly; or freedom of petition.

The effort has been to provide protection for all the most fundamental individual rights which might conceivably be infringed upon by the United Nations without, however, going into undue detail. Necessarily, as in the case of any constitutional guarantees of the rights of the individual, there will be room for judicial interpretation and application of a United Nations Bill of Rights. This function would be performed by the International Court of Justice which, in the exercise of its proposed jurisdiction to interpret the revised Charter and to declare void any law, regulation or decision conflicting with the revised Charter as so interpreted, would gradually build up a body of world constitutional law relative to the scope and application of the various provisions of the Bill of Rights.

(13) *Ratification*. The proposed requirements for ratification of the revised Charter are: (a) that ratification shall be by five sixths of the world's nations, including all the twelve largest nations, the aggregate of the populations of the ratifying nations to equal at least five sixths of the total world population; and (b) that each nation's ratification shall be by its own constitutional processes.

At first glance, the requirement that so very large a preponderance of the nations and people of the world shall be necessary for ratification may appear excessively difficult. But it must be remembered that it would be impossible to accomplish the main purposes of the whole plan, namely, total disarmament and the establishment of an effective system of world law, unless there is a preponderant acceptance throughout the world of the constitutional document which would provide for the necessary world institutions. In practice, this means that the eight or ten principal Powers—especially the Soviet Union and the United States—would first need to agree. But once these Powers (containing together a large majority of the world's people) had reached agreement on the essentials of a revised Charter, there can be no doubt that virtually all the other nations would, as a practical matter, give their assent. Thus the obviously desirable object of obtaining the unanimous or nearly unanimous assent of all the nations appears also to be a practical one—once the indispensable assent of the leading Powers has been obtained.

(14) *Amendment.* The proposed requirements concerning the procedure for amendments to the revised Charter are almost as strict as those provided for its ratification. Any future amendments would be submitted for ratification when adopted by a vote of two thirds of all the Representatives in the General Assembly, whether or not present or voting, or by a two-thirds vote of a General Conference held for that purpose. In order for an amendment to come into effect, ratification by four fifths of the member Nations would be required, including three fourths of the twelve member Nations entitled to fifteen or more Representatives in the Assembly.

It will be noted that while the proposed provisions for ratification of the revised Charter would require that the ratifying nations shall include *all* the twelve nations having the largest populations, the provisions relating to the ratification of amendments would require the assent of only three fourths of those twelve nations.

The reason for this difference is that, in order to ensure the necessary overwhelming support for the revised Charter in its initial stage, it is considered essential to have the prior assent of literally all the world's largest nations—defined as the twelve nations with the largest populations. On the other hand, in the case of future amendments *after* the strengthened United Nations is functioning under the revised Charter, it seems unduly severe to require absolutely unanimous approval by the twelve largest nations. Instead, it seems sufficient to require the assent of no more than a preponderant majority of those nations.

(15) *Continued Organs and Agencies.* It should be emphasized that far from impairing the existing organs and agencies of the United Nations, which despite all obstacles have accomplished important results, the intention is not only to preserve but also to strengthen them. Thus the General Assembly would have much greater scope through having the final responsibility for the maintenance of peace, through the new system of representation and voting, and through the new, although limited, power to legislate.

The Security Council would, indeed, be abolished, but would be replaced by the veto-less Executive Council, chosen by and responsible to the General Assembly. The Economic and Social Council and the Trusteeship

Council would be continued, with important changes as to their composition and functions, and with much stronger financial support under the new revenue system. The International Court of Justice would be continued with greatly enlarged jurisdiction and greater authority. And as to various other organs, and such agencies as the Food and Agricultural Organization (FAO), the United Nations Educational, Scientific and Cultural Organization (UNESCO), the International Labor Organization (ILO) and the World Health Organization (WHO), the revision would not only provide for their continuance but would also give opportunity for the enlargement of their activities and usefulness.

The intention is not to dispense with anything which has proved useful, but rather to revise, supplement and strengthen the existing structure so that the United Nations will be fully and unquestionably equipped to accomplish its basic purpose—the maintenance of international peace.

Whether to revise the United Nations charter or to create a new world organization

We have cast our proposals in the form of a proposed revision of the present United Nations Charter, retaining the structure of its 111 Articles and supplementing those very Articles, as revised, by seven Annexes.

We have done this because it seems logical and reasonable to utilize an existing organization of such scope and experience as the United Nations; because the primary purpose of the United Nations has been from the beginning "to save succeeding generations from the scourge of war"; because the name "United Nations" is very suitable to a world authority dedicated to the maintenance of world peace under effective world law; and because the creation of a new and separate world organization adequately equipped for the maintenance of peace would necessarily overshadow the present United Nations.

Nevertheless, we do not regard this question of method as one of principle, but merely of policy. It must be recognized that if the creation of adequate world institutions for the prevention of war is to be achieved through the medium of the United Nations, numerous amendments of the Charter will be required which would together amount to a fundamental change in the structure and powers of the United Nations. And if it should develop that for technical or psychological reasons it would be more difficult to accomplish these amendments than to create a wholly new world organization to take over the peace-maintenance functions of the United Nations, we wish to make it clear that we would not object to that alternative method. In other words, a thorough revision of the Charter is merely, as we see it, the most reasonable means to the end in view and not an end in itself.

For example, it has been suggested that, while continuing the United Nations in nearly its present form, there could be separately created by universal, or nearly universal, treaty an entirely new world organization wholly restricted in its functions to those matters directly connected with the prevention of international violence. Such a world organization existing parallel with the United Nations might be called the "World Peace Authority" and, to be effective, would necessarily have to possess institutions and powers similar to those formulated in the proposed Charter revision for the enforcement of total disarmament and of world law in the field of war prevention. In that case, the United Nations could continue as a forum for the exchange of views on all matters of international interest.

The existence of a new, separate and powerful world organization alongside the present United Nations would obviously be an awkward arrangement. And yet since it would be better to tolerate some awkwardness than to do nothing effective to achieve universal and complete disarmament and a genuine regime of enforceable world law, the idea should not be entirely dismissed.

We emphasize also that while an elaborate plan for universal and complete disarmament is included in the proposed revision of the Charter, this does not imply that the revision of the Charter must necessarily precede an agreement for total disarmament. It is quite conceivable that an agreement on the technical aspects of universal and complete disarmament will be reached first, and that a revision of the Charter would come about later as the most logical means of ensuring adequate supervision and enforcement of such a disarmament agreement.

What we wish to make crystal clear is that in casting our proposals in the form of a comprehensive revision of the present Charter, we are not dogmatic about advancing this as the only available means to the desired end; and that if it develops that some other method is more feasible, we would be very ready to adopt it in order to reach the end in view.

The practical prospects

What are the practical prospects for the realization of genuine peace, through universal and complete disarmament and enforceable world law, not in some indefinite future but, let us say, by 1980.

The question is crucial because the achievement of genuine peace will largely depend upon the persistent effort of many people and, unfortunately, only a small fraction of the human race seems capable of working persistently for a purpose, however desirable, that appears far off and uncertain. On the other hand, if convinced that the goal is attainable within a reasonably short time, they will work for it in greater numbers and with greater zeal, and by this very fact make it the more realizable.

I take a hopeful view on the question and will, in fact, venture a reasoned prediction as follows: (a) that by 1980 a comprehensive plan for total and universal disarmament and for the necessary world institutions to make, interpret and enforce world law in the field of war prevention will have been officially formulated and will have been submitted to all the nations for approval; and (b) that within four to six years thereafter (by, say, 1985) such a plan will have been ratified by all or nearly all the nations, including all the major Powers, and will have come into force. . . .

The most important single adverse factor I suppose to be the reluctance of the average person to make any drastic change in his traditional form of behavior. As experience shows, he will, of course, try hard to save himself from destruction when he is not only in actual and imminent danger but also comprehends that danger. Short of these circumstances, however, his tendency is to procrastinate and hold to his old ways, often until it is too late.

This deep-seated trait of human nature is very evident at the beginning of the 1960's as a grave obstacle to genuine peace. This is so because nothing is more certain than that under the conditions of our nuclear age the realization of genuine peace will require a truly revolutionary change in human thinking and behavior—a change so drastic that human nature almost automatically resists it, no matter how clear the necessity may appear. As the historian, Arnold Toynbee, has put it, "we shall have a hard struggle with ourselves to save ourselves from ourselves."

For many centuries the units into which mankind has combined— family, tribe, town, city, national state—have been accustomed to assert or defend their interests, real or supposed, by violence or the threat of it—culminating during our "advanced" twentieth century in the two greatest wars in history and, by 1960, in the maintenance of the most elaborate and destructive armed forces that the world has ever possessed. And yet, no matter how obvious it may be that, in order to achieve genuine peace, these forces must be abolished, along with the whole ancient method of international violence, it is foolish to ignore the strongly adverse influence of these habits and traditions and of certain special influences and vested interests created by them.

Of these special influences and interests, by far the most formidable, I judge, is that of the military profession which, in many nations, has sufficient influence to force their governments to resist rather than to aid the cause of total disarmament and the establishment of the world institutions that are essential to the settlement of all international disputes by peaceful means. Unfortunate as it may be, it is necessary to accept the fact that, as of 1960, there is throughout most of the world what has been aptly called a "vested interest in armament" on the part of the military profession, which is a constant and powerful influence adverse to the new conceptions which can alone suffice to achieve genuine peace.

In appraising the weight of this pervading military influence, it is nec essary to recognize its good faith in most cases. The typical professional soldier, sailor, airman or missileman does not deprecate or oppose disarmament because he is any less humane or less civilized than the average civilian. He does so because his training and environment have irrevocably *conditioned* him to assume that his profession is indispensable. In consequence, it is simply too much to expect that the military professions as a whole will do otherwise than oppose or at least "drag their feet" in respect of all propasals for total disarmament and all that this implies. It follows that there will be no solution for the problem of world peace until the "vested interest in armament" of the military profession everywhere is firmly overruled.

A less important yet significant adverse "vested interest" is that of traditional diplomacy. It must be remembered that for centuries a principal occupation of the professional diplomat has been to deal in "power politics," that is to say, in the making of alliances or in seeking to undermine counteralliances or in veiled or open threats of force as a means of advancing the real or supposed interests of his particular country. These habits of thought are almost as difficult to shake off as those of the professional military man; and, consequently, those who seek peace through total disarmament and enforceable world law will do well to discount the almost certain resistance of the "professionals" in many foreign offices in all parts of the world.

Another "vested interest" sometimes mentioned as an important obstacle to disarmament and peace is the presumed interest of many millions of armament workers in a continuance of their jobs and the corresponding interest of proprietors in their profits from armament contracts. But while the problem of readjustment to nonarmament work is certainly one that will call for attention and planning, this should not be regarded as a serious difficulty. What is often overlooked is that the process of disarmament would necessarily be a gradual one. At the outset there would almost surely be an interval of several years between the formulation of a comprehensive disarmament agreement and its coming into force through ratification by the respective nations, and this interval would serve as a warning period in which to plan for and partially carry out the shift of workers and materials to nonmilitary purposes. There would then undoubtedly follow a considerably longer period for the carrying out, stage by stage, of the process of actual disarmament, during which the conversion of the armament plants would be completed. Remembering also the immense tax burden which would be lessened year by year and the release of manpower and materials for such purposes as roads, hospitals, schools, urban renewal and other pressing needs even in the most prosperous nations, it seems clear that this particular obstacle to disarmament and peace will prove to be a minor one.

Far more serious is the factor of mutual fears and recriminations which as of 1960 so poison the East-West atmosphere as to bring under suspicion in the West almost any proposal coming from the East and correspondingly in the East almost any proposal proceeding from the West. This state of affairs is unfortunately deeply rooted on both sides. It has been built up over a long period and "conditions" the thinking of millions of people—East and West—who on other subjects are capable of unbiased judgment. There is little use in seeking to assess the blame which both sides must share, and we must accept this mutually poisoned atmosphere as a fact of life which cannot be got rid of for a long time. This mutual fear and suspicion is indeed a most formidable barrier to peace and we should recognize that success in the accomplishment of total disarmament and the establishment of enforceable world law will not be because this barrier will soon disappear but because it will be pushed aside under the pressure of necessity.

Apart from the just-mentioned deeply rooted obstacles, there are several others which are only less important because they are likely to be more transitory. These include the exclusion of mainland China from world councils, a lack of sufficient understanding as to the necessity for complete, rather than partial, disarmament and a similar lack of understanding of the necessity for a comprehensive and interrelated plan rather than a piecemeal approach.

Taking together all the adverse factors—especially the strong tendency to resist any drastic change, the certain opposition of the military profession and of traditional diplomacy and the mutual fears and suspicions between East and West—we have a truly formidable group of obstacles. What are the *favorable* factors which are capable of offsetting or overcoming them?

Of these favorable factors the most important single one seems very clearly to be the *steadily increasing risk* of world catastrophe resulting from a continuance of the arms race and a continuing lack of effective world machinery to settle international disputes by peaceful means.

In specifying the increasing risk of world disaster, it is realized that the likelihood of all-out nuclear war may not increase at all and may even diminish during the 1960's because of a greater mutual understanding of its destructive consequences. But more than offsetting this factor is, I believe, the rapidly mounting potentialities of destruction if a large-scale nuclear war should, nevertheless, occur. For while it may be true that the chances of an all-out nuclear war may not increase during the 1960s, it is a certainty that the potential damage from such a war, if it should occur, will steadily increase from year to year. It follows that, taking the two factors together, the real risk will, in the absence of universal and complete disarmament under effective world law, be a steadily mounting one. A greater comprehension of this fact will be, I judge, the major influence in bringing about the formulation and acceptance of an agreement for total disarmament under enforceable world law. . . .

Next in importance to the risk of appalling disaster from the increasing destructiveness of modern weapons and the increasing popular pressure on the governments to remove this risk is, I believe, an increasing impatience with the vast economic waste and burden of the arms race. In terms of money this burden as of 1960 amounts to not less than $100 billion per annum, while in terms of human energy it means the full-time employment in the armed forces of some 15 million men and of not less than 30 million civilians in the manufacture of arms and other military activities— or a total of at least 45 million persons.

In the United States the resulting cost of about $46 billion per anum in 1960-61 absorbs more than half of the total Federal budget and about 9 per cent of the gross national product, while in the Soviet Union the proportion of the national product devoted to military purposes is even higher. In many other nations the cost, although proportionately smaller, is nevertheless a heavy drain on their economies which prevents or handicaps the carrying out of many badly needed improvements. Even in so affluent a country as the United States, the vast military expenditure holds back such urgent needs as the improvement of education and of medical care for lower-income people, urban renewal and the conservation of natural resources; and in nations less economically fortunate, like India, the adverse effects of military expenditure are naturally much greater. As the years have passed, there has been a growing consciousness that the existence of these burdens is incompatible with economic and social reforms urgently demanded by the peoples of many nations. In the 1960s, this consciousness will almost certainly become a more powerful force in favor of total disarmament.

Another helpful development should be a clearer realization from year to year that it is impossible to arrive at any important political settlements in the absence of an agreement for comprehensive disarmament. There has been much ill-considered talk to the effect that the settlement of various difficult political problems—such as the problem of Berlin and German reunification, the problem of Soviet dominance in Eastern Europe, the questions of Korean and Vietnam reunification and the Quemoy-Matsu situation—must precede, or at least be simultaneous with, any comprehensive disarmament. The common-sense of the matter is, however, that *in an armed world* it is most improbable that any of these difficult East-West issues can be settled—for the simple reason that it is virtually impossible to settle any hard controversy between opponents of equal strength and pride when the opposing parties are armed to the teeth and, therefore, bitterly suspicious of each other. All experience shows that before such opponents can settle any important issue, they must first agree to dispense with violence and cease their mutual threats and insults.

It has taken a long time to grasp this simple truth as applied to the crucial disputes between East and West; but in the 1960s it will become more and more apparent to most reasonable men and women that an agreement for universal and complete disarmament must be reached *before* these thorny East-West issues can be resolved.

Another favorable factor will be the almost certain abandonment during the 1960 decade of the exclusion of mainland China from the United Nations and from normal relations with the United States and many other nations. The bankruptcy of this policy, which has so greatly prejudiced adequate negotiations for peace, has long been apparent and it is hardly conceivable that it can much longer survive. When China, with its more than one fifth of all the people of the earth, is admitted to full participation in world councils, an important barrier to the formulation of a comprehensive plan for peace will have been removed.

Still another encouraging sign is the increasing knowledge of the *ways and means* whereby genuine peace can be achieved. The persistent and rising *desire* since the end of World War II for the abolition of war has unfortunately been accompanied by considerable defeatism as to the feasibility of accomplishing this result. This defeatism has, however, been largely caused by an exaggerated view of the difficulty of the problem which has been due in turn to a lack of sufficient study and discussion of the concrete problems that are involved, *i.e.* the various interrelated questions as to the nature and form of the world institutions requisite for world order. At the start of the 1960s we can discern a marked change in this respect, in that a beginning has at last been made in a closer study of the specific problems—not only by private persons but even by public officials. There is a definite relation between the development of this study and progress toward the desired goal. This is true because the problems involved are by no means insoluble, and as more and more people begin to apprehend how these problems can be dealt with, the spirit of defeatism will naturally lessen and the better will be the prospect for the acceptance of an adequate plan for peace.

An important result of the more intense study just mentioned will inevitably be a more general understanding that *total, rather than partial,* disarmament will alone meet the situation. In 1960 it is almost universally recognized that, in order to induce acceptance of any important disarmament, a well-organized inspection system is essential, while only a minority as yet seems to understand that *complete* disarmament is equally indispensable. For this proposition there are three main reasons: (a) because experience has shown that it is virtually impossible to agree upon any plan of any consequence for merely partial disarmament, since one nation or another is almost certain to claim, and with some justification, that the particular proposed reduction would put it at a disadvantage; (b) because even if agreed upon any merely partial disarmament would not fulfill the purpose, since in the nuclear age the retention of even a small fraction of the armed forces of 1960 would be enough to keep in existence many pernicious fears and tensions between the nations; and (c) because, although an effective world police force is clearly indispensable as a condition for disarmament, there is a distinct practical limit upon the size and expense of such a force, so that if even as much as 10 per cent of the national armed forces of 1960 were retained, it would be impossible to maintain a world police of sufficient strength to ensure its capacity to deter or suppress any possible international violence. As the disarmament negotiations of the 1960s develop, it can safely be predicted that the validity of these reasons will be more and more recognized. And when it is generally accepted that total, rather than partial, disarmament is no less necessary than an effective inspection system, a long step forward will have been taken.

Along with a clearer understanding that nothing less than the abolition of all national armaments will suffice, there is badly needed a clearer realization of the necessity for a comprehensive rather than any piecemeal or partial plan. No intelligent person sets out to build an adequate house without a plan providing for all the elements necessary to make the structure fulfill its purpose. He knows from the start that foundation, sidewalls, floors and roof must all be provided and that they must be so fitted together that, with each performing its necessary function, the house will stand. It is deplorable, therefore, that even in 1960 only a small minority seems to realize that the necessity for a complete *initial* plan applies also to the structure of peace; and that, if the structure is to stand, all the basic organs necessary for the maintenance of peace must be included in that plan. A more general realization of this truth will almost certainly come in the 1960s and will be a powerful force for world order. . . .

What the whole question comes down to in last analysis is whether the human race will show enough intelligence to enable it to make the required adjustment to the nuclear age. In 1960 the issue as to the future of mankind is whether the human race is sufficiently *resourceful* to formulate and accept world institutions which will once and for all abolish war and utilize the great new discoveries of science for peaceful uses alone. This issue will, however, depend not upon any *inherent* lack of intelligence but upon whether sufficient *effort* is made to make effective use of our present fund of intelligence. If the peoples are so apathetic as to permit the domination of military and old-style diplomatic thinking, they can expect nothing better than an indefinite continuance of the arms race and ultimate disaster. On the other hand, if the peoples make an even reasonable effort to comprehend the danger and the available means to remove it, it lies within their power to solve the problem and to institute an age of genuine peace under world law. . . .

Purpose of the proposals

As already stated, the purpose of this book is to provide material for the extensive discussions which will be required before truly effective world institutions for the maintenance of peace are accepted by the peoples of the world.

It is true that the authors have *attempted* to present a complete plan whereby genuine peace, in a disarmed world, would actually be secured. It is true also that we have confidence in our work which is the result of so many years of study and of searching criticism by hundreds of qualified persons in many nations. Nevertheless, it would indeed be presumptuous to assert that we have the final answers to the various thorny problems. We well know that better, or at least more acceptable, solutions may be hammered out in the process of debate. We do believe, however, that these detailed and specific proposals will serve to encourage others to discuss the many and difficult questions that are involved.

The need is not for more generalities in recognition of the necessity for world law. There are already enough of these. Rather, the need is for alternative detailed plans to furnish a basis for discussion; and our purpose has been to supply such a plan. If by so doing this book hastens even slightly the day when enforceable world law actually prevails between all nations, it will have fulfilled its purpose.

For modern man the prevention of war is not only the most important of problems; it is also one of the most difficult. During our work we have often thought of Professor Einstein's remark on this point. When asked why it is that when the mind of man has reached so far as to solve the secrets of the atom it has not been able to devise means to protect mankind from destruction by the new discoveries, he replied: "The answer is simple. It is because politics is more difficult than physics."

Nevertheless, our proposals are advanced in the firm conviction that genuine peace through total disarmament and enforceable world law is now a practical prospect which practical men can work for with reasonable hopes.

GRENVILLE CLARK,
Dublin, New Hampshire, U.S.A.

April, 1960

❉ ❉ ❉ ❉

The following speech by Hugh Gaitskell, opposition leader of the La-
bour Party in Great Britain who died suddenly in 1963 at the age of fifty-
seven, was made on October 25, 1962, at a time when Great Britain was
negotiating entry into the Common Market. In the preceding months
the Cuban missile crisis and the crisis between China and India over
border territory had shaken international life badly. The speech is not
generalities but an explicit statement by a responsible leader in active
political life who believed he had many elections before him and therefore represents a serious political act. Gaitskell put himself on record as
firmly believing that the idea of some degree of world government was
not distantly utopian but a practical necessity for our time. Some of his
objection to the regional approach was undoubtedly related to his party's
opposition to Great Britain joining the Common Market, but it is an
argument that must be taken seriously in itself.

For many people the gap between a "here" and a "there" may appear so large they can see no connection between them. Political leaders
in particular tend to be submerged by immediate and short range problems. Gaitskell was a politician with a superior imagination who was not
only able to visualize a "there" that was a long range goal but to see
intervening steps toward it. Had he been addressing an American audience it seems certain he would have included, for instance, repeal of the
Connally Amendment, which allows the United States to refuse to submit a case to the International Court of Justice unless she wishes to.

An Eight Point Programme for World Government

HUGH GAITSKELL

A great debate is now taking place in Britain about our proposed entry
into the E.E.C. I shall not continue it here. But I would like to remove
one misunderstanding.

Because some of us hold that the terms so far negotiated do not ade quately fulfill the conditions which we consider reasonable and necessary before we enter, this does not mean that we are hostile to Europe or wish to isolate ourselves from our continental neighbours.

Indeed the popular description of the controversy "Should Britain go into Europe or not?" is misleading. Britain is heavily involved—militarily, commercially and culturally—in Western Europe and will remain so whether or not we enter the E.E.C.

If the terms should be such that we do not feel able to enter the E.E.C., the alternative is not isolation, but a relationship with E.E.C. which would be even closer and friendlier than at present, accompanied by the special links we already have with the overseas Commonwealth and with the rest of Western Europe through EFTA.

But it is not about the Common Market that I wish to speak this evening. Indeed, I doubt whether the problems of disunity or unity in Western Europe are today among the greatest problems confronting the world. Fifty years ago, perhaps twenty-five years ago, this was true— though it was not from Western Europe but Europe as a whole, including Russia, that the danger of international conflict sprang. Since 1945, however, no one has seriously worried about the danger of war between Britain, France, Germany and Italy.

There are, of course, differences of opinion within the NATO alliance, but so there are within the Communist bloc. I doubt whether these differences have much connection with the formation of the E.E.C. or would be resolved by Britain's entry.

No, the really grave problems today are not the problems of part of a continent, however much we who live there may be absorbed by them, but those of the whole world. Their solutions can only be world solutions. Remedies which might have been suitable in a steam age half a century ago are not likely to be adequate in the days of rockets and astronauts.

It is trite but true to say that the world has become exceedingly small. When one reflects that in a few years—if we survive—we shall probably all be sharing the excitement of celebrating the first voyage to the moon—regardless of who achieves it—it is clear that we are now more than ever before a human society. It is the unity or disunity of this society which must be our principle concern.

Looked at in this light, the two greatest issues which face us are, on the one hand, the relations between the Communist bloc and the Western alliance from which springs the major danger of war, and, on the other hand, the problems of world poverty and the inequality between rich and poor nations. Both problems are world problems. Neither can be solved by local action alone.

There could be no more vivid proof of this than the two grave crises with which we are now confronted—the Chinese attack on the Indian frontier and Cuba. Their possible repercussions and the way in which they may each link up with other sources of conflict are very much in the minds of all of us. They are only the latest examples of the indivisibility of peace.

So also the major steps which are really necessary in dealing with the problem of world poverty—the stabilising of commodity prices, the opening up of markets for the products of the developing countries and the proper organisation and allocation of aid—unquestionably require world action.

But when we say world action, we do not mean some casual and temporary arrangement; for this would obviously not be sufficient. At best we should then still be staggering from one crisis to another. We mean, really, that we have got to set up and operate institutions which will mean nothing less than a major advance towards world government.

Global solutions of this kind which not long ago were dismissed as the cloudy fantasies of well-meaning cranks have today become the necessary conditions of our survival. Schemes for world government which were once just an academic exercise are now thrust upon us by the very logic of current international negotiations.

For example, both the United States and the Soviet Union propose in their disarmament plans the setting up of an international force. Indeed, it is now generally accepted that such a step is an essential part of a Disarmament Agreement. But if such a force is to be effective in providing security, it must have real power. If it is to have real power, the problem of who is to control it has to be solved. I do not see how this can be satisfactorily solved except through the establishment of a World Authority responsible to a World Legislature.

But how is the gap between the ideal of world government and the reality of the cold war to be closed? How do we move forward from the conflicting aims and ambitions of over 100 independent sovereign states to the creation of a system of international law and order?

Again, the Cuban crisis underlines the urgency of this matter. For it shows only too plainly the inherent instability in the balance of power and the danger of relying solely on this to prevent war.

Some say that the right path is by sacrificing sovereignty at the regional level. This, they hold, will lead in time to the breakdown of barriers at the global level. The idea is that larger and larger blocs are formed until at the end the last remaining blocs merge into one great world federation.

I understand and sympathise with those who take this view. Something like it seems to happen in industry. But I cannot find any evidence that it is likely in international politics.

The federation of one group designed to enhance the power and protect the interests of those who compose it may well lead to other countries following suit. But this will be out of fear and for self-protection. For the continuing existence of a new state formed from several existing ones is too often dependent on the cult of a new nationalism. Moreover, while the whole process may seem admirable to those within, it is usually regarded as a threat by those who are left out. Thus, suspicion and fear, the chief barriers to disarmament and the sacrifice of sovereignty by the great powers are likely to be magnified rather than reduced. One must remember, too, that while a war between two small nations can be localized, this is scarcely possible if two super states are involved.

No doubt these objections would not apply if each merger remained open to other states to join, or the grouping took the form not of new nation states but simply of loose associations. But, in practice, the first does not happen and the second would not, of course, involve the same sacrifice of sovereignty upon which the whole argument for a regional approach is based.

I conclude, therefore, with regret that there is no reason to think that a world divided into—say—a dozen great powers will necessarily be more peaceful than the world of a hundred nation-states as we know it today.

As we must also reject the notion that world government should come about through world conquest—since in present circumstances this would also mean the end of civilization, we are left, I believe, with only two other possibilities.

The first is the idea of a joint American-Russian domination which would retain a monopoly of nuclear weapons, refrain from attacking one another and impose peace on the rest of the world. For various reasons, however, I cannot believe that even if this were not so fanciful, it would be either a stable solution or be tolerated by the rest of the world.

The second is what I shall describe inelegantly as the gradual, piecemeal approach on a global basis. I can explain this best by first considering what are the real obstacles in the way of the sacrifice of sovereignty necessary for the establishment of international authority. I call these obstacles "the four fears":—

1 The fear of nations—particularly the powerful ones—that they will lose an advantage which they believe their power still gives them in international relations.
2 The fear of nations that they will not be guaranteed the same security as would be provided by their own arms and alliances.
3 The fear that the decisions taken by the world authority will run counter to their national interests.
4 The fear that other nations will not observe or be compelled to observe the contract to accept world government.

How can these fears be overcome? The answer, in general, is no doubt that they should be outweighed by the even greater fear of world war. Clearly, today, this is a greater factor than ever before in history.

More specifically, the first fear should count for much less because it is today much harder for the great nations to use their power effectively. As my friend Denis Healey recently remarked— "You could do anything with bayonets but sit on them. The only thing to do with the H bomb is to sit on it!" The events of the last few days have not yet proved him wrong.

The nuclear stalement has also had another effect. It has increased the influence of less powerful, uncommitted nations. For both super powers are anxious to preserve good relations with them. The Soviet Union refrained from pressing its Troika proposal and its opposition to the U.N. operation in the Congo, because it did not wish to quarrel with the emergent states—especially in Africa.

For the rest I believe that these fears can be overcome gradually as the nations not only realize the disastrous dangers of the existing situation, but experience in one field after another the consequence of sacrificing sovereignty and realize that this is neither so dangerous nor so damaging as they supposed.

The fears are not indestructible. Far from giving up, therefore, we should redouble our efforts, which should take two forms.

First there is a great need to increase enormously the educational and propaganda work of World Government. I fully realize the almost insuperable difficulty of doing this in Communist States. But we should not be deterred by this. After all, we are not asking for any unilateral scrapping of defenses.

Somehow we have got to get more and more people seriously considering the prospect of World Government, thinking about it as a real possibility, getting more and more accustomed to the idea.

Can we not have a single definitive plan on which we could all agree —all the various Associations who really accept the same ultimate aim?

Can we not have, for example, debates on the subject in the Assembly of the United Nations—leading up to the Charter Review Conference of 1965? Can we not now set about the task of creating a great and powerful Movement for World Government to enlist the maximum volume of support behind it?

But major institutional changes are a long term aim. A Movement of this kind will only thrive if there are short term objectives as well.

In part these will be provided by the march of events. It should be one of the functions of the Movement to take a stand on particular issues—in favour of action which clearly leads in the direction of World Government, against action which is opposed to this. Admittedly, not every case is straightforward, but there have been enough instances in recent years, about which there has surely been no doubt.

But there should also be, I suggest, a specific short term programme to which the Movement commits itself. In effect, this would contain the next steps towards World Government. All of them involve sacrifices of sovereignty, all of them involve greater support for international institutions.

Here are eight points which might be included in such a programme:

1 The establishment of the nucleus of a permanent international police force.
2 The creation of a World Development Organisation to ensure that this decade really is a decade of development with the necessary supervisory authority over the international economic agencies.
3 The setting up now by the United Nations of a Disarmament Agency not only to supervise the execution of a Disarmament Agreement but to help to secure it.
4 Reform of the United Nations financial arrangements so that member states are obliged to pay their allotted share of the U.N. operations whether or not they approve of particular projects.
5 Fullest support for the diplomatic activity of the Secretary General and his staff—and firm opposition to anything like the Troika proposals.
6 Reform of the Security Council and the Economic and Social Council so as to make them more representative—particularly of the large number of newer nations which have come into existence recently.
7 A greater effort to make the United Nations universal, including in particular the admission of the Peking Government of China.
8 The acceptance by member states of decisions of the Security Council and recommendations of the Assembly when carried by an overwhelming majority.

There is no short cut to World Government. Nor can we see the road all the way, but a Movement which advances on the two fronts—long term aims and short term objectives—would, I believe, command a great volume of support.

One last thought. The progress of this cause requires the active support of governments. It has been suggested by a distinguished American, Mr. Grenville Clark, that the British Government is well qualified to take the initiative—because of its political experience, because of its world-wide connections through the Commonwealth, because it is not a super power, because, though an important and loyal member of NATO, it is not fanatical in its attitude to Communism. Whether these qualifications are valid or appropriate, it is for others to say. In any case, the less individual nations arrogate virtues to themselves the better. But for my part I should be proud to see the British Government, in association with other like-minded governments, take a full part in this great enterprise. It is very much the kind of role I believe my country should play in the world today. I am sure that many others—in Western Europe and the Commonwealth and elsewhere—would gladly join with us.

We hear today of the various "blocs" in the United Nations Assembly. How encouraging if there were also a Pro-World-Government bloc!

Or if Party is a more attractive name to the supporters of the World Parliament, why not make the first Party in the Assembly the Party for World Government?

It is even possible to detect in the recent history of the United Nations the beginning of such a group. What is needed now is to strengthen it, to clarify its principles and purposes and to put behind it the voices of millions of the world's citizens who see no other hope for humanity.

※ ※ ※ ※

Pope John XXIII well knew the crucial turning point at which man finds himself today: the choice whether to develop further cohesiveness, further realization that we are all part of the human family, citizens of a world community and to develop institutions which serve those relatively new conditions of practical life (although they have always been conditions of religious life), or to cling to an obsolete world picture which sees the nation-state as the top development of the political structure; the choice whether to use man's best tool, his mind, only for the development of weapons of mass destruction or to answer the challenge which these weapons pose in a creative way.

The Encyclical *Pacem in Terris* is for Catholics a summary of the Church's stand on almost all the important issues of our day as they relate to peace. It is for everyone a great social document of deep feeling and intensive thought. For the purposes of this Reader one should concentrate especially on Part III in which the subject of war and disarmament is introduced and on Part IV which deals with a world authority. In Part I, however, it is impossible not to point out the Pope's emphasis on the dignity of the human being as a person and to remark that nothing so totally destroys the dignity and meaning of the human being as a person than nuclear war. Part I is primarily a statement of the nature of man with his interlocking rights and duties as the Church sees them.

Although the term "authority" appears to be used in more than one sense, in Part II Pope John makes clear that authority is chiefly concerned with, and must rest on, moral force. Moreover, he states plainly that if civil authority conflicts with conscience, it is conscience that is to be obeyed:

> "Since the right to command is required by the moral order and has its source in God, it follows that, if civil authorities legislate for or allow anything that is contrary to that order and therefore contrary to the will of God, neither the law made nor the authorizations granted can be binding on the consciences of the citizens, since we must obey God rather than men. Otherwise, authority breaks down completely and results in shameful abuse!"

If we combine this with the denunciation of war that follows in the latter half of Part III and the statement, "For this reason it is hardly possible to imagine that in the atomic era war could be used as an instrument of justice," we see that Pope John, in the name of the Church, has taken a new and revolutionary position. The Church's age-old distinction between just and unjust wars has been wiped out. In the atomic age all war is evil. It is a stand that after hot debate has been reinforced rather than weakened by Vatican II. This is a new condition. For the Christian, and with added force for the Catholic, the moral authority of conscience comes into direct conflict with the civil authorities if these should wage war.

We must pursue the inquiry which we have undertaken: What do we do instead? In Part III, which deals with the relations between States, as throughout the encyclical, the principle of justice is strongly stressed—justice as opposed to force. The encyclical notes the utter bankruptcy of our present system and concludes that justice, right reason and humanity urgently demand that the arms race should cease. The encyclical urges that: stockpiles be reduced simultaneously, that nuclear weapons be banned, that a general agreement should eventually be reached about progressive disarmament and an effective method of control. What this would be is not spelled out and in the succeeding paragraph the encyclical appears to count more on enlightenment and on voluntary cooperation than would a plan such as that of Clark and Sohn, although there is firm agreement that to be effective the process must be *complete* and *thorough.*

The encyclical supports all thoughtful people in pointing out that not only is disarmament demanded by reason but that its advantages would be felt everywhere—by individuals, by families, by nations, by the whole human family. The encyclical further notes that relations between states should be based on freedom; no country may unjustly oppress others or unduly meddle in their affairs. The economically developed nations must come to the aid of those in the process of development, but the cooperation should be effected with greatest respect for the liberty of the countries being developed, so that they are the principal artisans of their own economic development and social progress.

Part IV deals with the Relationship of Men and of Political Communities (*i.e.* nation-states) with the World Community. By its very title, we observe that the encyclical (like the Clark and Sohn plan) considers that the individual man or woman, not just the nation-state, has a relationship to the world community—in other words, a *new level of allegiance* is being forged. Pope John may not have thought in terms of the federal principle, but it is this principle, which recognizes a higher allegiance for certain specified matters without destroying the existing one, which we as Americans should understand. The encyclical emphasizes the incapacity of nation-states to ensure the common good at any level, but especially as regards security and world peace "not due to a lack of good will or a spirit of enterprise, but because of a *structural defect which hinders them."* Our world institutions are inadequate. For the sake of the common good, public authority is needed which is capable of operating in an effective manner on a world-wide basis. This public authority must be instituted by common consent, not imposed by force. There would be reason to fear a supranational or world-wide public authority imposed by force by the more powerful nations. Moreover, nations are sensitive regarding their dignity and are right in not yielding to an authority imposed by force or in whose creation they had no part. (Could the Pope be thinking of China in relation to the U.N.?)

It would seem that the world authority envisioned by the encyclical is not unlike that envisioned by Clark and Sohn. It is of course more idealistically, less pragmatically, defined; but there are also certain real differences that are instructive to think about. The encyclical spreads before us a world authority with very broad powers. But as regards enforcement it, like the Soviet view, relies heavily on the principle of coexistence—which we could define as one simple rule or law, that the nations must coexist, which they would obey voluntarily because modern weapons had made war unthinkable. The Clark/Sohn model on the other hand is of a world authority with strictly limited powers—limited to the prevention of war, with ways for other problems to be worked out on a more voluntary basis and "leaving to later generations any enlargement of the world organization that they might find desirable." But those limited powers which their world authority had could be strictly enforced, through a carefully defined machinery not unlike that of other communities.

It is possible to say that the public authority of the world community is seen in the encyclical as broadly socialistic or paternalistic, as knowing what is best. And it is possible that Pope John, quite as much as Khrushchev, did see coexistence as a prelude to peaceful conquest. In Part V he opens wide the door for dialogue with the Communist world, stoutly maintaining that his view of the truth is the right one but that there must be respect and tolerance for the views of others and that we must never confuse the ideology with the human person. In sum, the tone, the mood of the encyclical which is open and positive like its author, its transparent feeling and concern for the human being and its wholehearted attempt to grapple with the problems that threaten him— in particular war—realistically and in terms of today's world makes it a very great document which gave courage and lift to the whole world.

The encyclical and the Tillich address which opens the next section are, I believe, read with far more meaning, both moral and political, for being examined directly in connection with the various other materials presented. The more permanent ethical statements point the way to what is probably most valid in the practical search for ways and means, and clear understanding of the practical problems and the solutions that serious and informed people are suggesting illuminate the thinking behind the religious and ethical statements. The two are interlocked, for one might well say that what the world now is desperately seeking is the course of "right reason."

Pacem in Terris*

POPE JOHN XXIII

PART I: ORDER BETWEEN MEN

Every man is a person with rights and duties

8. In the first place, it is necessary to speak of the order which should exist between men.

9. Any human society, if it is to be well-ordered and productive, must lay down as a foundation this principle: that every human being is a person; his nature is endowed with intelligence and free will. By virtue of this, he has rights and duties of his own, flowing directly and simultaneously from his very nature, which are therefore universal, inviolable and inalienable. . . .

Rights

11. Beginning our discussion of the rights of man, we see that every man has the right to life, to bodily integrity, and to the means which are necessary and suitable for the proper development of life; these are primarily food, clothing, shelter, rest, medical care, and finally the necessary social services. Therefore a human being also has the right to security in cases of

---

* Since we are regarding the encyclical as a social document the frequent quotations from other writings of the Church which Pope John introduces to support his argument have been deleted. Minor cuts have been made in Parts I, II and III where there was repetition for emphasis. Part IV is given complete. Part V, Pastoral Exhortations, is addressed specifically to Catholics as Catholics and therefore I have included only certain short excerpts which seem relevant to me here.

sickness, inability to work, widowhood, old age, unemployment, or in any other case in which he is deprived of the means of subsistence through no fault of his own.

12. By the natural law every human being has the right to respect for his person, to his good reputation; the right to freedom in searching for truth and in expressing and communicating his opinions, and in pursuit of art, within the limits laid down by the moral order and the common good; and he has the right to be informed truthfully about public events.

13. The natural law also gives man the right to share in the benefits of culture, and therefore the right to a basic education and to technical and professional training in keeping with the stage of educational development in the country to which he belongs. Every effort should be made to ensure that persons be enabled, on the basis of merit, to go on to higher studies, so that, as far as possible, they may occupy posts and take on responsibilities in human society in accordance with their natural gifts and the skills they have acquired.

14. Every human being has the right to honor God according to the dictates of an upright conscience, and therefore the right to worship God privately and publicly.

15. Human beings have the right to choose freely the state of life which they prefer, and therefore the right to establish a family, with equal rights and duties for man and woman, and also the right to follow a vocation to the priesthood or the religious life.

16. The family, grounded on marriage freely contracted, monogamous and indissoluble, should be regarded as the first and natural cell of human society. To it should be given every consideration of an economic, social, cultural and moral nature which will strengthen its stability and facilitate the fulfillment of its specific mission.

17. Parents, however, have the prior right in the support and education of their children.

18. We turn now to the sphere of economic affairs. Human beings have the natural right to free initiative in the economic field, and the right to work.

19. Indissolubly linked with those rights is the right to working conditions in which physical health is not endangered, morals are safeguarded, and young people's normal development is not impaired. Women have the right to working conditions in accordance with their requirements and their duties as wives and mothers.

20. From the dignity of the human person, there also arises the right to carry on economic activities according to the degree of responsibility of which one is capable. Furthermore—and this must be specially emphasized—there is the right to a proper wage, determined according to criterions of justice, and sufficient, therefore, in proportion to the available re-

sources, to provide for the worker and his family a manner of living in keeping with the dignity of the human person.

21. The right to private property, even of productive goods, also derives from the nature of man. This right, as We have elsewhere declared, is an effective aid in safeguarding the dignity of the human person and the free exercise of responsibility in all fields of endeavor. Finally, it strengthens the stability and tranquillity of family life, thus contributing to the peace and prosperity of the commonwealth.

22. However, it is opportune to point out that there is a social duty essentially inherent in the right of private property.

23. From the fact that human beings are by nature social, there arises the right of assembly and association. They have also the right to give the societies of which they are members the form they consider most suitable for the aim they have in view, and to act within such societies on their own initiative and on their own responsibility in order to achieve their desired objectives.

24. Moreover, as We Ourselves especially warned in the Encyclical *Mater et Magistra,* it is most necessary that a wide variety of societies or intermediate bodies be established, equal to the task of accomplishing what the individual cannot by himself efficiently achieve. These societies or intermediate bodies are to be regarded as an indispensable means in safeguarding the dignity and liberty of the human person, without harm to his sense of responsibility.

25. Every human being has the right to freedom of movement and of residence within the confines of his own country; and, when there are just reasons for it, the right to emigrate to other countries and take up residence there. The fact that one is a citizen of a particular State does not detract in any way from his membership in the human family as a whole, nor from his citizenship in the world community.

26. The dignity of the human person involves the right to take an active part in public affairs and to contribute one's part to the common good of the citizens.

27. The human person is also entitled to a juridical protection of his rights, a protection that should be efficacious, impartial and inspired by the true norms of justice.

Duties

28. The natural rights with which We have been dealing are, however, inseparably connected, in the very person who is their subject, with just as many respective duties. . . .

29. For example, the right of every man to life is correlative with the

duty to preserve it; his right to a decent manner of living with the duty of living it becomingly; and his right to investigate the truth freely, with the duty of seeking it and of possessing it ever more completely and profoundly.

30. Once this is admitted, it is also clear that, in human society, to one man's right there corresponds a duty in all other persons: the duty, namely, of acknowledging and respecting the right in question. . . . Those who claim their own rights, yet altogether forget or neglect to carry out their respective duties, are people who build with one hand and destroy with the other.

31. Since men are social by nature they are meant to live with others and to work for one another's welfare . . .

32. It is not enough, for example, to acknowledge and respect every man's right to the means of subsistence: one must also strive to obtain that he actually has enough in the way of food and nourishment.

33. The society of men must not only be organized but must also provide them with abundant resources. This . . . requires that they collaborate together in the many enterprises that modern civilization either allows or encourages or demands.

34. The dignity of the human person also requires that every man enjoy the right to act freely and responsibly. . . . This is to be done in such a way that each one acts on his own decision, of set purpose and from a consciousness of his obligation, without being moved by force or pressure brought to bear on him externally. For any human society that is established on relations of force must be regarded as inhuman, inasmuch as the personality of its members is repressed or restricted, when in fact they should be provided with appropriate incentives and means for developing and perfecting themselves. . . .

36. Human society, Venerable Brothers and beloved children, ought to be regarded above all as a spiritual reality: in which men communicate knowledge to each other in the light of truth; in which they can enjoy their rights and fulfill their duties, and are inspired to strive for moral good. Society should enable men to share in and enjoy every legitimate expression of beauty, and encourage them constantly to pass on to others all that is best in themselves, while they strive to make their own the spiritual achievements of others. These are the spiritual values which continually give life and basic orientation to cultural expressions, economic and social institutions, political movements and forms, laws, and all other structures by which society is outwardly established and constantly developed.

37. The order which prevails in society is by nature moral. Grounded as it is in truth, it must function according to the norms of justice, it should be inspired and perfected by mutual love, and finally it should be brought to an ever more refined and human balance in freedom.

38. Now an order of this kind, whose principles are universal, absolute and unchangeable, has its ultimate source in the one true God, who is personal and transcends human nature. Inasmuch as God is the first Truth and the highest Good, He alone is that deepest source from which human society can draw its vitality, if that society is to be well-ordered, beneficial, and in keeping with human dignity.

39. Our age has three distinctive characteristics.

40. First of all, the working classes have gradually gained ground in economic and public affairs. They began by claiming their rights in the socio-economic sphere; they extended their action then to claims on the political level; and finally applied themselves to the acquisition of the benefits of a more refined culture. Today, therefore, workers all over the world refuse to be treated as if they were irrational objects without freedom, to be used at the arbitrary disposition of others. They insist that they be always regarded as men with a share in every sector of human society: in the social and economic sphere, in public life, and finally in the fields of learning and culture.

41. Secondly, it is obvious to everyone that women are now taking a part in public life. This is happening more rapidly perhaps in nations of Christian civilization, and, more slowly but widely, among peoples who have inherited other traditions or cultures. Since women are becoming ever more conscious of their human dignity, they will not tolerate being treated as mere material instruments, but demand rights befitting a human person both in domestic and in public life.

42. Finally, the modern world, as compared with the recent past, has taken on an entirely new appearance in the field of social and political life. For since all nations have either achieved or are on the way to achieving independence, there will soon no longer exist a world divided into nations that rule others and nations that are subject to others.

43. Men all over the world have today—or will soon have—the rank of citizens in independent nations. No one wants to feel subject to political powers located outside his own country or ethnic group. For in our day, these attitudes are fading, despite their prevalence for so many hundreds of years, whereby some classes of men accepted an inferior position, while others demanded for themselves a superior position, on account of economic and social conditions, of sex, or of assigned rank within the political community.

44. On the contrary, the conviction that all men are equal by reason of their natural dignity has been generally accepted. Hence racial discrimination can in no way be justified, at least doctrinally or in theory. And this is of fundamental importance and significance for the formation of human society according to those principles which We have outlined above. For, if a man becomes conscious of his rights, he must become equally aware of his duties. Thus he who possesses certain rights has likewise the duty to

claim those rights as marks of his dignity, while all others have the obligation to acknowledge those rights and respect them.

45. When the relations of human society are expressed in terms of rights and duties, men become conscious of spiritual values, understand the meaning and significance of truth, justice, charity and freedom, and become deeply aware that they belong to this world of values. Moreover, when moved by such concerns, they are brought to a better knowledge of the true God who is personal and transcendent. Thus they make the ties that bind them to God the solid foundations and supreme criterion of their lives, both of that life which they live interiorly in the depths of their own souls and of that in which they are united to other men in society.

PART II: RELATIONS BETWEEN INDIVIDUALS AND THE PUBLIC AUTHORITIES WITHIN A SINGLE STATE

46. Human society can be neither well-ordered nor prosperous unless it has some people invested with legitimate authority to preserve its institutions and to devote themselves as far as is necessary to work and care for the good of all.

47. But authority is not to be thought of as a force lacking all control. Indeed, since it has the power to command according to right reason, authority must derive its obligatory force from the moral order, which in turn has God for its first source and final end.

48. Hence, where authority uses as its only or its chief means either threats and fear of punishment or promises of rewards, it cannot effectively move men to promote the common good of all. Even if it did so move them, this would be altogether opposed to their dignity as men, endowed with reason and free will. As authority is chiefly concerned with moral force, it follows that civil authority must appeal primarily to the conscience of individual citizens, that is, to each one's duty to collaborate readily for the common good of all. Since by nature all men are equal in human dignity, it follows that no one may be coerced to perform interior acts. That is in the power of God alone, who sees and judges the hidden designs of men's hearts.

49. Those therefore who have authority in the State may oblige men in conscience only if their authority is intrinsically related with the authority of God and shares in it.

50. By this principle the dignity of the citizens is protected. When, in fact, men obey their rulers, it is not at all as men that they obey them, but through their obedience it is God, the provident Creator of all things, whom they reverence, since He has decreed that men's dealings with one another should be regulated by an order which He Himself has established. Moreover, in showing this due reverence to God, men not only do not debase themselves but rather perfect and ennoble themselves. For *to serve God is to rule.*

51. Since the right to command is required by the moral order and has its source in God, it follows that, if civil authorities legislate for or allow anything that is contrary to that order and therefore contrary to the will of God, neither the laws made nor the authorizations granted can be binding on the consciences of the citizens, since *we must obey God rather than men.* Otherwise, authority breaks down completely and results in shameful abuse.

52. It must not be concluded, however, because authority comes from God, that therefore men have no right to choose those who are to rule the State, to decide the form of government, and to determine both the way in which authority is to be exercised and its limits. It is thus clear that the doctrine which We have set forth is fully consonant with any truly democratic regime.

53. Inasmuch as individual men and intermediate groups are obliged to make their specific contributions to the common welfare, it especially follows that they should bring their own interests into harmony with the needs of the community. They should direct their goods and services towards goals which the civil authorities prescribe, in accord with the norms of justice, in due form, and within the limits of their competence. Manifestly, those who possess civil authority must make their prescriptions not only by acts properly accomplished, but also by acts which clearly pertain to the welfare of the community or else can lead to the same.

54. Indeed since the whole reason for the existence of civil authorities is the realization of the common good, it is clearly necessary that, in pursuing this objective, they should respect its essential elements, and at the same time conform their laws to the needs of a given historical situation.

55. Assuredly, the ethnic characteristics of the various human groups are to be respected as constituent elements of the common good, but these values and characteristics by no means exhaust the content of the common good. For the common good is intimately bound up with human nature. It can never exist fully and completely unless, its intimate nature and realization being what they are, the human person is taken into account.

56. In the second place, the very nature of the common good requires that all members of the political community be entitled to share in it, although in different ways according to each one's tasks, merits and cir-

cumstances. For this reason, every civil authority must take pains to promote the common good of all, without preference for any single citizen or civil group. Considerations of justice and equity, however, can at times demand that those involved in civil government give more attention to the less fortunate members of the community, since they are less able to defend their rights and to assert their legitimate claims. . . .

60. It is agreed that in our time the common good is chiefly guaranteed when personal rights and duties are maintained. The chief concern of civil authorities must therefore be to ensure that these rights are acknowledged, respected, co-ordinated with other rights, defended and promoted, so that in this way each one may more easily carry out his duties. For *to safeguard the inviolable rights of the human person, and to facilitate the fulfillment of his duties, should be the essential office of every public authority.*

61. This means that, if any government does not acknowledge the rights of man or violates them, it not only fails in its duty, but its orders completely lack juridical force.

62. One of the fundamental duties of civil authorities, therefore, is to co-ordinate social relations in such fashion that the exercise of one man's rights does not threaten others in the exercise of their own rights nor hinder them in the fulfillment of their duties. Finally, the rights of all should be effectively safeguarded and, if they have been violated, completely restored.

63. It is also demanded by the common good that civil authorities should make earnest efforts to bring about a situation in which individual citizens can easily exercise their rights and fulfill their duties as well. For experience has taught us that, unless these authorities take suitable action with regard to economic, political and cultural matters, inequalities between the citizens tend to become more and more widespread, especially in the modern world, and as a result, a man's rights and duties in some way lack effectiveness.

64. It is therefore necessary that the administration give wholehearted and careful attention to the social as well as to the economic progress of the citizens, and to the development, in keeping with the development of the productive system, of such essential services as the building of roads, transportation, communications, water supply, housing, public health, facilitation of the practice of religion, and recreational facilities. It is necessary also that governments make efforts to see that insurance systems are made available to the citizens, so that, in case of misfortune or increased family responsibilities, no person will be without the necessary means to maintain a decent way of living. The government should make similarly effective efforts to see that those who are able to work can find employment in keeping with their aptitudes, and that each worker receives a

wage in keeping with the laws of justice and equity. It should be equally the concern of civil authorities to ensure that workers be allowed their proper responsibility in the work undertaken in industrial organization, and to facilitate the establishment of intermediate groups which will make social life richer and more effective. Finally, it should be possible for all the citizens to share in their country's cultural advantages in an opportune manner and degree.

65. The common good requires that civil authorities maintain a careful balance between co-ordinating and protecting the rights of the citizens, on the one hand, and promoting them, on the other. It should not happen that certain individuals or social groups derive special advantage from the fact that their rights have received preferential protection. Nor should it happen that governments in seeking to protect these rights, become obstacles to their full expression and free use. *Nevertheless, it remains true that precautionary activities of public authorities in the economic field, although widespread and penetrating, should be such that they not only avoid restricting the freedom of private citizens, but also increase it, so long as the basic rights of each individual person are preserved inviolate. . . .*

67. It is impossible to determine, once and for all, what is the most suitable form of government, or how civil authorities can most effectively fulfill their respective functions, *i.e.* the legislative, judicial and executive functions of the State.

68. In determining the structure and operation of government which a State is to have, great weight has to be given to the historical background and circumstances of the individual peoples, circumstances which will vary at different times and in different places. We consider, however, that it is in keeping with the innate demands of human nature that the State should take a form which embodies the threefold division of powers corresponding to the three principal functions of public authority. In that type of State, not only the official functions of government but also the mutual relations between citizens and public officials are set down according to law. This in itself affords protection to the citizens both in the enjoyment of their rights and in the fulfillment of their duties.

69. If, however, this juridical and political structure is to produce the advantages which may be expected of it, public officials must strive to meet the problems that arise in a way that conforms both to the complexities of the situation and the proper exercise of their function. This requires that, in constantly changing conditions, legislators never forget the norms of morality, or constitutional provisions, or the objective requirements of the common good. Moreover, executive authorities must co-ordinate the activities of society with discretion, with a full knowledge of the law and after a careful consideration of circumstances, and the courts must administer jus-

tice impartially and without being influenced by favoritism or pressure. The good order of society also demands that individual citizens and intermediate organizations should be effectively protected by law whenever they have rights to be exercised or obligations to be fulfilled. This protection should be granted to citizens both in their dealings with each other and in their relations with government agencies.

70. It is unquestionable that a legal structure in conformity with the moral order and corresponding to the level of development of the political community is of great advantage to achievement of the common good.

71. And yet, social life in the modern world is so varied, complex and dynamic that even a juridical structure which has been prudently and thoughtfully established is always inadequate for the needs of society.

72. It is also true that the relations of the citizens with each other, of citizens and intermediate groups with public authorities, and finally of the public authorities with one another, are often so complex and so sensitive that they cannot be regulated by inflexible legal provisions. Such a situation therefore demands that the civil authorities have clear ideas about the nature and extent of their official duties if they wish to maintain the existing juridical structure in its basic elements and principles, and at the same time meet the exigencies of social life, adapting their legislation to the changing social scene and solving new problems. They must be men of great equilibrium and integrity, competent and courageous enough to see at once what the situation requires and to take necessary action quickly and effectively.

73. It is in keeping with their dignity as persons that human beings should take an active part in government, although the manner in which they share in it will depend on the level of development of the political community to which they belong.

74. Men will find new and extensive advantages in the fact that they are allowed to participate in government. In this situation, those who administer the government come into frequent contact with the citizens, and it is thus easier for them to learn what is really needed for the common good. The fact too that ministers of government hold office only for a limited time keeps them from growing stale and allows for their replacement in accordance with the demands of social progress.

75. Accordingly, it follows that in our day, where there is question of organizing political communities juridically, it is required first of all that there be written in concise and limpid phraseology, a charter of fundamental human rights, and that this be inserted in the basic law of the State.

76. Secondly, it is required that the Constitution of each political community be formulated in proper legal terminology, and that there be defined therein the manner in which the State authorities are to be designated, how their mutual relations are to be regulated, what are to be their

spheres of competence, and finally, the forms and systems they are obliged to follow in the performance of their office.

77. Finally, it is required that the relations between the government and the citizens be set forth in detail in terms of rights and duties, and that it be distinctly decreed that a major task of the government is that of recognizing, respecting, reconciling, protecting and promoting the rights and duties of citizens.

78. It is of course impossible to accept the theory which professes to find the original and unique source of civil rights and duties, of the binding force of the Constitution, and of a government's right to command, in the mere will of human beings, individually or collectively.

79. The desires to which We have referred, however, do clearly show that the men of our time have become increasingly conscious of their dignity as human persons. This awareness prompts them to claim a share in the public administration of their country, while it also accounts for the demand that their own inalienable and inviolable rights be protected by law. Nor is this sufficient; for men also demand that public officials be chosen in conformity with constitutional procedures, and that they perform their specific functions within the limits of law.

PART III: RELATIONS BETWEEN STATES

80. Our Predecessors have constantly maintained, and We join them in reasserting, that political communities are reciprocally subjects of rights and duties. This means that their relationships also must be harmonized in truth, in justice, in a working solidarity, in liberty. For the same natural law, which governs relations between individual human beings, must also regulate the relations of political communities with one another.

81. This will be readily understood when one reflects that the individual representatives of political communities cannot put aside their personal dignity while they are acting in the name and interest of their countries; and that they cannot therefore violate the very law of nature by which they are bound, which is itself the moral law.

82. It would be absurd, moreover, even to imagine that men could surrender their own human attributes, or be compelled to do so, by the very fact of their appointment to public office. Rather, they have been given that noble assignment precisely because the wealth of their human endowments has earned them their reputation as outstanding members of the body politic.

83. Furthermore, authority to govern is a necessary requirement of the moral order in civil society. It may not be used against that order; and the very instant such an attempt were made, it would cease to bind.

84. Lastly it is to be borne in mind that also in regulating the relations between political communities, authority is to be exercised for the achievement of the common good, which constitutes the reason for its existence. . . .

86. First among the rules governing relations between political communities is that of truth. But truth requires the elimination of every trace of racism, and the consequent recognition of the principle that all States are by nature equal in dignity. Each of them accordingly is vested with the right to existence, to self-development, to the means necessary to its attainment, and to be the one primarily responsible for this self-development. Add to that the right of each to its good name, and to the respect which is its due. . . .

88. Some nations may well have reached different levels of culture, civilization or economic development. Neither is that a sufficient reason for some to take unjust advantage of their superiority over others; rather should they see in it an added motive for more serious commitment to the common cause of social progress.

89. It is not true that some human beings are by nature superior, and others inferior. All men are equal in their natural dignity. Consequently there are no political communities that are superior by nature and none that are inferior by nature. All political communities are of equal natural dignity, since they are bodies whose membership is made up of these same human beings. Nor must it be forgotten, in this connection, that peoples can be highly sensitive, and with good reason, in matters touching their dignity and honor.

90. Truth further demands that the various media of social communications made available by modern progress, which enable the nations to know each other better, be used with serene objectivity. That need not, of course, rule out any legitimate emphasis on the positive aspects of their way of life. But methods of information which fall short of the truth, and by the same token impair the reputation of this people or that, must be discarded.

91. Moreover, relations between political communities are to be regulated by justice. This implies, in addition to recognition of their mutual rights, the fulfillment of their respective duties.

92. Political communities have the right to existence, to self-development and to the means necessary for this. They have the right to play the leading part in the process of their own development and the right to their good name and due honors. From which it follows at one and the same time that they have also the corresponding duty of respecting

these rights in others and of avoiding acts which violate them. Just as an individual man may not pursue his own interests to the detriment of other men, so, on the international level, one State may not develop itself by restricting or oppressing other States. St. Augustine rightly says, *What are kingdoms without justice but bands of robbers?*

93. Not only can it happen, but it actually does happen, that the advantages and conveniences which nations strive to acquire for themselves become objects of contention; nevertheless, the resulting disagreements must be settled, not by arms, nor by deceit or trickery, but rather in the only manner which is worthy of the dignity of man, *i.e.* by a mutual assessment of the reasons on both sides of the dispute, by a mature and objective investigation of the situation, and by an equitable reconciliation of differences of opinion.

94. In this connection, especially noteworthy is the trend that since the nineteenth century has become quite prevalent and strong, namely, the desire of those of similar ancestry to be autonomous and to form a single nation. However, for various reasons, this has not always been possible, and hence minorities are found within the geographical limits of some other ethnic group, so that there have arisen problems of grave moment.

95. In the first place, it must be made clear that justice is seriously violated by whatever is done to limit the strength and numerical increase of these lesser peoples . . .

96. On the other hand, the demands of justice are admirably observed by those civil authorities who promote the human welfare of those citizens belonging to a smaller ethnic group . . .

97. It should be noted, however, that these minority groups, either because of a reaction to their present situation or because of their historical difficulties are often inclined to exalt beyond due measure anything proper to their own people, so as to place them even above human values . . . Reason rather demands that these very people recognize also the advantages that accrue to them from their peculiar circumstances; for instance, no small contribution is made toward the development of their particular talents and spirit by their daily dealings with people who have grown up in a different culture. This, however, will be true only if the minorities, in their relations with the peoples around them, show an interest in the customs and institutions of these same peoples. It will not be true if they sow discord, which can cause considerable damage and choke off the development of nations.

98. Because relations between States must be regulated by the norms of truth and justice, they should also derive great benefits from active solidarity, through mutual co-operation on various levels, such as, in our own times, has already taken place with laudable results in the economic, social, political, educational, health and sport spheres. We must remember that,

of its very nature, civil authority exists, not to confine its people within the boundaries of their nation, but rather to protect, above all else, the common good of that particular civil society, which certainly cannot be divorced from the common good of the entire human family.

99. This entails not only that civil societies should pursue their particular interests without hurting others, but also that they should join forces and plans whenever the efforts of an individual government cannot achieve its desired goals; but in the execution of such common efforts, great care must be taken lest what helps some nations should injure others.

100. Furthermore, the universal common good requires that in every nation friendly relations be fostered in all fields between the citizens and their intermediate societies. There are groupings of people of more or less different ethnic backgrounds. However, the elements which characterize an ethnic group must not be transformed into a watertight compartment in which human beings are prevented from communicating with their fellow men belonging to different ethnic groups. That would contrast with our contemporary situation, in which the distances separating peoples have been almost wiped out. . . .

101. As everybody knows, there are countries with an abundance of arable land and a scarcity of manpower, while in other countries there is no proportion between natural resources and the capital available. This demands that peoples should set up relationships of mutual collaboration, facilitating the circulation from one to the other of goods, capital, and manpower.

102. Here We deem it opportune to remark that, whenever possible, the work to be done should be taken to the workers, not vice versa. In this way a possibility of a better future is offered to many persons without being forced to leave their own environment in order to seek residence elsewhere which almost always entails the heartache of separation and difficult periods of adjustment and social integration.

103. The sentiment of universal fatherhood which the Lord has placed in Our heart makes Us feel profound sadness in considering the phenomenon of political refugees: a phenomenon which has assumed large proportions and which always hides numberless and acute sufferings.

104. Such expatriations show that there are some political regimes which do not guarantee for individual citizens a sufficient sphere of freedom within which they can lead a life worthy of man. In fact, under those regimes even the very right to freedom is either called into question or openly denied. This undoubtedly is a radical inversion of the order of human society, because the reason for the existence of public authority is to promote the common good, a fundamental element of which is to recognize freedom and to safeguard it.

105. At this point it is not out of place to recall that exiles are persons, and that all their rights as persons must be recognized. Refugees do not

lose these rights simply because they have been deprived of citizenship in their national State.

106. Now among the rights of a human person there must be included that by which a man may enter a political community where he hopes he can more fittingly provide a future for himself and his dependents. Wherefore, as far as the common good rightly understood permits, it is the duty of that State to accept immigrants seeking to become members of a new society.

107. Wherefore, on this occasion, We publicly approve and commend every undertaking, founded on the principles of human solidarity and Christian charity, which aims at making migration of persons from one country to another less painful.

108. And We will be permitted to signal for the attention and gratitude of all right-minded persons the manifold work which specialized international agencies are carrying out in this very delicate field.

Disarmament

109. On the other hand, it is with deep sorrow that We note the enormous stocks of armaments that have been and still are being made in more economically developed countries, with a vast outlay of intellectual and economic resources. And so it happens that, while the people of these countries are loaded with heavy burdens, other countries as a result are deprived of the collaboration they need in order to make economic and social progress.

110. The production of arms is allegedly justified on the grounds that in present-day conditions peace cannot be preserved without an equal balance of armaments. And so, if one country increases its armaments, others feel the need to do the same; and if one country is equipped with nuclear weapons, other countries must produce their own, equally destructive.

111. Consequently, people live in constant fear lest the storm that every moment threatens should break upon them with dreadful violence. And with good reason, for the arms of war are ready at hand. Even though it is difficult to believe that anyone would deliberately take the responsibility for the appalling destruction and sorrow that war would bring in its train, it cannot be denied that the conflagration may be set off by some unexpected and obscure event. And one must bear in mind that, even though the monstrous power of modern weapons acts as a deterrent, it is to be feared that the mere continuance of nuclear tests, undertaken with war in mind, will prove a serious hazard for life on earth.

112. Justice, then, right reason and humanity urgently demand that the arms race should cease; that the stockpiles which exist in various coun-

tries should be reduced equally and simultaneously by the parties concerned; that nuclear weapons should be banned; and that a general agreement should eventually be reached about progressive disarmament and an effective method of control.

113. All must realize that there is no hope of putting an end to the building up of armaments, nor of reducing the present stocks, nor, still less, of abolishing them altogether, unless the process is complete and thorough and unless it proceeds from inner conviction: unless, that is, everyone sincerely co-operates to banish the fear and anxious expectation of war with which men are oppressed. If this is to come about, the fundamental principle on which our present peace depends must be replaced by another, which declares that the true and solid peace of nations consists not in equality of arms but in mutual trust alone. We believe that this can be brought to pass, and We consider that it is something which reason requires, that it is eminently desirable in itself and that it will prove to be the source of many benefits.

114. In the first place, it is an objective demanded by reason. There can be, or at least there should be, no doubt that relations between States, as between individuals, should be regulated not by the force of arms but by the light of reason, by the rule, that is, of truth, of justice and of active and sincere co-operation.

115. Secondly, We say that it is an objective earnestly to be desired in itself. Is there anyone who does not ardently yearn to see war banished, to see peace preserved and daily more firmly established?

116. And finally, it is an objective which will be a fruitful source of many benefits, for its advantages will be felt everywhere, by individuals, by families, by nations, by the whole human family. The warning of Pius XII still rings in our ears: *Nothing is lost by peace; everything may be lost by war.*

117. Since this is so, We, the Vicar on earth of Jesus Christ, Savior of the World and Author of Peace, and as interpreter of the very profound longing of the entire human family, following the impulse of Our heart, seized by anxiety for the good of all, We feel it Our duty to beseech men, especially those who have the responsibility of public affairs, to spare no labor in order to ensure that world events follow a reasonable and humane course.

118. In the highest and most authoritative assemblies, let men give serious thought to the problem of a peaceful adjustment of relations between political communities on a world level: an adjustment founded on mutual trust, on sincerity in negotiations, on faithful fulfillment of obligations assumed. Let them study the problem until they find that point of agreement from which it will be possible to commence to go forward towards accords that will be sincere, lasting and fruitful.

119. We, for Our part, will not cease to pray God to bless these labors so that they may lead to fruitful results.

120. One must also bear in mind that relations between States should be based on freedom, that is to say, that no country may unjustly oppress others or unduly meddle in their affairs. On the contrary, all should help to develop in others a sense of responsibility, a spirit of enterprise, and an earnest desire to be the first to promote their own advancement in every field.

Progress of economically underdeveloped countries

121. Because all men are joined together by reason of their common origin, their redemption by Christ, and their supernatural destiny, and are called to form one Christian family, We appealed in the Encyclical *Mater et Magistra* to economically developed nations to come to the aid of those which were in the process of development.

122. We are greatly consoled to see how widely that appeal has been favorably received; and We are confident that even more so in the future it will contribute to the end that the poorer countries, in as short a time as possible, will arrive at that degree of economic development which will enable every citizen to live in conditions in keeping with his human dignity.

123. But it is never sufficiently repeated that the co-operation, to which reference has been made, should be effected with the greatest respect for the liberty of the countries being developed, for these must realize that they are primarily responsible, and that they are the principal artisans in the promotion of their own economic development and social progress. . . .

125. It is vitally important, therefore, that the wealthier States, in providing varied forms of assistance to the poorer, should respect the moral values and ethnic characteristics peculiar to each, and also that they should avoid any intention of political domination. . . .

Signs of the times

126. Men are becoming more and more convinced that disputes which arise between States should not be resolved by recourse to arms, but rather by negotiation.

127. It is true that on historical grounds this conviction is based chiefly on the terrible destructive force of modern arms; and it is nourished by the horror aroused in the mind by the very thought of the cruel destruction

and the immense suffering which the use of those armaments would bring to the human family. For this reason it is hardly possible to imagine that in the atomic era war could be used as an instrument of justice.

128. Nevertheless, unfortunately, the law of fear still reigns among peoples, and it forces them to spend fabulous sums for armaments: not for aggression, they affirm—and there is no reason for not believing them— but to dissuade others from aggression.

129. There is reason to hope, however, that by meeting and negotiating, men may come to discover better the bonds that unite them together, deriving from the human nature which they have in common; and that they may also come to discover that one of the most profound requirements of their common nature is this: that between them and their respective peoples it is not fear which should reign but love, a love which tends to express itself in a collaboration that is loyal, manifold in form and productive of many benefits.

PART IV: RELATIONSHIP OF MEN AND OF POLITICAL COMMUNITIES WITH THE WORLD COMMUNITY

130. Recent progress of science and technology has profoundly affected human beings and influenced men to work together and live as one family. There has been a great increase in the circulation of goods, of ideas and of persons from one country to another, so that relations have become closer between individuals, families and intermediate associations belonging to different political communities, and between the public authorities of those communities. At the same time the interdependence of national economies has grown deeper, one becoming progressively more closely related to the other, so that they become, as it were, integral parts of the one world economy. Likewise the social progress, order, security and peace of each country are necessarily connected with the social progress, order, security and peace of all other countries.

131. At the present day no political community is able to pursue its own interests and develop itself in isolation, because the degree of its prosperity and development is a reflection and a component part of the degree of prosperity and development of all the other political communities.

*Existing public authority not equal to requirements
of the universal common good*

132. The unity of the human family has always existed, because its members were human beings all equal by virtue of their natural dignity. Hence there will always exist the objective need to promote, in sufficient measure, the universal common good, that is, the common good of the entire human family.

133. In times past, one would be justified in feeling that the public authorities of the different political communities might be in a position to provide for the universal common good, either through normal diplomatic channels or through top-level meetings, by making use of juridical instruments such as conventions and treaties, for example: juridical instruments suggested by the natural law and regulated by the law of nations and international law.

134. As a result of the far-reaching changes which have taken place in the relations within the human community, the universal common good gives rise to problems that are very grave, complex and extremely urgent, especially as regards security and world peace. On the other hand, the public authorities of the individual nations—being placed as they are on a footing of equality one with the other—no matter how much they multiply their meetings or sharpen their wits in efforts to draw up new juridical instruments, they are no longer capable of facing the task of finding an adequate solution to the problems mentioned above. And this is not due to a lack of good will or of a spirit of enterprise, but because their authority lacks suitable force.

135. It can be said, therefore, that at this historical moment the present system of organization and the way its principle of authority operates on a world basis no longer correspond to the objective requirements of the universal common good.

136. There exists an intrinsic connection between the common good on the one hand and the structure and function of public authority on the other. The moral order, which needs public authority in order to promote the common good in civil society, requires also that the authority be effective in attaining that end. This demands that the organs through which the authority is formed, becomes operative and pursues its ends, must be composed and act in such a manner as to be capable of furthering the common good by ways and means which correspond to the developing situation.

137. Today the universal common good poses problems of world-wide dimensions, which cannot be adequately tackled or solved except by the

efforts of public authorities endowed with a wideness of powers, structure and means of the same proportions: that is, of public authorities which are in a position to operate in an effective manner on a world-wide basis. The moral order itself, therefore, demands that such a form of public authority be established.

Public authority instituted by common consent and not imposed by force

138. A public authority, having world-wide power and endowed with the proper means for the efficacious pursuit of its objective, which is the universal common good in concrete form, must be set up by common accord and not imposed by force. The reason is that such an authority must be in a position to operate effectively; yet, at the same time, its action must be inspired by sincere and real impartiality: in other words, it must be an action aimed at satisfying the objective requirements of the universal common good. The difficulty is that there would be reason to fear that a supranational or world-wide public authority, imposed by force by the more powerful political communities, might be or might become an instrument of one-sided interests; and even should this not happen, it would be difficult for it to avoid all suspicion of partiality in its actions, and this would take from the efficaciousness of its activity. Even though there may be pronounced differences between political communities as regards the degree of their economic development and their military power, they are all very sensitive as regards their juridical equality and their moral dignity. For that reason, they are right in not easily yielding in obedience to an authority imposed by force, or to an authority in whose creation they had no part, or to which they themselves did not decide to submit by conscious and free choice.

139. Like the common good of individual political communities, so too the universal common good cannot be determined except by having regard to the human person. Therefore, the public authority of the world community, too, must have as its fundamental objective the recognition, respect, safeguarding and promotion of the rights of the human person; this can be done by direct action when required, or by creating on a world scale an environment in which the public authorities of the individual political communities can more easily carry out their specific functions.

The principle of subsidiarity

140. Just as within each political community the relations between individuals, families, intermediate associations and public authority are

governed by the principle of subsidiarity, so too the relations between the public authority of each political community and the public authority of the world community must be regulated by the light of the same principle. This means that the public authority of the world community must tackle and solve problems of an economic, social, political or cultural character which are posed by the universal common good. For, because of the vastness, complexity and urgency of those problems, the public authorities of the individual States are not in a position to tackle them with any hope of resolving them satisfactorily.

141. The public authority of the world community is not intended to limit the sphere of action of the public authority of the individual political community, much less to take its place. On the contrary, its purpose is to create, on a world basis, an environment in which the public authorities of each political community, its citizens and intermediate associations, can carry out their tasks, fulfill their duties and exercise their rights with greater security.

Modern developments

142. As is known, the United Nations Organization (UN) was established on June 26, 1945, and to it there were subsequently added Intergovernmental Agencies with extensive international tasks in the economic, social, cultural, educational and health fields. The United Nations Organization had as its essential purpose the maintenance and consolidation of peace between peoples, fostering between them friendly relations, based on the principles of equality, mutual respect, and varied forms of co-operation in every sector of human society.

143. An act of the highest importance performed by the United Nations Organization was the *Universal Declaration of Human Rights,* approved in the General Assembly of December 10, 1948. In the preamble of that Declaration, the recognition of and respect for those rights and respective liberties is proclaimed as an ideal to be pursued by all peoples and all countries.

144. Some objections and reservations were raised regarding certain points in the Declaration. There is no doubt, however, that the document represents an important step on the path towards the juridical-political organization of the world community. For in it, in most solemn form, the dignity of a person is acknowledged to all human beings; and as a consequence there is proclaimed, as a fundamental right, the right of free movement in the search for truth and in the attainment of moral good and of justice, and also the right to a dignified life, while other rights connected with those mentioned are likewise proclaimed.

145. It is Our earnest wish that the United Nations Organization—in

its structure and in its means—may become ever more equal to the magnitude and nobility of its tasks. May the day soon come when every human being will find therein an effective safeguard for the rights which derive directly from his dignity as a person, and which are therefore universal, inviolate and inalienable rights. This is all the more to be hoped for since all human beings, as they take an ever more active part in the public life of their own political communities, are showing an increasing interest in the affairs of all peoples, and are becoming more consciously aware that they are living members of a universal family of mankind.

PART V: PASTORAL EXHORTATIONS

146. Once again We deem it opportune to remind Our children of their duty to take an active part in public life, and to contribute towards the attainment of the common good of the entire human family as well as to that of their own political community. . . .

149. We desire to call attention to the fact that scientific competence, technical capacity and professional experience, although necessary, are not of themselves sufficient to elevate the relationships of society to an order that is genuinely human: that is, to an order whose foundation is truth, whose measure and objective is justice, whose driving force is love, and whose method of attainment is freedom. . . .

157. The doctrinal principles outlined in this document derive from or are suggested by requirements inherent in human nature itself, and are, for the most part, dictates of the natural law. They provide Catholics, therefore, with a vast field in which they can meet and come to an understanding both with Christians separated from this Apostolic See, and also with human beings who are not enlightened by faith in Jesus Christ, but who are endowed with the light of reason and with a natural and operative honesty. . . .

158. Moreover, one must never confuse error and the person who errs, not even when there is a question of error or inadequate knowledge of truth in the moral or religious field. The person who errs is always and above all a human being, and he retains in every case his dignity as a human person; and he must be always regarded and treated in accordance with that lofty dignity. Besides, in every human being, there is a need that is congenital to his nature and never becomes extinguished, compelling him to break through the web of error and open his mind to the knowledge of truth. And God will never fail to act on his interior being, with the result that a person, who at a given moment of his life lacked the clarity of

faith or even adheres to erroneous doctrines, can at a future date learn and believe the truth. Meetings and agreements, in the various sectors of daily life, between believers and those who do not believe or believe insufficiently because they adhere to error, can be occasions for discovering truth and paying homage to it. . . .

166. These words of Ours, which We have wished to dedicate to the problems that so beset the human family today and on the just solution of which the ordered progress of society depends, are dictated by a profound aspiration which We know is shared by all men of good will: the consolidation of peace in the world. . . .

173. Given at Rome at St. Peter's, on Holy Thursday, the eleventh day of April, in the year 1963, the fifth of Our Pontificate.

JOHN XXIII, POPE

III

DOUBTS, DILEMMAS, PROBLEMS AND ARGUMENTS

It would be lovely to accept the idea of a world order based on the principles of law and of justice without question. But it is not that easy. Certain doubts arise in the minds of thoughtful people, even those most desiring some such system. Some doubts are very valid; some are less so. This section attempts to present the most persistent, recognizing their complexity and exploring them further, thereby revealing the areas in which more clarification is needed. We begin to consider for ourselves what we most want; what we would give up for what; what are the realities and potentialities of our world. In recognizing the difficulties we come to grips with world order and find it curiously actual.

On February 18, 19 and 20 of 1965 a convocation was held in New York's Hotel Hilton to examine the requirements for peace in the context of the encyclical letter *Pacem in Terris* of Pope John XXIII. It was organized and supported by the Center for the Study of Democratic Institutions of Santa Barbara, California, with financial assistance from a number of foundations, particularly the Johnson (Johnson Wax) Foundation of Racine, Wisconsin. To participate in it came scholars, authors, scientists, thinkers, statesmen from many parts of the world. No one from the Peoples Republic of China, unfortunately, whose population represents one fourth of the world, since the policy of our government would not have admitted them even had they been invited and had they accepted. But it is important that Communists from Russia and from Poland came, with the approval of their governments, to consider the practical implications of this document by a Catholic Pope.

It was at a moment when the United States had just commenced the bombing of North Vietnam with the escalation of the conflict that was implicit in this. It was a moment when the United Nations, which had hitherto been, at very least, an ameliorating presence at other conflicts, was at a helpless low—due in part to a financial crisis that was at bottom political, in part to the weakening effect of the United States' decision to act unilaterally in Vietnam, and in part to the fact that this war pointed up, as no previous one had done, the *incompleteness* of the U.N. For here was a conflict within which lay the possibilities of a major war and yet one entire side was not included in the U.N.—neither North Vietnam, North Korea nor China is represented there. Among the conferees and the audience there could not help but be a strong tragic sense. As Professor Gray expresses it (in Section I) "The tragic conviction acknowledges the fragile and exposed character of individuality but discovers meaning and purpose in the individual's struggle to locate himself in nature and society. Tragedy links us to what has been in the history of our species and binds us in faith to the future. It teaches that there are things worth living and dying for, ideas, ancestors and descendants." This tragic conviction was, I believe, the mood of the convocation.

As I sat among the audience day after day, listening to speech after speech testifying from one viewpoint or another the need to outlaw war, the need for a world authority based on the principles of law and justice, the need for a world authority to bring social justice to the underprivileged two thirds of the world—no speech seemed to me so full of disturbing questions that must be dealt with as that of Paul Tillich.

This address rewards very close reading. I will confine myself to only a few points.

Tillich hails the encyclical and finds most valuable its emphasis on the principle of justice and on the principle of the worth and dignity of the individual. This is valid for Jews and Protestants and Humanists as well as for Catholics.

Tillich feels, however, that the encyclical is limited to Western culture in certain attitudes that relate to the different views of the individual as seen in the East and the West, and that "This should restrain those who adhere to the *spirit* of the encyclical from attempts to force some of its consequences, *e.g.* particular ideas of freedom and equal rights, upon people with other principles."

He questions the role of power and points out that power is not identical with force, nor with authority. (I suggest that it has a kinship to what in this Reader we have called "legitimate authority.") He points out there is no effective authority (by inference, no effective world authority) without a structure of power behind it, and no power can become effective without coercion applied against those who try to undercut it. (What would be the enforcement means of a world authority?) Then, he says, "The great question arises: when is coercion a just expression of power, when an unjust one? We acknowledge just coercion in the enforcement of the law." But he does not elucidate why this is so. And we ourselves know that we do not acknowledge as just, even in the name of the law, coercion which is excessive. What makes us on the whole, however, acknowledge a law as reasonably just and accept coercion by something we recognize as a legitimate authority, which has power but may not always have great force behind it? This is a problem which Louis Lusky raises later on.

As regards the use of power, and therefore the effectiveness of a world police force—here what Tillich means is equivalent to the World Peace Force of Clark and Sohn—Tillich believes that only minor conflicts can be solved in that way. To suppress major war by military force it would be necessary to use coercion with *or without* justice in the necessary exercise of power: *i.e.* the exercise of power would have to be so destructive that it would lose all relation to justice. Tillich warns against a world dictatorship as the price of peace. Clark and Sohn also fear world dictatorship and build a careful system to prevent it. But the dilemma remains: in the nuclear age, what are the limits of just enforcement when we also grant that without any enforcement there is no legitimate authority to defend us? Would a weaker or stronger World Peace Force give us the more ease is the question.

I would call attention to Tillich's words on the ambiguity of man's moral nature—good as well as bad, bad as well as good. This is equally so for the other fellow as for ourselves, and is the reason why man desires law and authority. If his nature were perfect it would be otherwise.

I would call attention to his distinction between utopian expectation and genuine hope, recognizing that he uses the word "utopian" in the sense of something desirable but totally unrealizable. And to the bases he sees for genuine hope.

But I would particularly call attention to this: "[Man] can establish a legal structure which guarantees peace among those who are subject to it, not absolutely but to a certain degree. Not absolutely, for everyone subject to the legal structure can break through it for his own interest or conviction. Therefore, something more than the legal structure for peace is needed. One has called it 'consensus.' But it is not something as intellectual as this word indicates. It is communal *eros* . . ."

Certainly what he is asking for here is not only the use of reason but a tremendous stretching of our *awareness* or consciousness to include within ourselves, to at least some degree, ways of looking at the world, ways of being human hitherto nonexistent to us. Not to adopt them—simply to recognize them as expressions of humanness—and feel an added dimension, a growth, stir in us. It is this more developed consciousness or awareness that is Tillich's communal *eros.*

With this in mind we can examine again Tillich's statement that "there are large cultural groups, some of them shaped by thousands of years of different religious tradition, in which the dignity of the individual man is not ultimate." It is true that in Buddhism and even more so in Hinduism, which lies behind Buddhism as Judaism lies behind Christianity, the individual man is regarded differently than we do in the religions of our own culture. This is due in part to the fact that those religions have a cyclical view of history, while we have what might be called a linear view of history. It is also due in part to the concept of reincarnation inherent in both those religions, wherein present miseries are taken as punishment for sins in past lives beyond the control of *that* individual (as we think of an individual), and likewise a more fortunate fate can be won in another incarnation by right action in this. Reincarnation frees the individual man from one point in linear time and thus makes him not "ultimate."

One might say that in Eastern religions there is more emphasis on man's belonging to life as a whole (remember Lifton's description of the particular horror felt for the Hiroshima bomb as meaning that Nature itself was dead) while in Western development, especially since the Middle Ages, there has been emphasis on the particular individual, his supreme uniqueness, what he can accomplish, his innate worth and, logically following, his rights and duties. It is important to remember, however, that a basic concept of Buddhism is that every man has in him the seed, the potentiality, for becoming the Buddha, the Enlightened One. And a basic concept of Hinduism is that there are four ideal stages of life—the pupil dedicated to learning, the householder fulfilling his part in the active life of family and community, the retirement from this to the forest to contemplate, and finally the free wanderer released from particularities, aware that he is everywhere at home in the underlying oneness of life. These views do not hold the dignity of man cheap—simply different from ours.

Not long ago I asked Nancy Wilson Ross, a novelist who has for thirty years been a serious student of Eastern art and religions, to put very briefly the difference between East and West. After careful thought and after remarking that nothing so brief was entirely accurate, she said: "The West, particularly Christianity, says 'I am my brother's keeper' whereas the East gives us the insight 'I am my brother.'" (The first leads to an ethic of action, the latter is an awareness of a common ground of being.)

It seems to me that United States foreign policy, put in its best light and acknowledging the desire to do right that is genuinely there along with the hypocrisy, the arrogance and the reliance on power, could be expressed by "I am my brother's keeper." This also is the spirit of the encyclical. What Tillich is asking for in the guise of communal *eros* is something closer to "I am my brother." I could wish this awareness for U.S. foreign policy too.

Address At *Pacem in Terris* Convocation

PAUL TILLICH

It is my task to express some thoughts about the subject of this conference and its basic document, the encyclical *Pacem in Terris* by Pope John XXIII, as a theologian who comes both from a Protestant and a Humanist tradition and has tried for many decades to show their ultimate unity.

My first reaction to the encyclical is the general one that its appearance is an important event in the history of religious and political thought and may have practical consequences for man's historical existence. Most valuable seems to me the way in which is emphasized throughout the document the ultimate principle of justice, the acknowledgement of the dignity of every man as a person, from which follow his rights and his obligations in the manifold encounters of man with man. There is no difference in this point of view among Jews, Protestants and Humanists: Jews in whose prophetic tradition this principle has arisen and has been reformulated up to Martin Buber's description of the ego—the thou encounter between person and person; Protestants who should never forget that the backbone of love is justice and that without the solid structure of justice, love becomes sentimentality; Humanists who have in Immanuel Kant's unconditional imperative to respect every person as person the highest criterion of "humanitas." All three agree with the basic principle of the papal encyclical.

On this foundation, questions arise, some of which are rooted in other traditions and may serve as a transition to the practical work of the next days.

My first question stems from the fact that the agreement as to the determining principle of the encyclical reaches only as far as the Western,
Christian-Humanist culture, but not essentially beyond it. Therefore, if we
envisage "peace on earth," we must remain aware of the fact that there are
large cultural groups, some of them shaped by thousands of years of different religious tradition, in which the principle of the dignity of the individual man is not ultimate. Only a prolonged mutual interpenetration, in
which the West must take as well as give, can change the situation. This
should restrain those who adhere to the spirit of the encyclical from attempts to force some of its consequences, for example, particular ideas of
freedom and equal rights, upon people with other principles. Such attempts are hopeless even if they lead to external victory.

The second problem, concerning the encyclical, refers to the question
of resistance against those who violate the dignity of the individual. Such
resistance unquestionably belongs to the rights of the person as well as of
the group which has accepted and is willing to defend the dignity of the
person and the principles following from it. But such resistance can become rebellion, and rebellion can become revolution, and revolution can
become war; and history leaves no doubt that the wars over contrasting
ideas of justice are the most cruel, most insistent and the most devastating
ones. So it was in the religious wars when the rights of man were identical
with the truth about man. So it is now in the ideological wars when the
rights of man are identical with the social organization which guarantees
these rights. And there is hardly a situation in which the dignity of the
person is more deeply violated than in the struggles for the establishment
of conditions under which this dignity shall be guaranteed. This is true of
person-to-person relationships as well as of the relation of individuals to
groups and of groups to groups. There are situations in which resistance
without armed violence is possible; but even then, destructive consequences are hardly avoidable, be it through psychological, through economic or through sociological forms of compulsion. And there are situations in which nothing short of war can defend or establish the dignity of
the person. Nothing is more indicative of the tragic aspect of life than the
unavoidable injustice in the struggle for justice.

A third problem, which must be considered to create a transition from
the encyclical to the political thought of the conference, is the role of
power in relation to force and the principles of justice. Power can neither
be identified with force nor with authority. In several statements of the
encyclical, this has been done, and a direct discussion of the ambiguities
of power is lacking. But without it, a realistic approach to the peace problem is impossible.

There is no effective authority without a structure of power behind it;
and under the conditions of existence, no power can become effective

without coercion applied against those who try to undercut it. For power is something positive; it is a basic quality of being. It is the power to resist what tries to distort and to annihilate the structures of being. I remind the theologians of the fact that they open the majority of their prayers with words like "almighty" or "all-powerful God" thus consecrating power in itself. And I remind the philosophers that potentiality means "power of being." In every individual and in every group is some power of being and the affirmation of this power and the drive to defend and to increase it. In the encounters of power with power, union as well as conflict arises and the conflicts lead to the use of force for the sake of coercion. Then the great question arises: When is coercion a just expression of power, when an unjust one? We acknowledge just coercion in the enforcement of the law. Is there a just enforcement in the relation of power-groups? This question has been answered for many centuries by the concept of the just war. But this concept has lost its validity through the fact that in a serious atomic conflagration there is no victor and no vanquished, in other words, neither a coercer nor a coerced will be left.

Only in minor conflicts, the old concept has meaning and may lead to a kind of world police. But a conflict between those who give power and authority to such a police force could not be solved in this way. The problem is neither power nor coercion, but the use of coercion with or without justice in the necessary exercise of power.

In this connection, a fourth problem arises: the question to what degree a political group, for instance a social group with a center of power, able to act politically, can be judged in the way in which one judges human individuals. Such analogy, if taken seriously, has dangerous consequences. It considers a contingent government as the deciding and responsible center of the group. This makes it possible that the government is asked to follow moral laws like the Ten Commandments, or the Sermon on the Mount or the Natural Moral Law for individuals—as is often demanded by a legalistic pacifism. But no government can make a total sacrifice of its nation, such as an individual can and sometimes ought to make of himself. However, this does not and should not prevent a government to induce its nation to bring the sacrifice of self-restriction for the common good of a group of nations, including itself, even if some loss of the questionable and pernicious possession, called prestige, is involved. There is another consequence which the personification of a group can have. If the government is considered as the deciding center of the social body, no individual has the right to resist it. And this is the surest and most frequently used road to despotism. The group lies in another dimension of being than the individual; and the moral laws, valid for the latter, can be applied to the former only indirectly and with essential qualifications. A direct application of the rights and duties of the individual to the rights and duties of a group is impossible. This fact, together in unity with the three other problems we have mentioned, show the limits of any realistic hope for "peace on earth."

This statement forces me to lead you into a more universal and more basic consideration of the question of peace on earth. We must ask: which are the predispositions for the fulfillment of this aim in human nature and in the character of history? Most differences about the problems of peace are rooted ultimately in different interpretations of human nature and consequently of the meaning of history. At this point I must speak both as a Protestant theologian and as an existentialist philosopher. I see human nature determined by the conflict between the goodness of man's essential being and the ambiguity of his actual being, his life under the conditions of existence. The goodness of his essential nature gives him his greatness, his dignity, the demand, embodied in him, to be acknowledged as a person. On the other hand, the predicament in which he finds himself, the estrangement from his true being, drives him into the opposite direction, preventing him from fulfilling in actual life what he essentially is. It makes all his doings and all that which is done by him ambiguous, bad as well as good. For his will is ambiguous, good as well as bad. And one would not appeal to "all men of good will" as the encyclical does. One should appeal to all men knowing that in the best will, there is an element of bad will and that in the worst will there is an element of good will. This view of the ambiguity of man's moral nature has direct consequences for the way a peace conference should look at the chance for a future state of peace.

It should distinguish genuine hope from utopian expectations. The bearers of hope in past and present had and have to learn this, mostly the hard way. The classical book of hope, the Old Testament, is a history of broken and revived hope. Its foundation was in the first place the belief in divine acting, in the second, the confidence in man's right response to it. In both respects it was disappointed. "My ways are not your ways" says God through the prophet to the disappointed; and nothing is more often expressed in the prophets than the unreliable character of the people, who turn away from the covenant which justified this hope. Nevertheless, a genuine hope remained in Israel up to today and kept the nation alive.

There is a profound analogy between the history of the religious hope in Israel and the history of the secular hope in the Western world from the great Utopias of the Renaissance up to our day. In the movements which were striving for a state of peace and justice in modern times, hope was partly based on the belief in a universal law of progress, partly on the belief in man's growing reasonableness. Both hopes were disappointed, perhaps most profoundly in our century. We cannot close our eyes any longer to the fact that every gain produced, for example, by scientific and technical progress, implies a loss; and that every good, achieved in history, is accompanied by a shadow, an evil which uses the good and distorts it. And we know just through our better understanding of man's personal and social life that human reason is not only determined by the natural laws of reason but also by the dark elements in his total being which struggle against reason. In view of the two main examples for this predicament of man, the ambiguity of blessing and curse in the scientific penetration into the atomic structure of the universe, and the well reasoned outbreak of destructive antirationality in Hitlerism and Stalinism, it is understandable that hopelessness has grasped large masses in the Western nations, especially in the younger generations. And it is understandable that a conference like this meets a widespread skepticism, perhaps by some in the conference itself.

But there are not only utopian expectations, there is also genuine hope in our time and in what we are trying to do—here and now—just as in the men of the Old Testament. A realistic view of man and history needs not to lead to cynicism. But it may often ask for hope against hope, and certainly it demands the courage to risk, even if failure is more probable than success.

Where, then, lies the difference between utopian expectations and genuine hope? The basis for genuine hope is that there is something present of that which is hoped for, as in the seed something of the coming plant is present while utopian expectations have no ground in the present. So we must ask: Which are the seeds out of which a future state of peace can develop?

The first basis for genuine hope is something negative which, however, can have and partly has had positive effects: The atomic threat and the fear of mutual destruction. The limited peace, forced upon us by the threat, is in itself merely negative. But it does something which is somehow positive: It makes the conflicting groups of mankind feel that there is mankind with a common destiny. This experience of a "community of fear" is still weak and easily overwhelmed by a stronger feeling of national and ideological conflict. But it does exist as a small seed.

A second basis of genuine hope for peace is the technical union of mankind by the conquest of space. Of course, nearness can intensify hostility; and the fact that the first manifestation of the technical oneness of our world were two world wars proves this possibility. But nearness can also have the opposite effect. It can change the image of the other as strange and dangerous; it can reduce self-affirmation and effect openness for other possibilities of human existence and—particularly as in the encounter of the religions—of other possibilities of genuine faith.

A third basis of genuine hope for peace is the increasing number of cross-national and cross-ideological fields of cooperation, some of them desirable as, for example, exchange in the humanities and religion, some of them essential as, for example, collaboration in the sciences, some of them necessary for the future of mankind, as, for example, the problems of food, medicine, overpopulation, conservation of nature.

A fourth basis of genuine hope is the existence and effectiveness, however limited, of a legal roof for all these types of limited groups. But man can extend the realm of peace which nature cannot. He can establish a legal structure which guarantees peace among those who are subject to it, not absolutely but to a certain degree. Not absolutely, for everyone subjected to the legal structure can break through it for his own interest or his conviction.

Therefore, something more than the legal structure for peace is needed. One has called it "consensus." But it is not something as intellectual as this word indicates. It is communal *eros,* that kind of love which is not directed to an individual but to a group. It is said that one cannot love another nation. This may be true in relation to a national state; but it is not true with respect to the people of the other nation. One can have *eros* toward them in their uniqueness, their virtues, their contributions, in spite of their shortcomings and vices. It seems that no world community is possible without this *eros* which trespasses interest as well as law. Every expression of such *eros* is a basis of hope for peace, every rejection of such *eros* reduces the chances of peace.

And now a last word about what we as a peace conference can hope for. First of all: We can only *hope*. We cannot calculate, we cannot know. The uncertainty remains. All the seeds of hope mentioned can be destroyed before they come to fulfillment. And further: There is no hope for a final stage of history in which peace and justice rule. History is not fulfilled at its empirical end; but history is fulfilled in the great moments in which something new is created, or, as one could express it religiously, in which the Kingdom of God breaks into history conquering destructive structures of existence, one of the greatest of which is war. This means that we cannot hope for a final stage of justice and peace within history; but we can hope for partial victories over the forces of evil in a particular moment of time.

With this hope, without utopian expectations, this conference should begin its work.

※ ※ ※ ※

That there must be interpenetration of East and West is obvious. Indeed it seems necessary for the survival of both. There is no question that the East needs in a practical way much that the West has to bring. On the other side, particularly since the end of World War II, it has been apparent that many persons in the West, notably in the younger generation, have been turning to the East in search of something which they feel themselves desperately to need. Perhaps one can describe it as a restoral of *feeling* and the validity of direct, vivid experience. It is as if we had suddenly realized that it is by no means the whole of reality on which we have concentrated. Besides which, the split between science and religion has left us dry. Everyone is conversant with the fact that an interest in Zen and in Japanese art (which is based on religious principles), for instance, has swept the country. This is not merely fashion, craze, but is symptomatic of the area in which we the West will take: art and religion—a revitalization of the emotive side of life. Just as radios, bicycles, legal constitutions, elections are not mere craze but are symptomatic of the area in which the East will take.

On a scholarly level, hundreds of Westerners and Easterners both have been trying for many years to search out the underlying ideational differences between the two cultures. Since 1939 a group of Asian and Western philosophers have met at the University of Hawaii every ten years (three times thus far) to search ways of making the two civilizations assimilable to each other. F.S.C. Northrop of Yale University* has been a leading participant in these meetings, and in *The Meeting of East and West* and other books has proposed ways of bringing into vitalizing contact the very different methods of truth-seeking in which each of the two cultures has specialized—perhaps overspecialized.

Northrop believes that the presuppositions of a culture determine its behavior and its institutions. If analysis reveals that the basic assumptions of two cultures are compatible or complementary, then the total ideology which underlies them can, without destruction, be enlarged to incorporate the new insights. Not in an eclectic, patchwork way like the nineteenth century theosophists, but by a true growth from within. Northrop finds that the total cultures of East and West are complementary in just this way.

Northrop himself is a philosopher of many parts, being equally at

* *In the comments on Northrop I am greatly indebted to W. Warren Wagar for his book,* The City of Man, *published by Houghton Mifflin in 1963. I did not take Mr. Wagar's word for anything, testing whatever he had to say against my own background of reading. Nevertheless, he has done an excellent job of synthesizing and condensing much that is difficult in a way that is readily understandable.*

home in metaphysics, legal theory, political science, Oriental thought, epistemology and doubtless several other areas. Some more specialized scholars complain that his picture of "East" and "West" is oversimplified. Of course it is true that there is much diversity within each; nonetheless, nearly all would agree with a few broad statements: In habits of thought, the East prefers intuition and synthesis; the West, closely reasoned analysis, fact finding, and the drawing of distinctions. Eastern philosophies and religions tend to be monistic, to see the cosmos as single undivided reality. Western religions and philosophies tend to carve the cosmos into distinct realms: such as mind, matter and deity, or creator and creation. Eastern ethical thought emphasizes the search for inner peace and the *oneness* underlying all. Western moralists stress active and practical life (expressed by Nancy Wilson Ross as "I am my brother" and "I am my brother's keeper"). Eastern man tends to accept intuitively the unitary nature of the world process. Western man has to deal with a constant dualism between mind and matter, intellect and instinct, religion and science which helps to make him at war with himself.

Northrop, and others, have shown how the Western mind can be both practical and material and yet highly abstract and theoretical, whereas the Eastern mind can focus simultaneously on concrete experience and undifferentiated ultimate reality. What Northrop calls the *aesthetic* component of knowledge, which is the speciality of the East, is reached by immediate experience, which includes intuition. The *theoretic* component of knowledge, the speciality of the West, is reached through concepts by postulation, and it is through this method that the West has achieved such amazing successes in the natural sciences. But a theory cannot be touched, smelled or tasted, nor directly tested in any way. It remains *abstract*. Aesthetic knowledge, on the other hand, is always *vibrantly direct*. Now Western science, with the advent of the unified field theory in physics, has come around to the recognition that the entire universe can be regarded as a single continuum. This total continuum can be studied through theoretical differentiations as in Western science, or it can be felt in its entirety undifferentiated and inexpressible in any language as in Eastern philosophy and religion.

The following article by Northrop is introduced into this Reader for several reasons: As a continued discussion of an important point raised by Tillich and to *represent* the great amount that has been and is being done to make East and West creatively available to each other by such scholars as Edward Conze, Heinrich Zimmer, Sri Aurobindo, Radakrishnan, D. T. Suzuki and on a somewhat broader level by Erich Fromm, Alan Watts, Nancy Wilson Ross, Joseph Campbell and others. To suggest to those who fear cultural imperialism by the West, as the obvious facts of our culture spread everywhere, that we have much to take and that in truth the traffic is even now not all one way. But most especially this particular article is introduced here because it is not sufficiently recognized that law, quite as much as technology, is the genuine and acceptable contribution of the West. This should help those who worry that there could be no common legal meeting ground or that it would be decades before all nations could reasonably discuss a constitutional framework such as the Clark-Sohn plan. As further testimony on the growing world acceptance of Western legal concepts I submit two paragraphs by Oliver J. Lissitzyn, Professor of Public Law at Columbia University. After discussing the quarrels underdeveloped nations feel with present international law which they regard as the creation of the former colonial powers to whose interests they suspect it is more addressed than to their own, he says however:

> "As non-Western countries have moved toward fuller participation in present-day economic and political life, they have come to realize that many of their legal traditions are no longer adequate to their needs. Most of these countries are adopting, in varying degrees, modern institutions, largely derived from those of the West. In some, reception of Western law has already reached an advanced stage. In the West itself law does not stand still. The effects on law of greater state participation in economic life and the rise of the 'welfare state' are likely to be world-wide. In the long run, this factor should serve to reduce differences in attitudes toward international law. . . .
>
> "Some diversity in attitudes toward law is bound to remain in the non-Western world, as in the West. But as the process of reception of modern law continues, there should be less and less reason to fear that differences of cultural heritage have produced an unbridgeable gap between Western and non-Western attitudes toward law in general and international law in particular. The long-term trend is toward greater uniformity of legal systems and traditions." *

* P. 58 and p. 60 from "International Law in a Divided World" (*Carnegie Endowment for International Peace*, March 1963).

The Wedding of the World's Civilizations

F. S. C. NORTHROP

When one examines the present encounter between the world's major civilizations, one sees that the peoples of Africa and Asia are adopting two major things from the modern West. The first is its technology, which requires of its creative practitioners a deep understanding of mathematical physics. The second is its contractual law, which entails a somewhat similar kind of imageless abstract thinking.

The world-embracing impact of modern science and its instruments is well known. The similar influence of contractual law is less generally recognized, but even more important, since it transforms not merely the instrumental values, but also the religious and political ideals and *de facto* normative social customs of a people.

This becomes evident when one notes how the recent new nations of Asia and Africa arose. First, their respective peoples had to achieve political independence from their Western rulers. This they did by appeal to the Westerners' own contractual legal and political principles, which were stated most clearly by the Stoics, Locke and especially Jefferson in the Declaration of Independence and the Bill of Rights of the American Constitution, upon which he insisted. Having thus succeeded in achieving independence, the leaders then had to decide what legal and political form their new nation would take. Had they returned to their religious, political and social beliefs and customs antecedent to the coming of the Western imperialists, there would be as many nations in Africa today, each rooted in racial purity and hierarchical tribal loyalty and authority, as there are countless local African tribes; and there would be as many theocratic nations in geographical India, at the present moment, under racially pure Aryan Hindu, high-caste religious and legal leadership as there were countless Hindu maharajas, to say nothing about the many medieval, theocratic Muslim Princely States. Clearly, this was not the choice that they made. Instead, they appointed a constitutional committee, composed of members trained in the constitutional, fiscal, and other constructs of Western contractual legal science, and authorized them to frame a constitution and nation, together with its monetary system, in which normatively all individual persons stand equally before a democratically determined contractual common law. A typical result is the Constitution of Free India with its Fundamental Freedoms that explicitly repudiate racial purity, patriarchal kinship, sexual primacy or joint-familial loyalty as the good, religiously or secularly, in either the state or social customs.

The economic legal construct is as important as the political and the normatively social in each of these new nations. There is, for example, the Bank of India and the Bank of Ghana after the manner of the Bank of England or the American Federal Reserve System. The existence of these fiscal institutions demonstrates the error in the frequently stated affirmation that economics is the key to law and politics, history, and everything else in the contemporary world. This error overlooks the fact that all contemporary economic, as well as political, institutions and transactions are contractual legal agreements and constructs. Like the unobservable, but indirectly and empirically confirmed elementary scientific objects of mathematical physics, the economic entities and activities of today's world are unobservable constructs of thought, subject, when correctly understood and operated, only to the contractually legal properties assigned to them syntactically by the construct, and made concrete and existential only indirectly by operational rules and acts of incorporation, or the like.

Consider a contemporary example: The General Motors Corporation. What is this entity? If we try to think of it in common-sense terms, we may visualize large factories in Detroit and elsewhere, but we soon realize that these do not make up its essential nature. For the factories may burn down or be replaced, with the General Motors Corporation preserving its identity through all these changes. Nor does the answer become any clearer if we shift attention from the buildings to the persons who administer this Corporation. They, too, successively die, though the Corporation persists. Moreover, they find themselves in trouble with the law unless they behave in accord with the contractual legal norms of incorporated entities. This suggests the answer to our question. The General Motors Corporation is a material instance of a contractual legal construct. More specifically, being incorporated in Delaware, it has the properties assigned to that fictitious construct of the Delaware legislative statutes which define syntactically the meaning of a limited liability corporation. Were it incorporated in Maine, it would be a similar, but nonetheless, in specific respects, slightly different entity.

The more precise meaning of what is being imported today from the modern West should now be evident. Briefly stated, the leaders of the new nations everywhere are importing the fruits of imageless, syntactically relational construct thinking. They are doing this with respect to natural science and descriptive theory of what *is,* and also in the humanities, including law, politics and economics. with respect to the norms that prescribe what *ought to be*.

The educational implication is obvious. The domestic cultural and the international problems arising from the present wedding of the world's civilizations cannot be understood, to say nothing about being constructively and peacefully solved, unless our entire educational system everywhere is radically reformed to make imageless, many-termed relational construct thinking elemental and continuous throughout the entire educational process, beginning in the most elementary grades. The important point to realize is that such education is as essential for an understanding of human values and the humanities as it is for a comprehension of mathematical physics and contemporary scientific technology.

Up to this point, we have been concerned with those factors in the present encounter between the world's major geographical areas and cultures which the rest of the world is taking from the modern West. In the contemporary West itself a scientific and philosophical reconstruction of its basic beliefs has occurred which already shows signs of making necessary a converse influence of the oldest Asian and non-Western cultures on Occidental thinking and behavior. Briefly put, there are reasons for believing that the modern Western world has, in our century, come to its end in precisely the same fundamental sense in which the medieval Western world came to its end when Galilei, Newton, Descartes and Locke articulated what seemed to them to be the basic scientific and philosophical beliefs of the modern era.

Perhaps the best way for me to approach the more concrete and positive meaning of what has happened is in autobiographical terms. In the early 1920's I went to the Imperial College of Science and Technology in London, to study the fundamental concepts in the scientific and mathematical reconstruction that occurred at the opening of this century, when Whitehead and Russell wrote their *Principia Mathematica,* Planck discovered the quantum of what later became quantum mechanics, and Einstein formulated his Special and General Theories of Relativity. The first time that I saw Whitehead, he said two things to me. The first was, "You must spend your days and your nights with Hume." The second was, "One cannot be too suspicious of ordinary language in science and philosophy."

What do these two statements mean? It is only in the last few years that I have come to what seems to me to be an understanding of Whitehead's words. Korzybski, incidentally, utters the same warning in his epistemology and semantics, urging us to beware of Aristotelian thinking, which is what he calls ordinary language thinking. If we amend Whitehead's statement slightly, it comes to read, "One cannot be too suspicious of any ordinary Aryan language in science and philosophy." This, of course, includes Greek, Latin, French, German, Spanish, *i.e.,* all the ordinary languages of the Western world, and, in addition, the Sanskrit of Aryan-Hindu India.

Why should we be suspicious of this kind of language? Its nature is that it has what logicians and epistemologists call a two-termed relational, thing-property syntax. This means that when we make a descriptive factual statement of any kind, our sentence must have a noun and a predicate term related to that noun by some form of the verb "to be." This is a requirement for correct English or Greek, Latin or Sanskrit usage. Such a syntactical language structure has the effect of causing us unconsciously to describe the facts of our experience in terms of things and their properties. Aristotle's physics was of this character, and so is ordinary common-sense thinking. Let me illustrate.

I experience an immediately sensed color which I denote linguistically with the word *blue*. Our Aryan prose syntax then leads me to put a substance beneath, so to speak, this quality, thereby providing the noun of which the *blue* is a prdicate. The result is the apparently innocuous sentence, "The water is blue." But one finds, with further observation, that this language lands one in certain difficulties. In the summer I live on the top of Shepherd's Hill overlooking a lake in New Hampshire. On a beautiful sunny morning I look out from my open screened study to immediately experience an emotively moving, vivid panoramic aesthetic continuum that is differentiated by countless colors, odors, and delicate sounds and occasional coolnesses standing clearly in a many-termed relation to one another. Even so, if I don't watch out, my ordinary language will cause me to single out but one of these multi-relational aesthetic qualities and say, "The water in Squam Lake is blue." A little later I walk down through the woods to the lake for a swim and notice, when I cup up a handful of its water to cool my head before the shock of plunging into that spring-fed lake, that "the water in Squam Lake" directly before my eyes in my hands is not *blue* but colorless. Then, following the syntax of Aryan language, I am on second thought liable to say that "The water in Squam Lake *appeared* to be blue," since, of course, I now know that "It is *really* colorless." Thus it never occurs to me that I should throw out all these substances underneath the blue that I first saw, the crystal clarity that I now see, and the terrifying blackness which I may later see when a dense thundercloud fills the sky. Instead, keeping the two-termed noun-predicate syntax of ordinary language, I populate the universe, since "the water is *really* colorless" with completely unaesthetic and unemotional little billiard balls too small to see, called "material substances." Thus, the materialists are born and, in the name of a factual description of observable experience and of physical science, the entire world of emotive, concrete, factual and aesthetic immediacy is turned into a phantasmic projection called "a mere appearance." Forthwith, art becomes effeminate and superficial; religion and morals lose their aesthetic and emotive sensitivity. Worst of all, in international law and politics, where, as noted above, normative, interpersonal universal lawfulness is of the essence, the self-defeating, tough-minded, heavy hardware power politicians pose as realists.

But this is not all. If our two-termed subject-predicate ordinary language syntax is to be saved, there must be an underlying substance as the projector of the phantasmic appearance which is purportedly the world of both cosmic and human nature which we directly observe. Moreover, the immediately experienced fact of emotive experience and consciousness cannot be denied. Ordinary language thing-property thinking thus leads one to add to the underlying unconscious and unaesthetic material substances a similarly unobserved spiritual or mental substance, as the projector of the phantasmic appearances and the subject of both emotive consciousness and thought. In this manner we find ourselves with the basic scientific, psychological and philosophical beliefs upon which both Descartes and Locke articulated modern mathematical physics and reared the modern world. Everything in both nature and human nature was conceived as an interaction between an aggregate of mental and material substances.

The theory was no more than formulated, when Descartes was asked where, in terms of this belief, the mind contacts the body. His answer was more amusing than illuminating and made evident to subsequent psychologists and philosophers that it leaves one with an insoluble body-mind problem.

Seen from the standpoint of the syntax of language, this traditional modern belief may be described as the product of taking the many-termed relational concrete facts of immediate experience and the inferred many-termed relational constructs of mathematical physics, and completely misunderstanding and misdescribing them by thrusting them into the Procrustean bed which is the thing-property thinking of the two-termed syntax of ordinary Aryan prose.

One meaning, at least, of Whitehead's statement that one cannot be too suspicious of ordinary language in science and philosophy should now be clear. What of his other statement to the effect that one must spend one's days and nights with Hume?

Hume's importance in the modern Western world is that more than anyone else, except William James, he brings our attention back to the immediately experienced facts of concrete experience, including both those of the so-called outer senses and those of the so-called inner introspection; thereby he makes it evident to modern Western thinkers, as did the Buddhists and nondualistic Vedantic Hindus in ancient Asia, and the Sophists, Democritean, Platonic and Stoic Roman thinkers in ancient Greece, that neither outer nor inner radically empirical immediate experience warrants the belief in a substance of any kind, be it material or mental.

At this point, the contemporary Western civilization and the ancient

Asian civilizations which are meeting today find something in common. For both, the material substances of the materialists and the mental substances of the personalistic pluralists and spiritualists are linguistic and metaphysical nonsense.

It does not follow from this, however, as the aforementioned Asians, the Greek Sophists and the modern Humean radical empirical positivists concluded, that there are no persisting entities and relations. All that follows is that the latter type of entities must be known and acquire their meaning in some other way than by reference to the directly observed. This other way the Democritean, Platonic, Stoic and contemporary mathematical physicists and philosophers of this subject know to be that of the aforementioned many-termed relational syntactical constructs. It was the discovery of these imageless constructs first made by Democritean, Platonic and Stoic mathematical physicists, and then applied to normative subjects by the Stoic legal scientists, that produced the Western contractual law of constructs which is today transforming the normative beliefs and customs of people throughout the entire world.

There is a further similarity between the Asian Buddhists and nondualistic Vedantic Hindus and the contemporary Western radical empiricists who have spent their days and nights with Hume. The generally accepted theory of ancient India's philosophy prior to the Buddha was Vaisesika dualism. Its position is similar to, if not identical with, the Lockean-Cartesian doctrine of mental and material substances with which the modern Western world began. Like the modern materialistic Hobbes, the Buddhists began their attack on this position by denying the meaningfulness or reality of any mental substance, while retaining material substances. This version of Buddhism is called realistic Hinayana. Then they proceed, after the manner of Bishop Berkeley in the modern West, to show that direct observation gives no warrant for the meaningfulness or existence of material substances, or the belief that we directly sense external public objects of any kind. But unlike Berkeley, who retained the belief in mental substances, this second movement in Buddhism rejected mental substances also. In this respect they did for ancient Asia what Hume made clear to the modern West. Positively expressed, this Buddhist equivalent of Hume is like what was called earlier in this century "neutral monism." This is the thesis that a noun such as mind is but a tag for a sequence of directly inspected feelings and images succeeding one another in time and perpetually perishing. Similarly, the noun "matter" is but a tag for such a sequence of perishing images of the so-called outer senses.

Buddhism, like the later nondualistic Vedantic Hinduism of Sankara, does not rest here, however. Both go on to point out that there is one factor in directly experienced, radically empirical immediacy which is not relative to the observer and not a perishing particular, and which is and remains always the same, both cosmically in nature and psychically within each one of us. This timeless factor the Buddhist denotes by the word "Nirvana" and the Hindu by the words "the Atman that is Brahman without differences." I shall try to direct your attention to this immediately experienced factor in radically empirically known nature and human nature as concretely as I can. It can only be pointed at by words; it cannot be literally said.

First, we must attempt, as far as possible, to remove all speculative theory from our minds and to concentrate attention on what we immediately apprehend, without any inferences beyond that immediacy either to underlying substances of any kind or to the imageless determinate constructs of mathematical physics or contractual law to which we referred at the outset of this paper. We note, as did Hume, the Greek Sophists, and the aforementioned ancient Asians, that in the realm of directly observed or experienced fact any item of inspection which is different from any other is temporal and perishes. As Professor Takakasu said at the beginning of his lengthy course on Buddhism in Honolulu in 1939, Buddhism begins with the directly observable, empirical fact that all such directly observed, determinate things are transitory. A determinate thing is any factor of fact that is different from any other after the manner in which a color is different from a sound, a blue color from a yellow one, etc.

So far as knowledge warranted solely radically empirically by observation is concerned, this thesis is true. Anyone can test it for himself. St. Paul gave expression to this thesis when he said that the things which are seen, meaning thereby determinate things, are temporal; they all perish. I have at a given moment a specific set of images. I can observe determinate things only with my senses. The objects of each of one's senses are not persisting substances, but successive, perishing images. From moment to moment these images change, the present ones perishing to be succeeded by a different, similarly perishing set. The same is true of the data denoted by the word "self" as given introspectively. This, as William James noted, is a succession of perishing moods and feelings, rarely twice the same. I am elated at one moment and dejected at another. Moreover, the self is as relative to the perishing images which entice attention as the images are relative to the perceiver. As William James put it, a man is what he interests himself in, the stock market, his golf game, abstract art, or what have you. The Buddhist Burmese give expression to this fact and belief by assigning a different name to a person in his religious interests from the name which he carries during his secular concerns.

This relativistic and perpetually perishing character of our directly experienced images and selves generates the second thesis of Buddhism: because all determinate things perish, all determinate creatures, both human and nonhuman, are doomed to suffer. This is a plain empirical fact of existence, since every differentiated thing we interest ourselves in, work for, cherish and love perishes.

But this is not all. The American philosopher and psychologist, William James, went one step beyond Hume in noting, as did the aforementioned Asians, that in the realm of purely factual, radical empirical immediacy there is one factor that does not perish. This is the all-embracing continuum of immediacy within which the many-termed relational perishing particular images of both the so-called inner and outer senses come and go. James expressed this as follows: It is only the portion of our radical empirical experience which is in the focus of attention that is sharply differentiated into successive perishing particular images; the periphery of radical empirical immediacy is vague and indeterminate. James noted also that religious experience derives more from this indeterminate and undifferentiated peripheral factor of immediate fact than from the perishing, imageful sensed particulars.

Within this account of the totality of radically empirical immediate experience, the Buddha's cure for the fact of determinate human suffering becomes meaningful. Were one's cosmic and psychical emotive experience and consciousness wholly determinate, after the manner of Hume, the fact of one's perishing and its attendant suffering would be the end of the story. The radically empirically informed Buddhist, similar to James, points out that each one of us is not only his transitory, radically empirical, perishing particular self, who may be a Dr. Jekyl at one moment and a Mr. Hyde at the next, but is also the cosmically all-embracing, indeterminate ocean-consciousness "without differences" within which these perishing particulars come and go. To cultivate, by radically empirical meditative and other means, the experience of this timeless, undifferentiated consciousness is to gain the equanimity and the unperturbable blissfulness from the standpoint of which one can view the pleasures and the sufferings of one's perishing particular differentiated self with equanimity. To do so is to achieve the Buddhist solution of the problem of suffering.

With respect to the radically empirical, differentiated perishing particular part of ourselves, all persons are different; with regard to the undifferentiated cosmic field component of ourselves, we are identical, not merely with one another, but also with the Divine consciousness. In Buddhism, therefore, as in its equivalent nondualistic Vedantic Hinduism, it is not a heresy to say "I am God," as it is in any of the three theistic Semitic religions.

What grounds are there for thinking that this radically empirical, descriptive account is thus at once both empirically true for radically empirically experienced fact and an immanent philosophy of religion? An examination of the usages of the words "religion" and "divine" shows that they may be viewed as but tags to denote those factors in empirically verifiable knowledge which are timeless. In the merely radical empirical component, the purely factual, noninferential part of our knowledge, only one factor is timeless, namely, the immediately experienced, all-embracing, undifferentiated continuum of immediacy within which all differentiations come and go. It is, therefore, appropriately identified with the Divine.

What reason is there for supposing that this holds true for anyone? The reason is that the radically empirical undifferentiated can never be defined away in terms of anything determinate and differentiated; the undifferentiated must, therefore, be taken as a primitive.

There is a second reason born of the experience of modern scientists and philosophers. One of the outstanding contemporary mathematical physicists, Schrödinger, a creator of the mathematics of quantum mechanics, writes to the following effect in his important little book, *What Is Life?* After noting that the theory of the pluralization of minds, which breaks consciousness into local atomistic mental substances, or Leibnizian monads, leads to the invention of souls, as many as there are bodies, and thereby generates the aforedescribed insoluble body-mind problem, Schrödinger concludes that the alternative is simply to keep to the immediate experience that "consciousness is a singular." This is to accept the Buddhist-nondualistic Vedantic theory. In fact, Schrödinger in his later book explicitly refers to the profound effect which these Oriental philosophies have had upon his thinking.

Such is the classically Oriental factor in the present wedding of the world's cultures. We conclude, therefore, that just as there is the aforedescribed world-embracing transformation of the beliefs and customs everywhere by the construct thinking of Western mathematical physics and its technology and Stoic Roman and modern liberal democratic normative contractual law, so the Western conception of radically empirical immediacy and both the human and the divine consciousness is moving toward and being deeply and profoundly influenced by the classical ideas of Buddhist and nondualistic Vedantic Hindu Asia. The same is true, as Professor Gardner Murphy's recent paper in *Main Currents* shows, of contemporary psychiatry. A corollary is that, when the radically empirical and the construct thinking parts of cosmic and human nature are correlated, humanistic normative, moral, legal, aesthetic and religious man and scientific man become one and the same person.

※ ※ ※ ※

Louis Lusky raises the doubts about a World Authority supported by World Law to keep the peace that many thoughtful persons must feel, even though they, like Lusky, long for it. He believes, as many such persons do, that its postponement for too long may bring an end of life on earth—and yet the doubts exist. Just as Tillich addresses himself to the encyclical, so Lusky addresses himself to the Clark-Sohn model. You will probably wish to read his article first and then turn to the comments upon it.

Four Problems in Lawmaking for Peace

LOUIS LUSKY*

We have out-dared Prometheus. We have grasped the power to destroy mankind with our atomic fire. And now we feel the chill of ever-deepening peril.

To be sure, there are significant forces working against war. The United Nations provides a medium of direct communication between most (though not all) nations, and thus reduces the danger that war will break out—as World War I may have done—because governments are badly informed about each other's intentions. And the United Nations facilitates third-party mediation of international controversies. Without its services, civilization might have perished at any of several critical moments during the past two decades.

A measure of security is also provided by "stable deterrence," which results from the tremendous gap between offensive striking power and the means of defending national populations against it. So long as each of two or more nations is able to destroy any attacker utterly, even after absorbing an all-out attack itself—an ability which the United States and the Soviet

* Louis Lusky was a clerk to U. S. Supreme Court Justice Harlan F. Stone before practicing law in New York and later in his native Louisville, Kentucky. In 1960 he carried to the United States Supreme Court and won the case known as Sam Thompson versus the City of Louisville. Thompson, a Negro handyman, had been twice fined for "loitering and disorderly conduct." The Supreme Court ruled that Thompson's civil rights had been violated and that the charges against him were unsupported by any evidence of guilt. Mr. Lusky is now professor of law at Columbia University Law School.

Union, at least, now appear to possess—it is unlikely that any deliberately planned major war (such as World War II) will develop.

Yet the danger of major war is great and growing. The United Nations, designed before Hiroshima when the possibility of a third world war was dreadful but not downright unthinkable, does not purport to provide any sure means of preventing war between two or more of the five major powers. "Stable deterrence" does not in fact afford full stability. Granted that no rational government can now deliberately initiate a program of world conquest, there is still the danger of accidental war (*vide Fail-Safe*) or irrationally caused war (*vide Dr. Strangelove*) or mutually undesired escalation. The mathematicians tell us that although the likelihood of such an outbreak in any given week or month or year may be quite small, the probability that it will take place *at some future time* is virtually 100 per cent. The simple multiplication of opportunities—even if not compounded by the increasing complexity of weapons—is enough to make it so.

It therefore behooves us, if we are interested in the survival of our civilization and our progeny, to cast about for greater security. In seeking it, of course, we cannot reasonably throw away such security as the United Nations and our arms now afford us. On the other hand, we can afford to give up our present protections in exchange for something better—if something better is truly available. The problem is to increase our *net* security.

As a basis for the present discussion of the difficulties which that problem offers, we posit the following propositions: (1) That the "something better" must include complete and universal disarmament. (2) That such disarmament is not in itself sufficient, and indeed would be dangerous unless coupled with enforceable world law against rearmament and war. (3) That a world federal system would be the most appropriate institutional matrix for such law.

It is not suggested that these propositions are self-evident, or that no one can reasonably dispute them. They have been widely discussed elsewhere, however, and their pros and cons need not be reviewed here. For present purposes it is enough that the propositions have been demonstrated to our own satisfaction by Grenville Clark and Louis B. Sohn, in *World Peace through World Law* (Cambridge, Mass., 2nd ed., 1960), and that we now adopt them as our postulates. The Clark-Sohn illustrative model of a world federal system also serves as a useful aid to concrete visualization of the difficulties which such a system would encounter.

As a final preliminary, we define "war" and "law," as those terms are used here. We use the term "war" to mean the use of physical force by one nation against another, excluding indigenous revolutions and civil wars which (as will presently be seen) involve special considerations. We use the term "law" to mean a rule of conduct which is applicable to individual persons rather than nations, and which is enforced by governmental action —action taken with sufficient regularity and vigor to assure a high level of observance, and enjoying such accepted legitimacy that it will effectively settle controversy without stimulating reprisal or escalation.

1

We know that it is not inherently impossible for a group of nations to form a federal system, establishing a central authority empowered to keep the peace between them by means of enforceable law binding on their people. The United States and other national federations have been so established and have successfully executed the purposes of their creation. The question is whether the ability to form such a federation depends on the existence of certain conditions which may not be present in the world today. If so, it is useful to know what those conditions are. Even if they cannot be changed immediately, we can at least understand what changes must take place before we can gain relief from the instability of "stable deterrence."

The Clark-Sohn proposal calls for world law against the possession and use of national armies and armaments, but not for law resolving economic and political conflicts of interest. Thus it is designed to eliminate the physical *ability* to wage war, but it does not provide for the making of laws to reconcile the clashing objectives that give rise to the *desire* for war. In this respect, their proposed system of world law would differ significantly from existing legal systems. Law, as we know it, does not stop with prohibiting *violence*. It also affords a peaceable means of settling the *quarrels that breed violence*. In effect, it says to each of us:

"Fighting is a bad way to settle a controversy. It wastes human life. It wastes wealth that is devoted to unproductive use such as the making of weapons. It renders life and property insecure not only for the contending parties, but also for bystanders. Moreover, it rarely effects a *final* settlement. Unless the beaten party and his supporters are wholly exterminated, their defeat will rankle and they will watch their chance to gather fresh supporters and turn the tables. Therefore, for the sake of the common good, men should be forbidden to fight over their controversies.

"However, controversies will always be with us. Men will quarrel over the right to possession of land or goods or river water or women, or will differ as to the meaning or binding character of their contracts, or will disagree as to which is the true religion or the best form of government. If fighting were the *only* way to settle these myriad controversies, it would be difficult to enforce the prohibition against it. But it is not the only way. The community can bring its judgment to bear on the merits of controversies, and settle them in conformity with *justice*—that is to say, in accordance with a code of social values which the community deems valid. Such settlements are likely to be accepted as final; for a defeated party is more disposed to acquiesce in a collective determination which the community declares to be just, than in a settlement imposed by the superior strength of an adversary.

"Therefore, at the same time that the law forbids fighting and other forms of violence within the community, it will also declare rules for measuring the merits of controversies by reference to community standards. The community will establish courts with authority not only to decree punishment for those who commit violence, but also to adjudicate questions of right and wrong between man and man. And some person or agency, whether a monarch or an elected legislature or something in between, will have the recognized power—as spokesman for the community —to change the rules of law from time to time in order to keep step with changes in circumstances or community values.

"In short, each man can and should be made to forgo the power of self-help in exchange for the community's undertaking itself to help him if it deems his cause to be just. The exchange is a fair and advantageous one, and reasonable men will be content with it. Enforcement of the prohibition against violence will thus be reduced to a relatively simple operation against a minority of social misfits, as compared with the much more difficult task that would be encountered if the law kept aloof from the merits of controversies, and did not offer justice (as well as protection from attack) in exchange for the power of self-help."

What is the nature of this "justice" that is offered as part of the bargain? To this question different societies give different answers. In a theocracy, it is said that justice is the will of God as interpreted by an official priesthood. In a totalitarian autocracy, it is said that justice is the will of the community as articulated by a dictator. In a constitutional democracy the concept of justice is more complex; it connotes not only the substantive ideal of government for the people, but preservation of objectively fair *procedures* whereby the people can exercise effective though peaceable control over their government. Such differences do have a significant bearing on the problem of creating world law, and we shall discuss them presently. But before commenting on the dissimilarities between the various legal systems the world has known, let us take note of one feature that all of them appear to have possessed: they have gone beyond the direct prohibition of violence, and have undertaken to settle the right and wrong of underlying controversy. As the source of standards for determining right and wrong, they have tendered a code of values that has made a more than negligible claim on men's loyalties. To be sure, those values have sometimes been primitive or neurotic; but even in Hitler's Germany, the law represented a value system which (however perverted) made an affirmative emotional appeal. Obedience to the law was demanded of Germans in the name of justice; and brazenly cynical though the demand may have been, it connoted a promise of comprehensive personal fulfillment far beyond the bare assurance of continued life.

By way of contrast, the world law proposed by Clark and Sohn would be explicitly related to one social value, and only one—the value of physical survival. True it is that this is the fundamental value on which all others depend. Justice and beauty and truth would have no meaning in a world devoid of life, or populated only by insects or microbes. Yet, in making a choice between the perils of "stable deterrence" and the security of world law, men will not overlook the fact that world law is offered in the name of necessity rather than justice.

It is not impossible to imagine such a legal system. Conceivably, a government might limit itself to forbidding its people to fight each other, and provide no legislative and judicial system whereby community standards could be brought to bear upon the merits of controversies. If the United States Constitution had denied to Congress such powers as the power to regulate interstate commerce, and had confined our federal government to the prevention of armed conflict between the states, our government might nevertheless be worth having. But the shape of our national society would be quite different from what it is.

States such as New York, Louisiana, and California, where the great seaports are found, could levy tribute on goods passing to or from the hinterland. States possessing important and relatively rare natural resources such as petroleum could ally themselves together to fix monopolistic prices. States with high wage levels could raise immigration and tariff barriers against cheap labor and its products. These and similar measures would stimulate reprisal in kind, and tensions would develop. The question is, would the federal law against interstate war be ungrudgingly obeyed under such circumstances? Or would people throughout the land come to regard that law as an obstacle to achievement of their "legitimate aspirations"? Fear of war would pull one way; rage against foreign imposition or oppression would pull against it. Literally, a tug-of-war.

History affords no basis for predicting the acceptability of a world legal system that is limited to what may be called "survival law," since the menace of war has never before been so hideous. This much, however, is clear: a system which forbids violence without offering justice begets an ambivalence. Men cannot submit to the law as wholeheartedly as they do when it promises peaceable redress of grievances as well as security from deadly attack.

Perhaps the difficulty could be avoided by empowering the world authority not only to prevent war but to make and enforce laws dealing with the substance of international controversies, just as our Congress is empowered to deal with matters occasioning conflicts of interest between states of our Union. Clark and Sohn have not overlooked that alternative. They make the judgment, however, that it involves an even greater difficulty, arising from the deep estrangements that now fragment mankind.

A legislature must function according to some sort of majority rule. Gross unfairness to the minority is always a theoretical possibility, but the degree of actual danger depends on the attitude the legislators have toward one another. If minority legislators are regarded by the majority as *colleagues,* representing people whose needs and desires deserve attention and understanding and objective evaluation, the danger of gross unfairness is small. In that event, the end product of the legislative process will be a good-faith effort to accommodate the competing interests of all segments of the constituent population. That is the essence of just lawmaking. Most legislatures approximate it fairly well, and grant a receptive and sympathetic hearing to the views of the "loyal opposition." If, on the other hand, the majority regard minority members not as colleagues but as *enemies,* whose views can rightly be ignored and overridden, the danger of gross unfairness is great.

Nations which are considering whether to join with other nations in establishing a world legislature will be conscious of this danger and will try to appraise it. All of them must reckon with the chance that their representatives will be in the minority at least some of the time—for no one knows beforehand what coalition of legislators will be in control, and what nations or races or ideologies will be in the minority, on any particular issue. If it seems probable that the minority will be despised and ignored, the nations may not dare to submit their differences for disposition by the world legislature.

Clark and Sohn appear to believe that any proposal which included establishment of a broadly authorized legislature would be rejected because of such fears. In the present state of the world, the fears cannot be dismissed as fanciful. Rich nations such as the United States might fear the wiping out of tariff and immigration barriers. Communist nations might fear, at a minimum, that their borders would be opened and the discipline of their people impaired by the seductive appeal of consumer goods and individual freedoms. Asians and Africans might fear exploitation at the hands of wealthier nations. Whites might fear the accumulated resentments of the huge nonwhite populations.

These apprehensions might shrink to manageable dimensions if the peoples of the world formed a true community, bound together by feelings of kinship and mutual concern. But the somber fact is that, in many cases, they see each other less as brothers than as stereotyped caricatures in the form of beasts or devils.

Under these circumstances, Clark and Sohn think it necessary to recommend that the powers of the world legislature be limited to the one subject-matter on which the interests of all nations point in pretty much the same direction, namely, the prevention of war. They do propose a

World Development Authority, to make monetary grants and loans for alleviation of disparities in national wealth and productivity. Those disparities doubtless breed deep international discord, and yet it is hard to say that they are the only, or even the primary, source of hostile pressures. They do not appear to have been a major cause of either of the two World Wars. Nor can it be said with assurance that elimination of grave economic inequalities would relax the tensions that now convulse the nations. The Arab-Israeli confrontation; the racial hostility between South Africa and Black Africa; the civil wars in Cyprus and the Congo; the Indonesian threat to Malaysia; Communist expansionism in Latin America, Southeast Asia, and elsewhere, opposed by the determination of the Western democracies to preserve the fundamental personal freedoms—all appear to result, at least in part, from factors other than disparities of national wealth. Therefore the World Development Authority, valuable as it might be, would not constitute a full substitute for legislative power to deal with the causes of war.

To summarize: Without a closer approach to universal brotherhood, the nations may not dare to submit their differences to a world legislature. But unless and until they are ready for that step, world law must limit itself to the objective of human survival, disclaiming jurisdiction to settle international controversies on their merits. Law thus limited may become acceptable only if utter destruction comes very near, so near that survival law is the only visible alternative.

II

There is a second difficulty. Suppose that some catastrophe or near-catastrophy had convinced all governments that "survival law" was a necessity. Suppose that they were willing to create a world authority possessing a monopoly of military power, but with legislative jurisdiction strictly limited to the prevention of war. The limitations on its powers would necessarily be based on the words of the organic document creating it. Clark and Sohn have framed such limitations as clearly and unambiguously as words can do it. They propose that legislation be limited to (a) laws authorized by the agreed plans for disarmament and for establishment of a world military force (which they call the Peace Force); (b) laws bringing into operation sanctions against non-complying nations; and (c) laws prohibiting and prescribing penalties for injury to U.N. property or personnel, illegal acts of U.N. personnel, violations of the disarmament plan, and the threat or use of force by one nation against another. But the question would remain, how efficacious are the words?

Men have become skeptical of the force of words not backed by power. Organizations, once they have been created, have been found to develop imperatives of their own—imperatives that demand fulfillment of the felt needs of the present, and scorn restrictions stipulated by their founders. The United States Constitution specifies the powers to be exercised by the federal government, and declares that powers not so granted are withheld. Yet Thomas Jefferson—the prototype of the strict constructionist—found himself constrained to approve, as President, purchase of the Louisiana territory. The Constitution did not authorize it, but the needs of the nation demanded it. For like cause Lincoln repudiated the right of secession. And as the states grew economically interdependent to a degree probably unforeseen in 1787, the commerce clause (after some delay) was held in the nineteen-thirties to authorize congressional regulation commensurate with the twentieth century needs of the nation.

We have seen the beginnings of a similar development in the United Nations. The stultification of the Security Council has led to the assumption of peace-keeping authority by the General Assembly and the Secretary General, which was not contemplated in 1945. To be sure, certain characteristics of the U.N. structure, such as its lack of a reliable source of adequate revenue, make uncertain the continuation of this development. But for present purposes it is enough to observe the tendency to disregard the verbal structure of the Charter and press the organization to satisfy the needs of the present.

We do not say that such developments are to be deplored. The United States and the United Nations have rendered far better service because of them. Had the United Nations not been able to transcend the circumstances of its birth, World War III might already have come and gone. Nevertheless, nations contemplating the creation of a world authority empowered to prevent war cannot blink the possibility that it may elect to go farther and deal with the *causes* of war. And again the fear of legislative injustice might appear.

III

Consider a third difficulty. Assume that all governments were agreed upon the need for "survival law," and were willing to take their chances that the stipulated limitations on the powers of the world authority would be observed. In order to gain the one thing they were bargaining for—relief from the danger of war—they would have to obtain solid assurance that the world law against war would be fully enforced. The question is whether full enforcement would involve unwanted side-effects.

Enforcement of prohibitions against armaments would not be a simple matter. Stocks of nuclear materials would have to be searched out wherever they were. Laboratories would have to be policed for activities capable of support to chemical or biological warfare. Caches of conventional weapons would have to be uncovered. Informers would have to be encouraged. And even if there were no significant attempts at evasion of the law, constant vigilance and surveillance would be necessary to provide the continuing assurance of universal compliance which alone would dispel the fear of war. Moreover, at least in the early years, enforcement operations would have to be carried out in areas where nationalistic feeling remained strong and xenophobia was rampant.

It is no easy task to enforce the law in a hostile, or even an apathetic, community. The United States government, powerful and accepted as it is, has not yet approached full success in extirpating the narcotics traffic or protecting the long-established rights of Negroes in the Deep South. This is not to say that it is *powerless* to accomplish these things. But they cannot easily be accomplished, in the face of popular apathy or local resistance, without resort to official force on a scale so massive as to jeopardize treasured personal freedoms.

How large a force would be required for the sure enforcement of world law prohibiting the making or possession of tools of war? With the full cooperation of national and local police establishments, the job could perhaps be done by a virtual handful of world police. Clark and Sohn appear to assume that such cooperation would be forthcoming, since they recommend a civil police force of only ten thousand—less than half the number now employed by New York City. (Their proposed Peace Force, with a standing strength of two hundred thousand to six hundred thousand and a Reserve of six hundred thousand to 1,200,000, would evidently be trained for military operations rather than routine police duty; it would be available to cope with organized large-scale resistance, but does not appear to be designed for the day-to-day work of criminal investigation and arrest of individual lawbreakers.) The ten thousand world police— one for about every three hundred thousand people, or an average of a dozen or so for each of the fifty states of our Union—would offer little threat to personal liberty and privacy.

The question remains, however, whether national and local police in all (or nearly all) countries would in fact cooperate. Keep in mind our assumption that world law would consist of "survival law" only, guaranteeing physical security but maintaining neutrality with respect to national aspirations or grievances. It is at least possible that chauvinistic demagogues would condemn the world police as watchdogs of an unjust *status quo*. In the United Arab Republic they might be regarded more as protectors of Israel than as guardians of the lives of Arabs and Israelis alike. In China they might be assailed as defenders of Taiwan; in Pakistan, as defenders of Eastern Kashmir; in Nigeria, as defenders of South Africa; in Eire, as defenders of Ulster. In our own country, within the past few years, we have seen states elect governors on a platform of noncooperation with federal law. We have also witnessed the consequent inadequacy of federal law enforcement, when state and city police have withheld their aid. Such experience suggests that compliance with world law may be achievable only through the creation of a world police force big enough to function effectively without local help.

A force of this kind would have to be much larger and stronger than the one proposed by Clark and Sohn. The problem of equipping it with authority adequate for vigorous and effective discharge of its duties, without exposing the general public to arbitrary and intrusive abuses of that authority, may not be easily solved. The gravity of the problem is indicated by the persistent refusal of Americans to establish a federal police force for enforcement of federal rights, even when certain of those rights are persistently flouted by state and local authorities.

A related, though probably less important, question can be raised with respect to the revenue system through which the world organization would be financed. Clark and Sohn have refrained from recommending a system comparable to our Internal Revenue Service, which operates directly on the taxpayer. Instead, they have proposed that the several nations be left in charge of tax collection. In principle, this would appear to leave the world authority subject to the same danger of paralyzing default that the United Nations now faces. Yet a direct collection system would add still another tier to an already burdensome—though indispensable—bureaucracy.

The existence of such problems does not mean that enforcement of world law is impossible. It does mean that the social cost may be high.

IV

Institution of a world law system would involve yet another difficulty, with respect to nations whose governments are not fully identified with the interests of their people as a whole. In this category are totalitarian governments that rule without the check of free elections, and governments such as the South African, which substantially disfranchises a great segment of its people and rules with the consent of the Caucasian minority only.

We have already noted the terms of the bargain that underlies present legal systems: surrender of the power of individual self-help, in return for security from attack and "justice" in the resolution of controversies. As a common denominator, each system includes the affirmation of social values (which, in the aggregate, officially define the Good Life) through the medium of rules of conduct—laws—premised on those values. (In order to have a name for the institution that formulates the laws, let us call it the "legislature"—even though we recognize that the legislative function is performed in some nations by a dictator or council not ordinarily referred to as a legislature.) We have also noted, however, that there is wide variation in the quality of the "justice" that different systems offer.

In this country and other democracies, the legislature is subjected to the effective control of the people who are bound by its laws. The validity of officially approved values is always open to re-examination. By protection of the freedoms of speech, press, assembly, and political association, the government itself shelters the development of public opinion critical of present law. And by protection of the elective franchise, it preserves the people's power to choose legislators who will translate public opinion into new law.

The knowledge that the corrective political processes exist is a powerful inducement to voluntary compliance with the present law. Even if a man regards it as bad law, in the sense that he believes it to embody inferior values or believes that it implements poorly the values it purports to serve, he will very probably obey it. For its very existence is prima facie evidence that most of his neighbors disagree with him, and think it is good law. Moreover, if he is right in thinking that a change in the law would benefit the community, he can reasonably expect the change to be made as soon as his fellow citizens learn where their true interests lie. And if he wants to persuade the community to his view, law protects his right to try it.

Under a nondemocratic system, where the people have no effective control over the legislature, a man is likely to have quite a different attitude toward a law he considers to be bad. He has no reason to think that his *neighbors* disagree with him; all he knows is that the *legislature* does. He knows that if he breaks the law the government will disapprove and will punish him if it finds out; but he also knows that his neighbors may not frown on him, and may even admire his action. And so he will ordinarily be less strongly impelled toward voluntary compliance than if he thought the law enjoyed general approval. A nondemocratic system must therefore rely more heavily on official coercion than does a democracy, in order to achieve the same degree of obedience to the law. And that means it must have a stronger police force. The term "police state" is a description, not an epithet.

Moreover, revolution is an ever-present danger in a nondemocratic system. Since there are no established procedures through which the people can peaceably bring about changes in the law, they can do it only by violence. The government knows it, and knows that the people know it. And the government's uneasiness is intensified by the realization that in the absence of free speech and meaningful elections it is difficult indeed to know whether and how deeply the people are dissatisfied with the existing law. Self-preservation thus dictates the need for a military force, loyal to the government, which is strong enough to suppress any probable insurrection.

The fact that nondemocratic systems need stronger police and military forces than democracies, to cope with purely internal problems, has a bearing on the problem of creating world law. Clark and Sohn rightly observe that disarmament involves restrictions on the size and weaponry of internal police establishments. (Hitler showed how readily policemen can be turned into soldiers, and put to aggressive use.) They propose a maximum of two police per thousand of population, which is about the size of the state and local police forces in the United States. But they also observe, again quite rightly, that world law can be instituted only with the approval of the governments of all the large nations and most of the others. If a strict limitation of internal police forces were accepted by the rulers of such nations as mainland China, the U.S.S.R., Spain, Portugal, Hungary, Yugoslavia, Indonesia, and South Africa, would they be signing their own death warrants?

Perhaps this difficulty might be avoided if the world authority were obligated to protect the national governments from revolution as well as external attack, just as the United States government is bound to defend the states from domestic violence as well as foreign invasion (Constitution, Article IV, §4). But this would mean that the world authority, in order to obtain the governmental consent necessary to its creation, must commit itself to perpetuation of the servile status of those unhappy peoples who lack the means of controlling their national governments. This may be part of the price of survival, and perhaps it would be agreed to. But it would be deemed a high price by some other nations—including, it may be, the whole of Black Africa; and they might balk at it.

As a matter of fact, these latter nations might go farther. They might refuse to join in the establishment of world law unless the law included guarantees comparable to the Civil War amendments to the United States Constitution, which protect the fundamental liberties of individuals from invasion by their own state governments. But adoption of a world bill of rights of this character doubtless would exacerbate the objections of totalitarian and racist governments. The question is whether there is *any* course of action which will not render the proposed world law unacceptable to one group or the other.

Conclusion

An effort has been made to articulate what are believed to be the major obstacles to institution of a system of world law under present conditions. The obstacles arise not from lack of ingenuity in devising a plan, but from deficiencies in our human societies and institutions—the alienation which flows from men's inability to feel kinship with their brothers of different tongue or creed or color, at home and around the world, and the precariousness of the power held by governments not controlled by their people. If these things block us off too long from the establishment of world peace through world law, they must be changed; otherwise they may bring the end of life on earth.

※ ※ ※ ※

All of these objections must be thoughtfully considered. Let us list Lusky's four problems and examine whether they are as intractable as they seem to him.

Problem I—"Survival Law" is not enough. There must be a way for community standards to be brought to bear on the merits of controversies other than the prevention of outright violence. To gain this, should the power of the world authority be increased to more resemble the type of law we know? But this cannot be, he says, because there isn't enough *trust* between peoples to be willing to give the necessary power to a world legislature (the revised Assembly of Clark and Sohn); and yet men and nations want *justice*. What he means by this here is not exactly synonymous with social justice. He means that which makes people here at home obey a law even if they don't like it. They think of it as "just" because they know the channels of corrective action are kept open and because there is a legislature that is trying to take into account objections. There is nothing like this in sight on the world level.

It is true that the Clark-Sohn plan, viewed strictly, does provide only "survival law." It provides enforceable ways to settle disputes that threaten world peace only. But it by no means fails to promote and facilitate justice in many ways which Lusky virtually ignores. Louis Sohn says that their plan does provide for "justice law" as well, but in a novel way—not by legislation like common law, but through the Equity Tribunal. If this mediation fails, then, if the legislature (the Assembly) decides to enforce a certain decision of the court it is, in effect, a law for that special occasion. Many disputes over "the possession of land, or goods or river water" would be settled in this way, much as many labor-management disputes are settled in the United States.

None the less, one must return to the heart of Lusky's objection: there are no community standards for the world as a whole. Therefore world legislators cannot regard each other as "colleagues," able to settle varied controversies with reasonable fairness. Consequently he sees survival law as purely negative, frustrating, unable to inspire loyalty.

One can, however, look at it slightly differently: if one regards law as able to play a part in realizing certain strongly held values of a society —a point of view which is being demonstrated in practice by some recent decisions of our own Supreme Court (such as the one on reapportionment to one man one vote), and one which is increasingly recognized by legal scholars and teachers—one can study the Clark-Sohn plan and see that what they have done is to look at the world community and say; "There is one extremely important value that just about everybody agrees on today which no existing system takes care of, which is that the mass murder of modern war is intolerable. Mankind must be free of it." And they go ahead and create a system which gives prominence to this one value. This is as far as they judge right to go for the present.

As I see it, different values are uppermost at different historic periods in any society. Soon or late they get formally recognized through an interacting process between public sentiment (including the needs of the time), government (the sovereign), and law. Public sentiment must always be there, because in the long run and usually even in the short, both law and government are worthless without it. Often the value trickles down to law last. But law can also consciously assist a society to realize certain values which the times demand and which are widely supported by public sentiment. It seems to me that this part played by law is especially important in a large diffuse society like the world community. A commonly held law helps a society become conscious of itself—indeed, helps those diverse legislators to become "colleagues" in just the sense Lusky wants. I personally can think of nothing more exciting than a few genuine world laws.

It is the same system Lusky and I are looking at, with the same limitations. It is simply a shift from a negative to a positive approach to law itself, an approach which I suspect will be more and more needed by mankind.

Certainly the expectation of justice must be there. It seems likely, however, that a Clark-Sohn type world government, with powers only to eliminate war as an instrument of national policy, would create a climate more favorable to the evolution of justice in Lusky's sense for the nations than our present system since so many disputes between nations arise out of fear, and out of what they consider "vital interests" for security. Beyond question the opportunity for increased social justice under an Economic Development Authority such as Clark and Sohn would provide, and on the scale that would be possible in a disarmed world, is enormous.

It has been suggested (by Edgar Snow, at the Second Dublin Conference October 1965, among others) that the World Authority, in addition to its war prevention powers, should have one tool: The right to have full access to *information* as to conditions within a country (*e.g.* about apartheid in the Union of South Africa, about the absentee landlords and landless Indian population in many South American countries) and to *make these conditions known* to the rest of the world. The effect recently of massive television exposure of conditions in the South in this country would support this view. Even the briefest look at the future indicates that electronic communications and new programming based on computerized knowledge and new-developing learning techniques are revolutionizing our total environment even more radically than did the invention of the printing press, and in a way hard to realize. Electric circuitry, which is a fact of our environment, brings people in relation to each other on a scale and with a total involvement hitherto unknown. Nor is there even need to look ahead as regards the power and wide dispersal of modern means of communication. You will remember that Boulding comments (in his article in Section I) that he would not be surprised to find that radio (which is cheap, everywhere, and does not depend on literacy for its effect) is the most important agent of social change today. This does not overlook the grave possibilities of misuse of modern communications, such as the current "nationalization of truth" (*i.e.* managed news), but widespread reporting of actual conditions by a respected world authority would have a great effect.

It seems not only possible but probable that a sufficient minimum common sense of justice to underlie world law would evolve fairly rapidly. Through exposure, social ills are made known, conscience aroused, and also the less appropriate ideas of justice and procedures would wither away (as an extreme illustration: if trial by water as practiced in the Middle Ages were displayed along with other means of determining guilt accepted as a matter of course in civilized places today, it would soon be voluntarily abandoned—the idea of justice of the people who had used it would be changed and brought more in harmony with man-kind's). Our own views too might be changed or modified. Certainly the sense of justice of many white Southerners is being altered.

It seems reasonable, I believe, to consider that Lusky's Problem I, though serious, is not insuperable.

Problem II—"Survival Law" might grow and then what might you have? This is the exact opposite of the first worry which deemed survival law not enough.

One must risk something somewhere. Clark and Sohn have sought to walk between many risks. They concluded that the prevention of war was all that was safe or wise for this generation to undertake. They present institutions for that purpose designed not to increase in power until an immense majority of mankind wished it. They believe the creation of those institutions is a far less risk than the virtually inevitable catastrophe of continuing as we are. The risks of both I and II must be judged not against perfection but against the clear risks of our present course. If we judge the risks of World War III to be very great, and we desire to avoid it, we must consider just how much world law is required to prevent it. Our own emotional feelings about the degree to which we feel mankind to be one community, or capable of becoming one community, will enter into our feeling whether the dangers in Lusky's Problem I or his Problem II appear the greater.

Problem III—Enforcement of a law cannot be carried out where the local populace is against it without use of force so great as to destroy the very freedom and justice that we conceive law as designed to support. This is essentially the same dilemma posed by Tillich: with the nature of modern weapons, the use of overwhelming force, even in a "just" cause, destroys justice. And yet authority vanishes without the ability to maintain itself. Lusky points out that without the cooperation of the local (*i.e.* national) police the World Police could not succeed and could not use its full force to force success because of the paradox above. He cites the difficulty of enforcing Federal law in some of our own Southern states which deliberately chose not to cooperate. It is not that the Federal government lacks the physical power to enforce its laws— but to do so against local sentiment would be extraordinarily disruptive of the very life that we think of as supported by law—a sense of free will rather than dictatorial oppression.

This is true, and if we project this sort of occurrence (many of us, during the civil rights crises in Alabama, *wanted* the Federal strength to exert itself more forcibly) into the unfamiliar setting of the world level it can give pause. Yet if we look at our own Southern states, since Lusky wrote his article, we see that changes have been and are taking place. They have been achieved by a combination of factors. There has been *some* show of force by the Federal authority—not much, and by no means all of which the Federal government was capable, but enough to seriously question the local authority and to represent the presence of another "legitimate authority" than the local government, and another principle of what is right.

Moreover, with this has been that very important modern factor which Lusky does not take into account: widespread information—news and television coverage which showed the rest of the country what was taking place in those states. This forced them willy-nilly into a larger framework of public opinion—this prevented their being able to stay with their own views undisturbed—and the "sense of justice" that Lusky rightly says is a necessary part of satisfactory law enforcement became to a certain extent that of the whole aroused country, which began to be felt within the Southern states themselves.

It is possible that compliance with World Law in a reluctant nation-state might come about in much the same way: a relatively small World Police Force, which represents another "legitimate authority" than the nation-state with another view of what is right; plus widespread information—actual sight on television, for instance, of illegal military installations, of local (*i.e.* national) police clashing with the representatives of the world authority—which would bring into play the pressure of world opinion including undoubtedly some perhaps otherwise timid opinion within the arming nation itself. By both means "the law habit"—to use a phrase of Richard Falk's—presently very weak as regards international law but nonetheless existent, would be encouraged.

In Problem IV, Lusky asks, in effect, whether in order to *get* World Law you would have to bribe the dictatorships by promising to preserve the status quo from internal revolution.

For anyone who envisions the kind of system change, grounded in life, and the needs of peoples, that this Reader seeks to explore, the answer must be unequivocally No. Too many peoples live under governments from which they are totally excluded. The desire to have some say in determining one's destiny is, among a growing number of people in many places, stronger than hunger and stronger than the desire for life itself. There are too many changes that must take place to correct these situations to imagine that they can all take place in perfect peace and it seems clear that a period of internal revolutions is ahead of us. Moreover, in any living society there can never be a perfect status quo. In our own society, we have reasonably well solved the problem of peaceful change. But we must not forget that "in a real sense, voting is an approximation of picking sides before a street fight" (from H. L. Nieburg, *Uses of Violence* which is quoted again below). It is to the advantage of everyone to count heads, abide by the ballot box and call off the fight, the loser knowing that in the next election he has another chance. Moreover, "A democratic system preserves the right of organized action by private groups, risking their implicit capability of violence. By intervening at the earliest possible point in private activities, the totalitarian state increases the chance that potential violence will have to be demonstrated before it is socially effective. On the other hand, by permitting a pluralistic basis for action, the democratic state permits potential violence to have a social effect with only token demonstration, thus assuring greater opportunities for peaceful political and social change." But this system too recognizes that in the last analysis the deeply committed person can resort to violence to show the strength of his commitment. If, like Norman Morrison, his values prevent him from using violence against others he may turn it against himself. As one considers this problem of peaceful change, it is useful to ponder the conclusion of H. L. Nieburg to his study of the uses of violence: "No system can hope to survive unless it can live with and adjust itself to the multitudinous threats of violence which are the basis of social change. Democracies have shown a greater ability to do this. However, this is not to rule out the possibility that, even within totalitarian forms, substantial democracy can be achieved. On the other hand, democratic forms can be subverted to become totalitarian in substance, if the search for infinite security in the international forum is reflected internally by the search for infinite deterrence of threats against the social and political status quo. Major social changes have major social causes; they are not the result of isolated conspiracies and plots. They cannot be arrested by an effort to stamp out all conspiracies and plots." Needless to say, the drive to employ violence to achieve social change is immeasurably greater in societies where the ballot box is meaningless.

The problem that a limited world government with authority only to prevent violence between nations is faced with, is how to handle the internal revolutions which in many areas of the present world are the only means to obtain social change. The Clark-Sohn plan provides no solution, but it does not authorize the World Authority to guarantee the internal status quo. Only when more than one nation enters the conflict does the World Authority of Clark-Sohn become involved. This leads at once to a further problem—how do you make sure the revolution stays a purely internal one? Which at once brings up the question: What are the tolerable limits of indirect aggression and subversion (which is generally considered the practice of the Sino-Soviet bloc although the C.I.A. has not been entirely innocent) and of intervention (which is generally considered the practice of the United States)? Even without a disarmed world a thorough airing of this subject would be helpful—difficult though it is, as demonstrated by the lack of success to date of two recent special U.N. committees—with as much agreement as possible on standards of behavior in this respect. United States efforts to *maintain* the status quo in many parts of the world through military aid, through economic aid tied to "friendship" to the U.S., as well as through direct military intervention, can be viewed quite as much as a form of aggression as Soviet and Chinese efforts to penetrate and stimulate the *overthrow* of the status quo. Both techniques equally inhibit the freedom of the nation in question and create the danger that any internal revolution may escalate into world war. (Such an open discussion might also help the underdeveloped nations to understand that they too could do more to improve matters, by refraining from "shopping around" for aid which only augments the tension, just as with the children of quarreling parents playing off one parent against the other. Any good family counsellor would recommend a general discussion and some modification of behavior by everyone.)

A picture of how social change might take place in a disarmed world will be found in the article by Walter Millis at the end of this section. The problem of the World Authority's relationship to internal revolutions, however, remains a difficult one.

※ ※

Sovereignty I

Throughout this Reader to date has lurked the issue of *sovereignty*. It is now time that we meet it head on.

There are thoughtful, concerned persons who cling to the nation-state as inevitable, God-given and inviolate. (The political writing of Reinhold Niebuhr, for example, often seems to support the view that the nation-state is the best form of society possible.) They strive to find the "solution" to our many problems, particularly war, in terms of this image. They recognize that war must be prevented, and they see sovereign nations working together to this end. One can say that they see an *international* order. They think in terms of balance of power and spheres of influence and of *international* law.

There are others who see the nation-state as less important than the newly emerging concept of mankind. They see the nation-state as less useful today to serve the needs of men who make it up and ultimately are its source of power and its *raison d'être* than other structures and institutions might be. They see a *supranational* or *world* order. They think in terms of world institutions, of varying degrees of development, and of *world* law.

My own instinctive kinship is toward the latter or world view, and with it the view that sovereignty—which is the possession of people to bestow where it seems best to them—must be scaled up to world institutions for certain needs and functions, and scaled down to local communities for others—not necessarily to the old political communities but to the actual communities of today. I am thinking, for instance, of the great urban conglomerations of today which, like the global community, are a new development without adequate structures and institutions for their urgent and obvious needs. At the same time, I acknowledge a strong emotional attachment to my country. I am proud of her unique contributions in the past, I suffer when I see her fall short of herself in the present. I feel myself very much an American and that this is part of my *identity*, like my name, like the name of my mother and my father which I carry with me and is part of me. But it is not *me*. It is less necessary for my psychic well-being than it was even fifty years ago when patriotism, membership in my own special in-group, gave me greater strength and coordination to meet the real world. Today, the democratic ideal of the self-determining individual (which has come to full flower and which the young people feel so strongly), the inventions—from the power-driven machine to the computer, the development of the scientific method of research which has removed factual ignorance and shattered bondage to nature—have transformed modern life. The nation-state (in the case in question, America—although in this context I would probably choose to say "the United States") is not the carrier of mystical religious content any more but an economic-political organization in hard and unremitting competition for material supremacy and resources with other economic-political organizations. I am set free. The real emphasis is on me, the individual, and I can choose where I bestow power on institutions to serve my needs most effectively. The social unit that stirs me, and which can be said to carry mystical religious content for me, is the emerging world. At the same time I recognize that this same emotion, which I in my democratically and technologically advanced country have so lately begun to outgrow, is even now awakening in many peoples hitherto repressed by other nations who *need*, for their psychic self, this sense of national identity, and therefore, along with a nascent sense of mankind, there is also what is generally spoken of as a period of nationalism before us. Rightly understood, and recognizing that there is a still higher loyalty to mankind, nationalism fosters diversity which is a value I cherish.

Grenville Clark sees the central problem as more simple than either complete internationalists or complete supranationalists do. One might say that a particular relevance of the Clark-Sohn model to our period in history is that it partakes of some of the outlook of both.

The core of the problem, as Clark expresses it is: "There is no enforceable law against maintenance by any nation of whatever armaments it chooses; no enforceable law against war by any nation for any cause or no cause; no standing world police force; no tribunals to which all nations are required to submit their disputes." This leads to the present national military power system, *i.e.* the security of each nation is dependent on its power relative to its neighbors and potential enemies. Hence the arms race. Equally important is the fact that for *all* national governments the security of their nation is properly paramount. Again, hence the arms race. Clark says that if you can focus on and properly solve this one problem, the security problem, so that there isn't this justifiable fear, then all other problems and the opportunities to deal with them are seen from a totally different perspective.

Clark contends that the solution to the national security problem in the present age can only be found by a *radical operation*, a true system change. The Clark-Sohn plan proposes world law only in the field of war prevention. But it would have that much. To have even that much violates the perfect (in theory) sovereignty of the nation-state. That is the system change. The Charter of the United Nations does not take this step.

The following, almost passionate, article by Hans Morgenthau (from *The New York Times Magazine*, Sunday, March 14, 1965) deals with both the desperate need for a strong United Nations and the crippling inadequacies in its present structure due to national sovereignty.

He says at the beginning "The congenital disease [of the U.N.] is the insoluble contradiction between national sovereignty and an effective international organization." He says in the middle that the U.N. is "neither a luxury nor a nuisance but a necessity." And he says at the end "The potentialities of the United Nations are more important still. For the U.N. has taken the first hesitant step towards developing into a *supranational* authority which would protect the interest of its members and thereby insure order and peace throughout the world. In the nuclear age, nations can no longer afford to protect and promote their separate interests through the traditional use of force without risking their own destruction. They need a *supranational* authority which will do for them what they can no longer afford to do."

But, in between, it is as though he did not always take the consequences of his own thinking. It would seem that he wants the U.N. to function pretty much as do Clark and Sohn—with *authority* in the settlement of international disputes (although he sees always this bugbear of sovereignty lurking unsolved). Even his suggested possible change in the General Assembly—*i.e.* the delegation of some of its functions, especially in the peace-keeping field, to a small representative committee—has an interesting resemblance to the proposed seventeen-member Executive Council, chosen by the General Assembly from among their own members, of Clark and Sohn. At the same time, Morgenthau disparages "tinkering with the Charter," although he sees so clearly that the "congenital disease" of the U.N. which inhibits it at every turn is the absolute sovereignty of the nation-state which is written into the Charter. It is probable that Morgenthau thinks that changes in the Charter are useless because he sees no chance of achieving them, that there is not time to bring them about, that our need for the U.N. is so great that it is better to keep going as is than risk structural changes—rather than because he would not like to see them take place. I think it is possible that he overlooks the importance of analyzing those weaknesses in the Charter that inhibit the U.N., of constructive thinking as to what is really required, of sufficiently broad understanding of what it is we want, so that when opportunities for change occur—and they do occur—we will be able to seize them. And perhaps he underestimates the acceptability of certain carefully considered changes in which everyone could see a net gain.

The U.N. of Dag Hammarskjöld is Dead

HANS J. MORGENTHAU

"The United Nations is in crisis," I wrote in this magazine on Oct. 29, 1961. "Will it survive? The diseases from which it suffers are both congenital and acquired. The congenital disease is the insoluble contradiction between national sovereignty and an effective international organization. Its acquired debilities are the lack of political cohesion among the new nations and the hostility of the Soviet Union."

The General Assembly, which has just adjourned without transacting any business requiring a vote, has answered the question I then raised. The United Nations which Dag Hammarskjöld molded into "a dynamic instrument of governments" is dead. Why did it die? How can it be revived? How can the world get along without it?

The controversy that paralyzed the recent General Assembly was legal in appearance but political in substance. Article 19 of the Charter provides that "a member of the United Nations which is in arrears in the payment of its financial contributions to the organization shall have no vote in the General Assembly if the amount of its arrears equals or exceeds the amount of the contributions due from it for the preceding two full years." The Soviet Union was in that position at the opening of the recent session on Dec. 1, 1964; France and a number of small nations were in it on Jan. 1, 1965.

The Soviet Union and France maintain, despite a contrary advisory opinion of the International Court of Justice, that they are not obligated to pay for peace-keeping functions which the United Nations has established against their own vote. They argue that only the Security Council, in which the great-power veto protects them from being outvoted, is competent to order peace-keeping measures, such as those in the Gaza Strip and the Congo, which were authorized by a two-thirds majority of the General Assembly.

If the provisions of the Charter had been applied, the Soviet Union would have been automatically deprived of its vote at the beginning of the recent session and France and the other delinquent nations after Jan. 1 of this year. The United Nations would thus have asserted its authority even against great powers among its members. By doing so, it would have risked an open split within its ranks or even of defections from them.

A number of member states were unwilling to take this risk and even the United States, while emphatic in words about its resolution to apply Article 19, was unwilling to bring the issue into the open by asserting the authority of the United Nations. Instead of voting, the General Assembly operated through "unanimous consensus," that is, it transacted only that kind of business for which there was unanimous consent; and that consent was established not through formal votes in the assembly hall but through informal agreements in the lobby. And when, on the last day of the session, Albania tried to bring the issue into the open by moving that the General Assembly resume its ordinary voting procedure, that motion was voted down. In this vote the delinquent members participated—on the legally untenable ground that Article 19 covers only substantive but not procedural votes.

These legal positions and arguments are the mere surface manifestations of a conflict inherent in the very structure of the United Nations. It is the conflict between national sovereignty and effective international organization. These two concepts are irreconcilable in theory and practice. In the measure that an international organization is effective, it is bound to impair the freedom of action of its members, and in the measure that the member states assert their freedom of action, they impair the effectiveness of the international organization. The U.N. Charter itself testifies to that unresolved conflict by stressing, on the one hand, the "sovereign equality" of all member states and, on the other, assigning to the permanent members of the Security Council a privileged position amounting to a limited world government.

The Soviet Union from the very outset, and France since de Gaulle's ascension to power in 1958, have been the champions of national sovereignty. The Soviet Union has protected itself against being outvoted in the Security Council through the frequent use of the veto, and it violently opposed the first two Secretaries General, Trygve Lie and Dag Hammarskjöld, as the symbols and practitioners of the collective will of the United Nations. When Hammarskjöld transformed his office into a kind of prime ministership the Soviet Union countered with the proposal for a "troika," to make the office of Secretary General into a collectivity of three acting in unison, of which one third would be controlled by Moscow. Its refusal to be held financially responsible for the peace-keeping functions of the U.N. is consistent with the general policy it has pursued toward the United Nations from the outset.

Yet, while the Soviet Union in the past was unsuccessful in thwarting the collective will of the United Nations, it succeeded this time. What accounts for that success? The answer comes in two interconnected parts, the roles of the United States and of the new members.

The United States has been the most consistent and influential champion of the collective will of the United Nations. It was able to play that role because it could regularly count upon broad support for its major policies. This support has been virtually automatic in the Security Council where the Soviet Union has found itself regularly in a minority of one or two. It was also assured in the General Assembly during the first decade or so of the U.N.'s existence. The apogee of American influence was the Uniting for Peace Resolution of 1950 through which the General Assembly assumed the peace-keeping functions which the Charter had assigned to the Security Council before the Council became paralyzed by the veto.

The General Assembly session of 1955 was a turning point in the history of the United Nations, and from then on the influence of the United States has steadily declined. In that session, the U.N. admitted sixteen new members and thereby started the massive expansion of its membership from the original fifty-one to the present 114. This expansion destroyed the political cohesion of the General Assembly and rendered it incapable of forming a two-thirds majority in support of substantive policies of any kind. The best it could do was, as in the case of the Congo, to delegate broad discretionary powers to the Secretary General, who then had to devise policies of his own without being sure of the political support of two thirds of the membership.

This disintegration of the political will of the General Assembly is in good measure the result of the political weakness and disorientation of many of the new members. Most of them are former colonies, lacking one or more of the attributes of nationhood. They are united only in a fierce and now somewhat outdated opposition to colonialism. Proud of their new independence, they find it hard to admit that they are in need of being protected and supported by someone. Thus, while the new nations have a vital interest in a strong United Nations, they have been unable to translate that interest into effective policies.

When the Russians defied the U.N. last December, they were confronted not with a phalanx of two thirds of the membership united in defense of the organization under the leadership of the United States, but with a conclave of disorganized, timid, and uncertain members united only in the desire to avoid a showdown. It is a moot question whether stronger American leadership could have marshaled a two-thirds majority and whether in a showdown the Soviet Union would have backed down, as it had before. But that leadership was lacking, and the Soviet Union was able to win an easy victory.

This victory amounts to a veritable counterrevolution against the United Nations as it developed in practice. According to the Charter, the Security Council was to be the executive organ of the United Nations while the General Assembly was limited to discussions and nonbinding recommendations. The Security Council was to be dominated by the five permanent members—the United States, the Soviet Union, Great Britain, France and China—which, acting in unison and protected from being outvoted by the veto, were to operate as a kind of limited world government. The Secretary General was to be the administrative head of the permanent bureaucracy.

This constitutional scheme was never put into operation. For the Security Council fell into virtual desuetude; the General Assembly took over the executive functions the Security Council was unable to perform; and the Secretary General emerged as the chief executive of the United Nations.

These extraconstitutional developments made the United Nations an effective international organization, but the successful Soviet challenge has now nullified them. It has returned the United Nations to the original intentions of the Charter. That means in practice that the Security Council becomes again the chief executive organ, still threatened with paralysis by the veto, that the General Assembly is reduced essentially to a debating society, and that the Secretary General is stripped of the executive powers which the General Assembly had bestowed upon him. That is to say, the Security Council is powerless, the General Assembly is powerless, the Secretary General is powerless. The United Nations has ceased to be an effective international organization.

How can its effectiveness be restored? Three types of proposals have been advanced: revision of the Charter, procedural changes and political arrangements.

Whenever an institution does not operate as it is supposed to, the legalistic-minded among us, of whom there are many, seek to manipulate the rules by which it functions. Thus, when the League of Nations was in a similar crisis, after the failure of its sanctions against Italy in 1935, its friends tried to save it with revisions of the Covenant. It was to no avail. For the fatal disease of the League of Nations was not constitutional but political, and the constitutional changes were irrelevant to these political factors.

Secretary General U Thant, in his address of Feb. 20 before the convocation on *Pacem in Terris,* called for revision of Chapter VII of the Charter dealing with "Action With Respect to Threats to the Peace, Breaches of the Peace, and Acts of Aggression" because it is out of date. Even if one assumes for the sake of argument that this is so—I doubt that it is—the revision of these provisions could have no appreciable effect on the cooperation of the great powers upon which the effectiveness of the Security Council depends, nor upon the political cohesion of two thirds of the members upon which the effectiveness of the General Assembly depends.

Other proposals for the revision of the Charter appear to seek not so much to strengthen the U.N. as to assure its impotence. Thus President de Gaulle, in his press conference of Feb. 4, gave a brilliant analysis of the history of the United Nations, sharply disapproving of the extraconstitutional developments which made the General Assembly and the Secretary General more powerful than the Charter intended them to be. He suggested that the great powers "return to the point of departure" and to that end called for negotiations to reach an agreement on that point.

Yet if what President de Gaulle wants is a return to the intentions of the Charter, which under present political conditions signifies an impotent United Nations, no new agreement is needed. As we have seen, the original meaning of the Charter has already been restored and the impotence of the United Nations thus assured. What President de Gaulle obviously wants to achieve through an additional agreement is to prevent the United Nations from again becoming an efficient instrument of international government through developments not envisaged in the Charter.

Similarly irrelevant, if not counterproductive, are the proposals to enlarge the membership of the Security Council. This is the remedy upon which the League of Nations hit in the thirties, and it proved to be completely useless. The Security Council consists at present of five permanent and six nonpermanent members. What would be gained by enlarging the number of the latter?

It would satisfy the vanity of the new members and it would depreciate the value of membership in the Security Council. But it would do nothing to increase the Council's effectiveness, for its decisions would still be subject to the veto of any permanent member. At worst, it would make the Security Council even more unwieldy an instrument of government than it is now.

More promising are the attempts at changes in the procedure of the General Assembly. The expansion of its membership and its concomitant inability to fashion a workable two-thirds majority have paralyzed it as the Security Council has been paralyzed by the veto. If the General Assembly could delegate some of its functions, especially in the peacekeeping field, to a small representative committee, it might recover some of its ability to act effectively on behalf of peace and order. The Secretary General has appointed a committee to study this question; it deserves our constructive cooperation.

Yet the success of such a procedural device, like the revival of the United Nations itself, depends on the willingness of the member states, big and small, to accept the authority of the U.N., within clearly defined limits. These limits are set by the self-interest of the nations concerned. The Soviet Union has opposed the authority of the U.N. because the organization was identified with policies, such as those in Korea and the Congo, to which the Soviet Union was opposed. The disease of the United Nations, then, is political and so must be the remedy.

No single, simple formula will cure it, nor will tinkering with the Charter. The past successes of the United Nations were due to political configurations that no longer exist. Its future depends upon new political configurations, whose key is the relations between the United States and the Soviet Union.

They and the other great powers must at least try to create communities of interest on behalf of which the United Nations can exert its authority. In the nuclear age, these communities of interest lie primarily in the peaceful settlement of international conflicts. It is the task of statesmanship to define and circumscribe them and to use the United Nations to put them into effect.

The United States supported the United Nations strongly as long as it could use the U.N. for its political purposes. It has been much less enthusiastic in its support in recent years, and it probably regards the shift of executive power back again from the General Assembly to the Security Council, in which it, too, has a veto, with feelings short of dismay. The

Soviet Union, for very similar reasons of political self-interest, has from the very outset been opposed to the supranational powers of the United Nations.

The delegate of Mauritania was not far off the mark when, on the last day of the recent session, he blamed both super-powers for the disaster that has befallen the U.N. There is no clear indication today that either side has learned from the recent experience and is about to change its attitude. The recent increased activity of the Security Council, concomitant with the decline of the General Assembly is encouraging. But perhaps it will require a more drastic experience, similar to the Cuban crisis of 1962, to make clear to all concerned that the United Nations is neither a luxury nor a nuisance but a necessity.

Nations which are threatened with nuclear destruction have a vital interest in an international organization which is capable of making effective the interests they have in common. In the past, the United Nations has performed this function with considerable success. It has done so in four different respects.

First, while the United Nations has probably not prevented any wars, it has materially contributed to the shortening of four of them: in Indonesia in 1949, in Palestine in 1949, in Egypt in 1956 and in the Congo from 1960-64. Its success in the Congo was temporary only because it was deprived of the financial support necessary to continue its operations.

Second, the United Nations has provided opportunities for unobtrusive diplomatic negotiations; the classic example is the settlement of the Berlin blockade in 1948-49. In a period of history which has witnessed the decline of diplomatic contacts between hostile powers, such opportunities add a new instrument to the traditional methods of diplomacy.

Third, the United Nations can act as a buffer between hostile nations, as it does at present in Cyprus, and provide a face-saving formula for the settlement of international disputes. Many international disputes arise from considerations of prestige and cannot be settled because of them. A formula for settlement put forward by the Secretary General or neutral nations, may be acceptable to both parties, since it emanates from neither but from a neutral source.

Finally the United Nations is a forum through which member states can voice their aspirations and grievances by the formal means of speeches or by informal discussions. These opportunities for nations to become aware of each other are no less important for being intangible. For in an age in which nations tend to assess each other in terms of ideological stereotypes, these contacts can provide an invaluable corrective.

Such are the actual achievements of the United Nations; it would be a pity to lose them. Without an international organization which could duplicate them in a future crisis, the chances for maintaining peace would be materially decreased. One only needs to compare the pacifying role the United Nations played in the Berlin crisis of 1948 with its inactivity in the present Vietnam crisis in order to see how important the availability of such an organization can be when the question of war or peace hangs in the balance.

The potentialities of the United Nations are more important still. For the U.N. has taken the first hesitant step toward developing into a supranational authority which would protect the interests of its members and thereby insure order and peace throughout the world. In the nuclear age, nations can no longer afford to protect and promote their separate interests through the traditional use of force without risking their own destruction. They need a supranational authority which will do for them what they can no longer afford to do.

The United Nations is not yet such an authority, but it could become one. Its present retrogression into impotence runs counter to the rational requirements of the age. To revive and strengthen it is not just a matter of convenience. The interests of all nations, big and small, in their physical survival require it.

豢 豢

Sovereignty II

The best and most vivid analysis of sovereignty I know is the following chapter from the book *The Anatomy of Peace* by Emery Reves which was published 21 years ago.

This book was published by Harper Brothers in June, 1945, a few weeks before the United Nations Charter was signed and made public. In it Emery Reves stated the case for a far stronger world body than the one whose Charter was then being debated in San Francisco. When the book appeared, it received excellent critical reviews but generated no unusual excitement until, on August 6, 1945, at 10:45 A.M., President Truman announced that the first American atomic bomb had exploded over Hiroshima, totally destroying the city and its population. I remember this time well. It was as though the thesis set forth in *The Anatomy of Peace* had acquired great meaning to everyone and leading citizens in all fields urged its consideration, in particular Albert Einstein who so understood the dangers of the atomic weapons and the drastic nature of the remedy that would be necessary in world politics. The book rapidly sold nine large printings of the original edition; Pocket Books sold 100,000 of the king-size paper edition; it was condensed in three long installments in the *Reader's Digest*; and was translated and published in 23 foreign languages as well as in Esperanto and in Braille.

The reason this book was read with close attention by so many people in 1945 and 1946, and then faded, reflects the appalling callousness we have come to feel about nuclear weapons and the depressing pattern that characteristically seems to follow war. Immediately following a war there is a wave of strong idealism, a determination that this horror shall not take place again. Then the experience of war fades, idealists become discouraged, an age group who did not experience the war and are sick of hearing about it enters the picture, and there is a general desire to turn one's back on these disagreeable problems. A period of extreme materialism takes over, usually with corruption and debasement of values. This was the course after World War I with the materialism of the Twenties, and it is judged by some to be among the major costs of war.

Immediately after World War II there was a lively sense of "One World" (Wendell Willkie made his famous trip). Grenville Clark, an unusually foresighted individual who, like Emery Reves, saw the inadequacies in the new United Nations Charter, called a citizens' conference in Dublin, New Hampshire, to see what could be done. A number of groups, all aimed at strengthening the Charter and transforming the U.N. into a limited world government, merged in Asheville in 1946, calling themselves the United World Federalists. There was a strong "student group" of young veterans who had returned to the campuses which gave the movement great vitality. Then once again the experience faded, and prosperity and materialism took over. In the United States we also had "the McCarthy period." The United World Federalists still exists today as a small, dedicated, useful group of men and women (Senator Joe Clark says the Nuclear Test Ban Treaty could not have been passed without its active help). But it is a middle-aged organization. Twenty-one years is just about a generation. Maybe a certain length of time had to come and go. Most of you do not need to look back at the articles by

Professor Gray and Rochelle Gatlin in this book to know that a new generation of young people is questioning the values of this recent materialistic and self-satisfied period. They have grown up in the nuclear age. They understand it in their bones and they see what it has done to the quality of life. Moreover they are justifiably anxious to "have" their life. For many reasons therefore it seems appropriate to publish this analysis of sovereignty again.

It is important to recognize that in a small but definite way the sanctity of national sovereignty was eaten into after World War II in a way that did not take place after World War I. The Nuremberg Trials, which were instigated and emotionally supported by the United States, repudiated once and for all the doctrine that "my country right or wrong" was an adequate justification of inhuman behavior to other humans. We reject the excuse of the extermination camp commander that he was carrying out his government's orders and his government's policy. And we judge in our hearts with considerable self-righteousness the great numbers of German citizens who shut their eyes to what their government was doing and allowed it to happen. We know that the actions of our own government in Vietnam are very different from Hitler. Yet much of the world looks askance at the morality of what we are doing there. And it is disconcerting, in an age of high level bombing, napalm and chemical spraying, where ordinary people rather than fighting men are the chief sufferers, to allow the thought in the poem by Thomas Merton that Jerome Frank quoted to intrude upon us.

The Historical Meaning of Sovereignty

EMERY REVES

The fundamental problem of peace is the problem of sovereignty. The welfare, the happiness, the very existence of a miner in Pennsylvania, Wales, Lorraine or the Don Basin, a farmer in the Ukraine, the Argentine, the American Middle West or the Chinese rice fields—the very existence of every individual or family in every country of the five continents depends upon the correct interpretation and application of sovereignty. This is not a theoretical debate but a question more vital than wages, prices, taxes, food or any other major issue of immediate interest to the common man everywhere, because in the final analysis, the solution of all the everyday problems of two thousand million human beings depends upon the solution of the central problem of war. And whether we are to have war or peace and progress depends upon whether we can create proper institutions to insure the security of the peoples.

Schopenhauer pointed out that health is a negative feeling of which we are never aware, while pain produces a positive sensation. If we cut our little finger, we concentrate on that completely dominating pain, excluding from our consciousness the many other parts of our body which remain uninjured and healthy.

This observation has also been proved true in other fields of human activity—certainly in the field of social science. Great social and political structures and revolutionary ideas are usually born in times of crisis.

The very fact that today there is so much talk of sovereignty—a word that was hardly mentioned in political discussions a decade or two ago—proves the existence of a sore spot in the body politic. It leaves no doubt that something is wrong with sovereignty, that the present interpretation of this notion is passing through a crisis and that clarification, restatement and reinterpretation are necessary.

In discussing this most intricate problem, it is essential to make a clear distinction between its two entirely different aspects.

The first is scientific: a realization of exactly what sovereignty is, what it meant historically during the various phases of human development, and what it means in a democracy in the middle of the twentieth century.

The second—which we must *eliminate* from consideration while searching for definitions and principles is: What would the people be capable of understanding, and what would they accept politically right now?

In our endeavor to arrive at a clear definition and correct interpretation of democratic sovereignty, we must not be deterred by the argument that the quest is futile because the people are nationalist and would resist any changes in the present political construction of the world. Such an outlook—a sort of government by polls of public opinion—is not democracy, but its caricature.

New ideas always take shape within a small group of men whose task it is to spread them and get them accepted by the people.

When Pasteur discovered that contagious diseases were caused by living organisms and explained how such diseases could be cured, almost everybody, including the overwhelming majority of doctors, laughed at him. At the time Hertz and Marconi declared that sound and signals could be transmitted around the world by radio waves, a public opinion poll would certainly have shown that 99 per cent of the people believed such a thing impossible and for all purposes, impractical. Those who, at the time of the Thirty Years' War, declared that it was possible for Catholics and Protestants to worship in freedom according to their beliefs and to live together peacefully under law, were regarded as dreamers and most impractical men.

Democracy does not mean that governments have to ask the people their opinions on complicated issues and then carry them out. It is essentially a form of society within which the conception of new ideas, their diffusion in view of their acceptance by the majority, the fight for leadership, is open to everybody.

The first problem, therefore, is that those who, for one reason or another, are in a position to influence public opinion and events should know the exact meaning of the words they are using and clearly define the ideas they are advocating.

The first step toward realism is the clarification of principles.

It seems one of the absurdities of our unhappy generation that hopeless utopians who live entirely in the past and are incapable of visualizing the future otherwise than as a projection of the past, call themselves realists and practical men and deride any attempt at rational thinking as "idealism."

What does this word "sovereignty" mean?

By now most people must realize that human beings are exceptionally perverted and ferocious creatures, capable of murdering, torturing, persecuting and exploiting each other more ruthlessly than any other species in this world.

At a very early stage of human society, it was discovered that before we could live together, in a family, in a tribe, it was necessary to impose certain restraints upon our natural impulses, to forbid certain things we like to do, and to compel us to do certain things we do not like to do.

The day the first legal imposition of a compulsion was forced upon a community was the greatest day in history.

That day, freedom was born.

How did this happen?

Human nature is such that man does not accept rules unless they are imposed upon him by constituted authority. The first absolute authority was God.

So it was necessary to make people believe that the required rules and regulations were the express commands of God. They were proclaimed with all the magic at their command by priests, who had direct access to God and who know how to proclaim His will, amid so much thunder and lightning that the people were frightened into accepting them.

Here we have the first sovereign authority—the first source of law—a supernatural symbol.

Later on as human society developed and law and order grew, it was necessary to separate that which was Caesar's from that which was God's. During that long period of history when peoples were ruled by the divine right of absolute monarchs, chiefs, emperors and kings, to maintain their authority and lawmaking power, to make people recognize them as the supreme source of law, the rulers linked themselves as closely as possible with religion and proclaimed that they derived their power from God.

The monarchs ruling by divine right were called sovereigns and their lawgiving capacity was designated as "sovereign."

Between the Renaissance and the eighteenth century, as a result of the revival of learning and new methods of rational and scientific thinking, a revolutionary social ideal took shape and found fertile soil among the masses suffering under absolutism. This revolutionary ideal was the principle that no individual, no family, no dynasty, could any longer be regarded as sovereign, that the sovereign lawgiving authority was the people and that "sovereignty resides in the community."

This revolutionary principle led to the great popular uprisings of the eighteenth century, to the establishment of the American and French republics, and to the "king reigns but does not rule" parliamentary system in England and many other countries.

The ideal of national sovereignty and national independence springs from long eras of monarchy and colonization. At its inception, it was a great forward step and an incentive to human progress. The American Declaration of Independence, the French Revolution, following on the development of representative institutions in England, were an enormous incentive to other peoples to fight for their own sovereignty and independence. The climax of this evolution was reached in the peace treaties of 1919, when more nations than ever before became completely sovereign and independent. Twenty years later all those proud national sovereignties lay trampled in the dust and today more people than ever before in modern history are enslaved and plunged into misery.

Why did this happen?

It happened because the political system established in 1919, an apotheosis of eighteenth century ideals, was an anachronism, and in total contradiction to things as they are in the twentieth century. The great ideals of national sovereignty, independence, nationality as the basis of states, were wonderful achievements in the eighteenth century, in a world which was so vast before the industrial revolution had begun.

The democratic form of government adopted by the great Western powers brought about a century of wealth, a spiritual, scientific and material progress unique in history. But nothing is eternal in this world, and we are again in the throes of a crisis which demands reinterpretation of the foundations of our social life.

Our present conception of national sovereignty shows how an ideal, once realized, can be distorted in the span of a single century.

According to the eighteenth century French philosophers, the most articulate among the founders of modern democracy, the democratic conception of sovereignty meant the transfer of sovereign rights from one man, the king; to all men, the people. In the democratic sense, sovereignty resided in the community.

By "community" they meant the totality of people. It was quite clear that no individual or groups of individuals could exercise sovereign rights unless *derived* from the sovereignty of the community.

We must try to visualize the world as it was in the eighteenth century. The industrial revolution had not even begun. The stagecoach was the fastest means of transportation. Everybody lived a rural life and any territory of one hundred thousand or even ten thousand square miles was an entirely self-sufficient and self-supporting unit.

Under such conditions, the widest horizon of the forebears of democracy was—the Nation. When they proclaimed the sovereignty of the nation, they meant the sovereignty of the community; they meant sovereignty to have the broadest possible basis.

Today, a hundred and fifty years later, when we can fly around the globe in less time than it took to go from Boston to New York, from London to Glasgow or from Paris to Marseille, the situation is completely different.

As the world is organized today, sovereignty does *not* reside in the community, but is exercised in an absolute form by groups of individuals we call nations. This is in total contradiction to the original democratic conception of sovereignty. Today, sovereignty has far too narrow a basis; it no longer has the power it should and was meant to have. The word is the same. The conception it expresses is the same. But the surroundings have changed. The conditions of the world have changed. And this changed situation calls for corresponding changes in the interpretation of this basic principle, if we desire to preserve this, the only foundation of democratic society yet discovered.

The great change brought about by the technical and industrial achievements of the nineteenth century is that the nation, which in the eighteenth century was the *broadest* imaginable basis of sovereignty, today is far too *narrow* a basis.

The seeds of the twentieth century crisis began to germinate almost immediately after the establishment of the modern democratic nation-states. Quite independently of the organization of the nation-states and the political conceptions of eighteenth century democracy, almost at the same time something happened which was destined to become an equally strong movement and an equally powerful factor of human progress. That something was: Industrialism.

These two dominating currents of our age, nationalism and industrialism, are in constant and inevitable conflict with each other.

Industrialism tends to embrace the whole globe within its sphere of activity. Modern industrial mass production needs raw materials from all over the earth, and seeks markets in every corner of the world. It strives to achieve its purposes irrespective of any political, geographic, racial, religious, linguistic or national barriers.

Nationalism, on the other hand, tends to divide this world into smaller and smaller compartments and to segregate the human race into smaller and smaller independent groups.

For about a century it was possible for these conflicting currents to flow side by side. The political constitution of the eighteenth century nation-state structure of the world had some compartments large enough for industrialism to develop.

But since the beginning of this century these two forces have clashed with titanic violence. It is this collision between our political life and our economic and technological life that is the cause of the twentieth century crisis with which we have been struggling since 1914, as helpless as guinea pigs.

The meaning of this convulsion is clear. The political framework of our world with its seventy or eighty sovereign nation-states is an insurmountable obstacle to free industrial progress, to individual liberty and to social security.

Either we understand this problem and create a political framework in this world within which industrialism, individual liberties and peaceful human relationship are possible or we dogmatically refuse to change the foundation of our obsolete political structure.

We *can* remain as we are. It is perfectly possible. But if this is our choice, then democracy is finished and we are bound to march with increasing speed toward totalitarianism.

The first step toward ending the present chaos is to overcome the tremendous emotional obstacle which prevents us from realizing and admitting that the ideal of sovereign nation-states, with all its great record of success during the nineteenth century, is today the cause of all the immeasurable suffering and misery of this world. We are living in complete anarchy, because in a small world, interrelated in every other respect, there are seventy or eighty separate sources of law—seventy or eighty sovereignties.

The situation is identical with that period of history when feudal lords of the land had absolute sovereign power over their fiefs and spent their lives fighting and killing each other, until the over-all rulers, the kings, imposed a higher sovereignty upon them, based on a broader framework. Within such a broader framework, the knights continued to envy and to dislike each other. But they were obliged to envy and dislike each other—peacefully.

Our present system of national sovereignty is in absolute contradiction to the original democratic conception of sovereignty, which meant—and still means—sovereignty of the community.

Why is it so urgently necessary to revive this notion and to re-establish the democratic conception of sovereignty of the community, which means authority of the people, standing *above* any individual or any group of individuals?

We all reject the monstrous totalitarian conception that the state is the absolute ultimate goal, with supreme power over its citizens, that the individual is merely the abject slave of the Moloch—state.

We accept the democratic conception that the state, created by the people, exists only to protect them and maintain law and order, safeguarding their lives and liberty.

The significant thing about the present crisis is that the nation-states, even the most powerful, even the United States of America, Great Britain and the Soviet Union, are no longer strong enough, no longer powerful enough to fulfill the purpose for which they were created.

They cannot prevent disasters like the first and second world wars. They cannot protect their peoples against the devastation of international war.

However sincerely the American, British and Russian governments sought to keep out of this war, they were forced into it in spite of themselves. Millions of their citizens have died, hundreds of billions of dollars of their national wealth have been wasted, for sheer survival. They had to fight for their lives.

If the sovereignty of the United States of America, the sovereignty of Great Britain and the sovereignty of the Soviet Union do not suffice to protect their citizens, then we need not even talk about the fiction of sovereignty in Latvia, Luxembourg or Rumania.

To put it plainly, the ideal of the nation-state is bankrupt. The nation-state is impotent to prevent foreign aggression, it no longer serves as the supreme institution capable of protecting its people against war and all the miseries and misfortunes that war brings.

The second World War has finally demonstrated that not a single one of the existing nations, even the most powerful, is economically self-sufficient.

These indisputable facts prove that our present conception of national sovereignty is obsolete and pregnant with deadly danger to us all.

The inescapable economic and technical realities of our age make it imperative to re-examine and reinterpret the notion of sovereignty and to create sovereign institutions based on the community, according to the original democratic conception. Sovereignty of the people must stand *above* the nations so that under it each nation may be equal, just as each individual is equal under the law in a civilized state.

The question is not one of "surrendering" national sovereignty. The problem is not negative and does not involve giving up something we already have. The problem is positive—creating something we lack, something we have never had, but that we imperatively need.

The creation of institutions with universal sovereign power is merely another phase of the same process in the development of human history—the extension of law and order into another field of human association which heretofore has remained unregulated and in anarchy.

A few centuries ago, many cities held full sovereign rights. Later some portion of municipal sovereignty was transferred to provinces. Then to larger units and finally, at the end of the eighteenth century, to the nation-states.

In the United States of America today, the problems of fire prevention, water supply, street cleaning and other similar matters are under municipal authority.

The construction of roads, marital legislation, education, legislation regarding industrial and commercial enterprises, and endless other issues are under state sovereignty.

And finally, problems affecting the United States Army, Navy, foreign policy, currency and other matters, are under Federal sovereignty.

The development is crystal clear. As human progress continues, conditions require an ever-broader basis for sovereignty, for absolute power, to fulfill its purpose: the protection of the people.

New Yorkers are citizens of the city of New York, of the state of New York and of the United States of America. But they are also citizens of the world. Their lives, their security, their liberties are protected in a very wide field by the sovereign authority which resides in the people, who have delegated its exercise partly to the city of New York, partly to the state of New York and partly to the Federal government of the United States of America.

The situation as to the delegation of sovereign power by the people to authorities on different levels is the same in all democratic countries. Just as in the United States, so in Great Britain, France, Switzerland and in the other countries, the sovereign peoples have delegated parts of their sovereignties to muncipalities, boroughs, counties, departments, cantons and national state institutions.

But during the past three decades, we have learned that these highest sovereign units created by the people—the nation-states—are not strong enough, are not sovereign enough, to protect them against international war, against attack by a foreign power over which existing sovereignties have no control whatever.

If the state of New York enacted economic or social legislation that reacted harmfully on economic and labor conditions in Connecticut, and no higher sovereignty existed, such an act on the part of the sovereign state of New York could not be prevented by the sovereign state of Connecticut, except by war.

But a higher sovereignty—the Federal sovereignty—exists, and under it the state of New York and the state of Connecticut are equal. This higher sovereignty alone protects the people against such danger.

The same dangers would exist in the relations of counties in England, departments in France and cantons in Switzerland, without higher sovereign national authority.

Democratic sovereignty of the people can be correctly expressed and effectively instituted only if local affairs are handled by local government, national affairs by national government, and international, world affairs, by international, world government.

Only if the people, in whom rests all sovereign power, delegate parts of their sovereignty to institutions created for and capable of dealing with specific problems, can we say that we have a democratic form of government. Only through such separation of sovereignties, through the organization of independent institutions, deriving their authority from the sovereignty of the community, can we have a social order in which men may live in peace with each other, endowed with equal rights and equal obligations before law. Only in a world order based on such separation of sovereignties can individual freedom be real.

Such separation of sovereignties, such gradation of governmental functions, has proved to be the only real, enduring instrument of democracy in any country.

It is irrelevant whether the delegation of sovereignty proceeds from local government to national government, as in the United States, or from national government to local government, as in Great Britain. Whether the delegation of sovereignty develops historically one way or the other, does not modify the fact that democracy needs separation of sovereignties and separate institutions to deal with affairs on different levels, adequately to express the sovereignty of the community.

Existing anarchy in international relations, due to absolute national sovereignty, must be superseded by universal statutory law, enacted by a duly elected legislative body. Such universal law must take the place of the utterly fallacious, ineffectual and precarious rule of unenforceable treaty obligations entered into by sovereign nation-states and disregarded by them whenever it suits their purpose.

The conception of sovereignty is not an end but a means to an end.

It is an instrument necessary to create law and order in the relations of men. Sovereignty finds expression in institutions, but in itself is not and never can be identical with any institution.

Institutions derive their sovereignty from where sovereignty resides. In ancient times, in religion, in absolute monarchies—from God. In democracies—from the people.

If our inherited institutions, established in the past, are no longer capable of maintaining law and order and protecting us, then their claims to sovereignty, their insistence upon sovereign power jeopardizes our very lives and liberty, the well-being of society to which we belong, and the sovereignty of . . . "we, the people."

Institutions—churches, dynasties, municipalities, kingdoms, nation-states—can be recognized to exercise sovereign power and to incarnate sovereign rights only so long as they are able to solve concrete and tangible problems, to fulfill the purposes for which they were created. To identify sovereign institutions with sovereignty itself, to assume that sovereign rights must eternally reside in any specific institution—today the nation-state—to believe that the nation-state is *the* expression of sovereignty, is pure totalitarianism, the greatest foe of democracy, the greatest political and social heresy imaginable, ranking with the making of graven images of God and their identification with God Himself in the Christian religion.

The nation-states were originally instituted and received their power from their peoples to carry out clearly defined tasks, *i.e.* to protect their citizens, to guarantee security to their peoples, to maintain law and order. The moment established institutions fail to keep abreast of conditions in society and are unable to maintain peace, they become a source of great danger and must be reformed if violent social convulsions and wars are to be averted.

Through such reform and transformation of obsolete and ineffective human institutions into more adequate and more powerful institutions adapted to realities, nothing whatsoever is "sacrificed" or "surrendered." Quite certainly not sovereignty.

Such a reform does not require the abolition of nations and national boundaries. Within each nation-state, we still have state lines, county demarcations, city limits, boundaries of our home lots or of houses and apartments. Families have names of their own different from those of other families. We like, protect and defend our own families more than other families. We love our homes, pay allegiance to our own communities, our countrysides, our provinces.

But sovereign power is not vested in these units which divide us.

Sovereign power is vested in the state, which unites us.

Those who talk of "surrendering" the sovereignty of the United States, of Great Britain, France or of any other democratic country, simply do not understand the meaning of "sovereignty."

A democratic state cannot "surrender" sovereignty, for the simple reason that it is not sovereign. Only a totalitarian or Fascist state is sovereign. A democratic state is sovereign only to the extent to which sovereignty is delegated to it by those in whom, under the democratic concept, sovereignty is vested—the people.

The real source of sovereign power cannot be emphasized too strongly and must never be lost sight of if we would understand the political problem we face. It is the people who create governments and not—as the Fascists say—governments that make nations.

The nation-states as they were set up in the eighteenth century, and as they are organized in the democracies today, are nothing but the instruments of the sovereign people, created for the specific purpose of achieving certain objectives. Should the people realize and come to the conclusion that in certain fields they would be better protected by delegating part of their sovereignty to bodies other than the nation-states, then nothing would be "surrendered." Rather something would be created for the better protection of the lives and liberties of all peoples.

Sovereignty would continue to reside in the people in accordance with the original conception of democracy, but institutions would be created to give realistic and effective expression to the democratic sovereignty of the people in place of the inefficient and tyrannical institutions of the nation-states.

The people would "surrender" their sovereignty only if sovereign power to create law were abandoned to an arbitrary authority or a lawless power.

But to transfer certain aspects of our sovereign rights from national legislative, judiciary and executive bodies to equally democratically elected and democratically controlled universal legislative, judiciary and executive bodies in order to create, apply and execute law for the regulation of human relationships in the international field—in a field where such law has never existed—is not "surrender" but *acquisition*. It is an exchange of a phantom asset, the product of unfulfilled and unfulfillable promises, for a real and tangible asset.

A Postscript to Sovereignty

Nonetheless, the idea of a large, remote authority, backed by an overwhelming force (such as World Police force in a disarmed world), enforcing laws—even supposedly for our own good—arouses strong reservations in many people. One of the realest and deepest fears is fear of conformity—fear of the big powerful organization which crushes out differences.

I was personally very interested that, when a group of students from Sarah Lawrence College asked the World Law Fund to assist them in organizing a weekend conference on war prevention, their first concern was how, under a world authority, cultural diversity, which they saw as individuality, could be preserved. They felt acutely that there are different truths and no one culture has a right to impose its views on another. I passionately agree with them. If they had greater sophistication they might have expressed this more nearly as do the Vedas, "Truth is one; the sages call it by many names." No area today, East, West, South or North, is expressing itself through the old ways. As the new symbols and forms take their shape they will not be identical in the various parts of the globe. The circumstances of local life, race and tradition must all be taken into account and will have their effect in the resultant forms. We must face the fact that not everyone even *should* embrace ours.

Those students felt that the right to one's own individuality is the most precious right there is. With this, they tended to see "law" as repressive and as protecting the status quo.

This outlook reminded me of that of young countries to whom likewise freedom and independence are so new that they are jealous of it. I thought of some remarks of Sir Muhammad Zafrula Khan of Pakistan, judge of the International Court of Justice, in his speech at the *Pacem in Terris* Convocation. "Peoples who have been under domination are sensitive to anything that touches sovereignty. Independence and sovereignty are necessary conditions of international cooperation. Those who are not sovereign have neither the means nor the capacity of participating in international activities. The acceptance of international obligations and participation in international cooperation are beginning to be recognized *as an exercise of sovereignty and not as a negation of it.*" (In this connection, one can remember that Russia too is a young country.) I thought also of the difficulty of Professor Gray's students (in his article in Section I) in reconciling the thrilling assertion of personal freedom of Socrates in the Apologia with his decision in the Crito to submit to the law; until one student understood that law was a freely elected value of Socrates, that subjugating himself to it, even at his own cost, was an exercise of freedom, not a negation of it.

This point of view which is jealous of individuality should be given much attention, however. It has a relationship to the problems raised by Lusky.

About the tendency to view law as repressive, I was reminded of another group which, like young people and new nations, tends to feel itself outside the power structure—*i.e.* the poor, who often fear the policeman and consider "the law" an enemy. It is essential that those who speak in terms of World Law recognize these different connotations, brought about by being in a different position in the going power structure, and take the responsibility of showing law as an enabling force, not just a repressive one.

Viewed in one way, even "rules of the road" are enabling and freeing—allow greater freedom of movement than otherwise—and in a bad traffic jam almost everyone is glad to see a policeman arrive. In both New York City's recent emergencies—the great electric power blackout of the Northeast on November 9, 1965, and the twelve-day transportation strike of January 1-12, 1966—the police were everywhere looked on as a freeing agent. What is more, "legitimate authority" was accorded even those volunteers who acted as police.

※ ※

Rich Nations and Poor Nations

Pope John called specifically for dialogue between the world of Western Christendom and the Communist world, by which he seems to mean in particular the Soviet Union and the Soviet bloc. Tillich and Northrop have spoken earlier in this section for the interpenetration of East and West. (The term "East" as used by these two writers obviously refers to the area of the globe which has been formed by the cultural and religious traditions of Asia, as distinct from the other common use of "East-West" in which East refers principally to Communist Russia.)

What one might call the interpenetration of the Northern and Southern tiers of nations is no less necessary but of a different character. It may prove in the end more potentially explosive, more difficult and more persistent than the cold war; and although it partially overlaps in geographical area it is by no means identical with what is asked for in the East-West terms of Tillich. Its solution appears impossible without two requirements: The impartiality, even more than the resources, of world institutions, and a freedom from the distorting fear, as well as from the actuality, of major war.

The interpenetration in question means the contact, relationship, cooperation, reciprocal understanding and awareness of the needs and nature of the others between the "have" and "have-not" nations. The developed nations, who are so few and so rich, the underdeveloped who are so many (both in numbers of persons and in number of nations) and so without. The fact that color as well as geography, income and culture so often enters into this rough division increases everybody's sensitivity and does not make matters easier.

It is possible to say that there are two worlds on this one small planet and that the gap between them is widening fast. Professor Nathan Keyfitz states the case in drastic form in the *Bulletin of the Atomic Scientists*, March 1966, from which the following are a few excerpts:

> With the shift in perspective from our own national position to the world view, the presently underdeveloped countries take on the role of the poor of the nineteenth century. They include all categories: the industrious poor of India; the indoctrinated and disciplined proletariat of China, with their intensively cultivated resentment; the noisy and ineffectual street mobs of Indonesia. In the degree to which the rough figures given earlier for the three categories of countries apply both to birthrates and to wealth, we may think of the present world situation as involving one billion middle class or potentially middle class people—mostly Europeans and North Americans—and two billion poor. If the gap in per capita incomes and birthrates remains, a terrifying prospect, then in somewhat over three generations some three billion rich people will face some 16 billion poor . . .

Among the underdeveloped, intensification of poverty can cause whole nations, like the neurotic patient, to be caught in a web of necessity which they cannot perceive. Frustration is inevitable. An outlet in foreign animosity is one morbid result, and new countries need not take long to develop traditional hostilities. Indeed, war sometimes appears to be the lesser evil. As a brilliant representative of the underdeveloped world puts it: "Now war . . . is evil, war is cruel, war is inhuman. But still more evil, still more cruel, still more inhuman is the slow and agonizing death of daily hunger" (Abdus Salam, "World Security and Developing Nations," Bulletin of the Atomic Scientists, September 1964, p. 6). *He is speaking of a level of irrationality which disregards the fact that the outcome of war will be intensification of hunger. . . .*

Population growth in the poor countries and technical advance in the rich ones are two factors which weaken the economic links between rich and poor. . . . there is a degree of the bitterness in the potential world confrontation between rich and poor which goes beyond Marx, because its source is not possible exploitation but rather exclusion from industrial life, of which low raw material prices are an aspect.

The demand of the West for tropical products in the days when its industrial machine was yet imperfect necessarily contained some elements of genuine working together, with a hope on the part of the oppressed, who saw themselves as doing the main work, that the going enterprise would sooner or later belong to them. One may speak harshly of exploitation, but as long as men are engaged in common activity they can communicate with one another. The very hypocrisy of the ruler is a means by which he can be influenced, especially when hypocrisy is reinforced by material need of the rich for the poor. The colonial situation was certainly bad, but the prospect today is worse, for a time is coming when the rich no longer need the poor, and even hypocrisy may decline.

The rich countries are reaching ever higher levels of comfort and pleasure; if each rise of income makes the powerful industrial machine less dependent on the pitiful supplies of rubber or fuel or sugar or cocoa which have constituted the sole wealth of the underdeveloped world, what depths of hatred will not be stirred in those large and functionless populations whose numbers are in many instances a product of colonialism, now left high and dry with its retreat?

The citizen of the rich world sees himself as fully earning the privileged position in which he sits. To the poor he has earned nothing. And we should be humble enough to remember that it is west-

ern society which is productive, and not necessarily we as individuals. The economics of the matter are complex, but as a practical fact a cobbler or a college professor in Calcutta, working at his bench or addressing his class, can perform with exactly the same effort and skill as his opposite number in Chicago, and his real income is at the most favorable one-fifth as much. For a long while the citizen of Calcutta has thought this was so because in some invisible way the Chicagoan was exploiting him. With the advance of western technology and the consequent increasing separateness of the rich and poor on their opposite sides of the world the absurdity of the notion of exploitation will become more and more patent. One cannot expect that it will therefore cease to be used, and if it is dropped the frustration which it has expressed in the past is likely to be carried by other bitter slogans.

Even without so drastic a view, it is plain that both sides to the confrontation give different priorities to the issues of our day. The established, powerful, developed nations give first priority to *security*. They have much to lose, so the avoidance of violent change is of the highest interest to them. The underdeveloped countries give first priority to *social justice*, which involves *change*. They have nothing, including the implements of modern war; so they are less concerned about the dangers of war between the world's great powers than about securing what they so desperately need, the wherewithal for life for themselves. Jealous of their new independence they resent attempts to pull them into the cold war on one side or the other. But they do not sufficiently understand how much their tendency to "shop around" for aid increases the tension between the giant opponents.

Nothing more calls for a combination of the two religious viewpoints than this mutual involvement of the developed and undeveloped countries which is upon us. *Both* "I am my brother's keeper" *and* "I am my brother" are needed. Because we must, in truth, *do* much to help, and at the same time be aware (through expanding our consciousness) of them as persons, brothers sharing our humanity with equal pride in their own essence. The attitude of the Peace Corps, whose members learn as well as teach, who give themselves freely without strings, is the right one.

Awareness, on one level, is something neither side can escape, for as Myrdal has pointed out (in the first section of this Reader) unless large-scale action is taken quickly, within ten years the sight of mass starvation will enter into our living room daily on television. While the underdeveloped nations, through that same network of communications, know that it is no longer necessary to be poor.

Within this utterly disparate framework of developed and underdeveloped, the new nations of Africa have been rapidly born into world society in the wake of colonialism and in the very active context of the cold war. How can they possibly establish their own identity when the western powers and Russia and China all press upon them? Barbara Ward discusses their problem in the article below.

It is plain that these African nations, like small powers elsewhere, will founder if they are drawn into the maelstrom of the cold war. The only safe place for them to turn, both for aid and for peace-keeping, is a world structure—at present the United Nations. Following Barbara Ward, Abdul Monem Rifa'i, Representative of Jordan to the U.N., raises his voice for nonalignment and for freedom from coercion and pressure. There is something touching in the simplicity and frankness of his remarks. He asks that a larger proportion of economic aid be channeled through international agencies to preserve this independence and this nonalignment.

Whenever I think of the smaller nations I think at once of the Clark-Sohn plan, the so-called radical proposal. Not only would these nations benefit enormously and rapidly from the economic structure of a Clark-Sohn type world system, but it is the *only* way they can maintain their independence. The Santo Dominican crisis of May 1965 and the extraordinary way a superpower like the United States felt obliged to act, out of fear of communism, must point up to all small nations that newly won freedom is completely jeopardized by the power struggle of the giants. Their only way lies in a world system that removes this power struggle, without closing them into a Have-not world permanently separated from the Have.

Profile of African Independence

BARBARA WARD

When historians look back on the first phase of African independence in the modern world, they may be inclined to stress one overriding factor—the degree to which outside pressures impinge on the new states at a time when they are trying to establish at home their own national identity. No doubt Africa is not alone in this. The ending of empires, even peacefully, is often the signal for new forces to press in, seeking influence and even control. Europe fought two world wars to work out who should fill the "vacuum" of waning Turkish imperialism, and some would say the issue is still unsettled. Yet if one compares Africa's present position with, say, that of Latin America in the last century, it seems clear that Africa's evolution is proving much more "open" and hence vulnerable.

There are a number of reasons for this. Technology has pulled the world together. Under no conditions would Africa of the jet plane resemble Latin America of the packhorse. An embryonic world society, centered in the United Nations, has drawn Africa's new leaders instantly onto the world stage—and if they go to the world, the world inevitably comes to them. In the United Nations, they have discovered a majority of states with a similar background and heritage—that of coming out of a century of Western colonial control. Such a field of common experience beyond Africa's boundaries inevitably draws African interest outward, and outside interest is drawn back into Africa in return.

Something of the same magnetic field appears in the issue of race relations. A secular experience of racial discrimination at the hands of the white man, common to many nations of the world, keeps the current of interest and action flowing in and out of the African continent. In addition, the southern part of Africa—the last large area of the world under Western colonial or settler control—helps to keep world attention concentrated on the ending of the colonial century rather than on the problems of the postcolonial epoch.

Above all, the colonial issue in Africa has been drawn to the heart of the world's ideological dispute. The Leninist interpretation of imperialism and neocolonialism fits Africa into a world-wide theory of the cold war waged between "reactionary" and "emergent" states. It projects into Africa ideas and interpretations of a global nature. None of this universalizing of issues was apparent in earlier centuries. In fact, not since the wars of religion in Europe or the Moslem conquests of the seventh and eighth centuries have faith and force been so closely allied.

The difficulty about this central—and inevitable—preoccupation with the colonial issue in the context of the cold war, is that while it decreases the likelihood of an African consensus on the needs and future policies of the continent, it tends to increase the risks and complexities of outside interest and even intervention. The whole issue is ambiguous since at least two radically different interpretations of exactly where the colonial issue stands today confront each other in Africa. Broadly speaking, the Western Powers—with the exception of Portugal—believe that the phase has closed. In conformity with the principles of self-determination and national independence, first asserted in the American and French Revolutions and given world-wide application in President Wilson's Fourteen Points of 1918, they have, they believe, accepted their colonies' claims to self-government and peacefully agreed to remove outside control. The British are proud of the fact that African states, on achieving independence, have decided to stay in the voluntary partnership of the Commonwealth. A majority of French-speaking states have entered a voluntary but even closer association with the European Common Market. This, the Westerners think, would hardly have come about if long and bloody struggles had preceded the break. Even where the fight was prolonged and fierce—as in the single case of Algeria—not all good-will was lost, not all links were broken.

The Western Powers also tend to feel that the connection with Europe helped to give Africa some of the preconditions of nationhood. They point to the missionary effort in education, to the founding of postwar universities. They argue that Western investment and Western purchases of Africa's products have launched the states on economic modernization and that a continuance of close economic relationships in the future will serve the interests of both sides. They underline both the postwar reversal of earlier colonial policy—that colonies should pay their own way—and the rapid growth in direct economic assistance which, from all Western sources, has been running at an average of about a thousand million dollars a year, the bulk of it from French and other European sources. Western governments probably feel less confident now about their direct political legacy to the new states. They question whether either the "Westminster model" or a multiplicity of parties, European-style, best suits the new nations in their early attempts to build unity on the basis of varied ethnic and tribal groups. But Westerners believe that they did transfer power to genuine national leaders and left behind a valuable tradition of a plural society and the rule of law. They tend, therefore, to support and sympathize with existing leaders and to regard attempts to unseat them and radically to redistribute political power as subversion and treason.

It would be difficult to conceive of a more opposite interpretation of the African scene than that put forward from the other end of the political spectrum. One cannot perhaps talk of a single Communist view of the colonial situation, for there appear to be significant differences between the Soviet and the Chinese approach. The Chinese are in a better position to identify themselves with the "world-wide struggle against colonialism and racial discrimination" since they are themselves emerging from an uncomfortable century of being jostled and attacked by outside powers, first Western, then Japanese. They have also endured racial discrimination at the hands of white peoples.

The Russians, on the contrary, are European, white, and can, on some interpretations of history, be accused of maintaining dominion over colored peoples in Asia. This is a significant factor in China's desire to keep the Soviet Union *out* of the Afro-Asian association. And although, since Mr. Khrushchev's fall from power, the theoretical points at issue between Moscow and Peking have become more obscure, it does seem that the two Communist power centers differ on the degree of force that will be needed to produce a single world order of Communist states, the Chinese arguing that Western imperialism must be driven out by violence if necessary, the Russians suggesting that there may be nonviolent roads to socialism, and that violence could produce an atomic war after which, in Khrushchev's chilling phrase, "the living will envy the dead."

These differences—which are likely to produce varying emphases and interpretations in African policy—do not, however, extend to the whole field of Communist-African relations. In general, the Communist interpretation of what has happened is fairly uniform and the exact opposite of Western views. The Communists argue that only the "aroused will of the peoples of Africa" has enabled them to throw off imperial control and that even now the process is not complete. The Westerners are determined to maintain their economic dominance in Africa, which has been highly profitable to them but is sheer exploitation from the point of view of Africa, its peoples and its resources. The aim of Western economic aid is to tie the new, still weak economies to dominant markets and corporations abroad, thus ensuring that Africa's minerals are shipped off to the West without adequate returns to Africa and that its raw materials will be made available to the capitalist countries at low and fluctuating prices. And since the "strings" on aid may not tie up the deal adequately, Communists say, the Western Powers go further and set up local puppet governments whose members, in return for heavy bribes, are prepared to cooperate with the Western monopolists to sell the nation's economic birthright for what one might be tempted to call a mess of profits, if the profits remained in local hands, which, by definition, they do not.

From this Communist analysis follow the presumptions that national leaders who maintain friendly relations with the West are in all probability lackeys of capitalism, and that the "aroused will of the peoples," having got rid of their colonial masters, must now get rid of them. Liberation is thus not complete until every link westward is broken.

But at this point a Western countercriticism becomes relevant. Throughout human history, the withdrawal of one form of imperial control has often been the signal for other power systems to come in and fill the vacuum. True, in the twentieth century, the effort is being made—for the first time in human history—to affirm the basic right of small nations not to be ruled and controlled by powerful neighbors, and to build up, in the United Nations, an instrument that can safeguard their independence. But the Western Powers question whether the Communist recognition of this right may not be heavily overlaid by the presuppositions of Marxist ideology. If, by definition, no state is "free" until it is Communist, then non-Communist states cannot claim the rights of freedom. "Liberation" can mean not simply the end of old forms of control but the imposition of new ones. The Soviet army freed Poland from Nazi imperialism and imposed control from Moscow instead. If such an evolution is possible in Europe, so argue the Western Powers, may not the risk be the same in Africa? Russia and China are very large states in comparison, say, with the Congo (Brazzaville) or Burundi. Is it certain that complete reliance on the Communist giants may not substitute a new form of outside control for the diminishing influence of the French or Belgians?

An outside observer can define the terms of the dispute since it is a world-wide dispute and an essential part in the dialectical dialogue of mankind. It is much more difficult to describe African reactions to the debate since they are, by definition, African, drawn from the unconscious roots of Africa's own history and from a more and more conscious attempt to find a specifically African response. Moreover, there is not one single African response but a spectrum of reaction from radical to conservative, different leaders and different countries emphasizing differing aspects of the debate—and the debate itself shifting under the impact of changing events.

But perhaps from outside one can assess the weight of some of the arguments and thus gauge the often contrary pressures under which African governments have to work. Links with the West have the advantage of familiarity and custom. Language, education, professional experience make an African more at home in London or Paris than in Moscow or Shanghai or, for that matter, Bonn. And since thousands of Africans are now educated in America, the same familiarity, on the basis of the English language, is growing up. This direct contact with the old metropolitan powers presumably allows educated Africans to realize how widespread the local Western commitment to anticolonialism really is. This in turn underpins belief that the excolonial powers, once gone, are not likely to return. Even when, as in East Africa in early 1964, British troops were invited to reinforce local authority, they were gone again before the end of the year. On the other hand, residence in some areas in the West—for instance, the Southern states of America—gives the African visitor a less comfortable picture of Western liberalism.

Turning to economic interests, one can argue that Western links do give Africa access to the wealthiest countries in the world, with the largest markets and the greatest supplies of surplus capital. The flow of aid continues. In fact, British aid to East Africa has sharply increased. For over a decade, France has been paying its African associates more than world prices for such products as coffee and groundnuts, and even though these discriminations are to cease in the latest agreements between the Common Market and its African associates, the European governments have undertaken to increase their grants to the Africans to help them to diversify their economies. Meanwhile, in the wake of the United Nations Conference on Trade and Development (U.N.C.T.A.D.) at Geneva, most of the European governments are giving more serious thought to means of stabilizing the prices of raw materials and providing the developing nations with balance of payments support.

In the field of capital, the share of local states in the return to be gained from investment seems certain to grow. Not only can sovereign governments experiment more widely in tax policies that retain more of the enterprise's earnings in the host country; companies are themselves working out formulas that offer more of the realities of partnership. The fifty-fifty division of profits between LAMCO (Liberian American-Swedish Mineral Company) and the Liberian government is a case in point. The Nigerian government has been able to negotiate equally favorable arrangements with Shell. In a different field, the British government has started buying out European farmers in Kenya and giving long-term loans for the resettlement of Africans on the released land.

So far, no government in Africa has been ready to neglect these advantages. The government of M. Sékou Touré in Guinea is at the radical end of the spectrum. But it has achieved a workable relationship with FRIA, the aluminum consortium developing Guinea's bauxite. Similarly, Dr. Nkrumah enjoys excellent relations with the Kaiser Aluminum Company, whose cooperation is essential to the success of the Volta River Scheme. Most African governments underline their desire for foreign investment and betray little fear that they will not be able to control the local activities of foreign investors.

Yet the issue creates a malaise, and when we turn to the credibility of the Communist accounts of colonialism, high in the list are memories of past exploitation, of decades during which Africa itself gained little from foreign enterprise beyond the customs duties used to cover the costs of colonial administration and unskilled wages for Africans—often migrant at that. The vast mineral wealth of Africa's south has advantaged the local Africans only by the "trickle down" process, and only in the Union of South Africa has this had widespread economic effects—and there the economic effects are nullified by political discrimination.

The extreme fluctuations in the prices of tropical products, the degree to which all middlemen profit in such activities as shipping, marketing, insurance, remain in Western hands, Western tariff discrimination against local processing—all this can be made to add up to a pretty ruthless picture of the rich getting what they can out of the poor. The very disproportion in economic power between such giants as the United States or, indeed, the vast American corporations, and the micro-states of Africa reinforces the feeling that even if the elephant is amiable, there is hardly room for him in the bath. And past history—from the Kimberley diamonds onward —is used to argue that he is not always amiable.

Nor is it only the past. Foreign investment is linked with the recent carving out of mineral enclaves from preexistent colonial territories— Mauretania out of French West Africa, Gabon out of French Equatorial Africa and the setting up there of very large Western mining interests. Here, it is argued, are the archetypes of neocolonialism—complacent local governments kept in power by foreign interests and, when necessary, by foreign arms. The attempt at secession in Katanga has been interpreted in the same sense and its leaders marked as "neocolonialist puppets."

All this malaise and uncertainty are, of course, reinforced a thousand-fold by the continuance of colonial and racial domination in Africa's south. There is no need to labor the point, but it is important to underline its link with the picture of Western capitalist powers unwilling to give up their allegedly monopolistic exploitation of African wealth. Angola and Mozambique are not only under colonial domination. They control the internationally owned Benguela and Beira Railways and hence the major outlets for Rhodesian copper. South Africa is not only ruled by a racial minority. It contains about one billion dollars of British investment and about a quarter of America's lending to Africa. Imperialism and capitalism, racial discrimination and Western investment, African exploitation and white wealth are believed to meet in southern Africa and to nail together the Leninist identification of "late forms of capitalism" with the continuance of the colonial system.

What does Africa make of these rival interpretations of its destiny? In general, perhaps, it is learning to live with them. Most African governments approach the matter pragmatically, picking out now this thesis, now that, according to their local needs and interests. All are united on the urgent necessity of ending colonial and racial dominance in the south. All are anxious to encourage foreign investment under proper safeguards. All want to trade with West *and* East. All joined the seventy-seven nations of

U.N.C.T.A.D. to demand more equitable distribution of the world's commerce and capital. All, inheriting the paternalistic tradition of colonial economic control, and largely lacking local entrepreneurs, intend that government shall play a large part in economic activity. Most would describe this policy as some kind of version of "African Socialism" in which old communal traditions are combined with modern concepts of planning. Virtually all agree that for some time to come governments of national union or single party governments will be needed to make possible the forging of the nation and the unification of the state. In fact, it would almost seem that consensus politics might have a reasonable chance in Africa, since, on so many great issues, governments do not appear to be very far apart.

But, in practice, the issue is much more troublesome. Wherever governments are strong, frontiers stable, social pressures manageable, ethnic and tribal strains under control, the ideological debate about Africa's future does not impinge on local security. But many states are not in this condition. Colonial frontiers are often an arbitrary inheritance and irredentism is the result—as on the frontiers of Somalia. Internal cohesion between tribes is often far from complete. The social structures of some states include unresolved conflicts between privileged groups and the mass of the poor. Feudal leaders on the Saharan fringe, for instance, and dominant professional and business classes in the more developed communities, enjoy living standards and opportunities closed to the majority, and the gap becomes steadily more apparent as cities grow and unemployment tends to increase. Many African states are, therefore, exposed to strong pressures for change, and the more these pressures undermine the stability of government, the more the ideological debate becomes a further factor of division.

It is an old story. Local divisions in Southeast Asia were entry points for the outsiders. Japan was able to preserve her independence in the sixteenth century only by heroic self-isolation. India after the collapse of the Moguls presents the same picture. Internal weakness invites external intervention and when the world is polarized between rival doctrines, the intervention will be all the more likely and all the more lethal. What is a war of liberation to the Communists is an act of subversion to the West, and if either radicals or moderates turn to outside sources of help, the country is quickly sucked into the whirlpool of the cold war.

For this reason, the Congo has proved, so far, a turning point in the development of African independence. Up to 1960, the newly founded states were stable and united enough to determine their own destiny, to explore new relations with East and West, to decide their own part in the world's fierce debate. But the Congolese, lacking all proper preparation for independence, fell apart and have hardly recovered their unity since. In the struggle internal forces have looked for outside support; the various efforts of secession—in Katanga, in the eastern provinces—have not failed to call on outside assistance; and today, after the withdrawal of the United Nations experiment to secure international control above the pressure of rival factions, civil dissension still rages, embittering the internal divisions of all Africa, sharpening ideological differences and creating the climate for a possible renewal of external intervention.

Nor is it difficult, in the light of these last five anguished years, to project into the future the appallingly divisive effects of the existing crisis. The deep rift over the Congo is dangerous enough. But if the struggle for African liberation in the Portuguese territories, in Southern Rhodesia and in the Union of South Africa becomes entangled with the worldwide hostility between East and West, the southern lands could become not only the scene of a prolonged and bloody racial struggle but even conceivably the flash point of escalation to nuclear war.

Can Africa in its own interest abate its own divisions and lessen the risks of outside pressure and intervention? That there is a strong internal drive toward African unity seems beyond question. The Organization for African Unity (o.a.u.) exists. Various subsidiary organs of unity—the Economic Commission for Africa, the African Development Bank—exist. They do so in spite of the divisions of Africa into French-speaking states attached, in the majority, to a close association with Europe and to the *Union Africaine et Malgache,* in spite of the British Commonwealth partnership, in spite of such local associations as the East African Common Services Organization.

Again, a certain amount of economic assistance to Africa is already being channeled in through international agencies—the World Bank, the International Development Association, the Special Fund, the affiliated U.N. agencies. New organs of unity such as the Economic Commission for Africa at Addis Ababa could accelerate the trend.

At various times, the African states have attempted to mediate their own disputes—over Somalia, over the Sahara. Their *ad hoc* body to settle the Congolese dispute is still in being although it did not achieve a basis for mediation. And this fact is perhaps the key to the relative ineffectiveness so far of the o.a.u.'s attempt to secure the autonomy of its efforts. The organization is already deeply divided between conservative and radical elements and has not yet found a stance above the battle of its constituent members. A completely *African* interpretation of today's crisis has not yet emerged. Africa is, like other continents, caught in the toils of the cold war and its freedom of action is correspondingly reduced.

Yet the last five years seem to give some clues toward wider unity and more effective African initiatives. Wherever the o.a.u. can act on the basis of majority opinion, the risks of outside interference are correspondingly reduced. If wider authority and greater resources are needed, the United Nations is a safer instrument of pacification than rival appeals to rival

Great Powers. At present, the U.N. is hamstrung by the Great Power dispute over peace-keeping and over the authority to control peace-keeping. But it would seem to be profoundly in the interests of African states, moderate or radical, right or left, to ensure that the United Nations can still act as policeman, conciliator and assistance-giver, provided the states most concerned with a dispute or a region wish U.N. jurisdiction to be introduced.

This is not simply an issue of peace-keeping. In view of the fatal lack of preparation for self-government given to Africans in such territories as Angola and Mozambique, international assistance on a massive scale would be needed after independence to prevent even worse versions of the Congo's tragedy. But such assistance can only safely come from the United Nations. Thus, the present time would seem the very last time at which Africa should acquiesce in a weakening of the powers and responsibility either of the organization in general or in particular of the General Assembly.

In a world driven by ideology, the small powers will founder if they are drawn into the maelstrom. As Dr. Nkrumah has often remarked: "When the bull elephants fight, the grass is trampled down." But the African states will avoid the bull elephants and keep their freedom of action only if they know how to keep clear of the Great Power struggle themselves and how to establish their own independent bases for action. Ultimately, no outside power can intervene effectively unless the invitation comes from within. And the invitations will cease only when Africans themselves realize effectively and fully the implications of their own unity.

Address At *Pacem in Terris* Convocation

ABDUL MONEM RIFA'I

It is not impossible; in fact it is quite feasible for humanity to succeed in destroying weapons of total annihilation. But man will not lack the means of war—as he did not lack them in the past—if the seeds of hatred and the elements of hostilities are to stay.

With the same logic I submit that the settlement of a certain problem shall not bring about the peace for which we search if such a settlement is dictated by only political considerations and if it does not take into primary account the moral aspects of the issue.

This is why we, the people who do not possess the wealth and the might, base our doctrine of peace on justice and right as everlasting rules for a peaceful life in which there is no room for fear or weakness.

In our concept of peace we envisage freedom—freedom in its widest sense—freedom from supremacy of one nation over another, and from one policy over the other. For it is the desire for superiority and supremacy that creates inequalities and disturbs social and international order. Such inequalities are bound to give rise to hostilities and violence between the ruled and the ruler, the slave and the master, and the poor and the rich.

The theory of equality springs from this concept. It demands that the strong should altruistically assist the weak and the developed should aid unselfishly the underdeveloped.

For in their need to be aided and to develop, small nations do not wish to see their independence hampered or their freedom diminished so as to find themselves moving in a certain orbit or heading in a certain direction. Peoples who strove to achieve independence prior to their economic development will by no means give up their independence after they made the transitional step towards development. It is no doubt a problem for us, and one for international peace, we who have aspired to achieve national independence, to preserve this independence while we need to continue to rely on foreign and international aid.

The United Nations, in its present phase, and the future which we hope for it, is the superstructure for collective security as well as for the protection of individual states. The United Nations which has so far successfully undertaken the granting of Independence to dependent peoples and territories should include in this process the aspect of securing the economic independence of these nations. This requires the wealthier nations to channel larger proportions of their economic aid through international bodies so as to be utilized for the purpose of maintaining independence.

I still feel, however, that until the United Nations becomes capable of assuming such a task regional organizations continue to be a useful machinery for serving such objectives.

For in the absence of effective international dependence and economic cooperation, direct foreign aids might in certain cases entail special foreign interests which might disturb harmony and international stability.

These apprehensions are exemplified in spots of serious tension in the world today.

To avoid such conflicts of interests the policy of nonalignment finds its way to the minds of many nations. Nonalignment is a philosophy which does not advocate nor does it entertain any expansionist motives or aggressive intentions. It is therefore a basic pillar for the establishment of world peace.

※ ※ ※ ※

The incorporation of these newly emerging and underdeveloped nations (and I am now including ancient and large cultural areas such as India, which in a sense is also newly emerging and certainly underdeveloped) into the modern world is not easy or simple. It seems extraordinary how little serious investigation there has been done as to the best ways to approach this problem. As Kenneth Boulding indicated (in Section I of this Reader) it requires a research effort at least comparable to the Manhattan project, which was directed towards war. In a very interesting article in the Fall 1964 *American Scholar,* John Hersey the novelist took two small concrete U.S. pockets of poverty-discrimination-crowding-illiteracy and general downward spiral of hope and expectation (Prince Edward County in Virginia, and a certain area of New Haven), whose case histories he knew intimately, and demonstrated from what actually happened that it *is* possible to do something about this syndrome we call poverty but that it takes an enormous amount of money, energy, brain power and community action, on a scale that makes our present "poverty program" look like a pittance. Where are these in such quantity to come from for our own country where the problem, though shocking, is residual and is being solved and for the world where it is not? To me the answer is obvious. From the arms race. What is required may not even cost so much in terms of money; it is the brains and energy and attention that matters most. In any society there are only a limited number of people of high intelligence and creative ideas. These are now sucked off, in one way or another, into the arms race and it is for the most part our less brilliant minds who occupy themselves with these other grave human problems. The waste makes me weep.

There is another aspect to the problem than sheer aid. One might say it calls more for the spirit of "I am my brother," than "I am my brother's keeper." One can express the problem crudely thus: How is any agency to do the job which must be done *quickly* enough to meet the crisis that is seen by a Boulding, a Myrdal or a Gerard Piel (editor of the *Scientific American,* whom I have heard speak passionately on this subject and which is his personal reason for supporting a limited world government of the Clark-Sohn style) without (for want of a better word) pauperizing the recipients? I have heard Edgar Snow, who knows China well, speak of the immense pride the ordinary Chinese feels in the fact that China is pulling herself up by her own bootstraps, is doing it herself. This pride is a real power. And I have heard educated and intelligent Puerto Ricans talk about the essential failure (although surface success) of "Operation Bootstrap" in which money was simply poured in from the United States. Yet there is no question the job must be done, and soon.

The following selection by Gustavo Lagos dealing with *atimia,* which is from the Greek word meaning "loss of status," does not answer my problem but it does give a greater understanding of it and it presents a very important aspect of the North-South confrontation. There seems to be no disagreement that the job cannot be properly handled except through an agency in which the recipients themselves participate— whether on a regional or a world basis.

International Stratification and Atimia

GUSTAVOS LAGOS

International stratification, in terms of economic stature, power, and prestige, was produced at the same time that the ideology of equalitarianism was holding sway in the field of international relations. The distinctive trait of this ideology is the affirmation that all states, from the moment they are constituted as such and from the moment they acquire independence, are free, sovereign, and equal. Sovereignty implies that each nation has the supreme authority to manage its external and internal affairs, with the exclusion of authority from any other nation, "in so far as it is not limited by treaty or . . . common . . . international law." All nations have the obligation to respect that independence or sovereignty and, in consequence, cannot interfere in its internal or external politics; "equality

. . . is nothing but a synonym for sovereignty, pointing to a particular aspect of sovereignty. If all nations have supreme authority within their territories, none can be subordinated to any other in the exercise of that authority." Out of "the principle of equality a fundamental rule of international law is derived which is responsible for decentralization of the legislative and, in a certain measure, of the law-enforcing function: the rule of unanimity. It signifies that with reference to the legislative function all nations are equal, regardless of their size, population and power. . . ." The vote of Panama counts as much as the vote of the United States.

The ideology of equalitarianism was one of the basic principles of Wilsonian thought. "An evident principle," he said, introducing his famous Fourteen Points in January, 1918, "runs through all the programme I have outlined. It is the principle of justice for all peoples and nationalities and their right to live on *equal terms* of liberty and safety with one another, *whether they be strong or weak*." The ideology of equalitarianism has always been the basic principle of international law, and it inspired the system of the League of Nations. The Charter of the United Nations did not give full recognition to the principle, because the veto power of some great nations was established. This situation was explained as a consequence of the fact that the great powers had an additional function: the maintenance of peace and security. In the field of inter-American relations, the ideology of equalitarianism found full recognition in Article 6, the Charter of the Organization of American States: "States are juridically equal, enjoy equal rights and equal capacity to exercise these rights, and have equal duties. The rights of each state depend not upon its power to ensure the exercise thereof, but upon the mere fact of its existence as a person under international law."

This ideology is also in perfect agreement with the thinking of the classical economists for whom the differences of economic stature among nations seemed unimportant. As Professor Triffin pointed out, interpreting the classical economic thought, "They would also point out . . . that if each nation-state acted rationally and embraced free trade, little or no damage could be done by the existence of separate political sovereignties and that the size of nations would then be irrelevant to their economic prosperity."

The concept of formal status of a nation emerges from this ideology. All nations have the same formal status; their positions, their rights, their duties in the system of international relations are the same. The achievement of these rights and duties is not influenced by size, population, wealth, historical age, military power, or political power.

In opposition to the formal status of the nation, the real status is found. While the first is derived from the equalitarian ideology, we have seen that the second is derived from the position that the nation occupies in the system of international stratification in its three basic variables, economic stature, power, and prestige. While in agreement with the first concept—all nations are equal—the structure of the stratified system also determines relationships of superordination and subordination among nations.

Before the present system of international stratification was established, when all nations were underdeveloped, the differences between nations still existed, but they were less accentuated. In such a period, a political leader such as Jefferson could think of assigning equal roles to the Brazilian and United States navies in the defense of the Western Hemisphere; today the American military budget is three times greater than the gross national product of Brazil, according to the most optimistic estimates of the latter.

There existed in that period less distance between the formal status of the nation and its real status, but now the fact that only a few nations have increased their real status to a considerable fashion has meant a degradation of real status for the rest.

Let us use a Greek word, *atimia,* which signifies the loss or deterioration of status, to designate this situation, and let us call the evolution or social change that ends in a state of *atimia* the *atimic* process. *Atimia* has manifested itself in various forms. Always its essential characteristic is the lowering of status, but this lowering can acquire total or partial characteristics.

Total *atimia* occurs when a nation has not been able to develop the necessary capacities to reach economic and technological maturity. This incapacity impedes its social development and maintains the economic stature—measured in terms of gross national product—on its lowest level. *Atimia* is manifested here in the three elements that constitute the economic status of the nation. As a consequence, the nation sees itself impeded in reaching a status on the power level, requiring, as a basic condition, technological maturity and a high gross national product.

All of the so-called underdeveloped countries that existed as independent nations, when international stratification developed, have suffered this process; as typical examples let us point out the Latin American nations and those of the Middle East. On the other hand, countries that have recently gained their independence in Asia and Africa have been born into an independent life in an already highly stratified international system. Although they have not experienced an *atimic* process, since they previously did not exist and in consequence could not suffer a lowering of a status that they did not have, they acquired formal status in a world in which there existed enormous differences between the formal status and the real status. Their positions in the international system doubtless would have been different had they acquired their independence when the rest of the world was underdeveloped, as happened with the United States and

Latin America at the end of the eighteenth and beginning of the nineteenth centuries. To use a metaphoric comparison in describing the system of national stratification, we can say that the countries that suffered the *atimic* process became the lower class in consequence of their *atimia,* while the countries who recently gained their independence were born into the lower class.

Partial *atimia* is produced when the nation, in spite of having acquired technological and economic maturity and social development, has not had the necessary economic stature, measured in terms of gross national product, to participate in the technological race, which is interpreted as the creation of the maximum expressions of military power. As typical cases of partial *atimia,* we may point out France and England. Although the *atimia* is evidenced in this case in power status, its economic implication is also clear since the lack of sufficient economic stature limits the capacity of the nation.

The most notorious indicator of total *atimia* is the lack of social development that is expressed by low standards of living. The most notorious indicator of partial *atimia* is the incapacity for technological leadership.

Total or partial *atimia* is also manifested in the pattern of prestige of the nation, because prestige needs institutional bases. Total *atimia* implies the lack of institutional bases of prestige linked with economic and technological maturity and with social development, while in the case of partial *atimia* institutional bases that permit a technological leadership have been lacking.

In this study we shall limit ourselves to analyzing the international consequences of total *atimia,* which is the common characteristic of underdeveloped countries.

Underdevelopment and atimia as a general definition of the situation of the underdeveloped countries

The highly stratified international system that we have described has created interactions of a peculiar nature among the nations that have experienced the *atimic* process—or its consequences—and those that have achieved a high status in economy and power.

The first result of this interaction has been the comparison of inequalities—a comparison that is typical of every system of stratification, as T. H. Marshall has pointed out: "Comparisons sustain both the sense of superiority of the rich over 'the great unwashed' and the sense of resentment of the poor against the 'idle rich.' Such feelings may be shared by any number of persons from a single individual to a whole nation."

The comparison of inequalities has been expressed in various dimensions. The governing elite of the underdeveloped countries have been able to appreciate from a close perspective the *atimic* situation in terms of military power, economic stature, and institutional development. The common man has perceived the most evident aspect of international inequality, the difference in standards of living.

As a typical example of the perception of inequality by the political head of a country, let us cite the words of President Kubitschek of Brazil as he explained the objective of Operation Pan-America: "Upon hearing a stronger voice for Latin America in the community of nations, the Pan-American Operation is not unaware that, in the hard realities of power politics, that voice will not be given a hearing unless it has its origin in countries of healthy economy and perfectly stabilized social institutions. . . . We cannot affirm our action unless we resolutely affirm our capacity for action. We cannot express our opinion with assurance on our neighbors' problems if we show ourselves incapable of solving our own problems. We wish to join the Free World but we do not wish to become its proletariat."

The common man has perceived international inequalities through the modern means of mass communication that has spread the social goals of the advanced countries on a large scale in the underdeveloped countries and has made known the high standard of living that exists in them.

It is *atimia* in one of its dimensions——the lack of social development —that has reached him.

> *Poverty is not new. But now there is a new factor. This is the awareness of poverty, the realization that it is not the inevitable lot of man, and the determination to do something about it. This new awareness, often referred to as the revolution of rising expectations, has come about largely as an indirect consequence of modern science and technology. . . . The wealth-producing capacity of science and technology was demonstrated in the more developed countries, proving that dire poverty for the masses is not inevitable. . . . This vast movement can be characterized as a quest for change in man's affairs by large sectors of population who previously had lived within static social patterns. This accelerated transition and transformation causes many strains and pressures throughout the social organism. . . . The world is divided into two camps, the traditional and the modern, the rich and the poor, the hungry and the satiated, the illiterate and the educated, the free and the oppressed. Potentially the most tremendous social force in the world of the 1960s will be the people who know they no longer have to be hungry and poor, who want education and freedom, who want bicycles, refrigerators, movies and radios, who want to see the city, who want it now. This force, this revolution in expectations, may prove to be the principal modern impact of science on man—the impact on his way of thought and on his values.*

The expression "underdeveloped country" is recent. It was mainly the United Nations and its specialized agencies who coined it when the differences between these countries and the more advanced nations became apparent. The fact that, in 1947, when the creation of the Economic Commission for Latin America was discussed in the Economic and Social Council of the United Nations, they described all the conditions of underdevelopment, but still did not use the word, is significant. In 1952 the United Nations published "The Preliminary Report on the World Social Situation," in which the social conditions of the world are described in the following terms: "More than half the population of the world is still living at levels which deny them a reasonable freedom from preventing disease; a diet adequate to physical well-being; a dwelling that meets basic human needs; the education necessary for improvement and development; and conditions of work that are technically efficient, economically rewarding and socially satisfactory." Although it is still difficult to establish the date on which the term "underdeveloped country" began to acquire universal usage, it may be stated that its use is little more than ten years old.

As Myrdal has pointed out it is interesting to note, concerning the use of this term, that it has a dynamic connotation.

> *The expression commonly used until quite recently was the static term "the backward countries." Both terms . . . are value-loaded, and it is conducive to clarity in our thinking that we are aware of this fact. The use of the concept "the underdeveloped countries" implies the value judgment that it is an accepted goal of public policy that the countries so designated should experience economic development. It is with this implication that people in the poorer countries use the term and press its usage upon people in the richer countries. When they, in their turn, accept this term and suppress the old one, "the backward countries," they also accept the implication. The change from the static to the dynamic concept thus implies in the richer countries a registration of a positive attitude [toward] . . . the poorer countries and, therefore, an acknowledgment—given naturally, only in a general and therefore necessarily vague form—that those countries are right in demanding higher standards of income, a bigger share in the good things of life, and greater equality of opportunity.*

The principal result of the comparison of international inequalities and of their expression has been the appearance of a group consciousness in the underdeveloped countries of their underdeveloped condition. The indications of such a consciousness are rich and varied. Let us point out several examples:

I. The term appears frequently in the official documents of the governing bodies of the underdeveloped nations. On opening the third meeting of the Committee of Twenty-one of the oas, the President of Colombia, Alberto Lleras Camargo, stated: "It is probable that in human history there has been no other case of such rapidity in the extension and intensity of a public preoccupation as that which has occurred with the problem of development, so that, for the third time, the countries of Latin America have dedicated another meeting exclusively to this matter."

During President Eisenhower's trip to Brazil, Argentina, Chile, and Uruguay in February and March of 1960, joint declarations were formulated by the President of the United States and the presidents of each of the countries visited in which development appears as the essential theme.

II. The use of the term is not limited to governmental spheres alone but has also reached political parties, which means that it has penetrated the language of political communication on the national level.

III. The fight against underdevelopment has come to be the essential objective of diverse international organizations sponsored by contributions from the governments. As an illustrative example we may point out: (a) the organizations of the Inter-American System that compose the administrative bodies of Operation Pan-America and the Alliance for Progress; (b) the creation of the International Development Association whose goals are to promote the economic development, increase the productivity, and, in this way, to raise the standard of living in the less developed regions of the world; (c) the Colombo Plan for Co-operative Economic Development in South and South-East Asia.

IV. The emergence in the heart of the United Nations of a group of fifty-seven underdeveloped countries of Asia, Africa, Latin America, and Eastern Europe with common hopes and interests concerning the problem of underdevelopment.

V. The fact that the Soviet leaders, in their propaganda, make the U.S.S.R. appear not so much the leader of world communism but rather the sustainer of underdeveloped countries reveals that the concept is readily accepted by public opinion in these countries.

VI. The debate of the Second Committee of the Fifteenth United Nations General Assembly, in which speaker after speaker pointed out that the rich nations were getting richer faster than the less developed nations, with the result that year by year the gap between the living standards of the two groups was growing wider.

The contradiction between the formal status and the real status of the underdeveloped nations has tended to accentuate the group consciousness of the state of underdevelopment. In agreement with the ideology of equalitarianism, the nations know that they have "equal rights, equal capacity to exercise these rights, equal duties" along with the nations of high economic status or power. They know also that their rights "do not depend on their power." But next to this ideological world, they find also the realities of power, of economic stature, and of prestige, all built on a complex gradation of status that is characterized by relationships of superordination and subordination.

In this context, the underdeveloped nations arrive at a general definition of their international situations, characterized by their low status as a consequence of the *atimic* process. In this study, our principal hypothesis is that, within this general definition of the situation, diverse international actions take place and that their total orientation is the elevation of the real status of the nation.

As the real status is composed of economic, power, and prestige variables, our effort will be directed to the study of these variables. We shall try to construct a conceptual scheme that may serve for the analysis of the variables and of their interrelationships, a conceptual scheme that may permit the sociological investigation of the international actions of the underdeveloped countries by means of empirical investigation. Our task falls then within the scientific orientation that Merton calls "theories of the middle range," theories that have a delimited range of social phenomena and are not "all inclusive speculations comprising a master conceptual scheme."

The orientation of these systems of action throws new light on the interpretation of the nationalist phenomenon. Nationalism, understood as the promotion of national interests in a world of sovereign states, acquires new perspectives from the point of view of the *atimic* process. The rise in real status appears to be for the underdeveloped nations the correct interpretation of the international dimensions of their national interests.

In his study *The Stages of Economic Growth,* Rostow pointed out that "as a matter of historical fact a reactive nationalism—reacting against intrusion from more advanced nations—has been a most important and powerful motive force in the transition from the traditional societies, at least as important as the profit motive."

Nationalism of the underdeveloped countries is also a reactive nationalism—reacting against *atimia* or its consequences—attempting to enhance the status of the nation in a stratified world that is dominated by the values of wealth, power, and prestige.

Postscript to Rich Nations and Poor Nations

A number of thoughtful, informed persons are coming increasingly to believe that the chief commodity which the developed nations must supply to the underdeveloped is *education,* which is the only door through which they can enter the modern world in their own right. Even this is not simple. The poor countries suffer attrition in so many ways. Due to their late entry into the modern acceleratingly productive world there is now a recognized "brain drain" by which poor nations are losing their most talented youth to the already developed nations because they do not see sufficient facilities, scope and jobs for themselves at home. This too could be solved by an intelligent, carefully researched attack on the most glaring problems of the underdeveloped nations conducted under the nonpolitical auspices of a world institution. Those who directed this research would be wise to recognize that in the evolution of man *diversity*, and his ability to incorporate diversity into an ever more complex whole rather than relying on specialization, has been his special gift. In other words, industrialized man as we have known him may not be the *only* form of man for the future. It may not be necessary or advisable for all the underdeveloped nations, many of whom are in southern climates which induce a different mode of life, to follow a course of development exactly like our own. They might better follow a somewhat different course and develop *other* traits of which man is capable that might be lost to mankind as a whole otherwise. Lost to us too. We could die of our own specialization and industrialization. We have an interest in these people which is not charity, for as Dr. George Wald, Professor of Biology at Harvard University, pointed out in a lecture (March 14, 1966) at the Museum of Natural History in New York, moral values are not superfluous decorations but are essential to man's survival. That is why they developed in the first place.

※ ※ ※ ※

A great resistance to thinking about a world order is that it appears as static, lifeless, inhuman—either repressively authoritarian or impossibly utopian. Yet change *must* occur, struggles *will* continue. In this next article, Millis imagines what a disarmed world might really look like and thereby gives flesh and blood to the kind of world that actually might emerge, even under Clark and Sohn. He also suggests a relationship be-

tween supranational authority and local authority that is different from
Clark and Sohn and well worth examining.

Millis points out that two thirds of the population of the globe live
today under four or five great centers of power, of internal law and order
of one sort or another: *i.e.* the United States, the Western European
Democracies, the Soviet Union, China and perhaps India (whether we
approve of the system or not is irrelevant). These have more or less excluded violence and bloodshed from their domestic affairs as instruments
of practical politics. The remaining third of the global population—*i.e.*
Southern Asia, Africa and much of Latin America—is less well organized. Domestic change within these areas takes place violently.

Since there has been historically an intimate relationship between
domestic violence (revolution) and international violence (war), Millis
asks us to look at the relationship between internal and external power
structures. If we succeed in abolishing great wars can there be great revolutions, and, conversely, will great revolutions inevitably create great
wars?

A breakdown of the Russian or Chinese internal power structure,
for instance, could hardly be dealt with by any presently foreseeable supranational police force with sufficient force and authority to "restore
order" in a chaotic Russia or China. In other words, the system that
Millis foresees would not be perfect. But the concept of a legitimate
authority would have been introduced and "a politics that starts from a
universal and complete disarmament has a far better chance of meeting
this sort of situation than one which starts with the system of organized
war."

One cannot predict exactly what the removal of organized war
would do to the process of domestic revolution. In the present great
organized power centers it is unlikely that the removal of organized war
would affect the problem of necessary change. The real question lies
with the less organized areas.

It is because Clark and Sohn visualize so clearly the tensions and
power struggles and potential violence that would continue to exist in a
disarmed world that they would set up at the same time an obligatory
judicial system and strong powers of enforcement, plus built-in checks
on the global authority itself. Millis likewise does not see Utopia as fol-

lowing from disarmament. The chief difference in the disarmed world as envisioned by Millis and that of Clark and Sohn lies in the character and size of the police force. Millis visualizes it as small and relatively weak, although representing a legitimate authority. In a disarmed world, without the existence of the present enormous weapons systems, the world police force would be sufficient to ensure that rearmament did not take place, but it would not be militarily powerful enough—as Millis sees it— to fight a war against the remaining domestic police force of a large nation, any more than our F.B.I., which likewise represents a legitimate authority, is equipped to wage a successful armed battle with a state or municipal police force. For the supranational police force to perform its functions there would have to be a certain amount of voluntary restraint on the part of the domestic police force. The activities of the supranational force would be far more like the U.N. "police action" in the Congo than that in Korea. In Korea the U.N. was a military force which attempted to decide the power struggle. In the Congo it was a truer "police" force attempting merely to avert extremes of savagery, violence and irresponsibility.

Thus Millis concludes that in a warless world domestic changes of power structure will probably continue to take place pretty much as they do now, *i.e.* with reasonable lack of violence in the large areas of the world that have developed internal order, and with considerable violence which the supranational force can mitigate but not suppress in the areas of the world that have not yet developed internal order. We would have to put up with a good deal of violence and small wars for a long time. *But,* and it is a large "but," in a disarmed world it would be "without the corroding fear of catastrophe which today complicates and distorts every real problem of international politics."

The use of models as a technique for thinking about the complicated problems of war prevention is helpful in making us understand the present and in seeing ways to the future. One can take the Millis view as an intermediate stage on the way to the Clark-Sohn model. Or one can regard it as sufficiently different to be taken in this respect as an alternate model of its own.

It is perhaps useful to add one further note which is not a part of Millis' thesis: Failure to achieve disarmament as a precondition need not be taken as defeat of all progress toward world order under law. It is possible that the institutions might come first with rather little actual disarmament but disarmament following as simply the most practical and economical way of life. This, in essence, was the course followed by many of our own Western frontier towns which operated under the posse system until citizens appealed to the governor for a sheriff, a jail and at least a visiting judge. Local residents did not abandon their personal six-shooters at once, but as the new system proved itself both more reliable, more just and less prone to bloodshed than the old, they gradually did so. Chief Justice Warren, in a speech to the Jewish Theological Seminary (May 4, 1966) spoke of "how ethical insights, cultural change and law interact to change human nature on a broad scale." Law and institutions can in themselves pioneer and assist the climate for necessary change.

"If through some miracle" he said "it were possible to develop a superstructure of international cooperation and law, analogous to our Federal Union, the peoples of the world would in a few generations come to think of one another as neighbors and fellow citizens; and the perils of hyper-nationalism would disappear."

Order and Change in a Warless World

WALTER MILLIS

To imagine a warless world is to imagine a special kind of world order—a system of "law and order" which must nevertheless allow for the disorder, conflict, and change essential to the development of human institutions. An idea must be formed of how such change, which throughout history has been so often and so deeply associated with war, can come about with a minimum of physical violence.

That change through conflict will continue to come about, regardless, is scarcely arguable. The complicated struggles among individuals, groups, classes, communities, or nations for wealth, position, and power is inherent in human nature. No system of world law and order can eliminate these power struggles; it would be primarily a means of regulating or structuring them.

The relative "justice" of such regulation is highly important from the standpoint of support for the system, but it seems essentially secondary—a by-product, as it were—to the "order" which the system would impose. There have, of course, been highly unjust orders which have survived over long periods and others comparatively just which have suffered early collapse. The essential of any order, just or unjust, is that it forces the competitive struggles among those subject to it into other than lethal or violent channels.

In any system of law and order one finds three elements, which are the mechanisms through which it achieves its purpose: (1) a sovereign "monopoly" of legal force to forbid resort to violence; (2) a system of general rules (law) defining in generalized terms the rights, duties, and, therefore, the power positions of all involved; (3) a judicial system to apply the general rules in specific conflicts and to provide in its decisions a generally accepted alternative to trial by combat or violence.

No system of this kind, of course, is ever perfectly successful. An irreducible minimum of violent crime, usually a certain amount of rioting and group violence, remains under the most developed systems of law and order. Nor has any such system ever completely inhibited change; even the most static and somnolent of social orders has never been "frozen" into a coma. It is true that a developed system of law and order has the effect, at any given time, of defining—crystallizing—the power relations of the individuals, groups, and classes subject to it, and that this crystallized legal structure of power may survive after the actual power relationships in the community have changed. But when the actual power structure tends to get out of line with the legal definition, it is, sooner or later, the legal definition which is altered, not the newly emerging structure of power.

When the discrepancy between the fact and the form grows too great, such changes may be violent, reflected in great wars on the international stage or bloody revolutions within. But war and violent revolution are by no means the only or the necessary means of adjusting the system of law and order to changes in the underlying power structure. The modern world has recorded immense adjustments of the kind largely, if not wholly, effected by nonviolent means.

Nor is it true that these can occur only in those systems which, as in the Western democracies, include formal provision for popular participation in institutional change. Toynbee, in the opening article in this series, cites the abdication of the Tokugawa Shogunate in Japan—at the time anything but a democratic society—and the accompanying political and social revolution, all accomplished with very little violence. Since the death of Stalin, if not before, considerable shifts have plainly been occurring in the power structure both of the Soviet Union itself and among the constituent states of the Communist empire. But the Communist system of law and order (which is no less a system of law and order because it seems to us an unjust one) has accommodated itself to these changes in general without war or revolution. The one violent revolution of importance—that in Hungary—was suppressed by the Soviet police power, thus leaving Communist law and order outwardly intact. But the ruthlessness with which "order" was reimposed in Hungary does not mean that the system is perpetually unchangeable. The Hungarian revolt will still make its contribution toward those changes—hopefully nonviolent, but changes in any event—which shifts in the underlying Communist power structure are certain to bring about.

Even the existing international order, "anarchic" as it is commonly assumed to be, has since 1945 adjusted itself to very great changes in the basic power relations of peoples, states, classes, and groups with, on the whole, a rather surprising minimum of war or other violence. Discussions of a new world order usually overlook the fact that we already possess a more highly developed system of international law and order than ever before in history. It is a system not yet reduced to statutory form or fully embodied in treaty undertakings; and its institutional expressions, such as the U.N., are still quite rudimentary. It is a system, nevertheless. It is incapable, certainly, of "freezing" the political and social institutions of mankind into any perpetual mold; yet it is currently proving itself adequate to insure that for most peoples, most of the time, the infinitely complex struggle for power is carried on by essentially nonviolent means.

Perhaps two thirds of the population of the globe live today under no more than four or five great, stabilized, and mutually more or less invulnerable centers of power, of law and of order: the United States, the Western European democracies, the Soviet Union, China, and perhaps India. They appear rather effectively to have excluded violence and bloodshed from their domestic affairs as instruments of practical politics. Each has effectively developed the essentials of rule by law: a police force quite capable of forbidding anything more than merely casual resort to violence; a system of general rules to govern the internal power struggles, and at least some kind of adjudicatory and regulatory system to apply the rules and to offer an alternative to trial by violence which, however imperfect or unjust, can be accepted as preferable.

These great systems of law and order differ widely in their efficiency, their subtlety, and their sophistication as social organizations. It is difficult, for instance, to find much parallel between the deliberations of the Supreme Court of the United States and the intrigues within the Soviet power elite in the Kremlin, except that both serve the same broad purpose. Each offers an acceptable (or at any rate accepted) alternative to armed violence and rebellion in the settlement of basic power issues. Different as they are, each of these great systems appears to have established its ability to keep order, with yet enough flexibility to permit necessary change to take place without extremes of violence.

This at any rate, appears to be the common opinion. No one, for example, can seriously suppose that the United States will remain fixed in the particular mold of political, social, and economic relationships which it has attained in 1962. We all look for great changes of one kind or another in the American power structure; but it takes a John Birchite mentality to imagine that violent revolution either will or can accompany them. Much the same is true of the great Communist states. The shifting and uncertain power relations between Moscow and Peking are well advertised in the Western press; but no serious student has been rash enough to predict that they will end in a Sino-Soviet war. It is not the likelihood of armed rebellion in China or the USSR that impresses most, but its apparent impossibility in the foreseeable future.

Thus two thirds of the population of the globe already live under reasonably stable systems of law and order, so stable that no one predicts violent revolution or collapse for any of them (unless as a result of another world war), yet not so rigid as to be incapable of necessary change and development. By whatever paths of blood and misery the world has attained this result, it has attained it; one must recognize its novelty—for it is a phenomenon almost as unprecedented in history as are the nuclear arsenals themselves—as well as its obvious importance to the general problem of world law and order.

Unfortunately, much of the remaining third of the global population is less well organized. Southern Asia, Africa, and much of Latin America are being swept by the "revolution of expectations," inordinately complicated by nationalism, by racial and class conflict, by differences between the small educated elite groups, with their urban followers, and the peasant masses, as well as by the tendency of the great, stable power centers to exploit these difficulties for the advancement of their own power and influence. Speaking very generally, over much of this area the basic power structures (both domestic and international) are in a fluid state; it is the problem of the new leadership not so much to "seize power" as to discover the new bases on which a viable power structure may be erected. What rules (law) are available, whether derived from decisions in the U.N., from the principles of international law, or from domestic constitutional and institutional arrangements, are clearly out of line with the highly complicated actual power relationships.

Over much of this area no general rule of law and order, even a repressive one like that which the Soviet Union has successfully established over its many different peoples and different conflicts of interest, seems possible. And it would appear that a good deal of violence—whether in the savage form that occurred in the Congo or in Algeria, or simply the military coups d'états that have, with relatively little bloodshed, interrupted the processes of "democracy" in so many parts of the world—is inevitable. No system of law and order can hope to avert all violence, or dispense justice with a hand so even that men, groups, and communities will never seek to "take the law in their own hands." But it is still surprising that so little, not so much, violence and bloodshed has attended the enormous shifts in group, class, and national power relationships which have taken place since 1945.

Such is the situation in which we find ourselves today. We have developed a system of world law and order unprecedented in human experience. It contains no global monopoly of legal force adequate to forbid violent solutions to the problems of nations, classes, communities, and groups, although for the time being the great weapons-systems seem to be providing an effective substitute. Change is certainly proceeding as rapidly as most could wish; yet within an order sufficient to permit the vast majority of the world's peoples to live currently at peace and keep such violence as does continue to occur within tolerable bounds. It is an order sufficient to permit even more—to permit the growth of what Robert C. Angell has felicitously called the "interstitial tissue" of global organization: "Actually, an elaborate web of relationships is being woven among the peoples of the world. . . . There is live and growing tissue around us, interstitial tissue, if you will, which is spreading and becoming stronger every year." What would be the effect on this general situation of the assumed excision from it of the organized war system?

This is really the central question. All that we have been asked to assume in this series is an initial abolition of organized war, with the introduction of whatever (only vaguely specified) institutional arrangements may be necessary to maintain the abolition. How, so far as securing necessary social and political change is concerned, would the resultant warless system differ from the existing one? The easy answer is to say that it would differ very little; but there is an obstacle to the easy answer. This lies in the still obscure but clearly intimate relationship which has existed through most of history between domestic violence and revolution and international violence and war. The two have probably been intermingled in most of the major changes in human systems of law, order, and power-organization. Great wars have led to great revolutions; great revolutions have led to great wars. Perhaps the causal relationship was not in fact so simple as this would suggest; but the observation at least inspires an inquiry as to whether, if there are no more great wars, there can be any more great revolutions; or, conversely, if there are to be further great revolutions, will not great wars inevitably be revived?

Our presently existing world order seems to be both sufficiently flexible and sufficiently stable to meet the necessities of change without intolerable concomitants of violence. But so did the Atlantic world appear to its inhabitants on the eve of the French Revolution; so did the Western and the Russian imperial world appear on the eve of World War I. Both the Soviet Union and China today appear to represent stable systems of law and order. But the appearance may prove to be illusory. As power relationships continue to shift within the rigid frameworks of these great societies, it may be that nothing short of violent and bloody rebellion will suffice to break up the old power structures and institute the new.

Revolutionary violence in France after 1789 not only reorganized the domestic power structure; it fractured the international power structure of the time and led to the first total wars of modern history. Given an initially warless world, a similar violent breakdown of the Russian or Chinese power structures might have similar effects. No presently imaginable system of policed disarmament could deal finally or completely with such a situation. It is hard to picture an international police force endowed with either the physical force or, more importantly, the authority to intervene in a chaotic Russia in order to "restore order." It is easy to imagine the pressures upon the contiguous national police forces to intervene in one way or another in order to preserve their national interests; and to see that these pressures could lead to "escalation," rearmament, and war by processes which the international police would find difficult to control. All that one can say to this is that perfection is unattainable in this world; no system of politics will infallibly meet all the problems that may arise before it. But a politics which starts from a universal and policed disarmament, has a far better chance of meeting this sort of situation than has one which starts with the system of organized war.

There is the opposite case, often illustrated by the Russian Revolution of 1918, in which it is held that great international wars are necessary to break up encrusted and anachronistic power structures inhibiting human development. That wars have had this effect can hardly be doubted, but that major war is a necessary element in political and social advance is much more dubious. In the usual view, the Russian Revolution actually began with Alexander II's emancipation of the serfs in 1861, a voluntary recognition by the autocracy (not unlike the abdication of the Tokugawa Shogunate) that times were changing and that the legally established power structure in Russia would have to be modified accordingly. The process thereafter continued, haltingly, not without a good deal of violence on the part of government and revolutionaries alike, but rather steadily.

Even imperial Russia had within it the potentialities of necessary change; and many believe that the autocracy would have undergone a relatively peaceable "constitutionalization" of the new power relationships —rather as happened in Britain and was happening in Germany—*except* for World War I. The Russo-Japanese War of 1904-05 no doubt pushed the autocracy along the avenues to modernization; but World War I simply paralyzed and finally destroyed it, leaving it as helpless to promote as it was to resist the change which was overdue. Power passed by default into other and more ruthless hands, who built and imposed a new power structure, one which was at least somewhat more responsive to the realities than the Czarist system had been, though hardly an ideal case of political and social evolution. World War I, in this view, was not necessary to political and social change in Russia; all that it did was to distort this change into extreme, and generally inefficient, forms.

Organized war and violent domestic revolution have thus been closely associated, historically, with the processes of political and social change. But the exact nature of the association is not too clear; and it is not easy to be dogmatic about the probable effect of the removal of one, organized war, from the global order. One may hazard some guesses. In the absence of international war, certain processes of violent internal change could not go on as they have done. Revolutionaries, for example, would have less chance of acquiring small arms and financial and propaganda support from rival outside powers than they have today. At the same time, they would have less to fear from outside intervention. To revert to the eighteenth-century examples, another American Revolution could not count on the assistance rendered by France as a strategic move in her war with Britain; another French Revolution would not have to face the coalition of powers joined in defense of the *ancien régime*.

It is not easy to strike a plausible balance between such possibilities; but so far as the present great organized power centers are concerned, it seems reasonable to predict that the abolition of organized war among them would not seriously affect the problem of necessary change. After all, at the end of World War I, the Western Allies attempted to intervene with armed force in the Russian revolutionary situation, in a way they could not do in a world disarmed by assumption. Their lack of success at least suggests that the presence or absence of national armaments would not greatly affect such basic reorganizations of the power structure as were then taking place.

Perhaps the real question lies not with the great and relatively stabilized power systems, but with the less-organized areas. How far will a warless world order try to limit the more sporadic disorder and violence that one must expect here? In a generally disarmed world one may expect the simple absence of the hypertrophied weapon systems to supply an adequate equivalent for a global "monopoly of legal force." The want of the necessary weapons systems will generally forbid resort to violence by any of the great power centers. (The argument, it must be remembered, is based on the assumption that the weapons systems have been *voluntarily* laid aside and destroyed.)

But with the survival everywhere of national police forces, there will be no lack of at least light weapons in the world accessible to bold or desperate men and to their followers. Riots and mob violence, the more organized use of such weapons as plastic bombs, the even more highly organized forms of guerrilla war, will still be possible. The military coup d'état will still be possible through the manipulation of the national police. (Indeed, most of the "military" forces which have participated in such affairs have amounted to little more than what one would expect the national police in a warless world to be.)

How far will a warless order, through its international police force, attempt to control all these forms of residual violence? It seems improbable that the attempt will go very far. The assumed elimination of major organized war must, after all, eliminate the one great danger in current minor wars and violence—the danger of escalation into a great-power conflict. It seems evident that the warless order must have not merely an international but a supranational (that is, veto-free) police force to control disarmament and to ensure that rearmament does not take place. But a supranational, veto-free police force can take on reality only as its empowerment (authority) as well as the physical force at its disposal is strictly limited to that requisite for its police functions. It is difficult to envisage an international or supranational police force as a great army, capable of coercing the states which must support it and overawing the national police forces which they will retain. One sees this force rather as comparable to the American Federal Bureau of Investigation, which wields very great power within the American system, but does so precisely because its weapons are of negligible importance and its empowerment strictly limited. The FBI obviously could not wage a successful armed battle with any state or municipal police force. It has other means of ensuring its power in state and municipal police circles; and it seems obvious that the real power of the supranational police force vis-à-vis the remaining national police forces with which it must work will rest on similar bases.

The concept of an "international police power" has a long, though generally unfortunate, history. Experience seems to demonstrate that while some power of the kind is necessary to avert extremes of savagery, violence, and irresponsibility, it can succeed in this much only if it refrains from itself trying to settle or decide the power struggles out of which the violence arises. One may compare the U.N. "police action" in Korea with that which it was driven by circumstance to take in Palestine and the Congo. The attempt in the first case was to intervene in a major power struggle, and it ended, as probably it could only have ended, in a fairly major international war. In Palestine and the Congo the attempt has been to limit the savagery as far as possible, without authority to decide the power struggles involved. It seems probable that the patterns along which a supranational police force in a warless world order would tend to develop are to be found in the Congo, not in Korea. For its problems would, in a real sense, be police and not military problems.

Perhaps what was first advanced as the easy answer is the right answer as well. Assuming the removal of the organized war system, the political and social institutions reflecting the underlying power organization of the world, of its peoples, states, classes, communities, and groups, would continue to grow and change much as they are now doing in fact, but without the corroding fear of catastrophe which today complicates and distorts every real problem of international politics.

IV

TRANSITION STEPS —
AND AN ARROW
TOWARD THE FUTURE

In this last section are examples of transition steps, many of which could be undertaken tomorrow, which would further the creation of world institutions to eradicate war and alleviate the worst ills of mankind. They are of many kinds, for many temperaments; indeed no one is excluded from taking part. Those offered are by no means exhaustive, and certainly others will arise as events happen. On the whole they support a way of thinking and a general direction of acting. What is important is that we constantly define with increasing clarity the world order that seems to us relevant and desirable and that we examine all ways to reach it.

The last item brings us back to the beginning of this inquiry, to the dropping of the first atomic bomb and to individual people again. You will find the description of a law case which, with enough awareness and reason on our part, may be a straw pointing to a more human future.

N o great change—and probably not any small one—is brought about by reason alone. It is dependent on elements deep within us, on emotions and attitudes which are a subtle outgrowth of many things and are acquired from infancy onwards. It is difficult to change them on a large scale except in response to a trauma—such as the experience of Hiroshima was for the Japanese whose entire national attitude about the value of military power underwent a change such that they, as people, formerly valuing war high, determined to eschew war forever and wrote this into their constitution. But personal attitudes do change and are responsive to smaller traumas than World War III. They are also changed by expanded awareness which is arrived at in many ways and which I see as the chief index of growth in the human being. And personal attitudes are the components of a national attitude.

Nothing is so powerful an agent as direct experience. This is what the civil rights movement has had: encounters with persons, encounters with actual situations. It is our infinite debt to the Negro leaders that they have allied themselves, not to violence, but to our deepest values and thus brought our emotional value-life and our political life together again. Another invaluable lesson from the civil rights movement is that these immense issues are not to be left to governments but are the concern of all of us, and that everyone can act.

In relation to the abolition of war as an instrument of national policy (both the civil rights movement and the thesis of this book have law in common as the basis of the solution—law seen as a freeing agent, not as a repressive one), there are a number of simple things that should happen:

We must face the consequences of our present course of hedging and contingency.

Those whose instinctive responses tend to favor the sort of world order that is indicated by these readings must formulate what this means in political terms so that they may have a cohesive approach to the problems and crises of our time. Then they may begin to draw to their side those whose instinctive responses are similar to their own but whose attention is focused in other fields. Otherwise much energy is lost in emotion which is unrelated to a positive line of action and consequently frustrating.

Others, who at present favor political attitudes based on more traditional habits of thought, will perhaps ask themselves in the light of today's world what moral attitudes are implied in the political courses they favor. Some may find a split in themselves which they may wish to resolve. In short, the first step, as in the civil rights movement, is to bring our political attitudes and our value attitudes in contact with each other where they belong. Only as unified persons can we meet the psychological challenge to make drastic changes in our ingrained habits of behavior and thinking that the actual scientific conditions of life now demand.

In relation to the paradoxes involving the use of power, force and justice, freedom and authority that have been set forward, particularly by Tillich, we must embrace them fully because they are essential to the creative tension of life. But we must not be immobilized by them. There is a Zen proverb for this which is simply "Walk on" (*i.e.* take the next step—do the best you can).

Life is paradox. It is also process. As Betty Goetz Lall said, "World Law is not something you get to and say *Ah.*" Where the words "solution" and "answer" have been used in these readings they have had for-our-time, not teleological, meanings. I wish to emphasize that a system change such as advocated by Clark and Sohn is not something distinct from the evolutionary process, but is characteristic of it. A form is developed and elaborated as far as it will go. Then something happens which is a change in fundamental structure and organization; the shift may be tiny at first but it is not mere elaboration and mere development. Indeed, system change has carried the main thrust of life and one can say, as does Teilhard de Chardin, that the direction of evolution has been toward greater and greater consciousness and greater and greater cephalization (heading)—*i.e.* organization. This is not merely an analogy with biological forms, for, just as the emergence of thought and what flows from it takes place within the evolutionary process, so does the emergence of society and what flows from it. Seen in the vast picture the change that transfers *some* sovereignty from the nation to the world is minute. Seen from the point of view of ourselves it is a wrench to much of our habitual thinking, a big step, carrying with it, like all system changes in the framework of evolution, new possibilities for life and growth.

By the same token, when we speak of "transition steps" they are not to be thought of as between now and some ultimate, final goal, but immediate attitudes and acts that would push forward the creation *within* the foreseeable future of initial world institutions adequate for the world's most fundamental needs. We have focused on war prevention, both because modern war embodies the most devastating and immediate dangers, and because it usurps so much passion, energy, brains, attention and material resources that should be turned instead on the problems of starvation and overpopulation and the quality of life.

"Transition steps" are of all sorts: large and small, simple and highly complicated demanding specialization and research. Some are concrete acts. Some are changes in habits of thinking. As well as the selections following I hope you will look back at the important articles by Hugh Gaitskell and Jerome Frank.

The last entry in this reader is about a legal case which took place in December 1963 in Japan and which may be a first tentative crystallization of something new. As Richard Falk says, it is what *becomes* of the Shimoda case that is important—whether it is a first wisp pointing to the future, or an abortive flicker that is exterminated. It is a most interesting case: in the development of law, in the development of world order, in the development of the individual's relationship to that world order, and in the development of mankind becoming conscious of itself. It leaves us with a great deal to think about.

火 火

On the weekend of February 11, 12 and 13, 1966, a group of 38 students from seven colleges or universities met at Sarah Lawrence College on their own initiative to discuss war prevention and world order. They had to assist them a small panel of invited experts who made informal statements on the various parts of the students agenda and to whom they could address questions. In her brief talk, Betty Goetz Lall* touched on so many excellent points in regard to "transition steps" that I can think of no better way to introduce the subject. As her talk was not written down, I must simply enter my own notes which, however, have been checked over by her.

Notes on a talk by

BETTY GOETZ LALL

February 12, 1966

World law is not something we get to and say "Ah." It is a constantly evolving process, like all law. We must emphasize that what we are doing is evolving the law of the future, *not* imposing the law or procedure of the past. This is particularly important in regard to new countries which tend to see international law as a development of the Western colonial powers and overfavorable to those powers. People will accept the idea of world law, however, when rightly explained.

Within the complicated ways in which governments let each other know what they really mean and really intend, one of the things leaders can do when they wish to show they *want* an agreement is to *answer their critics at home*. In the case of Vietnam this is not being done. Now neither side on Vietnam really believes the other side wants a settlement.

In this connection it is well to remember there is danger in the tendency to believe the *worst* of your adversary. A good example of avoiding this difficulty occurred during the Cuban crisis: During those tense hours when messages flew back and forth between the government of the U.S.S.R. and the government of the United States, two different interpretations of a certain Khrushchev message were possible. We decided to choose the one *most favorable* to a peaceful settlement, and signaled back by the wording of our answer that this was how we were going to interpret it. This allowed the other side to make a reply that furthered this peaceful direction, which would not have been possible for them had we

---

* *Betty Goetz Lall was a State Department arms control expert and the staff director of the Senate Foreign Relations Committee's subcommittee on disarmament. She is a political scientist and is now attached to Cornell University's School of Industrial and Labor Relations.*

chosen the other interpretation. This is the sort of transition step toward peaceful solution governments can make in time of crisis.

In the long range and in the short, we must constantly look to immediate steps that will lead us in the direction we want to go.

Look at the U.N. What should we do there?

NUMBER 1: Bring in China. As *fast* as possible. It is obvious we must have all the parties in the club. To bring China in might, as some say, "make our life more difficult" but it would not "wreck the U.N." China may not accept at first, but we must keep asking her. The U.N. cannot be a world body without her.

NUMBER 2: Remove our self-judging clause re the World Court (*i.e.* repeal the Connally Amendment), and also remove as many self-judging clauses as possible from treaties. This would show our willingness to move toward world law that meant something, whereas our reluctance to do so sets a bad example.

NUMBER 3: Reevaluate Article 43 of the United Nations Charter. This has to do with military forces made available to the U.N. Some smaller countries have already designated certain forces over to the U.N. as permanently available. This whole matter presents an opportunity for *cooperation* with the U.S.S.R. and might lead to the formation of a small permanent U.N. police force. But the United States so believes there is so little possibility of constructive work on Article 43 that the offer of the small countries was never even discussed in the Security Council as part of a permanent arrangement. This is an example of distrust by one side shutting off action which might have produced useful agreement.

Look at economic steps

NUMBER 1: The major powers have been slow to channel aid through international institutions but this is changing fast now. Aid should be divided into purely development aid, which should be channeled through international institutions, and aid with political motivations, which would be kept under national control. This would have the merit of honesty among other things. If, for example, our aid to India were channeled through the U.N. this would make a great difference to the government of Mrs. Indira Gandhi.

NUMBER 2: In the trade field, there is a dollar flow abroad and an effort to protect the balance of payments. So what do we do? We cut down our free imports straight across the board, when our dollar flow is only difficult in a few countries. This is a small thing but it is unfortunate. We should *favor* the underdeveloped countries in our trade agreements (tariffs, etc.).

Look at our attitudes

We must work on our whole attitude toward communism. Communism has been and is changing. Coexistence used to be considered such a dirty word. Now one can say: What's the matter with it? It is important that we keep reexamining our attitudes.

Look carefully at our power

We are so powerful, so "right" and so "good." Look sometimes how we must appear to others, and remember that *we* can afford to take more risks than the other fellow simply because we are so rich and so powerful.

Look hard at intervention

We should try *not* to circumvent the U.N.

Look at our defense budget

Few people look critically at how huge it is and what it is used for. It goes through the Senate in one day while the disaramament agency budget is haggled over, thousand dollars by thousand dollars.

(In response to a question by a student as to how one could personally act toward getting China admitted to the U.N., Mrs. Lall said:)

When you think something's unpopular, you must find others who think as you do, to give each other courage. (This is a point stressed by Jerome Frank, that it is hard for one person alone to stand up against group consensus, but in company he can.) As an example in relation to the admission of China: A few of us—Dr. Harold Taylor, myself and a small group of Asian scholars—drew up a carefully reasoned petition, a sort of position paper, for the admission of China to the United Nations which

we sent to professors of Asian studies in all those universities which had
such departments. We got many more signatures than we had anticipated
and many were from people who were sympathetic but might otherwise
not have expressed themselves. There are often more people who are with
you than you know, and you must seek them out. (A month later, on
March 21, 1966, this petition and a news story about it appeared prominently in *The New York Times*. Like the China Conference conducted at
the University of Chicago's Center for Continuing Education [February 8-
11, 1966] and the follow-up public meetings a week later in Chicago,
Cleveland, St. Louis, Madison and Minneapolis, this petition played a part
in helping Americans to re-evaluate their extraordinary myopia toward
China. Mrs. Lall believes that education can be carried forward not only
through better understanding of facts but through reasoned advocacy of
carefully considered courses of action.)

(In response to other questions by students, Betty Lall said that we
must strive constantly to work through the U.N. She said there were
built-in difficulties in its structure but she, like Morgenthau, does not see
any way to change them in the foreseeable future. And she concluded:)

The advantage of peace education and peace research is that it enables
us to keep criticizing the structure and using brains and imagination on
alternatives, so that when the opportunities come—and they do come—we
can use them! Otherwise they go by. Every crisis presents an opportunity
to *move.* But we must have the ideas to put forward. We must have a
general vision of the kind of world institutions and world laws we want so
that we can keep moving towards them on every possible front. Remember that *after each act the situation is different.*

(And for this reason "the foreseeable future" is not necessarily as
long a span of time as it sounds.)

⚹ ⚹ ⚹ ⚹

At this moment (February 1966) the attention of the United States is so
consumed by our undeclared and growing war in Vietnam that we tend
to forget that we have other unresolved problems with the communist
world whose chances of progress toward peaceful solution are not aided
by the present conflict. In his testimony on February 10, 1966, before the

Senate Foreign Relations Committee, George Frost Kennan, career diplomat, Pulitzer Prize-winning historian and world authority on communism, reminded us (in answer to a question by Senator Gore) that "we
must have more important problems than Vietnam to thrash out eventually with the Soviet Union, problems of disarmament and problems of
the halting of the proliferation of nuclear weaponry, and the still great
and vital problem of Germany, which is, to my mind, the most important specific political-geographical problem in the world."

Almost exactly a year earlier, on February 18, 1965, speaking at the
convocation on Pope John's encyclical *Pacem in Terris*, Kennan addressed himself to European problems with emphasis on Germany.
Those remarks follow:

It is the *attitude* of Kennan (that same attitude which informed his
testimony to the Foreign Affairs Committee as anyone who watched him
on television knows) which is in itself a transition step. This highly regarded and trained specialist in our relations with communism states
simply that it is up to others to search their own consciences. "My own
loyalties and obligations of conscience relate to the West, of whose culture I am a child and where I bear the responsibilities of citizenship, and
it is to Western concepts and policies that I wish primarily to speak."

He gives practical ways, with examples re Germany, how *we* could
reduce the pervasive suspicion and fear—particularly fear addressed to
the inconceivable disasters of war conducted with nuclear weapons. He,
like Betty Lall, asks for a reexamination of our own established assumptions and attitudes. This, I believe, would come more easily if we took to
heart two points of Tillich's: 1) recognition of other valid viewpoints,
with consequent restraint about forcing particular ideas of freedom and
equal rights upon people with other principles; and 2) the ambiguity in
the nature of man—*they* are not all that bad, *we* are not all that good.
(Once again we are reminded of Frank's description of the stereotype of
the enemy.)

Kennan's plea for an "act of faith in the ultimate humanity and
sobriety of the people on the other side" (addressed to them and to us)
and his view that overcynicism can be as dangerous as naivety, is Tillich's
"importance of hope." It is as pertinent re Hanoi or Peking, as re Moscow.

It is therefore for this business of "attitude" that I have put this statement by Kennan under "transition steps." As regards specifics, there is no doubt but that if the United States would agree to the principle of no "first use" of "any and all weapons of mass destruction and thus place ourselves in a position where we could proceed more effectively toward the eventual elimination of these weapons, and above all their delivery systems, from national arsenals," it would be a tremendous step.

What Kennan does not say but what seems obvious is that in a disarmed world under enforceable world law there would *be* no German problem. This is not an economic problem, an underdeveloped nation problem, a civil rights problem; it is a problem directly resulting from fear and armaments, and it is one of the problems for which it is most difficult to see a solution outside such a framework.

Contribution to the Discussion of European Problems at *Pacem in Terris* Convocation

GEORGE F. KENNAN

Some seven years ago, in a series of lectures delivered over the facilities of the BBC, I ventured a statement of my own views about two of the greatest of the European problems of the day: that of German unification and that of the East-West military rivalry on the continent. These views proved strange and unacceptable at the time to much authoritative opinion in the western countries; and I have been content, in recent years, not to press them. If, however, we are now to speak once more of European problems, the spirit of the noble document to whose inspiration we owe our presence here today compels me to speak with utmost candor; and the limitations of time enforce a rigorous brevity. These are my apologies if what I say sounds harsh and/or blunt.

Let me also say, by way of preface, that I can speak here only to the Western position in the questions at hand. By doing so, I would not wish to imply that there has not been at times in the past, or is not today, serious fault in the Soviet and communist position as well. The communist governments of the Soviet Union and Eastern Europe will have to search their own consciences and render their own accounting on those many points— particularly the denial of true civil liberties to the peoples under their control, the resistance to adequate inspection in the case of disarmament arrangements, the oversuspiciousness, and the steady poisoning of international understanding by propagandistic distortion—where many of us would feel they had done a disservice to the future of Europe. My own loyalties and obligations of conscience relate to the West, of whose culture I am a child and where I bear the responsibilities of citizenship; and it is to Western concepts and policies that I wish primarily to speak.

For several years, now, the Western coalition has pursued a European policy marked, as I see it, by the following characteristics:

1. The assumption of a strong Soviet desire to attack, or at least to intimidate by superior military force, the Western half of the continent with a view to obtaining a commanding influence over its peoples and governments;

2. a belief that the Soviet government could be deterred from acting on this desire only by a Western defense policy relying heavily on nuclear weapons and including, as a primary component, the military power of a heavily rearmed Western Germany;

3. pressure for German unification, by procedures which apparently envisage a unilateral retirement of Soviet forces from Eastern Germany in the face of a continued Western military presence in the ensuing united Germany, plus a full-fledged association of that united Germany with the Atlantic Pact; and

4. the cultivation, not everywhere but in some instances, of a species of "little-Europism," in the form of efforts to organize the European community for peaceful purposes within the framework of the Western half of the continent alone, through institutions closely related to the Western military alliance and thus involving a heavy reliance on the United States, and so conceived that they would, if fully realized, serve to impede rather than to facilitate the ultimate overcoming of the division of the continent.

It is evident that the results of a policy embracing these elements have been sterile and unsatisfactory. No general agreement has been reached on European problems, and no perceptible progress has been made in that direction. German unification has been brought no nearer. The dangerous uncertainty surrounding the position of Berlin has been prolonged and intensified. Grievous disunity has emerged within the Western community, over the problems of economic unification and those of control and possible use of nuclear weapons by members of the Western coalition, in peace as in war.

None of this is surprising. Such a policy is replete with inner contradictions. Its military objectives—notably the inclusion of a united Germany, as a major component, in a Western defense system based primarily on nuclear weaponry—are in obvious conflict with its major political objective, which is the military and political retirement of the Soviet Union from Central Europe; for no Russian government, communist or otherwise, could afford to retire in the face of such a demand. The difficulties encountered in the control of nuclear weaponry within the Western coalition reflect merely the contradictions inherent from the start in the cultivation of weapons suicidal in their implications, indiscriminate and politically incoherent in their conceivable effects. Schemes for economic and political unification in the western half of the continent alone are in contradiction not only with the divided and uncertain state of the Germany they are supposed to include, but also with that heavy and unnatural dependence on the United States which the prevailing political and military approaches imply. Britain is placed in a difficult position by the confusion between Atlantic and continental principles of economic and political unification. France, animated now by a natural and basically sound desire to see Europe the main architect and guarantor of its own future, is frustrated by the difficulty of realizing this concept within the framework of a divided Europe, where the western part has been taught to look for its defense mainly to the American nuclear capability.

The elimination of these contradictions and the reshaping of Western policy on a more hopeful basis would not alone suffice to assure to Europe a future of greater security and promise. For this, a reciprocation on the communist side would be essential, too; and relations between the Soviet Union and the United States would probably have to be less disturbed by developments outside of Europe than is the case at this present sad and dangerous moment. But without the elimination of these contradictions and without such a reshaping of western policy, I must confess that I can see little hope for an advance of European life along the lines indicated in the late Pope John's encyclical; for such advances in the human spirit cannot take place in an atmosphere of pervasive suspicion and fear—particularly fear addressed to the inconceivable disasters of a war conducted with nuclear weapons.

I turn with some reluctance to the question of what would be required to make possible this change in Western policy; for the answers, as I see them, cut deeply into established assumptions and attitudes, and the mere suggestion of them will no doubt again encounter incredulity and rejection in many quarters. But our troubles are not trivial ones, and the cures cannot be other than drastic.

As the first of these essential changes I would name a basic review of our position with relation to nuclear weapons and their place in our defenses. I recognize with appreciation the changes that have been introduced into American policy, in this connection, in recent years. I consider them a step in the right direction, and commend the insight and courage that inspired them. But I believe we could go further. I see no reason why a primary reliance on nuclear weapons should be considered permanently essential to the defense of my own country or of western Europe. I fail to see why we could not at least explore and discuss seriously the various proposals that have been brought forward over the years by the Polish government, looking to a restriction of the place of nuclear weapons in Europe's defenses. I think we could usefully reexamine our acceptance of the principle of "first use" in the employment of any and all weapons of mass destruction, and thus place ourselves in a position where we could proceed more effectively toward the eventual elimination of these weapons, and above all their delivery systems, from national arsenals. Without such a change I can see no possibility of halting the present trend toward the proliferation of control over such weapons to a point where all hope of preventing their eventual use, somewhere and at some time, would have to be abandoned.

In the case of Germany, I should think there could be evolved a general Western policy less heavily geared to the domestic-political compulsions that bear on West German governments. Everyone would understand it if West German political parties could accept such a policy only under protest and with the reservation of their own position. We should not, I think, leave the rearmament of Western Germany effectively open-ended, as it must today appear to be in the eyes of people in the East. Greater reassurance could be given to Poland and to others on the question of Germany's eastern borders, if not as a unilateral concession then at least hypothetically, as one component in a possible accommodation of East-West differences. And if, as it appears, there is to be no military disengagement in Germany in this present historical period, then one must learn to accept with better grace at least the provisional existence of a separate East German political entity, avoiding, if you will, the recognition of it as a final solution for the problem of the relation of that area to the rest of Germany, but promoting closer contacts with it and a more intimate association of its people with peoples to the west. It is not unreasonable to hope that there could be created in this way an atmosphere in which the Berlin Wall would become redundant even in the eyes of its creators, and the natural forces pressing for uniformity in the development of all modern societies could have a chance to diminish contrasts and to alter in this way the terms of the very problem of unification itself.

Finally, I should like to plead for a basic revision of assumptions concerning Soviet intentions, both hypothetical and actual. Western policy is apparently based on an assessment of these intentions which has not changed appreciably from the days of the Berlin blockade and the Korean War, and which, even then, probably embraced serious elements of misinterpretation. The assumptions commonly made with respect to Soviet military intentions (assumptions reflected in the very word "deterrence") are ones that can be reconciled neither with communist doctrine (which does not envisage the bringing of socialism to peoples exclusively or primarily on the bayonets of foreign armies), nor with the moral commitments the Soviet leaders have assumed to their own people, nor with the present state of relations between Moscow and the communist countries of Eastern Europe. They impute to the Soviet leaders a total inhumanity not plausible even in nature, and out of accord with those humane ideals which we must recognize as lying, together with other elements less admirable in the eyes of some of us, at the origins of all European Marxism.

I should like, therefore, to end these observations with a plea for something resembling a new act of faith in the ultimate humanity and sobriety of the people on the other side; and I would like to address this plea to our communist contemporaries as well as to ourselves. History reveals that the penalties for overcynicism in the estimation of the motives of others can be no smaller, on occasions, than the penalties for naivety. In the case at hand, I suspect they may be even greater. For in the predication of only the worst motives on the adversary's part there lies, today, no hope at all: only a continued exacerbation of mutual tensions and the indefinite proliferation of nuclear weaponry. Our sole hope lies in the possibility that the adversary, too, has learned something from the sterility of past conflict; that he, too, sees—if only through the dim lens of ideological prejudice, suspicion and accumulated resentment—the identity of fate that binds us all; that some reliance can be placed, in the adjustment of mutual differences, on his readiness to abstain, voluntarily and in self-interest, from the wildest and most senseless acts of physical destruction. If this possibility fails us, we have little to fall back on. Let us make it our purpose, therefore, to nurture it, to give it the chance to bear fruit, to assure that it is not destroyed by fear, by suspicion, or by the reaction of others to what we ourselves do. The act of faith that this requires is something we must learn to see not only as the assumption of new risks to ourselves but as perhaps the only means whereby wholly intolerable risks could be avoided. Only in this way do we have a hope of approaching that state of mutual trust in international affairs which, in the words of the encyclical, "is something which reason requires . . . is eminently desirable in itself, and . . . will prove to be the source of many benefits."

※ ※ ※ ※

Immediately after George F. Kennan finished speaking, in the discussion of European problems at the *Pacem in Terris* Convocation, February 18,

1965, the Polish Communist Adam Schaff got to his feet. It is enormously interesting to read what he had to say, and to think back twenty years. It is hardly likely that this short speech, or indeed his presence at such a convocation would have been possible then. This thought may encourage us to reexamine our attitudes. It is also interesting to think ahead twenty years to a simliar convocation with Chinese participation. This speech, which once would have seemed impossible, may remind us to keep an open mind.

You will notice that Adam Schaff too speaks for diversity and, like Jerome Frank, for means other than war for a man to defend his ideals and values. To him, coexistence seems an adequate framework. To us it is not sufficiently defined. As has been pointed out earlier, the World Authority envisioned in Pope John's encyclical offers no more enforceable structure than does coexistence. It is, however, because on the whole we agree with Tillich about the ambiguous moral nature of man—bad and good mixed—that we tend to feel safer and *free-er* under a system of law and authority.

It has always been interesting to me that the children at the very free and progressive school Summerhill rapidly chose to construct a system of rules for themselves which they strictly enforced. This school government was acceptable to them, whereas other school governments were not, because they were in on, not excluded from, the decision making. This is something to bear in mind in relation to nations as well. Obviously the sooner we get China in on any discussions, the better.

Reply to Kennan at the *Pacem in Terris* Convocation

ADAM SCHAFF

I have no paper prepared. If I had one, I would reject it after what I just heard in the stimulating and, as I believe, realistic speech of Mr. Kennan and in the very unrealistic comments of Professor Schmid. I would like to speak not only as a Pole or as a representative of socialist countries, but, being a university professor, as a representative of the world-wide republic of "egg-heads." And I would like to start with the problem of coexistence and ideology.

I wish to begin with the encyclical—and with a confession. I come from a very different philosophical creed, and I cannot accept even the foundations of the reasoning of the encyclical. At the same time, I have the highest appreciation of the core of the encyclical in its search for the conditions of peace and of peaceful coexistence. Paragraph 159 said: "Who can deny that those movements, and those people belonging to those movements"—I am one of them—"insofar as they conform to the dictates of right reason and of the human person, contain elements that are positive and deserving of approval." This is an appeal for tolerance.

The two very fashionable concepts of our time are peaceful coexistence and the cold war. The nineteenth century would not have begun to understand what these terms mean. We coined them because they are adequate to the conditions of our life. When we talk of peaceful coexistence we are talking about international relations that consist in not using physical force—war—to decide conflicts or differences between peoples, nations, countries, governments. But that is not all. Coexistence has meaning only in the framework of different political, social, and economic systems. We do not talk about coexistence between, let us say, the United States and England, but we understand what it means when we talk about it in connection with, say, the United States and the Soviet Union.

There are three points to stress. The first is that peaceful coexistence is a fact. It is not something to be invented. These two big systems exist in the world, there is no war between them, and this means existing in peaceful coexistence. The second point is that the *shape* of peaceful coexistence can be different. The third is that peaceful coexistence is a necessity. It is a necessity if we wish to avoid the alternative, which is annihilation of humanity.

Nations are different, if only because they have different systems of values, and with them different ideologies. We have different evaluations as to the aims and goals of humanity, as to what human happiness means, as to which ways lead most directly toward this happiness. This is "ideology," a system of ideas and attitudes underlying the social activities of people and determining the goals of these social activities.

There is a logical consequence to our having different ideologies. In an age when "hot war" is rationally impossible, the role of ideologies, of ideological differences, of ideological conflicts, if you like, is increasing. And if one does not like it, he might recognize that it is better to throw ideologies at each other's head than to throw atomic bombs! There is an oversimplified theory that there cannot be true coexistence as long as these ideological differences and ideological stresses obtain. This is an enormous mistake. Look at the consequences. Americans would be supposed to drop their ideals, their ideology, what they call "the American way of life." Christians would be supposed to drop their ideals and ideology, and their fight for these ideals. Marxists and Communists would be supposed to do likewise. Nobody is prepared to do this. Nobody should. If a man has his ideals embodied in an ideology, it is a point of honor to go on fighting for it by peaceful means.

But does this mean that we cannot do anything at all, that there is a fatality of stresses and fights, and that there cannot be progress? Not at all. It means only that we began with a false definition, because coexistence in connection with ideology brings out some very important things.

One of them is tolerance—people coexisting, coming closer together, knowing each other better, realizing that neither side has horns and that we resemble each other more than we sometimes suspect. This is also mentioned in Paragraph 159 of *Pacem in Terris*. It means that none of us has a monopoly on truth and that all of us can learn from the writings and teachings of others.

Another is cooperation. If it is not true that we are prepared to drop our ideologies, it is true, nevertheless, that we can cooperate. When we Marxists, we Communists, stress that there is no coexistence in ideologies, we are saying at the same time that we can and wish to cooperate in all fields, including my own field of science and those fields which have ideological implications. This is a major fact of our time.

Coexistence is a fight, a competition, a noble competition for the hearts and minds of people. This will continue, but let us hope that our conduct will be rational. On your side you will go further and further in expanding your economy, increasing social security, and so on, not only because you recognize that this is the normal course of development but because there is pressure from the socialist countries. On our side we are rapidly changing our political situation, bringing in more and more democracy, liberalizing the internal life of our society. This is also the normal course of our development, but it is also the result of competition from you. We are coming closer and closer, and this is the great hope.

※ ※ ※ ※

There were many excellent statements made at the *Pacem in Terris* Convocation. Those of you who wish to read more of them should write to the Center for the Study of Democratic Institutions in Santa Barbara, California. I am including only this one more here.

His Excellency Abba Eban, Deputy Prime Minister of Israel, speaks for the need of *action* for peace. And this action includes a duty to look at structures, institutions and laws, for the structures, institutions and laws of peace are sadly in disarray. In the action he calls for, and in his approach to that action, you will be reminded of many subjects already examined in this Reader. It is an example of how these articles and statements by many thoughtful persons interweave, reinforce each other, throw sidelights on each other and reveal, when they are taken together as we have been trying to, a way of thinking with responsible authority behind it.

In this article you will, I think, be especially reminded of the Robbers Cave experiment described by Jerome Frank, for you will note that Abba Eban's seven joint projects of cooperation—each enormously useful in itself—really serve as a type of transition steps *toward joining* two hostile groups. It is interesting that, in No. 7, he puts the future structure of the world organization itself in the category of joint projects, cooperation in working toward which would in fact help produce the climate for creating it.

Statement at *Pacem in Terris* Convocation

ABBA EBAN

I left Jerusalem yesterday to join this dialogue on the requirements for peace. The journey is long in space but short in spirit. For thirty centuries, humanity has been searching for an ideal Jerusalem, that lives forever in the hearts and minds of men, symbol in every land and every tongue of the quest for individual and human perfection.

Peace is the destination of that quest. It is now the central idea, but also the central interest of mankind. It was not always so. War has too often been regarded as a part of man's essential nature, the source of nobility, heroism and redeeming sacrifice. Literature is full of such images of war. Today, the ideal of peace converges with its necessity. Whether men are moved by hope or fear, by active ideals or a passive institution of survival, the result is the same.

Everything in history that once made for war now makes for peace. In this I include our new and all-pervading vulnerability.

I hope that I do not introduce too shocking a note if I express a deep scepticism about the utility of peaceful talk without a new impetus to peaceful action. Peace is not something to be inherited by aspiration alone. It will be attained, if at all, by action in its service. This implies a duty to look at structures, institutions and laws. This is the first era of global history—the first in which an event happening anywhere has effects and echoes everywhere. There is an ecumenical spirit in modern life and thought, and letters—a new pluralism, diversity and tolerance. No ideological camp believes any longer that its doctrine must either perish or conquer all mankind. And yet the structures, institutions and laws of peace are in disarray. The grievous condition of the United Nations is a case in point. It lies weak before us amidst all the objective conditions for growing strength.

In a universal society, as in a national community, peace must have its code, its law and doctrine. Here I see no substitute for the U.N. Charter. The Charter is more impressive as a document than the U.N. has been as an institution. It is a document that strikes a correct balance between national identity and universal solidarity. The nation-state is still the main source of distinctive culture. In some respects all nations are like all others.

But those qualities which a nation holds uniquely to itself, its special memories and dreams, may well be its distinctive gift to human culture. National diversity can be reconciled in a fragmented world, with the requirements of an international order. We seek a family of states, separate in their rights and liberty of expression, but all united in a covenant of law and peace.

In this covenant the central law is that expressed by the U.S.S.R. in its message to the U.N. this year—the avoidance of the use of force in disputes between existing sovereign states. The West too is committed to this view by its own interest—the small states by the very condition of their survival.

With 90 per cent of mankind now living in sovereign states, the revolution against status quo—the ambition for progress and change, must now turn not to lenitorial change, but inward to the organization of a world community and the increase of economic and social equality.

The problem of peace will not be advanced unless it exercises the minds of nations at their highest level of responsibility. This is not the position today. Diplomacy is still conservative in its traditions, methods, and above all, its range. It is concerned with the crisis of today and the explosions of tomorrow—Vietnam, Cuba, Congo, Cyprus, the Near East. Diplomacy is local, not universal in its habit of mind and in its techniques of solution. Our Chairman has written a book called *Old Myths and New Realities*. Diplomacy is still obsessed by the old myths.

The new reality lies in the existence of problems which cannot be denied, still less solved except on a global scale.

Just as the leaders of communities within our nations assemble to survey the national problems, so should the leaders of nations come together for the first time in history to review the total human destiny. By this, I mean, a review of problems and action facing the City of Man during the next quarter of a century.

I propose for discussion that the heads of all sovereign governments, within and outside the U.N. devote a week of their time to consider the problems not of any nation but of the human nation.

An agenda for such an encounter must include:

1. The prospect opened up by the new technologies—both the danger and the hope.
2. The world will very nearly double its population within the next three decades. Is this a problem for our presidents and premiers in comparison with what exercises them now?
3. Over 1½ billion people suffer from malnutrition. There was a "campaign against hunger" conference a few years ago, but its participants were not heads of government with a capacity for action and commitment.
4. In this golden age of knowledge there are 700 million adults entirely illiterate—one third of the world's adult population—and a similar number at a low level of literacy. There is as yet an inadequate flow of scientific and educational skills from the advanced to the developing worlds.
5. Amongst the 115 sovereign states, ostensibly equal in their rights and status, there is a vast disparity of income and resources. There are groups of states where income is 2000 per cent higher than that of others. Within a national community such disparities would lead to violent upheavals. Are we sure that the same is not true of the international community? There should be a blueprint of a Great Society in international terms.
6. The fabric of our planet—its soil, water, minerals and air—faces depletion or pollution or both. Our generation has no special right to hand the planet onto our children in a worse natural condition than that in which we found it.
7. The future of international organization—and especially in the problem of peace-keeping—needs long-term planning by those who have knowledge both of the central political realities and of technical developments. Disarmament is a vain discussion unless we devise

instruments of security, beyond the national deterrents of sovereign states.

In proposing that the heads of 115 governments give a week to the survey of these vistas, I do not delude myself by the view that a solution will be found. The world was created, according to Biblical reckoning, in six days. It will take longer to repair the damage that we have been doing ever since.

But there have been, in each of our national histories, occasions of assembly to which we look back as points of departure toward uncharted seas. Let there be the first assembly of governmental leaders to survey, not the state of any nation, but the state of mankind.

The Papal message *Peace on Earth* was governed by deep compassion for man in his vulnerability. There is also a sense, in this wondrous age, of what man can achieve in his redeeming moments of grandeur.

As we look out on the human condition, our consciences cannot be clean. If they are clean, then it is because we do not use them enough.

It is not inevitable that we march in hostile and separated hosts into the common abyss. There is another possibility—of an ordered world, illuminated by reason and governed by law. If we cannot yet touch it with our hands, let us, at least, grasp it in our vision.

❧ ❧

A Short Note on Education

Implicit in all these statements is the idea that we are in an age when issues must be looked at from a world, rather than a national interest, point of view. This means a different way of thinking about them that is not narrowly nation-centered. It involves, as I see it, three things: the toleration and respect for the views of others that is the spirit of Locke and of our Founding Fathers (there is another strand in our national heritage that runs to messianic fanaticism); a genuine effort to judge issues objectively on their merits without the distorting attachment to any dogma; and the understanding (also held by Locke) that in the long run private happiness and the general good coincide, and therefore attention to this end is what is practical as well as virtuous. Such a way of thinking rests on enlightenment and education, on open discussion of courses of action and their implications and on examination of relevant facts. The issues that come under the head of "foreign policy" are no longer "foreign" or distant to the individual citizen. They are closer and more important to him than most domestic issues, although he quite accurately feels that he has less voice in them and less information on which to base his deeply concerned opinion.

This situation inevitably places increased importance on the part toward education our own government officials can play. On the Vietnamese issue, which is now a world issue as well as one of intimate concern and great complexity to all Americans, President Johnson has not (as of this writing) used his position to educate, but merely to state one side of the case as he sees it and has taken no steps to aid the citizens of the country to determine in a scientific and objective way the issues at stake and the facts. The split in the country which exists and which will undoubtedly grow is based on the utter disparity between the facts and issues as the administration presents them and as they are seen by many deeply concerned and informed persons.

Taking into account this condition that in today's world "foreign policy" is no longer "foreign" but of intimate concern to all citizens, I think one can say without question that Senator Fulbright, more than any other public servant in our government or any other government, has taken advantage of his position as Chairman of the Senate Foreign Relations Committee to use his Committee as a forum of education, using the world approach rather than the purely self-interest approach. On the transnational problems of the Vietnamese war and admission of China to the U.N. now confronting Americans, such education is a vital transition step.

※ ※ ※ ※

In relation to transition steps, particularly in the area of practical politics, one good rule is to look at what is "acceptable" and then think how we can act to extend the bounds of what is "acceptable." Genuine hope, as opposed to utopian expectation, is rooted in seeds that already exist. Here Louis B. Sohn, a noted expert in world law, outlines well-defined practical steps that could be taken at once in the political area to assist the achievement of the six basic components of a peaceful world.

He shows how *some* destruction of weapons could easily take place —in a way which would allow the Russians to get used to inspection slowly.

He shows how the U.N. might go about creating a *small* permanent force for immediate use. National contingents of the U.N. force could take over when they became available and where they were not in opposition to their nation's policy. But even a *small* permanent force, a mere 1,000 men to begin with, ready for quick action, trained and equipped, would make a big difference in many situations.

He describes how methods for the settlement of international disputes could begin to be improved, and points out that we already *have* some needed institutions, but *they are not used*. He shows how we could begin using them in a small way at first.

He shows how, *without* amendment to the Charter, the structure of the U.N. can still be strengthened, and money made available to the World Bank for a Development Fund while at the same time interest on these loans could contribute toward a Peace-keeping Fund.

In short, Sohn says, what is important is that we need not wait forever for the perfect treaty. There are lots of ways to begin now.

Practical Steps Toward World Peace

LOUIS B. SOHN

There are many roads to world peace and we should beware of those who single-mindedly insist that we must follow a particular road to get there. General and complete disarmament may be very important, but by itself it cannot bring about permanent peace. If the United Nations had at its disposal an international police force, it could help in many situations but many others would still remain intractable. International lawyers who put all their faith in the strengthening of world law or in a system of world courts frequently overstate the advantages which will accrue from such reforms. None of these radical remedies, if taken singly, can remove all the dangers to world peace. A greater measure of success might be achieved through an effective combination of various approaches and a concerted attack on several fronts. It is the purpose of this article to explore the practical steps which may be taken in the near future toward the achievement of the six basic components of a peaceful world:

1. General and complete disarmament of all the nations through gradual, simultaneous, proportionate and effectively verified measures;
2. United Nations Peace Force strong enough to enable the United Nations to deter or suppress any threat or use of force in international relations;
3. Adequate arrangements for the settlement of international disputes, both legal and political;
4. Development of international law into a supranational system of world law;
5. Cooperative development of economic and cultural resources of mankind for the common benefit of all;
6. Strengthening the United Nations by making its structure more representative and its powers more adequate.

While plans need to be prepared for the final solution of all these problems, many interim steps can be taken which will bring us closer to these goals.

Steps toward disarmament

Not all disarmament steps require immediate strengthening of the peace-keeping machinery of the United Nations. Today the major powers have so many weapons of mass destruction that they can easily destroy a large proportion of them without upsetting the existing balance of military deterrence, provided that the necessary measures are taken simultaneously by all the powers concerned and that the necessary minimum of inspection is accepted.

In view of the well-known attitude of the Soviet Union toward inspection, the first steps should be those which require only a small amount of inspection. The most difficult approach is the one which is based on a specified percentage of the total number of weapons, because it requires a large amount of inspection to ascertain the accuracy of each nation's total inventory of weapons. The only approach which overcomes this difficulty is one based on simultaneous destruction of specified numbers of weapons on both sides. If categories of weapons can be found in which the two parties have almost equal inventories, it should be possible to make arrangements for destruction on a monthly basis of specified numbers of weapons on both sides. The inspection in such a case could be limited to the verification of actual destruction of weapons at a location chosen by the state destroying them.

It is conceivable, however, that there is no category of weapons in which the holdings of both sides are about equal, and in such a case it would be necessary to provide for a compensatory arrangement in which either even numbers of different weapons or uneven numbers of similar weapons would be destroyed. For example, there have been proposals for destruction of even numbers of certain types of bombers. In addition, other bombers or strategic missiles could be destroyed in monthly installments in an uneven manner. Assuming that both the United States and the Soviet Union have about 2,700 strategic delivery vehicles each, including long and medium-range bombers and missiles, an arrangement to destroy 2,400 of them on a one-for-one basis would be in theory an uneven agreement, as some types of bombers and missiles have a higher military value than others, and in particular the West would have to exchange a large number of intercontinental missiles and bombers for Soviet medium-range missiles and bombers. The result would be, however, that both sides would be left with about 300 of their best vehicles of comparable value, and it would then be possible to reach an agreement on further reductions on a more even one-for-one basis. Nevertheless, such an agreement might be considered to be dangerous to the Western nations as on the one hand, it would establish parity in the nuclear field and, on the other hand, leave the Soviet bloc with a preponderant strength in the conventional field. In such a case, in order to balance the arms reductions it might be necessary to require that the Soviet bloc should supplement each step in strategic disarmament by a parallel reduction in tanks and heavy artillery so that parity between the West and the Soviet bloc in those weapons would be reached at the same time as the level of 300 delivery vehicles; for example, if 100 delivery vehicles were destroyed each month, together with a proper number of tanks and heavy guns, the point of parity in both areas could be reached after twenty-four months.

Destruction of these weapons would be, however, meaningless if not accompanied by a simultaneous freeze on further production of such weapons. Such a freeze would require more inspection than an agreement limited to destruction, but such inspection can be properly limited in several ways. In the first place, strategic delivery vehicles, tanks and heavy artillery can be produced only in large industrial establishments which assemble parts produced in many factories scattered throughout each country. If there are, for instance, some 240 principal industrial centers in the Soviet Union and 240 in the United States, a graduated inspection system might extend each month to only 10 of them, starting with the largest ones and in each step extending to 10 additional ones. With respect to each city thus opened to inspection, the inspectors would be allowed to verify that no large factories there engage in the prohibited production. Thus no inspection outside big cities would be required, and no locations of strategic delivery vehicles would be disclosed. Secondly, the intensity of each inspection might be limited at the beginning, increasing only in later stages. At the start, it might be enough to verify from the outside that a factory which previously produced prohibited weapons is no longer in operation. Later, materials coming into or out of a suspected factory might be checked to see that they do not contain parts for prohibited weapons. In another stage, an inside check of production lines would be allowed, and at the end it should be permissible to verify the present and past records of production and of shipments to and from the inspected plant.

This combination of the rapid destruction of a large number of delivery vehicles and other major weapons with a freeze on their production has the advantage of linking together an important disarmament measure requiring minimal verification with a limited disarmament measure (freeze) requiring a larger, though still limited, amount of verification. Together those two measures present a balanced blend of disarmament and inspection, and do not require disclosure of important strategic secrets, especially those relating to the location of strategic weapons. The acceptance of such a proposal would reduce the nuclear danger by almost 90 per cent, would establish parity in conventional weapons and would keep the inspection requirements within reasonable limits. It could constitute a decisive step toward effective disarmament.

Toward a U.N. peace force

The experience of the United Nations Forces in Egypt, the Congo and Cyprus has led to various studies for the improvement of the performance of such forces. In particular, the Scandinavian countries, Canada and a few other countries have pledged certain contingents or services for United Nations Forces, and are now investigating how to prepare their contingents for United Nations action. It would greatly increase the effectiveness of United Nations Forces if most countries other than the five nuclear powers would take similar action. Such pledges need not be universal in scope; they might be limited to action within a specified region.

It is likely, however, that almost all these pledges will be circumscribed by the requirement that a contingent will be available only if a particular action, including the rules governing the proposed activities of the force, is approved by the government concerned. If a country finds certain rules unsatisfactory, its contingent will not be forthcoming, and if the rules are revised, the contingent might be withdrawn. This situation is not likely to change, as states cannot be asked to pledge their forces for unknown contingencies and to train them not only for all the most likely tasks but also for some unanticipated ones.

A way out of this difficulty might be found if a small permanent United Nations Force were available for first-aid temporary measures until the national contingents can be brought into action. Thus, instead of our present method of sending national contingents directly to a trouble spot, a two-step approach might be adopted. First, the permanent United Nations Force would be sent to the trouble spot; second, the national contingents would temporarily take the place of the permanent force wherever it was employed before the emergency arose. For instance, as long as there is a United Nations Emergency Force in the Gaza Strip on the Egyptian-Israeli boundaries, its function could be normally performed not by national contingents, as at present, but by a directly recruited United Nations Force, composed of volunteers and owing its allegiance to the United Nations only. Such a force could be trained for a variety of tasks, and it could be used anywhere. Because of its international character, the current difficulties with respect to the acceptability of a particular contingent to the host state would be avoided. Of course, except in a case of an action ordered by the Security Council, the United Nations Force would enter a particular country only upon its request. But once such a request is made, there would be no necessity to obtain special consent to the bringing in of a particular unit of the internationalized United Nations Force. Should an emergency arise, the United Nations Force would be able to move immediately to the trouble spot as it would have the necessary transportation facilities and equipment. Once an agreement on the employment of the force is reached by the United Nations and the country concerned, quick action would be possible, thus avoiding the delay which in the past has often aggravated the situation and has made the task of the United Nations Forces more difficult.

In order to be able to use the new United Nations Force stationed in the Gaza Strip (or in some other place), it will be necessary to replace temporarily the units sent to the danger area with national contingents. Thus, in the second step, national contingents will be quickly flown to the Gaza Strip (or its future equivalent) to fulfill the duties of the United Nations Force there, while the Force is employed elsewhere. As this replacement obligation can be clearly defined in advance, will be limited in scope, will permit special training, and will involve practically no danger for the troops in view of the relative peacefulness of the area in which they will be stationed, it ought to be much easier for many states to accept this specific duty. It is likely that most countries will be able and willing to provide contingents for temporary replacement duty in a specified area though they will hesitate to sign a blank check committing national units to service anywhere in the world and to unspecified future tasks which might involve grave danger to the troops.

If such a two-step procedure were accepted, one could envisage the following developments. Should an emergency arise, similar to the one in Cyprus, a part of the new United Nations Force could be moved immediately from the Gaza Strip (or some other area where the force is then stationed) to the crisis area and, under the stand-by arrangements with a number of states, replacements would be flown quickly to the Gaza Strip (or the other area where the force might be located). If additional forces should be required, the rest of the permanent force would be moved into the emergency area and further replacements would be sent into the Gaza Strip (or its future equivalent).

The original United Nations Force need not be large, as its function would be local peace-keeping and not fighting a war against an aggressor. It will be a police force in the narrower sense of the word rather than a full-fledged military force. If the United Nations could have at least 1,000 men ready for quick action, well-trained and properly equipped, it would make an important difference in many situations where the speed of United Nations interposition is more important than the size or military strength of the Force. Later such a force might be increased to 5,000 or more, and some day it might become the nucleus of a United Nations military force which, in the language of United States proposals of April, 1962, would be so strong that "no state could challenge it." Though this goal might seem difficult to attain, that fact should not serve as an excuse for not taking at least the modest steps suggested here.

Steps toward improving the methods for settling international disputes

In the area of dispute settlement, we already have some of the needed institutions but the crucial fact is that they are not being used. The International Court of Justice at The Hague is well qualified to settle international legal disputes, and it is generally agreed that its decisions have been both sound and impartial. Nevertheless, only one third of the members of the United Nations have accepted the Court's jurisdiction, and many such acceptances are accompanied by broad reservations. Only a few cases have been submitted to the Court despite the large number of disputes which could be solved easily by submission to the Court.

The first step to be taken here is to try to overcome certain misconceptions about the use of the Court. In the first place, it should be clearly understood that submission of a dispute to the Court should not be considered as an unfriendly act. If two governments disagree on a point of law and cannot settle the question through diplomatic negotiations, they might as well submit it to the Court rather than continue to argue about it year after year. In fact, the more friendly two nations are, the easier it should be for them to transfer their disputes from a diplomatic to a judicial setting. Secondly, the Court should not be reserved for big disputes, as such disputes often have political connotations which make it difficult to submit them to judicial settlement. States should start with small issues and submit them to the Court in large numbers. In that way they would become used to the Court and to the fact that, while they cannot win all cases, they are likely to win a sufficiently large number. The law of averages works better in a larger number of cases than a smaller one, and it is not likely that a particular state will be wrong in every case in which it is involved.

The next step might be to make the Court more easily accessible by increasing the number of ways in which the Court's jurisdiction could be accepted. The present optional clause in the Statute of the Court which applies in particular to disputes concerning "any question of international law" is so broad that it scares many states away completely and invites others to include crippling reservations in their declarations of acceptance. States could be given several other options. They might find it easier to accept the jurisdiction of the Court over disputes involving only the interpretation and application of international agreements, because in such cases the obligations to be defined by the Court are specified already in an international document which has been voluntarily accepted by all the states concerned. Another proposal would make it easy for a state to accept the jurisdiction of the Court over those areas of international law with respect to which it has no difficulties, postponing until later the acceptance of such jurisdiction over areas which it considers more dangerous. A list of all the subjects of international law could be prepared, and each state would from time to time accept the Court's jurisdiction over a few of them. Thus, if there should be 50 subjects and each state would agree to accept the Court's jurisdiction over 10 of them in each five-year period, after 25 years the Court's jurisdiction would be complete. In the meantime, with each acceptance by a large number of states of the Court's jurisdiction over a particular subject, the Court's accessibility would be gradually increased and after a while it would be really universal.

Some states might be willing to accept the Court's jurisdiction with respect to states with which they have strong political ties, though they are doubtful about accepting it by an open-ended method easily accessible to less friendly states. Stronger commitments should thus be possible among members of alliances than in agreements which are open to all.

If some states are worried that their acceptance of the jurisdiction of the Court might open them to too many suits by unfriendly neighbors, they might qualify their acceptance by requiring that each case should be first submitted to the General Assembly or the Security Council of the United Nations and should be referred to the Court only if the United Nations should find that the dispute involves a legal question important enough to justify such reference.

Many other ways can be devised to strengthen the Court's jurisdiction, and parallel methods can be devised for dealing with political disputes and dynamic changes in relationships between states. The difficulty of further steps should not, however, stand in the way of the relatively simple ideas suggested here.

Similarly, preliminary steps can easily be taken in the other areas mentioned at the beginning of this article. The process of codification of international law and the development of new rules of international conduct could be speeded up either by doubling the number of sessions of the International Law Commission or by establishing a new commission of both lawyers and elder statesmen to deal with problems of international law which have not only a legal but also a political aspect.

Many improvements are possible in the work of the specialized agencies of the United Nations which deal with common economic, social and cultural questions. New resources may be put at their disposal if some of the savings from disarmament can be channeled in that direction.

Toward a peacekeeping fund

Finally, even without any amendments to its Charter, the structure of the United Nations may be strengthened in many respects. If the countries of the world should be willing to transfer to the World Bank $3 billion from savings resulting from disarmament, the money to be lent to developing nations at about 4 per cent interest and the interest to be paid to the United Nations, more than $100 million per year could be provided for the United Nations expenses. For instance, the United States might agree to lend to a U.N. Capital Development Fund $2 billion for 20 years on condition that the Soviet Union would contribute $1 billion for the same purpose. The money would come from present expenditures on armaments and would constitute a reduction in the military budgets of the great powers. Such reduction cannot be verified effectively as long as the money saved is spent within the country announcing such a reduction. But if the reduction is large enough and accompanied by an obligation to spend the money abroad, the possibility of diverting it to hidden arms production is greatly diminished.

Such diversion can be made even more difficult if the industrial capacity of the nation concerned is used for production of heavy machinery and transportation equipment for the developing nations. Consequently, it might be desirable to oblige the Capital Development Fund to spend the money received from the U.S. and the U.S.S.R. for capital goods produced in those countries. This would also diminish the danger of an economic depression caused by a significant cut in the arms budget and would help to solve foreign exchange problems which might otherwise complicate the situation.

The U.S. and the U.S.S.R. would forgo the interest on the loans made to the Capital Development Fund, but the Fund would be allowed to charge ordinary interest rates (about 4 per cent) on loans made by the Fund to the developing countries. The interest received by the Fund on these loans would amount to about $120 million per year once all the money is lent. The Fund would not keep that interest but would put it into a special United Nations Peace-keeping Fund, which could be used for paying past peace-keeping debts and for current peace-keeping expenditures.

Similar rules should apply if other countries should contribute to the Fund.

The secretary general of the United Nations might be authorized to draw upon the Peace-keeping Fund: (a) up to $20 million per year, when so authorized by a new Committee on Peace-keeping, which would be composed of the ten largest contributors to the Peace-keeping Fund and of ten members selected by the General Assembly to represent the various regions of the world, and which would decide by a two-thirds vote; (b) between $20 million and $100 million, when so authorized by the Committee on Peace-keeping by a two-thirds vote, provided that the United States and the Soviet Union do not vote against but either vote for it or abstain.

Once an agreement is reached on the Peace-keeping Fund, and pending the receipt of interest from loans, the United States and the Soviet Union might contribute $50 million each as a temporary advance to the Fund to be repaid from future receipts. To the extent necessary, a part of that advance might be applied by the secretary general toward the past indebtedness to the United Nations peace-keeping activities of the state making such advance contribution.

In this way four steps would be taken simultaneously: the current financial crisis of the United Nations would disappear, a cut would be made in armament expenditures, a permanent United Nations Peace-keeping Fund would be established, and significant progress would be made toward the development of the underdeveloped countries.

Toward a world parliament

A United Nations having all these responsibilities would need a more democratic structure. While it might be difficult to change the voting structure in the General Assembly of the United Nations where each state, regardless of size or population, has only one vote, the General Assembly could take the first step toward a more representative world parliament by granting special consultative status to the Inter-Parliamentary Union in which most parliaments of the world are represented on a weighted basis related to the population of the member countries. It would be very proper for the General Assembly to consult, in certain categories of cases, the parliaments of the world as represented in the Union. While the General Assembly would not be bound by the opinions of the Inter-Parliamentary Conference, in most cases they would have such a great weight behind them that the General Assembly might find it difficult not to follow such advice. In this manner, a democratization of the decision-making process in the United Nations could slowly be achieved.

Of course, many other first steps can be easily imagined. It does not matter in what sequence they are put into effect. What is important is that we need not wait forever for the completion of a perfect treaty on disarmament and peace-keeping, but that we should start going in the right direction and take immediately those steps which can be taken to increase everybody's security and well-being. While it is going to take some time before the major nations of the world will agree to a final document establishing an effective world order, this time need not be wasted but should be used for improving the existing order bit by bit. As President Johnson has said, "Peace is a journey of a thousand miles and it must be taken one step at a time." If simultaneous steps are taken on several fronts, the climate of world opinion can be changed and opportunities for further improvements will greatly increase.

※ ※ ※ ※

Louis Sohn has pointed out immediate practical improvements within the present system that would assist in achieving a desired end. It is also certain that every smallest action and shift of attitude that works for reason and awareness, that works for justice and peace and against the irrational violence of war as a means of settling disputes and realizing interests, is important. But it is possible that a more radical approach is necessary than a slow series of independent steps. The following selection is from a preliminary draft of a long paper on the case for a limited world government which will be included in a book of new materials to be called *The Future of International Law* and published in 1967.

Saul Mendlovitz is professor of international law at Rutgers University Law School. He is editor of the book *Legal and Political Problems of World Order*, and co-editor with Richard Falk of the four-volume work *The Strategy of World Order*. Both these are built around the Clark/Sohn *World Peace through World Law* used as a teaching "model" for organizing the subject and subjecting it to the strictest and most objective scrutiny from every angle. Since 1962 Mendlovitz has taught at Rutgers Law School a course of his own devising on world order problems, which in 1964 was made a compulsory course for all law school freshmen.

It is interesting that when Mendlovitz started teaching this subject he was, with respect to methods of transition to a warless world, very much on the side of what is referred to as the conventional wisdom. As a result, however, of his constant personal involvement in the search for a war prevention system, of the experience of teaching, and of his exhaustive familiarity with all the materials on the subject, he has come to feel that in our interrelated world, which is daily becoming more interrelated, one cannot advance appreciably by fragments. One must swallow the whole medicine if one wants to avoid war.

In this connection I would like to introduce some words of Albert Einstein, who, as is characteristic of genius, had the ability to penetrate to the heart of a problem. This was written in 1934, when Hitler was emerging and the League of Nations Disarmament Conference had just come to its disheartening close. The argument remains unshaken, staring at us today.

> *The greatest obstacle to the success of the disarmament plan was the fact that people in general left out of account the chief difficulties of the problem. Most objects are gained by gradual steps: for example, the supersession of absolute monarchy by democracy. Here, however, we are concerned with an objective which cannot be reached step by step.*
>
> *As long as the possibility of war remains, nations will insist on being as perfectly prepared in a military sense as they can, in order*

to emerge triumphant from the next war. *It will also be impossible to avoid educating the youth in warlike traditions and cultivating narrow national vanity joined to the glorification of the warlike spirit, as long as people have to be prepared for occasions when such a spirit will be needed for the purpose of war. To arm is to give one's voice and make one's preparations, not for peace but for war. Therefore people will not disarm step by step; they will disarm at one blow or not at all.*

The accomplishment of such a far-reaching change in the life of nations presupposes a mighty moral effort, a deliberate departure from deeply ingrained tradition. Anyone who is not prepared to make the fate of his country in case of a dispute depend entirely on the decisions of an international court of arbitration, and to enter into a treaty to this effect without reserve, is not really resolved to avoid war. It is a case of all or nothing.

It is undeniable that previous attempts to ensure peace have failed through aiming at inadequate compromises.

Disarmament and security are only to be had in combination. The one guarantee of security is an undertaking by all nations to give effect to the decisions of the international authority.

We stand, therefore, at the parting of the ways. Whether we find the way of peace or continue along the old road of brute force, so unworthy of our civilization, depends on ourselves. On the one side the freedom of the individual and the security of society beckon to us; on the other, slavery for the individual and the annihilation of our civilization threaten us. Our fate will be according to our deserts.

The Case for the Big Step

SAUL H. MENDLOVITZ

I

One of the issues faced by serious students and advocates of a world in which large-scale organized violence is eliminated concerns itself with the strategy for transition: How do we change the present system of international relations to a system better able to prevent the threat or use of violence? For some years now most sophisticated opinion has held that the strengthening of the U.N. Charter and of U.N. peace-keeping facilities would evolve gradually, on a more or less step-by-step basis over a long period of years, with community of interest developing first and only then —if at all—followed by institutional changes. More recently there has been developing a small but still significant body of opinion which believes that the notion of taking a set of interrelated steps rapidly which, when completed, would radically change the nature of the present international system, should be given far more careful consideration than it has received up to this time.

It may be clarifying to point out that what is sometimes referred to as the "big step" or the "radical proposal" is called so for two reasons which are distinct but intertwined: 1) It involves crossing the line between the present decentralized international system based on separate national sovereignties (albeit not equal in influence) and a reallocation of a portion of those sovereignties to a world body. The reallocation may in fact be small, but by crossing over a line hitherto uncrossed it is indeed a big step. And 2) As a *method* of transition, *i.e.,* as a method of achieving a war prevention system, the big step argues that it is more realistically feasible to do so by a number of inter-related proposals taken together—what might be called a bundle of elements—than through a series of strung-out, small, independent advances. In this sense of a "bundle" it is also a big step.

Since the conventional wisdom to date has been on the side of the gradualists, it may be useful to summarize their position, which covers rather a wide gambit.

Let us assume that those whom we call gradualists are in agreement with the proponents of the big step that some form of supranational organization or world authority or, if you will, world government is an essential ingredient for a stable and viable war prevention system, and that this world government should emerge or be created by voluntary acts of the people and/or states of the world. The gradualists, while recognizing the grave dangers in the present international system, state flatly that this is impossible in the foreseeable future. They assert such a goal can only be approached slowly, in small, separately negotiated steps. They acknowledge that at some point one of those steps would cross that line which transfers some real sovereignty to a world body but they tend to blur this eventuality. Although there is wide variation in their thinking on the degree of community on the world level that would be necessary before a world government could successfully emerge that would be acceptable, in general their arguments run somewhat like this: "There is not yet sufficient sense of community. What you propose is unrealistic. How can you expect to take this large interrelated step when you cannot repeal the Connally Amendment? The time is not yet ripe." Put more formally: In view of the present ideological divisiveness, lack of common value structures, strident nationalism, and a host of international tensions arising out of such problems as racism, over-population and poverty there is insufficient community to get agreement on government and we must work our way through a slowly accommodating process to that end. This entire approach rests on the assumption that a series of unconscious accommodations, tacit understandings and formal agreements on a large number of issues will culminate, over a long period of time, in such a way as to produce sufficient trust and community to allow the formation of government on the world level.

While some groups, particularly lawyers, have advocated the development of legal institutions, it is accurate to say that most gradualists—and, it must be underscored, of the variety who do indeed desire to bring about world government—have been much more attracted to proposals of a sociological and political nature. Thus, for example, gradualist proposals within the past decade which have received wide support have been people-to-people programs, maximizing the relationships that can occur in international sports competition, cultural exchange, and the like. At the same time there has been a set of proposals made within the political area espoused by many gradualists. Thus, for example, the signing of a treaty not to test atomic weapons, the advocacy of the establishment of nuclear free zones, the encouraging of states to submit to the compulsory jurisdiction of the international court of justice, and the advocacy of the expansion of the Security Council to make it a more representative political organ. The reader will judge for himself the extent to which these proposals, adopted and unadopted, have made significant contribution to the problem of preventing thermo-nuclear holocaust, or large-scale war, or more prosaically the incidence of international violence. It is my personal conclusion that they have been tragically insufficient. Despite the fact that Stalin is dead and the period of the most extreme tension between Communist Russia and the West appears past; despite the nuclear test-ban treaty between Russia and ourselves; despite the hot line between Washington and Moscow; despite the cultural exchange program with Russia opened up by President Eisenhower, out of which the Pugwash Conferences became possible—despite these and some rather few other favorable steps, the net *loss* every year in real progress toward war prevention is tremendous. We have simply to note that the number of nuclear powers has increased, that there has been not only proliferation of nuclear weapons but also cheapening in their manufacture and increase in their yield, that countless subsidiary armaments races now escalate—witness that in the Middle East, that the United States is now engaged in a fair-sized war with the real possibility of Chinese involvement, that the United Nations is at an all-time low as a peace-keeping factor, and that we are creeping up on entering a heightened stage in the armaments race in the anti-ballistic missile systems, with all the attendant waste, renewed instability and danger that this implies.

II

In view, then, of the failure of national governments, of the U.N., and of gradualism in general over the last twenty years to make progress on disarmament and peacekeeping, it would seem only sensible to examine another approach to the problem. The case for the big step as a form of transition to a warless world can be put quite simply. It is this: It is possible, through the development of a set of interrelated proposals of sufficiently broad sweep, to project a picture in which all states would see that it was to their net advantage to move rapidly from the present international political system to a system of government on the world level. This proposition is often considered unrealistic, utopian and not relevant to contemporary problems. On closer examination, however, it shows itself to have not only relevance but a considerable thrust not inherent in the other approach.

What are the important dimensions of international community from the point of view of responsible nation state officials? They may be summarized under four headings: political and military security; a share in the distribution of material goods in a naturally productive world economy; adequate participation in the decision-making with regard to the above two areas; and maintenance of national identity with home rule on domestic issues. The advocates of the big step argue that if a system of international relations takes account of these basic values not only do a myriad of other problems become manageable but it becomes highly desirable to both officials and publics to move into that system. They further point out that within the contemporary scene it is possible to categorize the various states in relation to certain attributes which, however, do not exist singly but in varying combinations. These attributes are ideology, military potential, economic development, and the extent to which each state influences international action.

What I wish to argue is that the proposals set forth by Grenville Clark and Louis B. Sohn in their book *World Peace Through World Law* take account of the above dimensions and the above attributes and are therefore highly relevant to the problems facing the contemporary world. Having set out to solve the one problem of security, through innate humanity and a profound knowledge of how government actually works, almost unintentionally they created a system which is responsive to the other essential values as well.

The Clark/Sohn proposals, in bare outline, include: general and complete disarmament achieved and maintained by a strong structure of formal authority of which an important element is a police force able to enforce disarmament and prevent international violence; world law expressed in explicit constitutional and statutory form against the use of international violence, which law to be directly applicable to the individual persons of the world as well as to the nations, with the result that an individual could, if need be, be brought to trial without the need to indict a whole nation; establishment of mediation, conciliation and compulsory court systems; creation of a reliable revenue base for the operations of the world authority which would cost the people of the world approximately 120 billion dollars less than their present combined military budgets, and which would also support an ambitious world development program; and the grant of legislative authority to deal with war prevention to a world body in which representation is weighted to reflect the population of each nation but in which every individual nation has some voice.

It may be illustrative to take two types of nation and show briefly how other interests which normally are not discussed with disarmament are taken care of in the Clark/Sohn proposals, thereby making these proposals not only acceptable but attractive. Regardless of ideology, the superpowers today have a real stake in disarmament since they are the ones most likely to be annihilated in the event of thermonuclear war and since the financial burden of their military budgets is staggering. If they disarmed and transferred their defense to a strong world body they would be safer and they would save money, but they must be assured that the system is able to protect their other interests and that their legitimate influence as a large power on the international scene remains high. If they disarm, they would remain in the same relative position vis-à-vis each other, but how would they look in relation to the rest of the world? Despite the danger of the present system, they feel there are advantages, in relation to their other policies, to their position of influence which their preponderance of weapons and their ability to give or withhold these from satellites gives them. In matters of trade, for instance, the Russians might fear that in a disarmed world the capitalist nations might combine to bring about an unfair situation in which they would establish a monopoly of trade in one or more large areas. Under a continuance of the present system, Russia, like many other nations in the past, would have recourse to her own military strength to influence others and prevent such a situation arising. Although the Clark/Sohn plan does not allocate to the world authority legislative power to redress such a social grievance, it does provide a World Equity Tribunal of the highest quality and impartiality for just such disputes which are not primarily of a legal nature. Should the recommendations of this body (made after full investigation, with public hearings, and within a specified time limit) not be taken, should the capitalist bloc continue unfair trade practices, a situation would be created which would ultimately threaten the peace. At this point the revised General Assembly, by a suitable majority, could order that in this special instance the recommendations of the Equity Tribunal be enforced exactly as though it were a judgment of the International Court of Justice. In that revised General Assembly both Russia and the United States would have an equal and large voice, and because of the multiplicity of interests of all states it is hard to imagine that there would be any set line along which voting, whether or not to make the recommendations of the Equity Tribunal enforceable, would occur. With this flexibility there is high probability that fair treatment would be received. And should the shoe be on the other foot—*i.e.,* were it the capitalist nations who were complaining that Russia took unfair advantage of her centralized economy to deliberately sell a certain commodity at a loss over a sustained period in order to capture a market at their expense, there would be the same avenues of redress open to them. Thus we see the many elements of a viable world system for war prevention. Under the Clark/Sohn scheme, which includes weighted voting, legitimate interests could be met and big powers would remain big powers.

The underdeveloped nations, on the other hand, have relatively few armaments to give up but have a high priority on a greater share in the distribution of the earth's material goods. This share is unlikely to be made available to them, however, unless the wealthy states are in a position to relieve themselves of the burden of armaments and divert some of their resources for developmental purposes. The developing states might well agree to relinquish some of their sometimes strident nationalism in return for a new system which gave them access to developmental funds, particularly if their integrity and dignity as states is assured.

What needs to be noted here, in addition to the urgent material needs of the underdeveloped areas, is that these newly developing states are populated largely by non-white peoples and for them especially the treatment of non-whites throughout the world has become a crucial world issue. The Clark/Sohn plan, published in 1958 and written out of the research of the preceding years, took note of this problem but did not calculate the extent to which racism would become generally recognized as morally and legally reprehensible throughout the world. It becomes increasingly clear, therefore, that the Clark/Sohn proposals will need elaboration in recognition of this value. It is to be hoped that the citizens of the newly developing states will themselves construct the specific blueprints to effectuate this as their contribution to the final scheme.

It must be evident that there are different ways of viewing the world, depending upon the position in which the viewer sits and the direction in which his main interests lie. For different reasons, men value certain interests even above life itself. In the western world the feeling underlying this has been phrased in the form, "I would rather be dead than Red." In the underdeveloped areas it may be phrased in another fashion: they would rather have bread; or, put in another way, without bread they will be dead anyway, and if it requires violence to achieve bread they are willing to use it. Still another form of this has to do not with bread but with a people's sense of dignity, and it touches therefore on the status which some nations are attempting to seek and on their willingness to use violence to achieve it. The point I wish to make is that whether your sympathies or your interests incline you to view the divisiveness of the world as a bi-polar, cold-war, ideological struggle, or as a three-cornered contention of communist bloc, western democracies and "third world," or as a developed-underdeveloped (plus race problem) confrontation between the northern and southern tiers of nations, or as any mixture of the above, it makes no difference. From whatever viewpoint, the Clark/Sohn scheme provides a framework which shows itself flexible and fair for the settlement of disputes without recourse to war, and this applies to the intra-block difficulties as well.

Nor is it surprising that it should be this way because government is, in essence, the process of mediating amongst various ideological, economic and power groups. Moreover, these matters are dealt with in the Clark/Sohn scheme by the ethically neutral imperative of population criteria which cut across all the divisions we have mentioned above. The one attribute that seems generally recognized as cutting across all others, in the matter of who has how much voice in decisions on the world level, is some notion of whether you are a unit with a large population or a small population.

Within concrete political-historical situations it is difficult to measure the impact of each of these elements (ideological, economic, decision-making) separately. In fact they represent an organic system, and the special characteristic of the Clark/Sohn scheme is that in almost every proposal the authors take into account all these variables rather than isolating them and handling them as separate elements. In the solution of social problems—in this case the problem of war—it is always sound theory to mesh variables. Thus I am led to believe that unless you have general and complete disarmament of nations, a centralized police force, compulsory jurisdiction by courts, weighted voting that reflects population, and some acknowledgment of responsibility toward underdeveloped areas, you will not get any agreement on war prevention in the real world today.

III

An immense thrust, too little discussed, which the big step has over gradualism as a method of achieving a warless world is that it offers tangible benefits to *people*. Stated most baldly, it removes the threat of nuclear catastrophe and all that this implies, psychologically and otherwise. It removes the suffering, waste, and moral degradation of lesser wars such as the one now being waged in Vietnam, which U.N. Secretary General U Thant has characterized as "the most barbarous in history." It releases brains, energy and resources for constructive purposes. It saves taxes. It tends to restore power to local areas within national governments such as the U.S. where the imperatives of the present international system and of the military have acted to concentrate greater and greater power in the hands of fewer and fewer men in Washington. It offers an idealism now singularly lacking and which in itself is a driving force.

No small step painfully negotiated by gradualists yields much visible benefit, and therefore it fails to generate much active enthusiasm. This is the fallacy of the argument which says that if you cannot repeal the Connally Amendment you cannot expect to win support for a world government in the field of war prevention. To repeal the Connally Amendment (although I earnestly believe we should do so) arouses all the opposition which the big step itself would engender and offers few rewards. As a tactical matter for achieving a warless world, unless one gets the political goals of the international community tied to a domestic pay-off, political action groups within various societies are unlikely to become attracted to it. It is the responsibility of those who wish to achieve the sort of warless world we have been talking about, therefore, to make clear what its domestic benefits in each nation would be. All governments, to varying but at least some degree, are responsive to the pressure of their publics. The outstanding gradualist step to date, the nuclear test-ban treaty, was the result of the pressure of an aroused public which saw in the increasing radiation the direct connection to itself.

There is so much work which should be done for peace today that we must choose our priorities. Once one has accepted the rationality of the propositions set forth above, how do those of us who believe that the big step offers the most feasible—and perhaps the only—means of transition to a war prevention system which is enforceable and just, see to it that its basic propositions become part of the discussion and negotiation and institution-building of the world community? In short, how do we embark on a world social movement, which becomes translated very rapidly into a world political movement, which calls for constitutional debate, which will permit the formal structure to emerge? One approach is through education, specifically by introducing an academically responsible study of world order into the curriculum of educational institutions throughout the world, thereby forcing substantive discussion of the problems. Another method would be to concentrate on political elites and to form a cadre of responsible and serious people throughout the world to commit themselves to a five-year period of contacting, discussing with and badgering all the relevant political officials of all the relevant political organizations so that the seriousness of intentions and depth of discussion can be carried on in a way equivalent to the discussions that were held prior to the formulation of our own Constitution of the United States. Another method would be to find the sources of authority throughout the world which are non-governmental. These would include clergy, who are a vital source of authority in some areas, business people, writers, artists generally, and perhaps most particularly students as an active political force. Other groupings come to mind. The recent history of the birth control movement illustrates how rapidly—when the need is great and enough people have been educated to understanding—public opinion can change.

I would like to suggest two final reasons why we should engage in such action. It is very possible that the gradualists seriously overestimate the life span of the present international system. In 1959, Herman Kahn who has shown enormous capacity for thinking about the unthinkable wrote, "For many reasons, I do not believe that the 20th Century will see a disarmed world but it may see a world government or the equivalent." His conclusion was based on an analysis of the problems of national security in an increasingly rapidly proliferating nuclear world. In the seven years since he wrote that sentence the conditions on which his analysis was based have not changed for the better. If there is this degree of chance that we will have a world government of some description I would argue that it is time that we gave more attention to how it will come into being and what form it will take. Furthermore it is possible that the gradualists underestimate the degree of community already existing on the world level. No one doubts the growing abhorrence of modern warfare on the part of citizens. Granted all the divisiveness which the gradualists emphasize, it may well be that the various peoples, while not able to agree on ultimate values and ways of realizing them, nonetheless have concluded that the threat or use of force has become clearly inappropriate for achieving and maintaining their interests, and would actually welcome a new system were one proposed.

If the above judgment is not deemed already valid today, I would ask anyone who has seriously taken into account the accelerated rate of technical change to imagine the year 1990 *without* some form of world government. Last winter my home was in Cohasset, Massachusetts. When a new form of flu developed in Geneva, Switzerland, the inhabitants of Cohasset, Massachusetts, took flu shots. This is not some extreme example of esoteric behavior but an incident from everyday life. By 1990 there will be a minimum of $4\frac{1}{2}$ billion people on earth. Instantaneous world-wide communication, transportation of men to any part of the globe in a few hours, the control of weather, the harvesting of the oceans for food will all be commonplace. As men continue the exploration of space it seems unbelievable that this knowledge and power be used for purely national purposes and that there not be some common authority to control it. Those social interactions and lines of communication which develop common understanding, that reliance upon functions based upon a division of labor, and that realization of the extent to which man's condition is common—these elements which are the underpinnings of community and which are already present to some degree will be self-evident. The desirability of achieving order in an incredibly rapidly changing world will itself lead to government. Law, which is commonly associated with justice as well as order, seems the appropriate vehicle both for organizing such a government and for bringing it into being. Law becomes the natural focus for the discussion of what is necessary to transform the present ordering of international relations into one in which a world authority has a significant part. What the big step involves is, in fact, a discussion about and agreement on the laws and legal institutions necessary for an adequate and acceptable war-prevention system. Unless we are prepared to undertake this we may wait too long.

✹ ✹ ✹ ✹

This Reader will end where it began: with the dropping of the first atomic bombs—and with people. It is interesting that the article by Professor Lifton in the *American Scholar* and the article by Richard Falk in *The Nation* appeared only one month apart. Group standards about violence *are* changing. Perhaps we are ready to be aware and to think.

The Shimoda case leads us back to Hiroshima and Nagasaki and the inauguration of nuclear weapons, when war finally lost whatever redeeming features it ever had and was extended totally to include the lives of civilians as well as soldiers. We have spoken very briefly of having become a death-oriented culture—in so many ways, but many of them are curiously wound up in the compelling fascination of the arms race which draws us from life-oriented pursuits. We have considered Boulding's analysis that normal response to a collision course is a system change, and we have looked to law for a guideline.

The Shimoda case also leads us—tentatively, to be sure—*forward*, because, for the first time in an ordinary courtroom, law and war and ordinary people are brought together. Although the Shimoda case so carefully restricts itself to the specific instance, as a proper legal case should, by implication the actual *legality* of modern war, with the suffering to innocent bystanders, is called into question. The questions are asked, who is responsible? Who can actually be sued? Has the innocent individual any leg to stand on, any redress? (It is interesting that the Johnson administration felt it necessary, in February, 1966, to encourage a committee of the American Bar Association to declare that the current U.S. war in Vietnam *is legal*. It is something new that the matter even came up.)

We have also taken note that law is not simply a matter of edict enforced from the top, but a mixture of group standards, custom and formalized statement enforceable by some authority recognized as "legitimate." It is a recognition of sufficient consensus of public opinion on a given value so that it is crystallized into law.

There is no doubt that there is a growing world opinion against war, and in particular against the use of nuclear weapons. A step in this trend was the passage in 1961 in the General Assembly of Resolution 1653 by a vote of 55 — 20 — 26, the United States voting against and the Soviet Union in favor. The text of this resolution expressive of at least a moral consensus in the world community is as follows:

DECLARATION OF THE PROHIBITION OF THE USE OF NUCLEAR AND THERMO-NUCLEAR WEAPONS

The General Assembly,

"Mindful of its responsibility under the Charter of the United Nations in the maintenance of international peace and security, as well as in the consideration of principles governing disarmament,

Gravely concerned that, while negotiations on disarmament have not so far achieved satisfactory results, the armaments race, particularly in the nuclear and thermo-nuclear fields, has reached a dangerous stage requiring all possible precautionary measures to protect humanity and civilization from the hazard of nuclear and thermo-nuclear catastrophe,

Recalling that the use of weapons of mass destruction, causing unnecessary human suffering, was in the past prohibited, as being contrary to the laws of humanity and to the principles of international law, by international declarations and binding agreements, such as the Declaration of St. Petersburg of 1868, the Declaration of the Brussels Conference of 1874, the Conventions of The Hague Peace Conference of 1899 and 1907, and the Geneva Protocol of 1925, to which the majority of nations are still parties,

Considering that the use of nuclear and thermo-nuclear weap-

ons would bring about indiscriminate suffering and destruction to mankind and civilization to an even greater extent than the use of those weapons declared by the aforementioned international declarations and agreements to be contrary to the laws of humanity and a crime under international law,

Believing that the use of weapons of mass destruction, such as nuclear and thermo-nuclear weapons, is a direct negation of the high ideals and objectives which the United Nations has been established to achieve through the protection of succeeding generations from the scourge of war and through the preservation and promotion of their cultures,

1. Declares that:

(a) The use of nuclear and thermo-nuclear weapons is contrary to the spirit, letter and aims of the United Nations and, as such, a direct violation of the Charter of the United Nations;

(b) The use of nuclear and thermo-nuclear weapons would exceed even the scope of war and cause indiscriminate suffering and destruction to mankind and civilization and, as such, is contrary to the rules of international law and to the laws of humanity;

(c) The use of nuclear and thermo-nuclear weapons is a war directed not against an enemy or enemies alone but also against mankind in general, since the peoples of the world not involved in such a war will be subjected to all the evils generated by the use of such weapons;

(d) Any State using nuclear and thermo-nuclear weapons is to be considered as violating the Charter of the United Nations, as acting contrary to the laws of humanity and as committing a crime against mankind and civilization;

2. Requests the Secretary-General to consult the Governments of Member States to ascertain their views on the possibility of convening a special conference for signing a convention on the prohibition of the use of nuclear and thermo-nuclear weapons for war purposes and to report on the results of such consultation to the General Assembly at its seventeenth session.

Under the present structure, of course, such a declaration by the General Assembly does not constitute law. The present official position of the United States on the legality of nuclear weapons is indicated in the field manuals prepared for the guidance of military personnel. For example:

There is at present no rule of international law expressly prohibiting states from the use of nuclear weapons in warfare. In the absence of *express prohibition, the use of such weapons against enemy com-batants and other military objectives is permitted.*

(Article 613 of the Rules of Naval Warfare)

and

The use of explosive "atomic weapons," whether by air, sea or land forces, cannot as such be regarded as violative of international law in the absence of any customary rule of international law to the contrary.

(Paragraph 35 of the U.S. Army Rules of Land Warfare)

Note that the Army formulation seems the more permissive as it does not confine the use of nuclear weapons to military objectives nor call attention to the distinction between combatants and noncombatants.

Nonetheless, there is a strong movement of world opinion in support of a no-first-use of nuclear weapons formal treaty agreement. It would seem that the United States feels obliged to oppose such an agreement because our military posture depends so heavily on our ability to use nuclear weapons. (Certainly our government would not repeatedly risk major war with China if we did not have a vast preponderance of nuclear weapons and were willing to use them extensively. Thus, while it is sometimes argued that our possession of nuclear weapons has, on occasion, averted World War III, in this instance it seems to be inviting it. And this time there is no excuse that we do not fully know what nuclear bombs—now one thousand times more destructive than the original atomic bombs—do to human beings.) A further reason perhaps is that to certain extremist groups such an agreement would symbolize an entering wedge of encroachment on untrammeled national sovereignty. But even though the United States does not sign a formal agreement on this, if, at each time that temptation to use nuclear weapons appears great, citizens put tremendous pressure on the government to refrain, the tradition of nonuse will grow. The longer such a restraint can exist in practice, the greater will be its chance to mold world opinion and to act as an effective deterrent, both on ourselves and on others. It is likely that the precedent of the Shimoda case, as it becomes known, will contribute to this deterring pressure.

But it is the long-range precedent of this case that stirs both our imagination and our hope. One can here detect the first signs of world law, generating from world public opinion, recognized in a municipal court (which means common-garden law, of the sort that we know), involving individuals. In the big picture of evolution, what is coming up as the form in which the main thrust of life expresses itself is the individual and the world social unit. Here the large unit, the world, and the small unit, the individual, vaguely, tentatively, inconclusively, begin to speak to each other.

Richard Falk was the first to introduce *Shimoda* to American readers. I learned of it first through his article in *The Nation*, February 15, 1965. The case itself is long—too long to reprint here—and the layman's understanding is immensely helped by informed commentary. Yet the *Nation* article, excellent though it is, seemed to me too slight for both the interest of the subject and its implications to stand alone. In order to give it something approaching its proper weight, and to make the case, as a legal case, stand out in the mind, I have added a few excerpts from the far longer, more extended and detailed article which Richard Falk also wrote for the *American Journal of International Law*.

The Claimants of Hiroshima

RICHARD A. FALK

On December 7, 1963, the District Court of Tokyo handed down a decision involving claims against the state brought by injured survivors of the atomic attacks on Hiroshima and Nagasaki. The opinion of the Japanese court in the case of *Shimoda and Others* v. *Japan,* recently translated into English, suggests that the time is ripe also for a moral reckoning in the United States.

The *Shimoda* opinion is long. Only its main features can be outlined and some tentative interpretations suggested. Five residents of Hiroshima and Nagasaki sought compensation from the Japanese Government for damages sustained by the atomic blasts. Japan was made the defendant because in the Peace Treaty it had waived the claims of its nationals against the United States, but the United States was the real defendant—

that is, the state whose alleged wrongs gave rise to the damage. It is an irony of the proceedings that the role of the Japanese Government as defendant required it to argue in behalf of the legitimacy of atomic attacks on two of its own leading cities. One senses the reluctance of Japan to press "its side" of the case. In the complaint, which is printed with the opinion, the claimants set forth the facts of the attack, the legal basis for their recovery, and specify the damage that they have individually sustained. The defense does not dispute the facts of the attack or damage, but confines itself to arguing that international law did not prohibit the use of atomic bombs by a belligerent and that, in any event, the Japanese Government has no responsibility to compensate individual victims of atomic damage.

The court recites the agonizing facts, examines, with the help of three expert advisers, the status of atomic weapons and arrives at several important conclusions. First, that it is neither possible, nor necessary, to conclude expressly that international law forbids the use of atomic (or nuclear) weapons, although the reasoning used suggests that such weapons would almost always be illegal if used against cities. Second, that the attacks upon Hiroshima and Nagasaki caused such severe and indiscriminate suffering that they did violate the most basic legal principles governing the conduct of war. And third, that these claimants had no remedy, since international law does not yet allow individuals, in the absence of an express stipulation in a treaty, to pursue claims on their own behalf against a government, especially against their own government.

These conclusions have great interest for international lawyers because they constitute the sole attempt by a legal tribunal to assess the relevance of the laws of war to the realities of the nuclear age, including especially the legality of nuclear weapons if used against cities and civilian populations. The decision has an added interest in that it was rendered by a domestic court of a leading Asian country on the basis of Western legal concepts and sources of authority. It is also an opinion in which a principal belligerent policy of the victor in a war is brought under legal scrutiny by a tribunal of the defeated state. It should be noted, however, that the court, and even the complainants, make every effort not to pass judgment on the United States or its President, but to examine only the acts complained of. Reading the opinion, one feels a far greater sense of impartiality than that which pervaded the Tokyo and Nuremberg War Crimes Trials, those being trials conducted by the victors sitting in judgment over the defeated.

The *Shimoda* opinion also grapples in an interesting way with the status of individual claims for relief in international law in the absence of treaty rights, and thereby touches on the widely discussed question of whether individuals, as well as states, should become subjects of an evolving international legal system. This is not just an issue fit for academic speculation. Most abuses of human rights are perpetrated by governments against their own nationals. It is a crucial matter whether the victims have the status and a forum within which to assert their claim, embarrass their government, and perhaps arouse a response by the organized international community.

It is probable that the Tokyo opinion will be received favorably by international lawyers throughout the world, admiration being expressed for its dispassionate approach, careful and exhaustive examination of all the legal questions presented, and its conservative conclusions. The court was careful to refrain from making extravagant claims about the relevance of international law to the conditions of atomic attack and to avoid "legislating" on the delicate matters before it. At the same time, it reached the clear and momentous conclusion that the attacks on Hiroshima and Nagasaki were illegal. The court acknowledged the delicacy of its role in characteristic Japanese manner by rendering the decision on December 7, the anniversary of Pearl Harbor, thereby linking the aggressive Japanese initiation of World War II with an appraisal of its brutal termination. This was a most graceful way to impart a sense of humility to the whole proceedings and to express the moral ambiguity of the judge's role in a legal controversy drawn from the events of a major war. The District Court of Tokyo deserves commendation for its competence and tact in handling the case.

But it is not for its contribution to international law that the *Shimoda* case is most important. It is rather that the specific context of the claim, with the vividness supplied by the details of the injuries, has produced a text for the study of the whole relationship between nuclear weapons and human destiny. For we are here confronted with suffering and with an attempt to assess the acts causing it in light of the moral and legal traditions of mankind. The magnitude of the horror caused at Hiroshima and Nagasaki, though at a level far below the destructive potential of current bombs, deprives us of the numbing abstractions about national security, credible deterrents, and the like. It is important to go back, and this decision by the Tokyo District Court leads us back.

The *Shimoda* case may also supplement existing attempts to prohibit the use of nuclear weapons in international conflict. In 1960, the United Nations General Assembly passed a resolution supported by most of its membership, but not by the United States, declaring nuclear weapons illegal and proposing a conference to implement the declaration. Plans are going forward for such a conference. This may eventually induce the Great Powers to consider more sympathetically the movement to create a tradition of no-first use of nuclear weapons, or—what amounts to the same thing—the restriction of nuclear weapons to reprisal for prior nuclear attack.

In my judgment, a tradition of no-first use, if seriously supported by the official proclamation of principal governments, would considerably improve the prospects for avoiding nuclear war. One doubts, for instance, that the United States would have defied the moral and legal tradition against poison gas or lethal germs if it had developed chemical or bacteriological weapons of mass destruction comparable to atomic weapons. We refrained from using poison gas against the Japanese, despite its relevance to the successful conduct of island and jungle warfare. We refrained more because the weapon was illegitimate than because we feared retaliation. If nuclear weapons could be banned by common tradition, then our defense planning would have to be changed so that security interests could be satisfied without reliance upon them.

However, such a tradition will lack its true moral foundation until Hiroshima and Nagasaki are reconsidered and responsibility accepted for the wrongs done there. Hiroshima and Nagasaki are not yet properly implanted in our imagination. There is reluctance to consider the moral question, an impatience with it, and a widespread sense of its irrelevance. To the extent that the issue has been discussed, it has been in technical and strategic terms: whether the Japanese were ready to surrender anyway; whether lives were ultimately saved, and how many; whether a comparable result could have been achieved by a demonstration blast in an uninhabited region. These questions are virtually unanswerable; they do not assess the moral responsibility of the United States for having set a precedent in favor of using nuclear weapons to achieve normal belligerent objectives, and for causing so much indiscriminate grief that lingers on because of the peculiarly grotesque qualities of radioactive diseases. And what does this precedent signify for the future? Has Pandora's box been let open forever, or is a nation, contemplating the use of nuclear weapons in the future, more likely to refrain by thinking back to what happened at Hiroshima and Nagasaki?

We must appreciate what it means to have crossed the nuclear threshold. It is hardly mitigating to suggest that the attacks upon Hiroshima and Nagasaki were no worse than the saturation bombings of Dresden and Hamburg, or the fire raids on Tokyo. To begin with, these attacks were themselves awesome rather than routine examples of what war at that time was like. Furthermore, the terrifying impact of atomic devices is enhanced because so much destruction can be achieved by a single detonation. The towering mushroom cloud and the huge blast that obliterates everything within a certain radius are ineradicable aspects of the experience. The impact of atomic war upon the political imagination is suggested by the reaction in Japan, where a widespread revulsion to war is formalized in a clause of the new constitution that permanently forbids Japanese participation in or preparation for war. Pacifist feelings remain strong, especially among the younger generations, and there is a great distaste for any security arrangement that involves relying upon nuclear weapons. Is it necessary to suffer the trauma of nuclear attack to question seriously the wisdom and legitimacy of relying upon nuclear weapons to uphold traditional sovereign interests?

The United States' refusal to question the status of nuclear weapons reflects much more than an unwillingness to face unpleasant features in our nation's past. Since the end of World War II, our leadership in world affairs has depended upon our ability and willingness to use nuclear weapons against our enemies should circumstances warrant. Especially in Europe, we have made clear that we require nuclear weapons to offset what is alleged to be Soviet conventional superiority. And throughout the world we have tried to intimidate our adversaries by making the conditions of nuclear response uncertain so that acts of provocation might seem more risky. In the years immediately following World War II, our military preeminence was allowed to rest principally upon our nuclear monopoly. More recently, it has rested upon our nuclear superiority, insofar as that exists. Therefore, to withdraw legitimacy from nuclear weapons would be, as has been gleefully pointed out by some of our defense intellectuals, a species of unilateral disarmament. For the United States would be giving up a military advantage without getting anything in exchange.

Some of the military objections to making nuclear weapons illegal, or even to reducing the stockpiles of such weapons, have grown weaker in the last few years. First, the United States is itself now vulnerable to awesome destruction by the Soviet Union. Second, the prospect of widespread dissemination of nuclear weaponry has increased since France and China acquired a nuclear capability; this undermines the security and strategic value of nuclear weapons for both the United States and Russia. Third, it seems quite possible to arrange the defense of Europe on the basis of conventional weapons, and there appears to be much less fear that the Soviet Union will resort to military aggression for expansionist ends. Fourth, it becomes more plausible, although still by no means likely, that satisfactory disarmament agreements can be negotiated. Fifth, the main arenas of international conflict are now internal wars (Vietnam, Laos, Congo) where nuclear weapons have little or no application; that is, the outcome of the cold war is seen to depend much less on the relative capacity to deliver nuclear destruction than upon the ability to influence political developments in certain crucial states of Asia, Africa and Latin America. In short, there is less reason now than earlier to resist the suggestion that it would be proper and sensible to ban these weapons.

But it is not easy to reverse the direction of technological progress. Nuclear weapons have been used; the technique for their manufacture is now known throughout the world. Peaceful uses of atomic energy and the exploration of outer space assure the survival, even in a totally disarmed world, of the know-how and industrial capability to achieve rapid nuclear rearmament. No political system of constraint has ever managed either to avoid war permanently, or to prevent the use of any weapon that a belligerent thought would give it a decisive advantage; no nation has been willing to lose a major war rather than refrain from using some novel weapon thought more destructive than the weapons of its opponent. Present prospects for eliminating the danger of nuclear war are thus bleak, but a beginning can be made if we, the citizenry of the country that initiated the nuclear age and exercised leadership over its development, view with belated alarm our role in creating this unprecedented hazard to the future of man.

The Tokyo decision is a useful focus for thorough appraisal of nuclear weapons because it is rooted, as such an appraisal must be, in human tragedy. Let me give some pertinent extracts from the opinion itself:

The plaintiff, Ryuichi Shimoda, was a healthy man, 47 years old when the atomic bomb was dropped on Hiroshima. He lived with his family at No. 945 Nakahiro-machi, Hiroshima, and ran a small factory. His eldest daughter, Reiko (16 years old then), his third son, Kiyoshi (12 years old then), his second daughter, Yoriko (10 years old then), his third daughter, Kazue (7 years old then) and his fourth daughter, Toshiko (4 years old then) were killed by the atomic bomb. The plaintiff, his wife, Hina (40 years old then) and his fourth son, Katsuji (2 years old then), were injured by bomb-shell blast, heat ray, and radiation. The plaintiff now has keloid [tumor] in the right upper arm which is functionally disordered, and he also has keloid over the abdominal region and the left back which suppurates in the mild season of every spring. Also, he has physical handicaps in the kidney and liver, and he cannot find employment at the present time. His wife, Hina, is suffering from a feeling of languor in the whole body, a feeling of adynamia, and headaches. There sometimes appear symptoms of potential atomic bomb injury to his fourth son, Katsuji. On account of this situation, the family has no income and they barely live by the help of a little money and a few things sent monthly by the plaintiff's elder sister in Honolulu, Hawaii, the United States.

The plaintiff, Maki Tada, resided at No. 2-262, Minami-machi, Hiroshima, when the atomic bomb was dropped, and lived a healthy and happy life with her husband who was an employee of Hiroshima Dentetsu Kabushiki Kaisha [Hiroshima Electric Railway, Inc.]. She was injured on the face, shoulders, chest and feet, and keloid is left in them. She has pains in her body even at the present time, and cannot continue working at daily wages. As her husband left home, disliking her disfigured looks, and has been missing ever since, she lives a miser-able life with the help of government livelihood assistance.

The injuries of the other three plaintiffs are recited in similar detail. The complaint presents remarkably modest claims for compensation: between $550 and $825, plus 5 per cent interest from May 24, 1955, the day the suit commenced.

Within this setting the court examines various prohibitions directed at weapons in the past, beginning in 1886 with the St. Petersburg Declaration that prohibited explosives of less than 400 grams (explosive bullets), and continuing up through the twentieth century when various formal efforts have been made at international meetings to outlaw poisonous gases, and to circumscribe rights to engage in aerial bombardment and submarine warfare. A painstaking examination is conducted to reach the conclusion that atomic bombs cannot be said to be legal just because they were new weapons at the time of their use. The emphasis in the opinion is less upon the status of the weapons themselves than upon the specific occasions of their use. Especially, the opinion concentrates upon the inability of an atomic attack to discriminate between military and nonmilitary targets in a metropolitan area: *"Therefore, the act of atomic bombing . . . should be regarded . . . as a blind aerial bombardment; and it must be said to be a hostile act contrary to international law of the day."*

The court then examines the counter argument, advanced by the Japanese Government, that the concept of total war eliminates the distinction, traditional in international law, between combatant and noncombatant, and between military and nonmilitary objectives. The opinion rejects this argument, pointing to the continuing immunity from attack of such objects as schools, churches, shrines, hospitals and private houses. It rejects also the related argument that Hiroshima and Nagasaki represented targets where military objectives were so concentrated that zone bombing could be justified. It notes simply that military objectives were not particularly concentrated in those two cities.

The court examines the claim that the atomic bombing of the cities was "contrary to the principle of international law that the means which give unnecessary pain in war and inhuman means are prohibited." Here, the court recognized that the law of war is formed by weighing considerations of humanity against those of military effectiveness. But it goes on to examine the various prohibitions of weapons—and decides that "however great the inhumane result of the use of a weapon may be, the use of the weapon is not prohibited by international law, if it has a great military efficiency." The court emphasizes the bombings, not the weapons, and concludes that they violate the most fundamental of all principles in the history of the law of war: "The destructive power of the atomic bomb is tremendous; but it is doubtful whether atomic bombing really had an appropriate military effect at that time and whether it was necessary. It is a deeply sorrowful reality that the atomic bombing on both cities . . . took the lives of many civilians, and that among the survivors there are people whose lives are still imperiled owing to radiation, even today, eighteen years later. In this sense, *it is not too much to say that the pain brought by atomic bombs is severer than that from poison and poison gas, and we can say that the act of dropping such a cruel bomb is contrary to the fundamental principle of the laws of war that unnecessary pain must not be given."*

Here, then, is the full and direct charge against the United States: We used these cruel weapons for doubtful military purposes, in an unusually inhumane way that has permanently seared the imagination of men, and has left an unextinguished legacy of actual suffering among civilians selected arbitrarily as victims of terror practiced on a gigantic scale. Note the analogy to the throwing of handmade bombs into crowded cafés during the Algerian War, a practice that properly provoked editorial writers of *The New York Times* to indignation. Note, also, that these same writers have not as yet seen fit to take notice of this momentous Japanese decision.

I have tried to indicate the character of the opinion in the case of *Shimoda and Others* v. *Japan* and some of the reasons for taking it seriously. Its full force can be felt only by reading the whole document, accompanied by an informed interpretative commentary. We can redeem our past only by comprehending it. At least, we must have the courage to confront what we have done through the eyes of others. This distinguished opinion by the Tokyo District Court deprives us of our last excuse for forgetting the past. Several books have been written about the Eichmann trial. As yet, I have not seen in the United States a sentence printed about the *Shimoda* case.

There are some concluding issues. It can surely be argued that a reconsideration of the past does not reduce the prospect of its repetition. However, such an argument is hollow when made by Americans, for we have insistently urged the Germans to bring their war criminals to justice, conceiving such an encounter as an occasion for a moral catharsis.

Also, the augmented horrors of war in the nuclear age should not be allowed to diminish the horror of pre-nuclear war. One of the more bedeviling ambiguities in this subject of nuclear war arises because the existence of nuclear weapons may have avoided World War III, or at least postponed it.

Finally, there is the question of whether it makes any sense to contend that there exists a national responsibility for Hiroshima and Nagasaki. For is it not true that the decision to drop atomic bombs was made in secret by President Truman and a small number of close advisers? I would claim that the citizenry cannot so easily separate itself from moral participation in the decisions of its government. For one thing, our entire social and political system elevates to authority those whose values accord with the moral consensus. For another, national reactions to the bombings have ranged from apathy to endorsement. The response certainly seemed equivalent to a mass ratification. As Americans, then, we remain implicated, at least so long as we shun the experience of Nagasaki and Hiroshima as being without interest or importance.

From *"The Shimoda Case: A Legal Appraisal of the Atomic Attacks upon Hiroshima and Nagasaki."* (American Journal of International Law):

[From Falk's summary of the Argument of the Five Plaintiffs:]
To recapitulate, the main steps in the argument of the plaintiffs are as follows:

1. The use of the atomic bomb by the United States violated international law.
2. A violation of international law is necessarily a violation of municipal law.
3. The municipal law of Japan governs the controversy before the court.
4. Individuals are entitled on their own behalf to assert claims for injuries arising from violations of international law.
5. The waiver in Article 19(a) of the Peace Treaty bars claiming directly against the United States Government.
6. The Japanese Government violated the constitutional and vested rights of these claimants by agreeing to the waiver provision and is legally responsible for paying the claims wrongfully waived.

[From his summary of the Defense of the Japanese Government:]

The defense concedes, of course, the facts of the atomic attacks, although it submits that the casualties were considerably lower than the plaintiffs contend. On the main issue of legality, the Japanese Government contends that the atomic bombs were new inventions and hence not covered by either the customary or the conventional rules of the international law of war. Since the use of atomic bombs was not expressly forbidden by international law, there is no legal basis upon which to object to their use by a belligerent . . .

Even if international law covers the atomic bombing, there is no cause of action, the defense contends, created in municipal law. The law of war is a matter of state-to-state relations and there is no expectation that individuals injured by a violation of the laws of war can recover directly or indirectly from the guilty government. . .

The Japanese Government also denies the standing of the claimants to institute action on their own behalf. The defense subscribes to the traditional theory that it is the government on behalf of national victims, and only the government, that has the capacity, in the absence of a treaty conferring capacity on individuals, to assert claims against a foreign state.

[From his long and detailed summary of the Judgment of the Tokyo District Court:]

The principle holding of the court is, of course, that the attacks with atomic bombs upon Hiroshima and Nagasaki on August 6 and 9 of 1945 were in violation of international law. The principal reasons given were as follows:

(1) International law forbids an indiscriminate or blind attack upon an undefended city; Hiroshima and Nagasaki were undefended; therefore, the attacks were illegal.

(2) International law only permits, if at all, indiscriminate bombing of a defended city if it is justified by military necessity; no military necessity of sufficient magnitude could be demonstrated here; therefore, the attacks were illegal.

(3) International law as it has specifically developed to govern aerial bombardment might be stretched to permit zone or area bombing of an enemy city in which military objectives were concentrated; there was no concentration of military objectives in either Hiroshima or Nagasaki; therefore, no legal basis exists for contending that the atomic attacks might be allowable by analogy to zone bombing, because even the latter is legal, if at all, if directed against an area containing a concentration of military targets.

(4) International law prohibits the use of weapons and belligerent means that produce unnecessary and cruel forms of suffering as illustrated by the prohibition of lethal poisons and bacteria; the atomic bomb causes suffering far more severe and extensive than the prohibited weapons; therefore, it is illegal to use the atomic bomb to realize belligerent objectives:

(a) that is, the duty to refrain from causing unnecessary suffering is a principle of international law by which all belligerent activity is tested, whether specifically regulated or not;

(b) that is, specific prohibitions embody a wider principle and this principle extends to new weapons developments not foreseen at the time when the specific prohibition was agreed upon.

Having reached these conclusions favorable to the plaintiffs, the opinion goes on to examine whether a Japanese court is able to award compensation to these individuals injured at Hiroshima and Nagasaki. The main issues in this part of the case are as follows:

(1) Assuming that there was an injury caused by a violation of international law, is there also a violation of domestic law that can be relied upon by a domestic court as the basis for recovery?

(2) Are the municipal aspects of the case governed by Japanese or United States law?

(3) Can Japan be made responsible for waiving the international claims of its nationals?

(4) Can the United States be made responsible either in a Japanese court or by hypothesizing the outcome in an American court?

The court summarily concludes that, despite the absence of a specific provision in the Imperial Constitution of Japan (in force at the time of the atomic attacks), it was generally understood that a violation of Japanese municipal law. The same legal result, the opinion finds, occurs in the United States, and there treaty law has the benefit of an explicit constitutional provision, Article VI, paragraph 2. Therefore, a violation of international law is *ipso facto* a violation of the domestic law of both Japan and the United States. But, as the opinion notes, the violation of municipal law is of no relevance unless these plaintiffs have the standing to present a claim and the court before which it is brought is competent to adjudicate such a suit on the merits.

The court affirms that when a belligerent injures another belligerent by an illegal act then it is liable to pay damages. But the liability is possessed by the United States and it is discharged by paying Japan. The only proper defendant is the United States and not, as the plaintiffs alternatively contended, the public official who ordered the illegal acts, President Truman. But is there a legal claim possessed by the injured individuals as well as the injured state? The opinion does not endorse the pure form of the traditional view that states, and only states, have the standing to pursue claims arising from violations of international law. The language used in the opinion is not entirely clear, but the court seems to affirm the potential capacity of the individuals to enforce international law. At the same time, the court denies that this capacity always, or even generally, exists in present-day international law. On the contrary, the individual only possesses a legal capacity to proceed on his own when the capacity has been specifically conferred in an international agreement. In the italicized formulation of the court:

It is still proper to understand that individuals are not the subject of rights in international law, unless it is concretely recognized by treaties. . . .

[Those who wish to know more of *Shimoda* will find the English translation of the text in Volume I of *The Strategy of World Order,* edited by Richard A. Falk and Saul H. Mendlovitz and published by the World Law Fund. Preceding it are comments from which I have drawn. Those who wish an informed, detailed legal commentary on the case are referred to *The American Journal of International Law,* October 1965, from which I have quoted. In this commentary on the case, Richard Falk says in part:]

Shimoda views military necessity in a fairly orthodox way. It refuses to exonerate the bombings because they may have hastened the Japanese decision to surrender and thereby achieved a net saving of lives, even of Japanese civilian lives, although these arguments were presented to the court by the defense and are frequently offered in the West as the principal justification for the atomic attacks.

As the *Shimoda* court notes, such reasoning, if accepted, would tend to legitimate any belligerent act, however extreme and horrible. Thus the Japanese court rejects the extreme view of a contextual approach to legal valuation that tends to account for any act by reference to an acceptable goal, the surrender of the enemy and the restoration of peace. . . . As soon as the motivation of conduct, as well as conduct itself, enters into the determination of what is legal, the conclusions of legal analysis are almost certainly likely to be self-serving and those with contradictory motivations can generate an equally convincing, albeit contradictory, set of legal conclusions. This process of legal analysis impairs the actual and potential ordering role of international law in stabilizing relations between rival states pursuing incompatible objectives, and yet sharing a common interest in maintaining peaceful relations, a common interest that might take increasing precedence over the goals of conflict in view of the mutual commitment to avoid nuclear warfare. . . .

[At the same time, Falk calls attention to the fact that there is a]

strain placed upon legal approaches based on intrinsic modes that seek to prescribe standards and yet allow for reasonable expectations about probable courses of behavior. It is commonplace to assume that a state confronted by a choice between subjugation and victory will do whatever is likely to promote victory, just as a man confronted by a choice between starvation and theft is likely to steal. All law, not just international law, is ineffective in extreme situations.

❧ ❧ ❧ ❧

As Tillich too pointed out, in the last analysis the individual, out of necessity or conviction, can break through the law.

These diverse thoughts, together with *Shimoda* whose details so vividly demonstrate the necessity of preventing any future use of the bombs that gave rise to it, lead me to see that, since nuclear weapons, if they remain in the possession of nation-states, will be used in extreme situations analogous to the man stealing to avoid starvation (*i.e.*, to avoid final subjugation by an enemy), we cannot merely outlaw nuclear weapons. We must eradicate the institution of war itself if we sincerely wish that no government find itself with the extreme choice of subjugation by an enemy or using them. Thus a law prohibiting the use of nuclear weapons, although a humane and much to be desired step forward and one that would create a climate of hope and progress, is not enough. Nor indeed is a law prohibiting war unless some other means of settling vital disputes is set up. And just as something within us recognizes the human right of the man who steals bread because he or his children are starving —particularly if the causes of his starvation are not of his making and he sees about him a flagrant display of abundance and riches—just as we know that if we truly wish to keep respect for that law against stealing, or indeed for law itself, something must be done to ameliorate extreme conditions which force men to break it, so too on the world level does some sort of a world development authority seem an inextricable part of the solution.

This brings us once again to the closely woven interrelatedness of the whole problem, awareness of which permeates the Clark-Sohn proposals. And we must ask ourselves whether not necessarily this one, but some such complete set of interrelated proposals is not the only way in which the world can move forward. Buckminster Fuller in his extraordinary summary speech at the Vision 65 Conference* about the meaning of man, the rapidity of change in his own lifetime, the utterly new conditions of life that are coming—all unrealized—upon us in the next single generation due to the immense technological breakthroughs man himself has evolved, concludes by saying that the choice before us is of oblivion or utopia. My personal conclusion has been that the time has

* See *American Scholar*, Spring, 1966.

come when quite literally everyone must concern himself with the study and definition of what seems to him the relevant utopia to meet our needs, our values and the realities of the present; and to ask himself what is the essence of the system change that is necessary for it.

A short list of suggested reading for those who wish further study

ON WORLD ORDER:

Grenville Clark and Louis B. Sohn. *World Peace through World Law.* Cambridge, Mass.: Harvard University Press, third edition (enlarged), 1966.

Richard A. Falk and Saul H. Mendlovitz, editors. *The Strategy of World Order,* in four volumes: I. *Toward a Theory of War Prevention,* II. *International Law,* III. *The United Nations,* IV. *Disarmament and Economic Development.* New York: The World Law Fund, 1966.

Marion H. McVitty. *A Comparison and Evaluation of Current Disarmament Proposals.* New York: The World Law Fund, 1964. This short study may be used in conjunction with *Current Disarmament Proposals,* also published by the World Law Fund.

Emery Reves. *The Anatomy of Peace.* New York: The Viking Press, 1961.

ON THE SPIRITUAL UNITY OF MAN:

Pierre Teilhard de Chardin. *The Phenomenon of Man.* New York: Harper, 1961.

ON EASTERN THOUGHT FOR WESTERNERS:

Nancy Wilson Ross. *Three Ways of Asian Wisdom.* New York: Simon and Schuster, 1966.

ON AGGRESSION:

Konrad Lorenz. *On Aggression.* New York: Harcourt, Brace and World, 1966.

ON UTOPIAS:

Daedalus (Journal of the American Academy of Arts and Sciences), the issue of Spring 1965.